Sport and Corporate Nationalisms

Sport Commerce and Culture

Series ISSN: 1741-0916

Editor:
David L. Andrews, *University of Maryland*

The impact of sporting issues on culture and commerce both locally and globally is huge. However, the power and pervasiveness of this billion dollar industry has yet to be analyzed deeply. Sports issues shape the economy, the media and even our lifestyle choices, ultimately playing an unquestionable role in our psychology. This series examines the sociological significance of the sports industry and the sporting world on contemporary cultures around the world.

SPORT COMMERCE AND CULTURE

Sport and Corporate Nationalisms

Edited by
Michael L. Silk, David L. Andrews and C.L. Cole

Oxford • New York

First published in 2005 by
Berg
Editorial offices:
1st Floor, Angel Court, 81 St Clements Street, Oxford OX4 1AW, UK
175 Fifth Avenue, New York, NY 10010, USA

Berg is the imprint of Oxford International Publishers Ltd.

Library of Congress Cataloging-in-Publication Data
Sport and corporate nationalisms / edited by Michael L. Silk, David L. Andrews and C.L. Cole. — 1st ed.
p. cm. — (Sport, commerce and culture)
Includes bibliographical references and index.
ISBN 1-85973-794-3 (cloth : alk. paper) — ISBN 1-85973-799-4 (pbk. : alk. paper)
1. Nationalism and sports. 2. Corporate sponsorship. 3. Sports — Marketing. 4. Sports — Economic aspects. I. Silk, Michael L. II. Andrews, David L., 1962- III. Cole, C. L. IV. Series.
GV706.34.S617 2004
306.4'83—dc22
2004023158

British Library Cataloguing-in-Publication Data
A catalogue record for this book is available from the British Library.

ISBN 1 85973 794 3 (hardback)
1 85973 799 4 (paperback)

Typeset by JS Typesetting Ltd, Porthcawl, Mid Glamorgan
Printed in the United Kingdom by Biddles Ltd, King's Lynn

www.bergpublishers.com

Contents

Notes on Contributors

John Amis is an associate professor at The University of Memphis, where he holds joint appointments in the Department of Health & Sport Sciences and the Department of Management. Amis' research interests have predominantly centered on organizational change and the identification, utilization and management of intangible resources. His work has appeared in journals such as *Academy of Management Journal*, *Journal of Applied Behavioral Science*, *Journal of Sport Management*, *European Marketing Journal*, *European Sport Management Quarterly*, and *Leisure Studies*.

David L. Andrews is an associate professor and a member of the Physical Cultural Studies Research Group located in the Sport Commerce and Culture Program, Department of Kinesiology, and an affiliate faculty in the Department of American Studies, at the University of Maryland–College Park, USA. He has been guest editor of the *Sociology of Sport Journal*, and is currently on the editorial board of the *Journal of Sport and Social Issues* and the *Sociology of Sport Journal*.

C. L. Cole is an associate professor of Women's Studies, Sociology and Kinesiology. Her teaching and research investigate the production of deviant bodies and national identity in post-World War II America. Cole is a core faculty member of the following interdisciplinary units at University of Illinois at Urbana, Champaign: Unit for Criticism and Interpretive Theory; Cultural Studies and Interpretive Research; and Science, Technology, Information, and Medicine. She teaches courses on queer studies, body politics, sport & post-civil rights America, cultural studies of race & sport, masculinity & American identity, and consumer culture & the politics of health and fitness. Currently, she is the editor of the *Journal of Sport & Social Issues* (Sage) and the co-editor of the book series "Sport, Culture & Social Relations" (SUNY Press). She also serves on the editorial board of *Cultural Studies-Critical Methodologies* (Sage) and the advisory board of *GLQ* (Duke University Press).

Mark Falcous received his doctorate from Loughboough University, UK. He is currently a lecturer in the sociology of sport at the University of Otago, Aotearoa/New Zealand. His research focuses on sport, the local-global nexus and identities.

Michael D. Giardina is a doctoral candidate in kinesiology, cultural studies, and interpretive research at the University of Illinois, Urbana–Champaign. He has published on a variety of topics related to flexible citizenship, stylish hybridity and global sport, as well as numerous performative pedagogical texts that engage with the popular cultural response to/in post-9/11 "America." He is currently completing a book (Peter Lang Publishers, 2005) titled *Sporting Pedagogies: Performing Culture and Identity in the Global Arena.*

Jean Harvey is a professor and the Director of the Research Centre for Sport in Canadian Society, School of Human Kinetics, University of Ottawa, Ontario, Canada. He has published extensively on sport policy, globalization and the political economy of sport. His research interests also include inequalities and sport, citizenship, social capital and the governance of sport

Brendan Hokowhitu is a lecturer in Te Temu: School of *Mäori*, Pacific and Indigenous Studies at the University of Otago. Brendan received his Ph.D. in the School of Physical Education, University of Otago and his research interests include the social construction of *Mäori* in "mainstream" discourses, specifically *Mäori* masculinities, education and sports media.

Fan Hong is reader in the Department of Sport Sciences at De Montfort University in England. She was an editor of the *Journal of Sports Culture and History* published in Beijing by the Sports Ministry in the 1980s. She is an editor of *Sport in Society* and a member of the editorial board of *The International Journal of the History of Sport* and the *International Encyclopaedia of Women and Sport.* Her main research interests are in the areas of gender and sport, politics and sport, with particular reference to China and Asia.

Jeremy Howell is an associate professor in the Sports and Fitness Management Graduate Program at the University of San Francisco. He has extensive sports industry experience and serves as an advisor to a number of national and regional organizations, including Western Athletic Clubs Inc, Brian Boitano's Youth Skate Foundation, Senior Assisted Living, Inc, and The Joy of Sports Foundation. He is also on the editorial board of the *Journal of Sport & Social Issues.*

Steve Jackson is an associate professor in the School of Physical Education, University of Otago, New Zealand, where he teaches courses in sport, media & culture and sociology of sport. His research interests include globalization and sport, media and sport and sports advertising. Currently General Secretary for the International Sociology of Sport Association, Steve has published (with David Andrews) *Sport Stars: The Cultural Politics of Sporting Celebrity* (Routledge) and has a second volume forthcoming titled *Sport, Culture & Advertising* (Routledge).

Samantha J. King is an assistant professor in the School of Physical and Health Education at Queen's University. Her research explores the cultural politics of sport, health, and the body, including, most recently, a project on the role of consumer-oriented activism in the cultural reconfiguration of breast cancer in the United States. A member of the editorial board for the *Journal of Sport & Social Issues*, her recent publications have appeared in *Social Text*, the *International Journal of Sport Marketing & Sponsorship* and the *Journal of Sport and Social Issues.*

Alan Law is an associate professor of Sociology at Trent University in Ontario, Canada. His research and teaching interests center primarily on the sociology of sport, leisure and tourism in addition to research methodology. Professor Law also has a background in industrial sociology, which, together with his experience as a corporate accountant and public sector consultant, energizes his interests in political economy and citizenship.

Joseph Maguire, PhD is past-president of the International Sociology of Sport Association and currently Co-Director of the Centre for Olympic Studies and Research at Loughborough University, UK. Professor Maguire leads the Sociology of Sport within the School of Sport and Exercise Sciences. He has published extensively in the area of sport, culture and society. Areas examined include violence, pain and injury, sport and the body/emotions, sport and the media. Currently, his work focuses on the area of sport and social theory, the body, and sport and globalization. His latest book is *Power and Global Sport* (in press) (Routledge).

Jennifer L. Metz is a Ph.D. candidate in women's studies and kinesiology at the University of Illinois and is an instructor of kinesiology at Northern Illinois University. Her research interests include feminist criticism, gender, ethnography and qualitative research methods.

Mary G. McDonald is associate professor in the Department of Physical Education, Health and Sport Studies and an affiliate with the Women's Studies Program at Miami University in Oxford, OH, USA. Her scholarship focuses on feminist and cultural studies of sport, media and popular culture, and explores power relations as constituted through race, class, gender and sexuality. She is co-editor with Susan Birrell of *Reading Sport: Critical Essays on Power and Representation* (Northeastern University, 2000), an anthology that ties particular highly publicized sporting events and personalities to larger cultural, economic and political realms.

Philip Rosson is the Killam Chair of Technology, Innovation and Marketing in the School of Business Administration at Dalhousie University. Between 1999 and 2002, he served as co-editor of the *Canadian Journal of Administrative Sciences*. He has published widely, with an emphasis on the growth strategies of small and medium-sized companies, particularly in foreign markets. Dr. Rosson was educated in England, where he earned MA (Lancaster) and PhD (Bath) degrees.

Michael L. Silk is an assistant professor and a member of the Physical Cultural Studies Research Group located in the Sport Commerce and Culture Program, Department of Kinesiology, at the University of Maryland. His work is committed to the critical, multidisciplinary and multi-method interrogation of sporting practices, experiences and structures. Dr Silk has published a number of book chapters and journal articles in *Media, Culture, Society*, the *Journal of Sport and Social Issues*, the *Sociology of Sport Journal*, the *International Review for the Sociology of Sport, Sport, Culture and Society*, the *Journal of Sport Management* and *Media Culture: A Review*.

Trevor Slack is professor and Canada Research Chair at the University of Alberta. His interest is in the organization of sport. His articles have appeared in *Journal of Sport Management*, *Organization Studies*, *Human Relations*, *Journal of Management Studies* and *Academy of Management Journal*. He is currently on disability leave from the University of Alberta.

Alan Tomlinson is professor of Leisure Studies at the University of Brighton, where he is the area leader of Sport and Leisure Cultures in the Chelsea School, Head of the Chelsea School Research Centre and Deputy Chair of the university's Research Degrees Committee. He teaches and writes on the social history and sociology of consumption, leisure and sport. His latest research concern is the changing nature of popular spectacle.

List of Tables and Figures

1

Corporate Nationalism(s)? The Spatial Dimensions of Sporting Capital

Michael L. Silk, David L. Andrews and C.L. Cole

Despite being published more than twenty years ago, Theodore Levitt's provocative *Harvard Business Review* article, "The Globalization of Markets", continues to underpin debates pertaining to the nature and influence of economic globalization (Quelch, 2003). Indeed, in many respects, it represented the stimulus – in terms of being a critical point of comparison and departure – for the current project. Widely lambasted at the time of publication by academics for its all-encompassing relentless homogenization, Levitt's thesis was embraced by corporate executives who marketed standardized products globally – consumers worldwide, after years of "deprivation", were thus able to consume the forbidden fruits of American brands (Quelch, 2003). Levitt (1983) predicted the sophisticated attempts by global corporations to command the widest possible market base (through penetration of local cultures by the economics and imagery of global capitalism), and thereby accrue the benefits derived from the realization of colossal economies of scale. In this early stage of corporate globalization, Levitt famously identified that companies operated "as if the entire world (or major regions of it) were a single, largely identical entity" and subsequently attempted to sell the "same things in the same way everywhere" (Levitt, 1983, p. 22).

Despite enthusiasm from within the corporate ranks, Levitt's mantra appeared to stall with increased competition and responses, from local brands and from backlash against global brand saturation. Most organizations soon realized the impracticability of treating the global market as a single, homogenous entity. The advancement of capitalism has always been about the overcoming of spatial constraints as a means of improving the flow of goods from producer to consumer (Hall, 1991; Morley, 1995), but this intrinsically rationalizing logic of market capitalism came unstuck when faced by the "warm appeal of national affiliations and attachments" (Robins, 1997, p. 20). So, rather than attempting to neuter cultural difference through a strategic global uniformity, many corporations realized that securing a profitable global presence necessitates negotiating with the local, "and by negotiate I mean it had to incorporate and partly reflect the differences it was trying to overcome" (Hall, 1991, p. 32). Levitt's detractors may well view the national as a stumbling block to global brand saturation, yet it is timely to explore global corporatism's negotiations with the local, thereby adding to the small yet growing body of knowledge that critically interrogates global corporate engagement with national sensibilities. For some, like Levitt, this has meant a rampant global homogenization in which organizations, or more accurately, brands, roam freely, a vision in which national difference becomes all but obliterated and replaced with a global culture. For others however, the boundaries remain clearly demarcated; global brand saturation is met with (sometimes violent) resistance and the local triumphs over the threatening and placeless brand universalism.

Of course, and as has been played out in the literatures neither position is adequate: the relationships and nuances between global brands and local cultures are far more complex and, at different times and in different locations, throw up a range of issues in regard to the exploitation of local peoples, the superficial re-imagining of local cultures, the connections (and thereby disconnections) between global brands and certain segments of a nation's populace, the re-emergence of "local" brands (although often a veneer as this local expression is often owned by various global corporations), or the adaptation of global brands to local tastes, as well as wholehearted remnants of Levitt's mantra and his opposers. This text explores these issues critically by focusing on those global corporations that have, to varying degrees, crossed geographic boundaries and, in varying ways, negotiated with the specificities of particular locales. In this sense, while recognizing that in political and economic terms we may well be inexorably and seemingly irreversibly heading toward a "post-national world" (Smith, 1991, p. 143), this text sets out to explore the "changing", as opposed to the "withering", of the nation under the logic of global corporate capitalism (Hannerz, 1996, p. 89).

Spaces of Capital: Transnationalisms *and* Localities

The modern nation-state emerged as a cohesive political, economic, and cultural entity designed to consolidate and regulate capital accumulation within the boundaries of a specific geographic location, contemporary conditions of advanced globalization have seriously undermined the economic and political autonomy that helped constitute the modern nation. Although these processes can be traced further back, increased global interdependence and interconnectedness intensified in the 1970s due to the state regulation of many Western national economies that focused primarily on industrially based production being fatally undermined by "rising wages and declining productivity, overcapacity and market saturation, competition from low-wage countries, [and] increasing costs for public services" (Morley and Robins, 1995, p. 27). The lack of confidence in Fordist/Keynesian economic policy, aided and abetted in the 1980s by concomitant shifts in the Reaganite and Thatcherite geopolitical landscape that espoused a superficially *laissez-faire* approach to economic development centered on the primacy of free markets, deregulation, and unfettered international trade (Sassen, 2000) institutionalized by the formation of transnational political structures, alliances, and treaties (NAFTA, IMF, WTO), saw many major corporate entities shift focus from commodity production and capital accumulation within individual national economies (a strategy that largely existed within, and helped constitute, national boundaries) to a more flexible and dynamic approach. Within this approach the corporate footprint transcended national borders in the search for more rational and efficient commodity chains. These conditions provided the backdrop for the birth of the transnational corporation – nomadic economic institutions (such as Toyota, Philips, Pepsi Co., Sony, and Nike) that scour the globe for the ever cheaper labor costs and underexploited markets that would ensure expected rates of growth. Working beyond national boundaries, these transnational corporations evidence the degree to which "'the nation' today is visibly in the process of losing an important part of its old functions, namely that of constituting a territorially bounded 'national economy'" (Hobsbawm, 1990, p. 173). These placeless, decentered, supranational organizations, operating in the interests of a global market and global circuits of cultural production (Hardt and Negri, 2000), along with the global flow of peoples, goods, services, capital, images and symbols, has caused some, within academe and the business communities, to decry the demise of the nation at the hands of rampant globalization. Given the degree to which the process of globalization has infiltrated the contemporary imagination (both popular and intellectual), there has emerged a widespread *global panic* rooted in the fear that global corporations have sought to rationalize their products and strategies, as Levitt (1983) predicted, into single globally focused directives; the corollary being the instantiation of a globally homogenizing commercial culture. This line of thought derives from the presence of corporations possessing the technological wherewithal (in terms of networks facilitating the instantaneous global flow of capital and information), political approval (derived from the major Western democracies' perception of market globalization as an irresistible force of nature (Held, 1995)), and economic structure (in regards to the deregulationist initiatives that have lowered trade and tariff barriers), to transcend national boundaries, and thereby benefit from the massive economies of scale derived from global marketeering. Certainly the global ubiquity of McDonald's golden arches, the Nike swoosh, and David Beckham's latest coiffure, all seemingly corroborate the pessimistic "vision of the globe flattened into a low-level monoculture, a gigantic K Mart with no exit" (Buell, 1994). It is at this point that some critics infer that globally focused corporate capitalism is inalienably leading to the demise of the nation as an economic, political, and perhaps most pertinently, cultural entity. These scholars posit that the nation-state is losing control of its territoriality (Sassen, 1996) and is limping on its last legs (Appadurai, 1996). Others go even further to argue that globalization may eventually lead to the hallowing out (Jessop, 1994), the decline (Held, 1990) or even the end (Ohmae, 1995) of nations and/or nation-states.

However, and as Jenkins (2002) argues, the proliferation and spatial reach of the transnational corporation, while affecting the activities of national state powers, does not necessarily transcend the local in respect to national loyalties. Conversely, and as part of the global brand backlash to Levitt's form of relentless homogenization, some display a steadfast belief in the enduring relevance of the nation as a source of identity and differentiation whose symbolic resonance has continued far beyond the nation's shelf-life as a largely autonomous and distinct political and economic formation in spite of the cultural threat posed by the cosmopolitanism that accompanied the increased transnational flow of products, capital, images, and institutions. Such discussion problematizes the *end of the nation* rhetoric that punctuates the globalization debate, by demonstrating the apparent contradiction exposed by the continued presence and importance of the nation as a cultural entity, within the "borderless world" of the domineering global marketplace (Ohmae, 1995). That is, in spite of the global cosmopolitanizing logics of transnational corporatism, "geography still matters" in a very real sense as local and national specificities continue to shape production and consumption processes in many sectors in different ways (Preston and Kerr, 2001).

Such debate raises crucial questions for scholars attempting to understand if the global ecumene (Hannerz, 1996) has taken a single shape – at least for the present, recognizably American, relentlessly commercial – reflective of transnational corporate control over the flow of media goods and services (Foster, 1991). Further, if the nation, at least as a cultural identity, retains resonance, then how is the construction of national boundaries sustained in a world now more than ever open to cultural flows (Appadurai and Breckenridge, 1988; Foster, 1991)? These debates and questions frame our present focus on the spatial reach of transnational corporate capital and the promotional strategizing that, to differing degrees, engages with, negotiates with, surpasses, or (fictitiously) revises the "nation".

Reconsidering the Nation

The contemporary form and influence of the nation – steeped as it is in an historical veneer of tradition and mythology – belies what are relatively recent origins within the history of human civilization. Futuristic visions of twenty-first century life routinely depicted civilizations within which, amongst other things, entire meals were ingested in pill form, mass transit systems comprised of intricate networks of air corridors, and mega-corporations governed every sphere of human existence, from the cradle to the grave. Within such populist prophesies the specter of nations and nationalism – the threads that organized modern communities and conflicts – were noticeably absent. National formations were effectively subsumed in the wake of a rampant corporate imperialism, thus vindicating science fiction's function as a form of contemporary social commentary, these fictions critiquing the excesses of either modern nationalism, corporate capitalism, or indeed both. As we edge our way into the new millennium, it would seem an appropriate time to celebrate the endurance of the square meal, rue the absence of more efficient forms of transportation, and, more pertinently, reflect on the present relations between national and corporate interests. For, today, when the political and economic sovereignty of nation-states is being increasingly undermined by an array of "national and supranational organisms under a single logic of rule" (Hardt and Negri, 2000, p. xii), the very idea of the nation continues to be a virulent force in the structuring of individual lives and consciousness.

Despite appearances of antiquity, the genesis of the modern nation-state can in fact be traced to the relatively recent past in history of human civilization. Premised on a multilateral recognition of states' rights to autonomous constitution and development, the Peace of Westphalia in 1648 brought the Thirty Years War to an end, and simultaneously heralded the demise of the Holy Roman Empire. More importantly, this covenant instantiated the very idea of the sovereign state – and indeed that of an international community of states – through a mutual agreement as to the common independence of state formations. The establishment of a philosophy and system of sovereign nation-states did not automatically lead to the firmament or dissemination of national popular cultures and identities, around which state citizens could unite. Rather, notions of national belonging developed haphazardly within Western Europe, until the industrializing tumult of the nineteenth century, when national governing elites became instrumental in advancing the nation as the "political and cultural organizing principle of mass-industrial modernity" (Hedetoft, 1999, p. 71). In a Durkheimian sense, through the advancement of emotive symbols, anthems, rituals, and institutions, the state acted as a producer of "authorized definitions and representations of the national community" around which rapidly changing, urbanizing populations congealed to form a coherent sense of collective self (Foster, 1991, p. 248). This "foundational, existential, thick" (Hedtoft and Hjort, 2002) national collective, no matter how mythical, divisive or exclusionary, is produced, reproduced and spread by actors in concrete contexts, and thereby appropriated, (re)configured and manifest in discourse (De Cillia, Reisgel and Wodak, 1999). As Hardt and Negri identified, as well as being a political economic structure, the nation was thus constituted in, and through, "a cultural formulation, a feeling of belonging, and a shared heritage" (2000, p. 336), of which sport was to become an important aspect.

Within a couple of decades either side of the turning twentieth century the power elites within most, if not all, Western nations capitalized on sport's entrenched popular appeal by selectively inventing sporting traditions in order to help concretize the nation's very being (Hobsbawm and Ranger, 1983). So, the "badges of membership" (Hobsbawm, 1983, p. 11) of the nation came to include the participating in, and/or the spectating of, the particular sporting practices with which national cultures became associated; sport effectively playing a crucial role in "the construction and confirmation of national identity" within modern industrializing societies (Maguire, Poulton, and Possamai, 1999, p. 441). As Hobsbawm famously described:

> What has made sport so uniquely effective a medium for inculcating national feelings, at all events for males, is the ease with which even the least political or public individuals can identify with the nation as symbolized by young persons excelling at what practically every man wants, or at one time in life has wanted, to be good at. The imagined community of millions seems more real as a team of eleven named people. The individual, even the one who only cheers, becomes a symbol of his nation himself. (Hobsbawm, 1990, p. 143)

Having gained a foothold in the national psyche, the twentieth century witnessed a strengthening of the bond between the discursive (re)production of specific national cultures and select sporting practices, such that sport has become arguably the most emotive – peacetime – vehicle for harnessing and expressing bonds of national cultural affiliation.

There has been a small, yet growing number, of academics investigating the devotion, emotion, and sometimes violent sensibilities associated with the expression of national sentiment in, and through sport (for example, Cronin and Mayall, 1998; Bairner, 2001; Bale and Cronin, 2003), but the cultural nationalisms presently sweeping the developed world are qualitatively distinct from those that helped to constitute the symbolic boundaries of maturing nation-states during the nineteenth century. While human civilization is being increasingly corporatized, the nation and national culture have become principal accomplices within this process, as global capitalism seeks to – quite literally – capitalize upon the nation as source of collective identification and differentiation. For instance, the increased synergy between sport and media interests in the latter twentieth century encouraged the growth of nationally evocative, yet truly global, sport spectacles, most notably the Olympic Games, and the FIFA World Cup. Such transnational events are populated – and indeed popularized – by a coterie of sport celebrity figures, acting as representative subjectivities of the national collective configurations with whom they are affiliated (Marshall, 1997). Hence, it is easy to discern the paradox of an increasingly global sport economy within which national difference has, if anything, become ever more significant (see also Cole and Andrews, 2001; Hargreaves, 2002; Rowe, 2003). In this manner, transnational capital's encroachment into the symbolic orchestration of national cultures has usurped the productive role of modern political institutions. As recently noted by the advertising maven, Rance Crain, without a hint of foreboding, "You can make a good argument that our government should subsidize the brand-building and even nation-building activities of companies that market products tailored to the needs of developing countries" (Crain, 2001). The nation is thus corporatized, and reduced to a branded expression of global capitalism's commandeering of collective identity and memory.

The *context* then and the *processes* through which national cultures are produced and reproduced are being transformed (Held, McGrew, Goldblatt and Peraton, 1999). Not that the internal political forces previously responsible for harnessing and contouring national cultural identity have been rendered obsolete. Rather, their position of influence is being eroded by external, commercially driven, forces. In this scenario, the locus of control in influencing the manner in which the nation and national identity are represented becomes exteriorized through, and internalized within, the promotional strategies of transnational corporations. Simply put, and prefigured on the operations and machinations of multi-, trans- and supra-national entities, the politico-cultural nation of the nineteenth century has been replaced by the corporate-cultural nation of the twenty-first century. We have termed this process, corporate nationalisms, processes that are qualitatively distinct from those that helped to constitute the symbolic boundaries of maturing nation-states during the nineteenth century. As human civilization becomes increasingly corporatized, the nation and national culture have become principal (albeit perhaps unwilling) accomplices within this process, as global capitalism seeks to, quite literally, capitalize upon the nation as a source of collective identification and differentiation.

This collection draws together a number of leading scholars who address points of negotiation between transnational corporatism and local cultures. In differing yet complementary veins, these scholars point towards the operations, practices and strategizing of the global sport marketplace with regard to the examination of the corporate structures at the vanguard of transnationalizing processes, the human agents responsible for realizing these expansionist corporate goals, and the various commercially inspired inflections of culture produced. Taken together, the contributions provide critical insight into the important place of sporting structures, organizations and experiences in the understanding of the contemporary corporate nation.

In Chapter 2, Mark Falcous and Joe Maguire address the presence and cultural reception of a global brand – the National Basketball Association (NBA) – as it encounters local cultures. Falcous and Maguire point to the co-presence of the NBA alongside "indigenous" basketball and highlight how the reception of the NBA is mediated by existing cultural identities and affiliations that surround "local" sporting practices. Through exploration of the dynamics of local cultural impacts and response to the activities of the NBA, Falcous and Maguire are able to provide insight into the complex set of synergies that form influential and powerful global flows.

Alan Tomlinson's focus in Chapter 3 is on the era of global expansion for the world football governing body, FIFA. Tomlinson traces the evolution of the FIFA World Cup into a global commercial spectacle, complete with its coterie of indispensable corporate sponsors and partners. Crucially, Tomlinson highlights the contradictions and tensions that emerge in the relationships between, and effects of FIFA as a supra-national organization on individual, national, sporting cultures and organizations. In Chapter 4, Steven J. Jackson and Brendan Hokowhitu address the politics of identity associated with global sports company adidas and its use of the traditional New Zealand All Blacks *haka* as part of its promotional strategizing. Framed within contemporary political debates related to indigenous culture and intellectual property rights, the chapter highlights the problem of maintaining and protecting cultural spaces when indigenous identities and constructed and affirmed through the promotional strategizing of transnational corporatism.

In Chapter 5, Samantha King explores the emergence of global strategic corporate philanthropy and community relations programs as part of the practices and operations of transnational corporatism. Through a case study of the Avon Corporation's Worldwide Fund For Women's Health and the Avon Running Global Women's Circuit, King's focus is on the social commitments that are enabled and constrained when "economic freedom" is pursued through the language and structures of global corporate philanthropy. King suggests that global strategic corporate philanthropy has developed into highly measured strategies that are integral to the profit-making activities of business. In respect to Avon, seeking to produce and sell goods in an ever-expanding number of locations, King proposes the organization has increasingly deployed philanthropy and community relations not merely to further some social good but as techniques for market penetration and retention.

Michael D. Giardina and Jennifer L. Metz provide an interesting corollary to King in their discussion of women's soccer, corporate identity and neoliberal citizenship in Chapter 6. Through a contextualization of the structural formation of the Women's United Soccer Association (WUSA), the entrenchment of family values within the US and the role of corporate sponsors in the WUSA, Giardina and Metz read the WUSA as a key site from which to excavate the construction of a (re-)emerging neoliberal national symbolic – an inclusive, race-neutral, global face of America's post-national future – organized around "all-American" notions of family and identity in post-Reagan/Clinton America.

Following Giardina and Metz's account of a post-racial America, in Chapter 7, Mary McDonald critically examines the role of sport in the media response to the terror attacks of September 11, 2001. Through a focus on the debates over whether or not to postpone play in the aftermath of September 11 and the symbolism surrounding the 2001 Major League Basketball (MLB) World Series, McDonald proposes that mediated versions of elite sport legitimated the capitalist workplace, multi-national corporations and consumer culture as stabilizing forces in uncertain times. In Chapter 8, John Amis focuses on the vagaries and complexities associated with competing in a global marketplace. Through a focus on the sporting strategizing of Guinness, Amis examines the practice and decision-making of cultural intermediaries responsible for the development and implementation of brand positioning in three different locales: Ireland, Great Britain and Africa. In this chapter Amis not only points out the role that sport plays in depicting a gendered and inevitably superficial simulacra of a particular society, but addresses the ways in which "organizational knowledge" – the structure, practice and operation of an organization – has been transformed by the perceived need to act globally, but think locally.

In Chapter 9, Phillip Rosson provides an account of the global strategizing of computer-game giant, SEGA. Through a focus on SEGA's shirt sponsorship relationship with Arsenal FC, of the English Premier League, Rosson investigates the ways in which Sega attempted to ingratiate itself, through Arsenal's tradition, history and global appeal, within the specificities of the complex European marketplace.

Jean Harvey and Alan Law, in Chapter 10, focus on the oligipolisitic authorship of mediated global sport culture. Harvey and Law suggest that an emergent commodified global sport culture has had a substantial impact upon the regulatory environment that surrounds the Canadian (sport) media. The focus in this chapter is how the space for resistance and for conjuring up imagined versions of competing Canadian national identities through (sport) media products has been ceded to global media oligopolies. Harvey and Law point out that this has not necessarily been in the form of a monolithic invasion of the Canadian media system. Rather, they point to how – in order to 'protect' Canadian culture and identity – Canadian telecommunication corporations reacted to the emergence of the global media conglomerates in ways that modified substantially traditional regulation policy.

Jeremy Howell addresses the morphing of the business structure of MLB in Chapter 11. Howell explains the passage America's national pastime has taken from "economic national champion" to "global enterprise network", pointing to the potential new symbolic mythologizing of the game in line with the logics of global capital accumulation. Howell suggests that the local fortunes of MLB are being shaped by distinctly global capitalist criteria, global conditions that shape the choices of the individual franchises that produce the global conditions out of which they have emerged. Finally, in Chapter 12, Trevor Slack, Michael Silk and Fan Hong address the "emergent" Chinese marketplace as it articulates, engages with, rejects and operates within a new global ecumene. In particular, these authors examine the impact that the globalizing forces of transnational corporations are having upon China and the Chinese sportingscape. The chapter focuses on the miscalculations of transnationals attempting to engage the Chinese market, negotiations with local particularities and complexities and the refinement of the Chinese economy, cultural identities and sport system in line with global consumer capitalist discourse.

References

Appadurai, A. (1996), *Modernity at Large: Cultural Dimensions of Globalization*. Minneapolis: University of Minnesota Press.

Appadurai, A. and Breckenridge, C. (1988). Why Public Culture. *Public Culture*, 1: 5–9.

Bale, J. and Cronin, M. (2003), *Sport and Postcolonialism*, Oxford: Berg

Bairner, A. (2001), *Sport, Nationalism and Globalization: European and North American Perspectives*, New York: State University of New York Press.

Buell, F. (1994), *National Culture and the New Global System*, Baltimore: Johns Hopkins University Press.

Cole, C. L. and Andrews, D. L. (2001), The Nation Reconsidered, *Journal of Sport and Social Issues*, 26(2): 123–5.

Crain, R. (2001), From Brand-building to Nation-building: Commentary – How US Businesses can Help Market Freedom, *Adage.com*, December 3, http://www.adage.com/news.cms?newsId=33535.

Cronin, M. and Mayall, (1998), *Sporting Nationalisms: Identity, Ethnicity, Immigration and Assimilation*, London: Frank Cass.

De Cillia, R., Reisgel, M., and Wodak, R. (1999). The Discursive Construction of National Identities, *Discourse and Society*, 10(2): 19–173.

Foster, R. J. (1991), Making National Cultures in the Global Ecumene, *Annual Review of Anthropology*, 20: 235–60.

Hall, S. (1991), The Local and the Global: Globalization and Ethnicity. In A. D. King (ed.), *Culture, Globalization and the World-system*, London: Macmillan, pp. 19–39.

Hannerz, U. (1996), *Transnational Connections: Culture, People, Places*, London: Comedia.

Hardt, M., and Negri, A. (2000), *Empire*, Cambridge MA: Harvard University Press.

Hargreaves, J. (2002). Globalization Theory, Global Sport, and Nations and Nationalism. In J. Sugden and A. Tomlinson (eds), *Power Games: A Critical Sociology of Sport*, London: Routledge, pp. 25–43.

Hedetoft, U. (1999), The Nation-state Meets the World: National Identities in the Context of Transnationality and Cultural Globalization, *European Journal of Social Theory*, 2(1): 71–94.

Hedetoft, U. and Hjort, M. (2002), *The Postnational Self: Belonging and Identity*, Minneapolis: University of Minnesota Press.

Held, D. (1995), *Democracy and the Global Order: From the Modern State to Cosmopolitan Governance*, Cambridge: Polity Press.

Held, D., McGrew, A., Goldblatt, D. and Perraton, J. (1999), *Global Transformations: Politics Economics and Culture*, Stanford CA: Stanford University Press.

Hobsbawm, E. J. (1983), Introduction: Inventing Traditions. In E. Hobsbawm and T. Ranger (eds.), *The Invention of Tradition*, Cambridge: Cambridge University Press.

Hobsbawm, E. J. (1990), *Nations and Nationalism since 1870: Programme, Myth, Reality*, Cambridge: Cambridge University Press.

Hobsbawm, E., and Ranger, T. (eds) (1983), *The Invention of Tradition*, Cambridge: Cambridge University Press.

Jenkins, R. (2002), Citizens, Residents, and Aliens in a Changing World: Political Membership in the Global Era. In Hedetoft, U. and Hjort, M. (eds), *The Postnational Self: Belonging and Identity*, Minneapolis: University of Minnesota Press.

Leslie, D. A. (1995), Global Scan: The Globalization of Advertising Agencies, Concepts, and Campaigns, *Economic Geography*, 71(4): 402–25.

Levitt, T. (1983), *The Marketing Imagination*, London: Collier-Macmillan.

Maguire, J., Poulton, E. and Possamai, C. (1999), Weltkrieg III? Media Coverage of England versus Germany in Euro 96, *Journal of Sport and Social Issues*, 23(4): 439–54.

Marshall, P. D. (1997), *Celebrity and Power: Fame in Contemporary Culture*, Minneapolis: University of Minnesota Press.

Miller, T. (2001), *Sportsex*, Philadelphia: Temple University Press.

Morley, D. and Robins, K. (1995), *Spaces of Identity: Global Media, Electronic Landscapes and Cultural Boundaries*, London: Routledge.

Ohmae, K. (1990), *The Borderless World*, New York: HarperBusiness.

Quelch, J. (2003), The Return of the Global Brand, *Harvard Business Review*, (August): 22–3.

Preston, P. and Kerr, A. (2001). Digital Media, Nation-states and Local Cultures: the Case of Multimedia "Content" Production, *Media, Culture and Society*, 23: 109–31.

Robins, K. (1997), What in the World's Going On? In P. D. Gay (ed.), *Production of Culture / Cultures of Production*, London: The Open University, pp. 11–66.

Rowe, D. (2003), Sport and the Repudiation of the Global, *International Review for the Sociology of Sport*, 38(3): 281–94.

Sassen, S. (1996), *Losing Control? Sovereignty in an Age of Globalization*, New York: Columbia University Press.

Sassen, S. (2000), Whose City Is It? Globalization and the Formation of New Claims. In F. J. Lechner (ed.), *The Globalization Reader*, Malden MA: Blackwell.

Smith, A. D. (1991), *National Identity*, London: Penguin.

2

Making it Local? National Basketball Association Expansion and English Basketball Subcultures

Mark Falcous and Joseph Maguire

> I think it's really about excellence, I don't think anyone cares what country a . . . star comes from. If people are interested in a particular discipline, they seek out the best and are interested in watching the best.
>
> Rick Welts, President NBA Properties

> No amount of hard cash will ensure that the sport is nothing more than just another transient American import.
>
> *The Observer*, November 6, 1994

A divergent set of views on the reception of American basketball beyond the US can be discerned when examining the key groups involved in its diffusion and development. On one hand, National Basketball Association (NBA) executive, Rick Welts, emphasizing "excellence", perceives American basketball as transcending all national boundaries, whereupon, due to the high standards of play, its cultural acceptance is inevitable. Similarly, NBA commissioner David Stern has saluted the NBA presence within Europe, suggesting that "If you haven't seen it, you can't appreciate how much a part of the European culture the NBA is" (*Sports Illustrated*, June 3, 1991, p. 86). On the other hand, sections of the British press expressed skepticism regarding the impact of the NBA. Such popular speculation regarding basketball is symptomatic of wider discussions central to globalization debates. These debates include questions regarding the propensity for local processes and cultures to be shaped by heightened global interdependence. Central to questions of the local-global nexus are issues of cultural hybridity, interpretation, consumption, disjuncture and resistance (Featherstone, 1991; Robins, 1997; Held et al., 1999; Held, 2000).

The presence and cultural reception of "global brands" such as the NBA are characterized by multiple nexuses. That is, there are several convergence points that contour the NBA encounter with local cultures. For example, negotiations and interpretations of NBA imagery with youth culture are particularly prominent (see Andrews et al., 1996; Andrews, 1997, 1999). Likewise, the development of the local commercial sports market contextualizes both opportunity and receptivity toward the NBA presence. Similarly, the nature of television audiences and markets (sporting or otherwise) contour the impact of mediated images. Reception across such indices is patterned along stratified, most notably, "racialised" lines (Wilson, 1997; Andrews, 1997, 1999; Kanazawa and Fund, 2001). Furthermore, there are encounters that center upon the existing cultural space occupied by "indigenous" basketball, which is confronted by the NBA co-presence. This chapter focuses upon this latter nexus as a "critical case". It considers the expansion of the NBA to Britain[1] with reference to an English case study of the development and consumption of "indigenous" basketball.

Brief attention is given to the theoretical debates concerning the local-global sports nexus. This discussion provides the conceptual basis to consider the NBA presence in the context of local consumption of basketball. Subsequently, we outline NBA expansion and strategies in Britain. Questions regarding the co-presence of local sports with the British game are then addressed with reference to interview, questionnaire and focus group data exploring the consumption of "local" basketball. Finally, we make explicit the link between our observations and the theoretical debates surrounding the local-global sports nexus.

Global Sport: Conceptual and Theoretical Considerations

Within the globalization of sport debate attention has increasingly swung to the relationship between global and local processes (Jackson and Andrews, 1999). Pivotal to questions surrounding the local-global nexus are "dialogues" between and within global flows and local cultural identities. Transnational promotional strategies have become a feature of the local-global interplay that surrounds sporting events, leagues, stars and teams. These are predicated on the creation of corporate alliances, international media synergies, corporate and state sponsorship and concerted promotion on a global scale. Indeed, transnational industries have emerged as a "significant feature of the global sport system" (Maguire, 1999, p. 128). Symptomatic of these developments are the attempts of North American professional sports leagues to expand globally. The National Football League (NFL), National Basketball Association (NBA), National Hockey League (NHL), and Major League Baseball (MLB) have actively sought out global markets (see Maguire, 1990, 1991; Bellamy, 1993; Guttmann, 1994; Wilcox, 1994; Miller et al., 2001, 2003).

The activities of these groups have a range of implications for localized cultures and identities. Conceptual debates on these processes, which have tended to be formulated in dichotomous terms, have centered on whether we view the dynamics of the local/global nexus as powered by either monocausal or multicausal processes. In addition, researchers argue about whether such processes are flowing unidirectionally or multidirectionally. Further, consideration is given to whether these processes are shaped by the outcome of the intentions of more powerful groups such as transnational corporations (TNCs), or are they contoured by "disjunctures" and unintended dimensions?

A range of observations have been made with specific reference to the NBA (see Emerson, 1993; Mandle and Mandle, 1990, 1994; Andrews et al., 1996; Andrews, 1997, 1999; Jackson and Andrews, 1996, 1999). The presence of "American commodity signs", such as the NBA, Jackson and Andrews (1996, p. 57) argue does not "inevitably lead to the creation of globally homogenous or 'Americanized' patterns of popular cultural existence". Alternatively, they emphasize the cultural dialectic at play in relation to the presence of transnational brands and images in influencing local identities and experiences. At one level, Jackson and Andrews (1999) speculate the presence of the NBA may actually energize multiple popular and local cultures. There is a need to clarify such issues and to detail the nature of any such "energizing".

Correspondingly, scholars have cautioned against the simplistic allure of the homogenization thesis. For example, Maguire highlights the need to be aware of the "celebration by global marketing strategies of difference and individuality" (Maguire, 1999, p. 213). Reflecting this, Silk and Andrews (2001) claim that sport "[acting] as a de facto cultural shorthand – has been appropriated within . . . the advertising campaigns of transnational corporations as a means of contributing toward the constitution and experiencing of national cultures" (p. 180). In this manner, they argue that TNCs may be implicated in the re-imagining and reconstitution of local cultural identities. These observations remain speculative at the textual level and therefore await empirical grounding in terms of reception.

Notwithstanding such strategies of "localization", the NBA is more akin to the "global-product" (Robins, 1997) in presenting a largely consistent product – at the textual level – across worldwide markets. In this way, Jackson and Andrews (1999) argue it holds specifically "American signification". Yet, even this presence is characterized, as we will demonstrate, by locally specific initiatives, as the NBA seeks resonance with differentiated markets. Subsequently, "local" promotional initiatives and the concerted promotion of migrant players to the NBA in specific countries are evident. For example, migrants have become important in promotional strategies, as the league seeks local resonance. Examples include John Amaechi (England), Detlef Schrempf (Germany), Vladi Divac (Yugoslavia), Yao Ming (China) and Dikembe Mutombo (Zaire), Peja Stojakovic (Yugoslavia), Pau Gasol (Spain), Andrei Kirilenko (Russia), Hedo Turkoglu (Turkey) and Tony Parker (France) who have been prominent in NBA promotions in their respective home countries. As Miller et al. (2003) clarify, such migrants, both in basketball and other sports, have become crucial in the global appeal of US sports. Subsequently, several caveats are required to Jackson and Andrews' (1999) contention that the positioning of the league is premised upon an operational strategy which "explicitly promotes itself as a signifier of cultural difference" and aims towards "*not* becoming an accepted armature of the local culture (p. 35, emphasis in original). Alternatively, elements of a quest for local resonance are a feature of NBA operations.

At the level of reception, the blend between the explicitly "American" signification of NBA promotion and local resonance is worked out within specific national contexts across a range of nexuses. In the case of New Zealand, Jackson and Andrews (1999) note the manner in which the juncture of the NBA with youth culture may be implicated in the re-articulation of local identities – characterized by the co-presence, and co-consumption of local sports stars and commodities. In this way, they suggest, localized popular cultures may be "energized". Yet, they document simultaneous media censorship of NBA-corporate imagery as linked to discourses of the threat of "Americanization". Similarly, the case of Poland illustrates the scope for varying responses within locales. These include simultaneous resistance, retrenchment and active solicitation resultant from the NBA presence (see Andrews et al., 1996).

For us, approaching these issues is best served by adopting a long-term perspective and avoiding of theoretical dichotomization. At the center of the analysis must be multidirectional processes, marked by power struggles of different kinds, which are contoured by unintended consequences stemming from the disjunctures between local-global flows and an uneven power geometry. On this basis, researchers are better able to grasp that, in making sense of the local-global equation, we must also grapple with a model of local cultures and local knowledgeability (Maguire, 1999). Too often research either romanticizes the local or sees it as obliterated by outside forces. Yet, local people make sense of the local-global nexus in quite complex ways. Texts, defined as powerful by "experts", don't always achieve the anticipated outcomes, as we shall observe, or have as powerful effects as transnational corporations may wish.

In this regard we also seek to explore the emergence of new varieties of "British" identity. For analytical purposes we focus, in this chapter, on a city in the English East Midlands: Leicester. While TNCs develop national and transnational marketing strategies for developing awareness and consumption of products, these strategies are always played out at the local level. Hence, our attention to this local scene and contention that it can act as a "critical" case study. Bearing these conceptual issues in mind, and in the context of a discussion of the NBA, the research presented addresses questions concerning political economy, TNC strategies, local-global co-presence, global brands, receptivity, and knowlegability. These issues lie at the heart of unravelling the local-global nexus in the context of the strategies and operations of TNCs.

National Basketball Association Expansion to Britain: A "Full-Court *Press*"

The starting point of concerted NBA involvement in the British market was the October 1995 "McDonalds Championship" held in London. The establishment of a "satellite" office in London to coordinate the NBA's operations followed this event. This direct, "on the ground" presence had been preceded by the appearance of NBA games on the satellite broadcast channel BSKYB, during the 1994–5 season. The following season, satellite coverage was complemented by terrestrial programing on Channel 4. Crucially, such free-to-air exposure was open to a much larger audience than the subscription-dependent satellite broadcaster. The strike-shortened 1999 NBA season was subsequently aired on Independent Television (ITV) and its digital "arm" ITV2. The appearance of the NBA on ITV, the main commercial rival to the BBC, is indicative of increasing penetration of the mainstream media. Alongside scheduled game and highlights coverage, NBA players visiting the UK also appeared on programmes such as BBC 1's *Record Breakers*, Channel 4's *The Big Breakfast*, *Nickelodeon*, *SKY News* and *SKY Sportscentre*.

A key element of the NBA strategy in the UK was to target the youth market. Reflecting the centrality of this market segment, and hinting at the strategy employed, Paul Smith, NBA Media Officer, observed:

> If you talk about the UK specifically, our main goal is to grow the sport, we need to grow the sport of basketball, we need to get more balls in more kids' hands bouncing them, and playing, and having an interest. That then affects the whole rest of our business, it affects . . . whether they wanna watch it on TV, whether they wanna buy a T-shirt, whether they wanna read about it in a magazine. (Interview, NBA London Office, March 23, 1998)

Accordingly, alongside television programing aimed at the younger audience segment, they embarked upon several "grassroots" initiatives to establish their brand, primarily amongst British youth. These strategies featured three main dimensions. First, the "Jam Session"; a traveling road-show of NBA-related items, trivia and exhibits visited major outdoors events and major towns and cities in its own right. Second, the "Mad Skillz" tour; a program of one-day coaching sessions that travels to different towns and cities. The first year of this initiative, 1997, featured fifteen dates. This number was subsequently increased to thirty dates for 1998. Third, a school-based initiative known as "NBA-2-ball" targeted children in schools. A two-person shooting game, the "2-ball" initiative was initially established in 500 schools in 1996, through the distribution of teaching resources and inducements in the form of NBA paraphernalia. The program was expanded to include 1,200 schools by 1997. In addition to these initiatives, an NBA "showtime tour" toured shopping centers throughout Britain from April–June 1997, displaying NBA merchandise.

The targeting of British youth has also been apparent with NBA TV programing being oriented specifically toward the adolescent market segment. For example, the NBA programing *NBA Raw* and *NBA 24/7* shows appearing on Channel 4, and *NBA '99,* aired on ITV, represented a marked departure from the systematically punctuated, journalistic style of traditional British sports programing (Blain et al., 1993; Boyle and Haynes, 2000). Spectacular game action interspersed with personality interviews and features, youth-oriented terminology and team histories, presented against a backdrop of rap music, and fast-cutting editing was reminiscent of the "staccato" style of American TV. Programming also featured explanation of the rules, nomenclature and conventions of basketball, in the quest to "educate" new consumers.

Indicative of the emerging NBA presence was the appearance of related magazines: *XXL Basketball*, *Hoop* and *Slam Dunk* on the shelves of Britain's newsagents. Further media penetration was evident in the appearance of a weekly basketball column in the *Sun* newspaper. NBA features also occasionally appeared in national dailies such as *The Times* and the *Daily Express*. Features on the league and its players also began to appear in general sports titles such as *Total Sport* and *Inside Sport* magazines, alongside articles in various lifestyle, youth and fashion publications.

The formation and extension of existing strategic alliances also accompanied expansion into the British market. The NBA's "global partners" such as Nike, Coca-Cola and McDonalds, have been involved. Nike, for example, acted as title sponsor to the "Mad Skillz" tour of 1998 – the promotional material featuring the imagery of their endorsees and the "swoosh" logo. Additionally, Nike television advertising, aired extensively on the ITV channel throughout 1999, featured Seattle Supersonics endorsee Gary Payton. Similarly, Coca-Cola involved its "Sprite" brand in promotions with packaging featuring the NBA logo and players imagery. Burger chain McDonalds also used NBA logos, imagery and paraphernalia in a prize draw promotion. In addition to these synergies forged with "global partners", UK-specific partnerships were developed. For example, KP Foods used NBA logos on packaging of its "Hula Hoop" brand during February 1997, involving over 80 million packs of product, supported by advertising and promotion fronted by well-known British television comedians Harry Enfield and Paul Whitehouse. National Basketball Association player cards were also distributed within "Hula Hoop" multi-packs.

Further reinforcement resulted from promotional campaigns, such as that undertaken by Adidas which featured NBA player, Kobe Bryant, in television and magazine advertisements throughout Britain during 1999. Similarly, the breakfast cereal manufacturer, the Kellog Company used player imagery on its "Frosties" and "Start" brands, the latter of which included give-away badges featuring NBA team logos. The Kellog Company also acted as title sponsor of the 1999 NBA-2-ball initiative, its logos featuring prominently on promotional material. The forging of these mutually reinforcing strategic alliances served as a further element of the NBA presence in Britain.

The final element of NBA strategy was the sale and promotion of licensed merchandise in British shops. Using a technique widely employed in North America, the NBA granted licenses for the production and distribution of goods to a select number of "official licensees". Licenses were granted for goods in six identifiable areas: school supplies, sports equipment, apparel, cards and stickers, novelties, home videos and computer games. In total, twenty-three different licensees were involved, notably some of whose agreements extended to a pan-European level, although several were confined to Britain alone. Bearing the logos of teams and the league itself, this merchandise became widely available, most notably in "high street" sports chains, such as JJB Sports.

During the late 1990s, TV exposure alongside "grassroots" initiatives established the NBA within the British marketplace. The presence of the league was further augmented by the use of the league's logos and imagery by corporate accomplices in the form of product promotions and television advertising. Additionally, the appearance of merchandise in British "high-street" stores contributed to the visibility attained by the league. The various strands of the approach adopted by the NBA are illustrated in Figure 2.1.

Gauging the relative impact and success of these strategies is complex. Relatively small amounts of sports print media coverage, mainly confined to the play-offs, reflect the lack of widespread infiltration of the NBA into the mainstream British sporting press. Furthermore, although NBA television coverage gradually attained greater penetration of the mainstream outlets, it has remained at the periphery of sports programming dominated by football, rugby union, rugby league, cricket and horse racing[2] (see Table 2.1; see also Whannel, 1992; Boyle and Haynes, 2000). As Table 2.1 illustrates, viewing figures for NBA broadcasts were modest. At no point did they surpass the

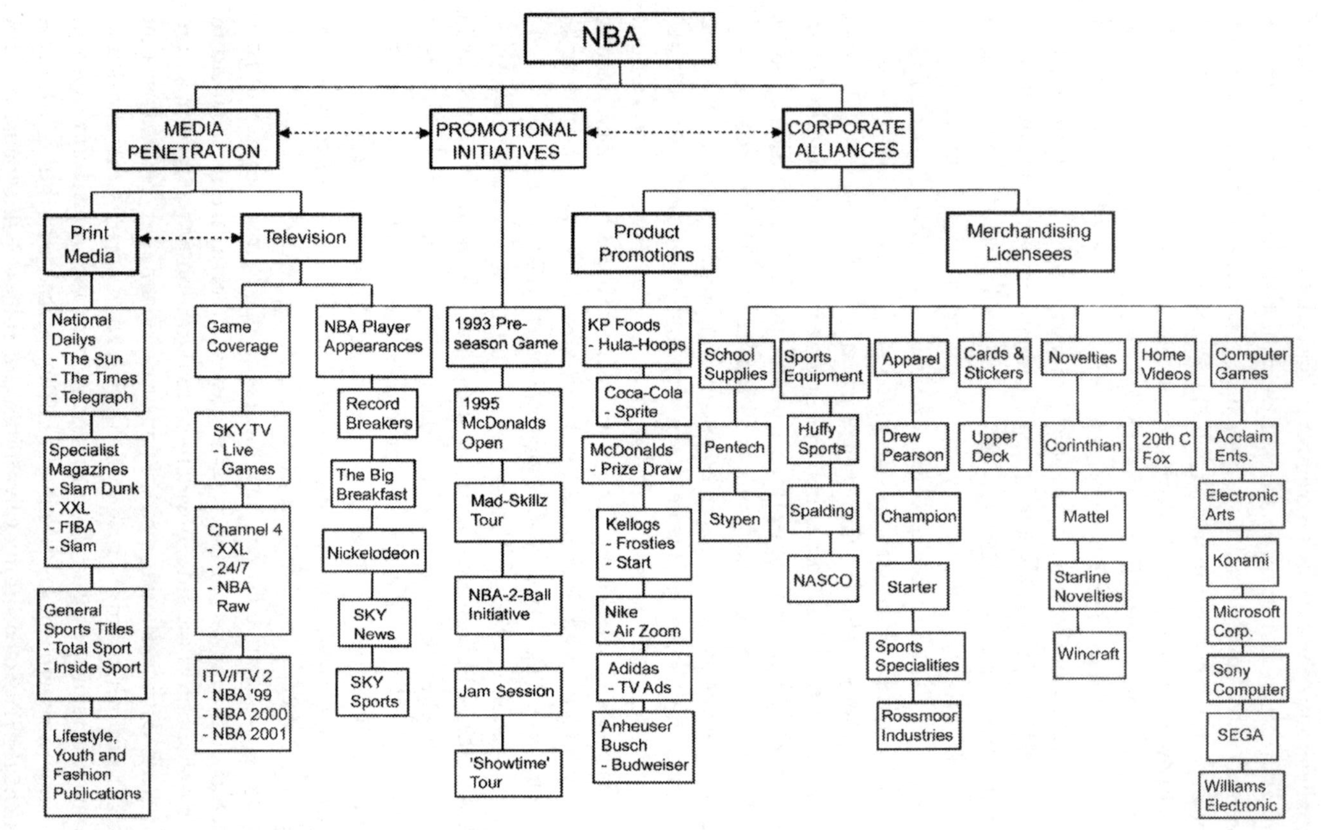

Figure 2.1. *NBA strategies of expansion in Britain 1993–2002.*

1 million viewer mark. The audiences are well below those of dominant indigenous sports and previous American imports. During the late 1980s, for example, the NFL attracted average audiences of close to 4 million viewers (Maguire, 1990). This marginal status of the league highlights aspects of the local reaction to the marketing strategies employed. Indeed, symptomatic of the relative lack of success of the corporate alliances and media synergies documented above, in generating popular appeal, the NBA disappeared from British terrestrial television altogether. For the 2002–3 season, access to NBA basketball in the UK was limited to the subscription based BSKYB. Given this, it is to the dynamics mediating local reception that this chapter now turns, with particular reference to the NBA–British basketball nexus.

Table 2.1. *NBA Viewing Figures in Britain (1996–2001)*

Year	*Viewing figures (average audience)*
1996	507,333
1997	263,800
1998	521,000**
1999*	720,000
2000*	659,000
2001*	766,380

Note: * ITV took over coverage of these seasons from Channel 4.
** Figures only available for February 1998.

The NBA–British Basketball Nexus

The presence of "global" competitors alongside local sports raises several questions regarding the potential homogenization of the scope of global sport, the room for local and global "brands" to co-exist, and scope for antagonism. For example, the NBA's global market expansion has brought it into conflict with both the Munich-based International Basketball Federation (FIBA) and a series of national leagues. Despite speculation about expansion to Europe and Asia (see McCallum, 1988), Rick Welts, President of NBA Properties asserted: "we don't believe that the NBA has in its future a league that's operating franchises in far-flung continents around the globe" (cited in Rosenberg, 1994). Such reassurances were received skeptically, however, in the light of the exposure afforded NBA "stars" at the 1992 Barcelona Olympics[3] and subsequent expansive NBA merchandising operations and television coverage.[4] Such expansion is potentially threatening to indigenous leagues, governing bodies and commercial interests. Indeed, in 2000, NBA commissioner, David Stern cryptically raised the prospects of an NBA-run feeder league based in Europe itself, outlining:

> we might be the first league that decides to have a minor league in one season and move it lock, stock and barrel to a different continent for another . . . in some cases there may be entire leagues which seek affiliation, and in some cases there might be some proposals that the NBA operates an entire league. We see nothing but opportunity and the market place is talking. (http://www.britball.com/, accessed July 27, 2000)

Highlighting underlying tensions, these proposals provoked negative responses from within the existing infrastructures of European basketball. The chairman of FIBA, Boris Stankovic, for example, with a hint of sarcasm, defensively noted, "The NBA is a member of FIBA and I can't imagine that even the NBA would violate the rules. We now have two big basketball organizations in the world. Both have to work together" (http://www.britball.com/, accessed July 27, 2000). Expansion of the NBA has been characterized by tensions and friction with local interests and groups. Since these skirmishes Stern has predicted that by the end of the current decade "there will be multiple NBA teams in Europe" (cited in Eisenberg, 2003). Such projections forewarn ongoing tensions.

The case of Britain demonstrates the specific and nuanced nature of interpretations at the local basketball-NBA nexus. In documenting the early commercial development of English basketball, Maguire (1988) detailed the conflicts between investing entrepreneurs and those concerned with the wider development of the game – specifically regarding indigenous players, junior development and national teams. Following the consolidation of the power of entrepreneurs, the speculative commercial optimism and marketing hype within the indigenous game during the mid-1990s has not been realized. In fact, the game underwent a retrenchment during the late 1990s, with little sign of the much-heralded "boom around the corner" (Falcous, 2002).

Several commentators had initially viewed the onset of NBA activities as a turning point for the commercial status of the British game. Reflecting such optimistic rhetoric, David Stern forecast benefits for the indigenous game. He noted "there is a need for continuity and consistency, working with the [indigenous] leagues, working with television and sponsors so that we can have a cumulative effect" (cited in Longmore, 1995, p. 26). That "cumulative effect", it was argued, would have consequences for the commercial success of the British game. Indicating that NBA interests extended to the development of the sport in the broadest possible sense, Stern continued "[we] have to work harder to make the sport work at the grass roots level. In the end, it's all about kids being drawn to the sport" (cited in Longmore, 1995, p. 26). Suggestions that NBA interests in promoting the broader game are philanthropic, however, require due skepticism. Similarly, speculation regarding the apparently positive effects of the NBA on the broader British game requires critical consideration. The presence of the NBA raises several questions for the "indigenous" game – itself heavily influenced by American playing and coaching personnel, marketing and presentation (see Maguire 1988, 1994). In turn, and for present purposes, there are questions regarding its consumption.

Local–Global Consumption: The NBA and English Basketball Fans

As the previous section has noted, the development and consumption of British basketball since the mid-1990s is marked by the co-presence of the NBA in terms of identification, television audience appeal and merchandising. What we wished to establish is how 'consumers' of the local game perceived, experienced and reacted to those developments. As Table 2.2 illustrates, the local basketball audience was dominated by white, middle-class family groupings.[5] The perceptions of Leicester Riders fans, probed via questionnaire, interview and

Table 2.2. *Demographic Profile of Leicester Riders Fans*

Gender	Female	Male				
	48% (n84)	52% (n90)				
Age range	15–20	21–30	31–40	41–50	51–60	61 and over
	15% (n26)	17% (n31)	25% (n44)	32% (n56)	8% (n14)	3% (n5)
Ethnicity	Black-Caribbean	White	Other			
	4% (n7)	94% (n165)	2% (n4)			
Occupational classification	Professional	Intermediate	Self-employed	Lower supervisory	Manual	Other
	43% (n75)	14% (n26)	6% (n10)	9% (n15)	3% (n5)	25% (n26)
Educational achievement	University/ post-graduate degree	Professional qualifications	16–18 qualifications[5]	Secondary school		
	27% (n44)	19% (n30)	25% (n40)	29% (n47)		
Household income	<£7,000	£8,000–£15,000	£16,000–£25,000	£26,000–£35,000	£36,000–£45,000	>£46,000
	5% (n7)	16% (n22)	23% (n32)	23% (n32)	22% (n30)	11% (n7)

focus-group techniques,[6] were revealing in the light of NBA marketing. This presence is characterized by the rhetoric of the league as the "world best", reinforced in NBA television coverage. In this way, the marketing of the game assumes that the NBA version will have a higher status, relegating its British counterpart by comparison.

The evidence, however, reveals greater complexity. In the case of TV coverage, a greater number of questionnaire respondents expressed a preference for viewing indigenous basketball (55 per cent) compared to the NBA (45 per cent). Hence, a small preference for watching the British game was evident, although clearly the presence of the NBA commanded the preference of a substantial proportion of fans. Such findings point to a complex interplay between attachments to the British game and perceptions of the NBA. Caution is necessary, however, in interpreting TV preferences, due to the mediating factors of accessibility and broadcast times of coverage. The British game appears primarily on the satellite, subscription-based SKY network, whereas the NBA during the late 1990s and early 2000s has been freely accessible on terrestrial channels. Nevertheless, it is significant that the figures point to marginal preferences for the British game, despite its subordinate status and greater difficulty of access, and warrants further exploration.

Expenditure on merchandise also reflected a relative preference for the British game. Of those purchasing merchandise (a total of 46 per cent of the questionnaire sample), 67 per cent reported buying the indigenous equivalent, compared to 51 per cent purchasing NBA merchandise. Hence, as with television coverage, a preference for the home game was apparent. Such a finding points to a further disparity between local fans identification of the "better" American game and their preferences for consumption. That is to say, they prefer to consume that which is associated with the lower status brand (in terms of a global hierarchy). Also significant to note is that goods associated with the British game are not as readily accessible in contrast to the NBA brand which appears in prominent "High-Street" shops and outlets. In sum, the local appears to have a stronger and deeper resonance with a majority of basketball supporters.

Further qualifications, however, are required. The figures are also suggestive of "overlap" between indigenous and NBA 'brands'. This latter finding points toward a process of pluralization, in that some fans come to identify with and consume the merchandise of both forms of basketball. Although limited, these questionnaire findings present interesting leads in the context of local-global identity politics. Specifically, they concur with Jackson and Andrews' (1999) observation on the co-presence and consumption in the case of New Zealand. Yet, and in contrast to previous work by Andrews (1997), despite attempts by the NBA to "locate" their brand as "world best", in terms of merchandising and television coverage there is an overall preference amongst fans for the domestic game. This highlights issues of relevance and identity that mediate the discourse of NBA marketing in Britain among Riders fans. The key questions in this light surround the lines of distinction that local consumers draw between them.

Using a technique based upon the work of Klein (1988, 1991), we further explored the co-presence of NBA and English basketball amongst Leicester Riders fans by posing a hypothetical question designed to explore fans' sense of cultural identification. Fans were asked if, price and quality being the same, they would rather wear the cap or clothing of the Riders, or an NBA cap or clothing. They were also asked in an open-ended manner to explain their choice. Results were revealing, pointing to a greater propensity for identification with the English game. Sixty-seven percent of fans said they would rather wear a Leicester Riders cap or clothing, the remaining 33 percent expressing a preference for the NBA equivalent. The reasons given for these selections highlighted several dimensions of fans identification with the local team and city.

A series of responses can be highlighted that help explain the preference for the Riders. These responses related to an identification with, and sense of emotional attachment to the team, on the basis of relevance to the fans own identities and leisure lives. Steve,[7] for example, explained: "I identify more with the Riders and don't particularly care about 'street cred' of branded clothing". That is to say, identification with the Riders outweighed the fashionable status associated with the NBA. Similarly, others noted, "[I] want to support my team – feel more 'in touch' with them" (Dan). "Riders are the team we support – no emotional interest in NBA teams" (Pat). Finally, in reference to recent poor team performances, Shelia explained, "You need to support your own team. God help us!!!"[8] This reasoning powerfully illustrates the sense of emotional obligation inherent in the preference for the Riders, irrespective of the presumed or prescribed quality of the "brand". Specifically, it highlights Sheila's affiliation to the Leicester Riders despite the potential unattractiveness of that identification due to the losing team.

Further responses explaining a preference for identification with the Riders emphasized the strength of civic affiliations and identities. Several fans explained their local preference with reference to: "local team and spirit of pride", "home town club", "Riders has more significance for me living in Leicester", "Local pride", "Loyalty to our side", and "Local pride and loyalty to team". These preferences for affiliation to the Riders rather than the NBA illustrate the importance of local identities and civic pride in mediating NBA imagery. The strength of such affiliations, for these fans, supersedes the "street cred" and cultivated image associated with the NBA. As Catherine confirmed, "I'm a Riders fan and would rather be associated with my local team than any other team". Such senses of affiliation, it is clear, transcend the "world-class" brand prowess of the NBA. Such explanations reinforce the association of the Riders with the city of Leicester and with the club as a source of local pride for fans. Significantly, these provide an "anchor" for identification with local basketball (in the guise of the Riders) in preference to the NBA which is not associated with such characteristics.

In addition, a series of fans' responses illustrate national identities and pride, as paramount to some preferences for identification with the Riders. Hence, forms of identification with the Riders were also based upon identification with the country more generally. For example, one fan in explaining his preference simply asserted: "Patriotic". Furthermore, identification specifically with the indigenous game was noted as a source of preference for the local over the global. Fan responses included: "I support British basketball", "I like British basketball, not the NBA", "Loyalty to the home game". Also evident was anti-American feeling. For example, Nick bluntly questioned "Who wants Yankee crap?" Further highlighting a lack of resonance, Keith reasoned, "Why wear something that's nothing to do with you?"[9] On the basis of these examples, it is clear that links with national identities and loyalty to British basketball are also a component feature of affiliations to the local in preference to identification with the NBA. Thus, claims in the global sport research that the NBA dominates the local may be over-stated. Yet, we do need to account for why the NBA brand had some limited appeal.

Those responses that opted for the NBA product were largely characterized by reference to the greater recognition of the league and the fashion "kudos", or "street cred", of NBA brands. Fans explanations along these lines included: "Better known name – more street cred", "Because they are famous teams known around the world", "More people recognize NBA than any other merchandise". Similarly, the higher status of the league relative to the British game was noted as a factor. Thus, Graham explained: "Because the NBA has the image of being the best basketball league". Likewise, Alan simply explained his hypothetical selection: "Because NBA is better". These responses demonstrate associations of the NBA with a particular, fashionable image, which appealed to a minority of fans. This was explained by fans in terms of the higher status and global "presence" of the American league compared to the British game.

These observations highlight several lines of distinction drawn by fans between the two "brands". Those fans opting to identify with the British game drew upon the emotional attachment, local identities and pride, and identification with British basketball more broadly. Fans also pointed to a lack of relevance or identification with the NBA, and/or anti-Americanism, as a reason for identifying with the British game. Alternatively, those with a preference for the NBA drew upon the status and worldwide recognition of the league, relative to the British game. Exploring this co-presence with reference to ethnographic data demonstrates how engagement with the NBA, whilst being contoured by the senses of identity and consumption above, is also patterned by a series of subtle variations associated with fans interpretive understandings of basketball. These subtle variations involve the specific conditions, circumstance and meanings associated with fans consumption of the local game. Let us examine these variations more closely.

Amongst several fans the experience of live Riders games, often with little "wider" interest in the sport of basketball, was a feature of a lack of interest in the NBA. Specifically, this was a consequence of television coverage failing to fulfill the form of entertainment they found at Riders games. That is to say, it was specifically the *live*, and *local* experience, which appealed in their consumption of basketball. The wider concerns of the sport were not necessarily their affair! Reflecting this, Delia explained: "we don't make an effort [to watch the NBA], if it was on the right time of day, on a day and we weren't doing anything else, but I wouldn't make an effort, I like the live game" (focus group, March 24, 2000). Similarly, Dot, expressed no interest in the NBA, and reinforced the attraction of basketball to her was the live experience of Riders games: "Err, no, its very hard to watch basketball on television I think, trying to follow it, it's not like being in the flesh, I'd rather be in the flesh" (interview, March 3, 2000). Hence, Dot's affiliation to the Riders was neither accompanied by or stimulated interest in NBA television coverage. Alternatively, she drew a distinction between the opportunity to watch live Leicester Riders games and viewing the NBA on television.

In a similar manner, other fans expressed a lack of interest in NBA coverage. For example, Teddy noted "I think it's the difference between seeing something on television and seeing something in the flesh. The advantage here is that you are very close to the action" (interview, March 4, 2000). Similarly, Jenny noted, "I don't really go out of my way to watch it, because I don't really get the same feeling watching it on TV as I do here . . . I don't really keep up with the NBA, I just like doing, like England and the matches round here and things, so I don't really watch it on TV" (Jenny, focus group, March 24, 2000). Likewise, Davina explained: "I don't think its quite the same either just watching it on TV . . . I think because of the involvement between you and the players and the other people in the crowd, I think its one of those things that you have to go and watch live" (Davina, focus group, March 24, 2000). Specifically, Davina highlighted that the attraction of basketball for her was related to the atmospheric experience, close proximity to the court and identification with players.

The specific attraction of basketball and affiliation to the Riders for some was linked to the experience of live spectatorship. Significantly, these opinions did not mean that fans necessarily favoured the British game on television because, likewise, it did not fulfill the specific form of entertainment these fans sought from the live game. Notably though, as televised coverage of the NBA is the *only* source of access to the American league (British fans cannot watch it live), these fans expressed little interest. Again, we may have to reconsider how we conceptualize mediated global sports images and how such images relate to or are offset by local meanings and experiences. Textual analysis alone is not enough.

When pressed on comparisons, fans largely expressed a greater identification with the televised British game as a consequence of "relating" more closely with that version, due to their identification with live games. Katie, capturing the sense of relevance explained: "I like the British, because with playing a lot of the teams, you know the faces, and then you can relate to it a bit more" (focus group, April 4, 2000). This contrasted with her view of the NBA: "its exciting to watch the NBA games, but you don't tend to know who people are" (focus group, April 1, 2000). Hence, despite acknowledging the potential excitement of the NBA, she favored the "British" game on the basis of relevance to her engagement with basketball, in that she knew and could identify with the teams and players. Of course, as previously observed, there is a degree of irony evident in this preference. After all, given the domination of the game by Americans, the "Britishness" of the local version is questionable (see Maguire, 1988, 1994).

Reflecting this identification with the indigenous game in preference to the NBA, a discussion between Denise and Alan illustrated the greater personal relevance of the British game (BBL) to fans:

MF: Which do you get more 'worked up' about, the BBL or the NBA?

A: I think the BBL, because if Bob Donewald's[10] on the telly being thrown out of a game or whatever, I can go "yeah Bob and . . ." 'cos I know Bob a bit or whatever.

D: **It's more personal is the BBL.**

A: It's a bit more personal.

D: You know, **you know the players**, the arena's are small, **you've got your friends down there.**

[emphasis added]

This dialogue illustrates how these fans' knowledge of the players, coaches and personnel of the British game renders it more "personal" than the NBA. Extracts such as these demonstrate identification with the British game, resulting in a preference for watching it on television, rather than the NBA version. They did so, on the basis that it is more relevant to their own lives, and experiences, of supporting their "local" team – the Riders.

In keeping with the broader attempt to capture the complexity of fandom and the heterogeneity of responses, it should also be noted that a small number of fans expressed an appreciation of and interest in watching the NBA due to knowledge and interest in the sport of basketball more broadly. Thus, Alan explained that when it came to TV coverage "I can engage with BBL [the British game] and get excited and shout at the television, erm and the odd time when NBA games are on . . . I can get screaming and shouting the same" (interview, September 19, 2000). In a similar manner, Graham acknowledged the playing superiority of the NBA, and expressed a keen interest, stating, "I follow it with interest, it's one of the best sources of basketball in the world". In this way, his appreciation of basketball contoured his interest of the NBA as the highest standard of basketball available. Notably, such views appear to be premised on a broader engagement with the sport of basketball per se, rather than an emphasis on the experience of live attendance at Leicester Riders games. Yet, such responses were infrequent.

These data point to a differentiated sense of engagement with the British game and NBA by fans. The relevance of the British game is associated with local identities, civic pride and national identities, whereas the NBA was alternatively linked to "fashionable", though not practiced images and status. Fans' perspectives are, once again, complex and highly contextualized. Simplistic notions of resistance, or acceptance, fail to capture the nuanced nature of engagement with the presence of the NBA. "Readings" are grounded in fans sense of engagement with locality and place. Subsequently, perspectives on the NBA are contoured by fans' understandings of their own consumption, broader affiliations and identification with the sport of basketball, as well as the strength of local identities – not solely with the mediated "product" *per se.*

Conclusion

Though preliminary in scope, the results highlighted in this chapter warrant some discussion in the context of the operations of TNCs and the dynamics of the local-global sports nexus. The evidence presented highlights the complexity of local-global consumption of sport within a global sports figuration characterized by the intended practices of TNCs such as the NBA, yet also shaped by local sporting identities and associations (Maguire et al., 2002). In the case examined, local cultural affiliations are a resilient factor mediating local-global sports consumption. Notably, the reception of the NBA is mediated by existing cultural identities and affiliations that surround "local" sporting practices. Central to fans' affiliation were issues of local pride and collective representation through place, space and national identities. In the response to the presence of carefully packaged and commodified "global" sports, these factors exercise an important influence over the response to what may be acknowledged as "world class" or the "best". Hence, issues of relevancy and affiliations to "community" (sporting and otherwise) are pivotal in the local reception, rejection, accommodation and/or consumption of the imagery and paraphernalia of TNCs, such as the NBA.

The dynamics of global sports, however, highlight the potential contradiction inherent in such local sporting affiliations when set in broader contexts, characterized by a global labor market and commodified sports structures. In this way, local affiliations to British basketball are undermined by a political economy that positions the elite game in a broadly dependent relationship with global, specifically American, influences (see Maguire, 1994). As Maguire (1999, p. 149) notes "sensitivity to local responses to global flows has to be stressed. But so does the balance of power between the groups involved". Hence, local affiliations to elite men's British basketball are played out within the broader dynamics of a commodified sport product. This product, while acting as a source of *local* meaning in relation to the "global" NBA, acts more broadly to underdevelop the wider British game. Specifically, local players and coaches and the interests of the national team are marginalized in favor of the American-dominated spectacle. Yet, within the everyday lives of British basketball fans, the game is a source of meaning and identity, notwithstanding the broader political economy. What counts is a sense of local space, place and identity, always relative to other local East Midland, regional and national identities. Clearly, the British game, although dominated by American personnel, is imbued with local affiliations acting as a source of local cultural meaning and identity for fans. Leicester Riders fans may or may not like American domination of the indigenous game, or respect or consume the NBA-mediated products, but they overwhelmingly take meaning from beating their closest local rival, the Derby Storm![11]

Given that powerful mediated texts do not always have the intended effects that TNC's representatives, such as the NBA's David Stern, hope for, further empirical work and conceptual clarification is needed. As we have attempted to highlight, it is necessary to explore the dynamics of local cultural impacts and response to the activities of organizations such as the NBA, and the complex synergies that inform the pervasive global presence they constitute. In particular, the data observed represents one local context, within a singular broader national context characterized by a unique set of historical and sporting antecedents. Comparative work from a diverse range of localities is required to establish further evidence of the identity politics and established/outsider relations we have observed in a preliminary way. Furthermore, sensitivity to the full complexity of the local, contoured along gender, ethnic, class and generational lines, is necessary to discern the dynamics that in turn may herald differing elements of response and reaction within local contexts.

Notes

1. It is appropriate to note here that NBA activities were not differentiated according to the varying national contexts within Britain. The case study that is the focus of this chapter, however, is based upon an English town. To complicate this issue the English team around which the case-study is centered plays within a British league – the BBL (British Basketball League). Hence many of the fans identified with the "British" game. We are conscious of the need to differentiate the Britain-wide marketing of the NBA, the indigenous British game, and the English context of the findings presented herein. In this regard, although the terms "English" and "British" appear within this chapter we do not use them interchangeably.
2. Viewing figures for NBA broadcasting indicate small audiences relative to competitors. At no point did average audiences surpass the 1.000,000 viewer mark. See Table 2.1 for the exact figures:
3. The vast media attention afforded the American "dream team" projected the NBA's carefully cultivated star players to a global audience. The significance for the NBA, Rick Welts, President of NBA properties suggested, was to "move our international effort ahead 10 years" (cited in Desens, 1994). The sales of NBA merchandise in Europe jumped from $56 million in 1990 to $259 million after the Barcelona Olympics (Connor and Russell, 1995).
4. By the 1998-99 season, television coverage of the league extended to 199 countries on 104 telecasters in 40 languages, reaching over 600 million households worldwide (http: www.NBA.Com/television, accessed April 12, 2000). The majority of this broadcasting takes the form of pre-packaged highlight shows designed to promote the league to new consumers (see Emerson, 1994).
5. The wider ethnographic project from which this data is drawn employed a questionnaire. The data revealed an audience with the demographic characteristics shown in Table 2.2. The basketball audience was, in terms of demographic composition, dominated by the middle and younger age cohorts, divided roughly equally by gender, overwhelmingly white in ethnicity, and dominated by the professional occupations with higher than average incomes and educational achievement. It is significant to note that this profile does not mirror that of the wider city. In particular the large Asian population of Leicester is absent. The ethnic minority profile of the basketball audience (6%) shows an under-representation of the city's ethnic population which stands at 28.5% (2001 Census).
6. As part of a wider ethnographic strategy a total of twenty-eight fans were engaged in either interview or focus group situations. Questionnaires were distributed on

an 'opportunist' basis to adult fans at a regular season game. In total 269 questionnaires were distributed; 177 useable questionnaires were returned

7. To protect the identity of fans, all names used are pseudonyms.
8. This humerous response was made in relation to a string of poor team performances.
9. Questions of "race" may also be "at play" here. Aside from issues of national identities that are expressed, there may be an unspoken resistance on the basis of the black-dominated playing base from a largely white, middle-class audience.
10. Bob Donewald, a frequently flamboyant and controversial figure in British basketball, was a former Leicester Riders coach.
11. Derby is located approximately 15 miles away from Leicester. Due to this geographical proximity matches between the two are the most eagerly awaited by the two sets of fans. Games themselves are parochial affairs with a strong sense of rivalry and civic pride evident.

References

Andrews, D. (1997). The (Trans)national Basketball Association: American Commodity-Sign Culture and Global-Local Conjuncturalism. In A. Cvetkovich and D. Kellner (eds), *Articulating the Global and the Local*, Boulder CO: Westview, pp. 72–101.

Andrews, D. (1999), Whither the NBA, Whither America? *Peace Review*, 11 (4): 505–16.

Andrews, D., Carrington. B., Jackson. S. and Mazur, J. (1996). Jordanscapes: A Preliminary Analysis of the Global Popular, *Sociology of Sport Journal*, 13: 428–57.

Blain, N., Boyle, R. and O'Donnell, H. (1993), *Sport and National Identity in the European Media*, London: Leicester University Press.

Boyle, R. and Haynes, R. (2000), *Power Play: Sport, the Media and Popular Culture*, London: Longman.

Bellamy, R. (1993). Issues in the Internationalization of the US Sports Media: The Emerging European Marketplace, *Journal of Sport and Social Issues*, 17(3): 168–80.

Conner, B. and Russell, N. (1995) *Slam Dunk: The Raptors and the NBA in Canada*, Scarborough, Ontario: Prentice-Hall.

Desens, C. (1994), The NBA's Fast Break Overseas, *Business Week*, December 5: p. 94.

Eisenberg, D. (2003, March 17), The NBA's Global Game Plan: As the world's best hoopsters flock to the US, the sport grows more popular and profitable abroad, *Time*, http://web1.infortrac.galegroup.com/itw/infomark/750/42275037w1/purl=rc1_EAI

Emerson, R. (1993), Globalball, *The Bulletin*, November 8, 77–82.

Falcous, M. (2002), *Globalisation and Sport. Local Identities, Consumption and Basketball*, unpublished Ph.D thesis, Loughborough University, Loughborough, England.

Featherstone, M. (1991), Global and Local Cultures, *Vrijetijd En Samenlevig*, 9 (3–4): 43–57.

Guttmann, A. (1994), *Games and Empires: Modern Sports and Cultural Imperialism*, New York: Columbia University Press.

Held, D (ed) (2000), *A Globalizing World? Culture, Economics, Politics*, London: Routledge.

Held, D., McGrew, A., Goldblatt, D. and Perraton, J. (1999), *Global Transformations: Politics, Economics and Culture*, Stanford CA: Stanford University Press.

Jackson, S. and Andrews, D. (1996), Excavating the (Trans) National Basketball Association: Locating the Global/Local Nexus of America's World and the World's America, *Australiasian Journal of American Studies*, 15: 57–64.

Jackson, S. and Andrews, D. (1999). Between and Beyond the Global and the Local. *International Review for the Sociology of Sport*, 43(1): 31–42.

Kanazawa, M. and Fund, J. (2001). Racial Division in Professional Basketball: Evidence from Nielsen Ratings. *Economic Enquiry*, 39: 599–608.

Klein, A. (1988), American Hegemony, Dominican Resistance, and Baseball, *Dialectical Anthropology*, 13: 301–12.

Klein, A. (1991). Sport and Culture as Contested Terrain: Americanization in the Caribbean, *Sociology of Sport Journal*, 8: 79–85.

Longmore, A. (1995), NBA orders Limited Retreat from Decibel Hell, *The Times*, October 19, p. 42.

Maguire, J. (1988), The Commercialization of English Elite Basketball 1972–1988: A Figurational Perspective, *International Review for the Sociology of Sport*, 23(4). 305–23.

Maguire, J. (1990). More Than a Sporting "Touchdown": The Making of American Football in England 1982–1990, *Sociology of Sport Journal*, 7: 213–37.

Maguire, J. (1991). The Media-Sport Production Complex: The Case of American Football in Western European Societies. *European Journal of Communication*, 6(3): 315–35.

Maguire, J. (1994), American Labour Migrants, Globalization and the Making of English Basketball. In J. Bale, J. Maguire (eds), *The Global Sports Arena. Athletic Talent Migration in an Interdependent World*, London: Frank Cass, pp. 226–55.

Maguire, J. (1999), *Global Sport: Identities, Societies, Civilizations*, London: Polity.

Maguire, J., Jarvie, G., Mansfield, L. and Bradley, J. (2002). *Sport Worlds: A Sociological Perspective*, Champaign IL: Human Kinetics.

Mandle, J. and Mandle, J. (1990). Basketball, Civil Society and the Post Colonial State in the Commonwealth Caribbean, *Journal of Sport and Social Issues*, 14(2): 59–75.

Mandle, J. and Mandle, J. (1994), *Caribbean Hoops. the Development of West Indian Basketball*, Gordon & Breach: London.

Miller, T., Lawrence, G., McKay, J. and Rowe, D. (2001), *Globalization and Sport*, London: Sage.

Miller, T., Rowe, D., McKay, J. and Lawrence, G. (2003), The Over-Production of US Sports and the New International Division of Cultural Labor, *International Review for the Sociology of Sport*, 38(4): 427–40.

Robins, K. (1997), What in the World is going on? In P. Du Gay (ed.), *Production of Culture/Cultures of Production*, London: Sage, pp. 11–67.

Silk, M. and Andrews, D. (2001). Beyond a Boundary? Sport, Transnational Advertising, and the Reimagining of National Culture, *Journal of Sport and Social Issues*, 25(2): 180–201.

Whannel, G. (1992), *Fields in Vision Television Sport and Cultural Transformation*, London: Routledge.

Wilcox, R. (1993). Imperialism or Globalism? A Conceptual Framework for the Study of American Sport and Culture in Contemporary Europe, *Journal of Comparative Physical Education and Sport*, 15(1): 30–40.

Wilson, B. (1997). "Good Blacks" and "Bad Blacks": Media Constructions of African-American Athletes in Canadian Basketball, *International Review for the Sociology of Sport*, 32(2): 177–189.

3

The Making of the Global Sports Economy: ISL, Adidas and the Rise of the Corporate Player in World Sport[1]

Alan Tomlinson

Introduction

The last quarter of the twentieth century was a crucial phase in the remaking of the political economy of world sport. Many sports rooted in particular histories, traditions and cultures, and in many cases seen as the embodiment of political values and a national identity, were remade in the image of a burgeoning international economy and a rapidly expanding global communications infrastructure. These were not by any means smooth and seamless transitions, and an incipient globalization process was not a simple alternative to forms of nation-building and nationalist rivalries as expressed in international competition. Indeed, international sporting competition is a very public realm that demonstrates the interdependency of the national and the global. But few national sports cultures would remain untouched by the increasing influence of the corporate and media interests that began to see in sport the perfect vehicle for their own expansionist, supra-national ambitions. In the 1960s in the USA, new models of sports finance, and the associated business of sport marketing and event management, began to be established as the vestiges of amateurism and voluntarism in sport were swept aside by rapacious entrepreneurs. In the 1970s and onwards, sports in the US/North American canon – the Big 4 team-sports of American football, baseball, basketball and ice-hockey – were further commercialized and remade around a logic of commodification. Individual sports such as tennis and golf were revolutionized as television coverage, concomitant revenues and associated sponsorship laid down the foundation for the Golden Triangle of sport, television, and corporate sponsor, so brilliantly consummated later in the century in mega-events such as the Olympic Games and the men's soccer World Cup, and on a more everyday scale in the UEFA (European

Football Union) European Champions' League (Sugden and Tomlinson, 1998; Chapter 4). At the beginning of this process, Leigh Hunt led the professionalization of tennis, and Mark McCormack established IMG (International Management Group) as the market leader for this new form of sports entrepreneurialism, making household names, across the world, of golfers such as Arnold Palmer and Jack Nicklaus of the USA, and South African Gary Player: Arnie's Army, as Palmer's fans became known, led the march towards a transformation of the economy and culture of sport. Meanwhile, the big sports bodies – the International Olympic Committee (IOC), La Fédération Internationale de Football Association (FIFA), the International Amateur Athletic Federation (IAAF) – slumbered in the background, not yet alert to the possibilities of the financial bonanza available to them once the corners of the Golden Triangle were linked up, and the right sympathetic agent or organizational broker placed at the center of any such triangle.

Simson and Jennings (1992) have shown how new men in key positions were to change the infrastructure of world sport as positions of presidential power were won by the likes of Spaniard Juan Antonio Samaranch in the IOC, Brazilian João Havelange at FIFA, and Italian Primo Nebiolo at the IAAF. What Sugden and Tomlinson (1999, Chapter 2) have called the "blazers and slacks brigade", an Anglo-Saxon paternalist élite, was swept aside as world sport was developed as a set of interlocking fiefdoms delivering undreamed-of riches to the opportunistic few. More positively, the sports organisations were modernized, the events expanded and better-funded, and worldwide sport culture given an unprecedented profile in the mediated global culture. None of this was possible without an intensifying presence of private capital in the sport economy, without the attraction of the corporate sponsor.

Internationally, the 1984 Los Angeles Olympics also symbolized this trend towards the corporate. The city, as the only bidder for those games, rewrote the rules for the staging of the event, drew widely on corporate sponsors, private capital, and volunteer labor, and triumphed jingoistically in the media ratings, benefiting from the Cold War rivalries and the absence of the Soviet Union and its allies, in the tit-for-tat boycotts following the US-led boycott of the Moscow 1980 games. Some commentators noted the uniqueness of this, a corporatization and McDonaldization of the world sporting event (Gruneau, 1984). The success of the 1984 games, as a media show and in reported financial terms (reporting a US$225 million surplus), opened the eyes of sports entrepreneurs to the money-making potential of top-class sport. Havelange had already expanded the soccer World Cup finals from 16 to 24 participants, in Spain in 1982, with an eye to the global markets that increased participation in the hallmark event could secure.

In the consolidation of these developments, multi-national companies, sports equipment and clothing retailers among them, saw sport and sport stars as irresistible vehicles for the marketing of their products. Regionally based national sponsors such as the brewer Steinlager, long-term sponsor of the New Zealand Rugby Union side the All Blacks, have subsequently given way to the multi-national takeover by companies such as adidas. As Jackson et al. put it: ". . . the adidas-All Black alliance is an important site for the exploration of the dialectic of the nation-making and global-marketing capacity of sport" (2001, p. 187). In advertisements and marketing campaigns adidas sought to present a legacy and tradition of its own within the history of the sport. Jonah Lomu was soon one of the featured individual names heading up the adidas Web site: "designers and developers take my input and feedback seriously when developing rugby footwear", he tells the cyberpunters. Adidas had two soccer players, England and Manchester United's David Beckham, and Real Madrid and France's Zinedine Zidane, both speaking in praise of the Predator brand of football boot. Other male stars in the Adidas stable were Ato Boldon, Trinidadian former world champion sprinter, and Sergio Garcia, Spanish golfer. The three women featured were US basketball player Tracy McGrady, and two tennis players: Czech-born Swiss Martina Hingis, pictured with breasts protruding in the forward lurch of a smash or a serve; and the icon of feminine sexuality in contemporary sport, Anna Kournikova, long shapely legs completely exposed in the action shot welcoming you to her trite utterance: "My relationship with adidas is a very good one". Whatever significant progress has been made in denting the steel surrounds of the patriarchal sports culture has been achieved and sustained in spite of the sponsorship of figures such as Kournikova (Bernstein, 2002; Harris, 2002). Adidas's contribution has been prominent in this regard.

Sponsorship is not new. Individual sports stars have had promotional, advertising and sponsorship deals throughout the modern era (Huntington-Whiteley, 1999). In England, cricketer Denis Compton smeared his hair with cream and became known as the "Brylcreem Boy" in the 1940s; boxer Henry Cooper advertised the men's fragrance Brut in a playful word association and appeal to his physical ruggedness. The amateur cricketer Ted Dexter, nicknamed "Lord Ted" in playing circles for his haughty demeanor, modeled men's clothes, and starred in celebrity golf tournaments in the 1960s. In the nineteenth century the professional cricketer W.G. Grace (1848–1915) widely exploited his image and reputation in a range of domestic products. But it is the scale of commercial involvement that is the difference in the contemporary political economy of sport. Corporate sponsorship now targets whole sports, not just individuals; establishes exclusive rights for set periods, not just one-offs. Early Olympic games may have generated some forms of sponsorship, but these were on a diminutive scale, little more, in London 1908 for instance, than opportunistic forms of orthodox descriptive advertising for health or body-related products (Tomlinson, 2004). International sports organizations had little sense of the commercial potential of the event, and corporations in an essentially print-based media saw little scope for highly developed forms of product or service promotion by association.

Nevertheless, the turn of the nineteenth and twentieth century saw a major growth of sport beyond national boundaries, with the formation of the IOC in 1894 and of FIFA in 1904. For generations a precarious balance between professional and amateur values, between voluntarism and commercialism, characterized the cultural and economic basis of sport. The more explicit exploitation of the commercial possibilities of sport was a long drawn-out process through the twentieth century but the pivotal phase was that century's last quarter. By the end of that phase, the prominence and dominance of the corporate sponsor was uncontested and complete. Visit Lausanne and take a tour of 'The Olympic Movement' exhibition at the IOC's Olympic Museum. On entry you pass between a Rodin sculpture of a (white) *American Athlete* (1904), and Antoine Boudelle's *Heracles Archer* (1921). This precedes a mounted display of replicas of all the torches (winter and summer games) used since the ritual's introduction at the 1936 Nazi Games in Berlin, a display of ancient Greek ephemera and memorabilia, an introduction to the philosophy of de Coubertin the founder, an astonishingly prominent photo gallery of all current members of the IOC, and then a tribute to the IOC's primary partners, the televison companies and corporate sponsors that have filled its coffers. In summer 2002 the museum reported that sponsors between 1997 and 2000 had "generated more than US$550 million in revenue to support the entire Olympic movement". In what was now the fifth cycle of these sponsorship deals since 1985, the IOC had ten exclusive commercial partners: Coca-Cola; John Hancock; Kodak; McDonald's; Panasonic; Samsung; Sema; *Sports Illustrated*; Visa; and Xerox. This constituted a veritable line-up of predominantly US economic global power, already etched in marble, within the museum. By now the centrality of the corporate sponsor in sport's political economy was a simple fact of life in the self-representation of the IOC.

Even in the early 1980s some commentators could express disquiet at the English Football Association's decision to allow its member clubs to do shirt-sponsorship deals. By 1992, all the teams in the inaugural Premier League had lucrative sponsorship deals, with sports kit and food retailers, media, electronic and communications businesses, and alcohol retailers. A decade on, in 2002, few of these sponsors had stayed the course. Only Liverpool – with the brewer Carlsberg – had the same sponsor, and almost half of the sponsors were now telecommunications companies. Manchester United – plugging Sharp computers in 1992 – embodied this shift, sponsored by mobile phone giant Vodaphone in 2002. To some traditionalists, the scale and degree of this form of sponsorship was still an issue, with the name of the club and the symbol on the team shirt subservient to the global media product or brand. To the newcomer to the game, it is as if the contest is between Team Fly Emirates (Chelsea) and Team O2 (Arsenal). That it might seem odd to many to raise this as an issue confirms the tight grip that sponsorship now has on high-performance sport, yet the turnover of sponsors is a warning as to the fragility of such a basis for long-term planning and development in the sport. This chapter, focusing now upon football in its global context, tells one important strand of the story whereby sport has been remade on the basis of a new political economy at the heart of which is the corporate sponsor.

The growth of world football and the increasing profile of the World Cup have been overseen by FIFA. From its headquarters in Switzerland, the world governing body of the game has established partnerships that have changed the financial base of the game, and established the football World Cup as a major global spectacle and, concomitantly, a marketing opportunity for the world's most powerful corporate investors. This chapter now traces FIFA's relationship with its most influential marketing partner, ISL (International Sport and Leisure). The former Minister of Sport for the UK, the late Lord (Denis) Howell, in his capacity as chair of the Central Council for Physical Recreation's (CCPR) committee of inquiry into sponsorship of sport, questioned this relationship. Drawing upon previously uncited documentation and sources, this chapter throws light upon the nature of FIFA's marketing initiatives, and demonstrates the interlocking corporate interests of a sports organization such as FIFA and its commercial partners. The article describes how FIFA was transformed through the expansion of its commercial base, and is offered as a case-study of the ways – sometimes innovative, and some might argue corrupt – in which the commercial side of world sport and the partnership relations between sports organizations and corporate sponsors have operated.

Finding FIFA Funds

In 1974, Dr João Havelange was faced with a huge problem on succeeding Sir Stanley Rous as President of football's world governing body, FIFA. He had little chance of fulfilling his campaign commitments to the African and Asian allies who had helped him win the Presidency (Tomlinson, 1994, p. 21), unless effective partnerships were established, and his commitments to the Third World allies who had helped him oust Rous had no economic base whatsoever. For Rous (1978, p. 192), television was an educative rather than a money-making medium. Havelange allied television's increasing interest in the football product with the recognition, by multi-national companies, of the global marketing potential of the game, for their own products. Vital to this was the story of how the German sports goods manufacturer Horst Dassler of Adidas, through the mediation of Patrick Nally, secured Coca-Cola as a global partner, and how the World Cup then acted as a magnet for international companies in FIFA's marketing strategy.

The French Connection

Patrick Nally had been involved, with the sports commentator Peter West, in the early growth of sport sponsorship in Britain. Through an advertising agency and then his own company West Nally, he had established sponsorship deals by brewery companies, Green Shield Stamps, and companies such as Benson & Hedges, Kraft, Ford, Esso and Cornhill Insurance: "In those early days of sponsorship, when men like him were inventing the genre, he was the international cavalier for whom the British market was a base from which to conquer the world" (Wilson, 1988, p. 176). Nally's marketing initiatives paved the way for remarkable marketing deals such as that achieved by ISL for the IOC, in initiating the inaugural TOP (The Olympic Programme) scheme for the 1988 Seoul Summer Olympics.

International Sport and Leisure was formed, Nally himself claims, as Dassler's own version of the West Nally Company and the Monaco-based SMPI (Société Monaquesque des Promotions Internationales) – this latter described by Wilson as "Dassler's money and contracts allied to Nally's ideas and marketing experience" (Wilson, 1988, p. 179). The model for ISL had therefore been the principle of exclusivity of marketing rights pioneered by Nally, on behalf of Dassler, for FIFA.[2]

Prominent in the UK sports market, with a unique portfolio of clients in the new world of sports sponsorship, Nally had been approached by John Boulter, the British runner, on behalf of Adidas, and initially became involved in the promotion of Adidas's Arena swimwear line, fronted by Mark Spitz in the wake of his phenomenal profile during and after the 1972 Munich Olympics where he won seven gold medals. Adidas was expanding its textile/clothes range, and "team sports like soccer with shirts was becoming more and more important". In late 1974 or early 1975, Boulter arranged for Nally to meet with Dassler, head of Adidas's French arm, in the latter's retreat in Landersheim in the Alsace hills in France, where the host "explained to me what was happening to international federations":

> . . . out of it evolved this very determined, eager person that fully understood that international sports federations were going to become extremely important, as tennis became professional,

> as other sports became professional, as soccer was very much on the outward trend. I think he'd seen the election of Havelange as being a big watershed because here you had the gentlemanly old school of Sir Stanley Rous suddenly ousted. The story Horst told me was that he was called by Sir Stanley Rous prior to the election when Sir Stanley suddenly woke up to the fact that he was about to be bumped off by this Brazilian . . . the story goes, from him to me, that at the last minute he was asked to help out, to try and help Sir Stanley Rous.

Havelange, already aware of the importance of Dassler for international sports networking, recognized the potential to FIFA of a fuller relationship with the Adidas man. Dassler became the key figure in the commercialization of the Olympics and the World Cup. He was trained in a tough school of sports business. He is reputed to have been sent by his father, Adi Dassler, founder of the company (and, of course, the source of its name), to the 1956 Melbourne Olympics, to market Adidas's sports equipment, particularly the shoes with the distinctive Adidas triple stripe. Amid cut-throat competition with Puma (founded by his uncle, in a bitter family competition in the sports industry), there were reports that people at docks in Europe and Australia were persuaded to prevent the dispatch or import of any Puma equipment. Adidas achieved a near monopoly of brand marketing at that event, and Dassler conceded that he allegedly paid officially amateur athletes to wear the Adidas brand. This was normal business practice borne of a strongly competitive approach, and was allied with effective communication skills in five languages:

> He became very adept at moving around and getting to understand people. He knew how to get things from people, in other words, he always knew who he could approach and offer money and he also knew who he could approach and not offer money . . . if an IOC membership was more attractive than trying to say . . . I'll give you a bung.

Nally claims that Dassler "traded in IOC memberships . . . I think Denis Howell was even offered an IOC membership . . . I think he would reaffirm it". Lord Howell refuted this claim in no uncertain terms. "It is certainly not true that Horst Dassler ever offered me an IOC position" (personal communication, April 25 1997). But the fact that the networks and rumour-mongers of this incestuous business world could suggest such possibilities is revealing of the level and aspirations of its *modus vivendi.* Dassler was clearly adept at business "intelligence" and astute commissioning, and what became known as the Shoe Wars in athletics were a fruitful training ground for Dassler, also training him in paranoia:

> . . . a total paranoia that someone was always trying to trip him up. So his whole life was secrecy and looking over his shoulders and spying on the opposition and paying. Everything was

> intriguing, everything was suspicion. So he would have spies, all of his sports people who were out there to look after the athletes would always spy on the opposition. They'd all be trained to bug telephones. They'd all be trained to go into other people's brief cases . . . it *WAS* the shoe wars. You were out there to do what you could to the enemy. He would keep information, you would get people drunk, you would be trained to investigate and find out what other people were up to.

Dassler foresaw the increasing professionalism of international sports federations and the huge possibilities of television money, and recognized that he would have to "go very much more within the system, within the federation system and the IOC". It was at this point, as outlined at the beginning of this chapter, that the new commercial logic of world sports began to take shape in football, and the chain of sport-sports industry/marketing and sponsorship/ television coverage emerged as critical for the development of world sport: "what Havelange needed was somebody to help him make his dreams a reality. The man he went to was Horst Dassler, and the man Horst Dassler went to was me [Nally] because this was the beginnings of how [we would] now work with the international federations and how we would get world sponsors to come and support world sport".

Nally saw this challenge as a "monster exercise", and relates with relish the way in which this seminal deal was done. He travelled the world for eighteen months negotiating with key figures in Coca-Cola: "at times it was very delicate because it was the first time it had ever happened". His key contact, Al Killeen, was number two in Coca-Cola, and had been involved in soccer in Africa through English football legend Sir Stanley Matthews. The Coca-Cola company had a federal structure, and did not typically make central decisions concerning worldwide policy and investments. Nally took Killeen to a match at Brazil's Maracana Stadium, "which absolutely blew his mind. He couldn't believe these 110 thousand screaming Brazilians that were there for the warm-up, before the real match". Thus converted to the marketing and branding potential of a sport that could mobilize commitment and passions on such a scale, and across the globe, Killeen battled inside the company at board level, with the support of the company's number one, JP Austin, and won the decision to:

> agree to do a world-wide sponsorship programme and that all of the various markets would contribute. But it wouldn't be that they were asked, they were told and had to contribute a small percentage of their money to a central pot in Atlanta, which Atlanta would then disperse on this and other programmes. But it was a nasty tough fight to get through the Coca-Cola company.

It was a close call, it seems. Havelange's eight-point manifesto, or "Programme" as it was titled in his campaigning brochure, was a long way from a development program:

> . . . what was a development programme? How do you take the best of Europe and the best of South America and teach it to the rest of the world? So we had to develop a whole concept of what the development programme was. Horst Dassler introduced me to an excellent teacher/sports administrator called Klaus Willing who was in Germany . . . and wrote the strategy of taking administrators, coaches, medicine trainers etc. into various countries around the world as part of the development philosophy. We actually wrote the regulations together of the World Youth Championship . . . The Development Programme was taking the knowledge of the strong soccer nations on to 100 countries . . . on an organized programme to Africa, to Asia, to all those places where the votes were important.

Dassler also recognized that the FIFA administration as it stood, inherited from Sir Stanley Rous – a Dickensian scenario comprising General Secretary Dr Käser, his secretary and the dogs, as Nally disparagingly caricatures it – would lack sufficient capabilities for the implementation of such a programme. Via a key figure of the time, Tommy Keller – who worked for Swiss Timing-Longines, and ran the international rowing federation as well as the General Association of International Sports Federations (GAISF) – Dassler was introduced to Joseph "Sepp" Blatter, an administrator working in Swiss Timing. Blatter was 'brought in to manage the programme and part of his management was a training session at Landersheim for a number of months . . . to work alongside Horst, to get to know what the Adidas operation was, to work with us on the planning preparation of the development programme. So the point is, he was very much cemented into the relationship". Blatter joined FIFA, married the daughter of the General Secretary and succeeded to that position himself, after successfully implementing joint FIFA-Coca-Cola initiatives, particularly the third World Youth Championships in Australia in 1981. The Adidas-FIFA interrelationship had already been a long-lasting one: Sir Walter Winterbottom recalls the importance, from the 1970s, of Havelange's connection with "Horst Dassler's underground movement" (interview with author, Cranleigh, Surrey, November 24 1996). This was cemented with Blatter's arrival at FIFA, and when the new FIFA House was under construction, former FIFA press boss Guido Tognoni recalls, Blatter worked from premises made available by Dassler (interview with author, Zurich, May 21, 1996). The manner of Blatter's appointment demonstrated, too, the characteristic Havelange style, Havelange announcing the appointment ahead of the date set aside for FIFA's executive committee to make its decision. Blatter had impressed Havelange and other FIFA officials in Australia, by administering the Coca-Cola sponsored World Youth Championships there, and stepping in and saving the local organisers from a situation of administrative chaos. On the spot, Havelange telexed FIFA his decision that Blatter was the man for the job.

Clearly, Havelange saw at first hand – and acted decisively upon his understanding of the situation – the necessity for efficient liaison with partners as important as a major sponsor: and such liaison would best come from within his own organization, rather than being left to independent and unpredictable sports administrators in any corner of the world. For the outcome of the negotiations with Coca-Cola had been that, for the first time, the company would back, worldwide, one sport: "Previously local countries and bottlers had made their own sports sponsorship policy. Killeen was brave enough to dictate to the whole Coke world that they would back one sport – soccer. The result was an enormous FIFA programme – giving Havelange the ability to honour his election mandate: to develop Africa and Asia, create a World Youth Cup, bring more Third World countries into the World Cup". Nally's fund-raising initiative was not just a God-sent (or Dassler-sent) package to the new president of FIFA. It was a revolutionary moment in the political economy of modern sport. Nally saw himself as "a third arm. You had your conventional shoe partner, you had your political team which was obviously keeping tabs on who and what in the federations, now this was the third element in Horst's operation whereby I represented a whole new era which was commercial sponsorship with commercial interests."

For Nally, the importance of getting a big name such as Coca-Cola into the soccer programme was twofold. First, it gave the right credibility and image for that sort of work. Second, "if you're into Coke, you're into the biggest bluechip company on a global basis". Bringing Coca-Cola into the sponsorship of world soccer "became the blueprint for everyone who wanted to try and bring money into international federations through this source". The multi-million investment package put together for FIFA concentrated initially upon the new World Youth Cup, which could guarantee Asian and African participation on the world stage. Complementing the flow inwards of the development areas of coaching, administration and medical expertise, the competitive platform of the youth cup (first held in Tunisia in 1977) provided the opportunity to create a flow outwards, from Africa and Asia, of teams that could then compete at international level against European and South American nations. This was revolutionary, and although the champions of the first two youth (under 20s) tournaments produced established winners, in the Soviet Union and Argentina (the young Maradona scoring the decisive goal in the 1979 final in Tokyo, against the Soviet Union), by the third tournament the value of the new initiative was becoming clear for developing football nations: Qatar, though losing 4-0 to West Germany in the final in Sydney, had beaten Brazil (3-2) and England (2-1) on the way to the final. African nations were soon to emerge on this stage: Nigeria won the third-place match, in and against the Soviet Union, in 1985, and in Saudi Arabia in 1989 lost the final by just 2-0 to Portugal. Ghana lost only 2-1 to Brazil in the 1993 final in Australia, having won the 1991 Under-17 title in Florence, Italy, beating Spain 1-0 in the final. The Under-17 World Championship had been inaugurated in 1985, Nigeria beating West Germany 2-0 in the final in Beijing, having defeated Italy (1-0) and Hungary (3-1) *en route* to its triumph. However skeptical the established football nations might have been about such events (some seeing them as peripheral, in comparison to their own apprenticeship systems and fully developed professional leagues), the FIFA initiatives clearly offered valuable international experience and competition that were to stand Asian and African footballing nations in good stead on the larger world stages of the World Cup and the Olympic Games. These developmental initiatives would not have been possible without FIFA's Coca-Cola monies.

A worldwide skills program was also created, to ensure widespread promotional activity for the sponsoring company. The base established in the development programmes and the youth cup, a deal was then concluded whereby, at the cost of between US$8 million and US$12 million, Coca-Cola was brought into the 1978 World Cup in Argentina, and "financed and funded the whole of the marketing programme." The external negotiations with Coca-Cola were conducted by Nally; the internal fixing was accomplished by Dassler and Havelange: "All the politics, he wanted handled through him and his team . . . the selection of putting Sepp Blatter in as Gen Sec of FIFA – the selection of Sepp out of [Swiss Timing] Longines, the training of Sepp at Landersheim . . . the convincing of Havelange to put Sepp in as the new development man as he then was – all that political selection of personnel was done by them."

Nally and Dassler established sponsoring clients' exclusivity in all aspects of merchandising and franchising, not just in stadium advertising: "Never again has FIFA released any rights to the World Cup from their central control", Nally observes (Wilson, 1988, p. 181). By the first World Cup of Havelange's Presidency, in Argentina in 1978, Nally had contracted six major sponsors to FIFA, including Coca-Cola, Gillette and Seiko, though he was still juggling the advertising billboards of companies contracted with different national teams. This was soon to be streamlined, and FIFA used the TOP (The Olympic Programme) scheme of the IOC as a template. From then on, the only option open to sponsors was the complete marketing package: "The sums were so vast that lots of companies couldn't touch it but it was a lot easier to work with the few who could", recalled Nally (Wilson, 1988, p. 182). This new scale of football finance involved the acquisition and distribution – with minimal accountability – of huge sums of money. Havelange had made major commitments to the development of African and Asian football. Dassler "would commit himself to help Havelange to get the money" to, for example, "take an event that's been running at 16 teams and go to 24 teams – to get the Spanish to agree to do it – politically it's important for the Africans and Asians." It was then Nally's task to "create a marketing programme to justify bringing big money into that sport to help Horst fulfil his obligations." The cost of the marketing rights for international football was, therefore, unprecedentedly high because of the range and scale of deals needed to fuel this expansionist programme: as Nally states – "because", for instance, "Horst committed to give 36 million Swiss Francs extra to Havelange to enable him to bribe the Spanish to take the World Cup up from 16 teams to 24 teams as part of his commitment to get more Asian and African teams in . . . in Spain, in the Placo de Congresso, in the gentlemen's toilets, Horst said the going rate with the Spanish organizing committee wasn't going to be $4 million which I'd already negotiated and agreed, we had to pay an additional 36 million Swiss Francs." Nally sees the effects of such financial flexibility as "good", evidenced by improving African and Asian performances in the World Cup following on from the developmental youth programmes, and such large amounts of money being poured in was made possible by the scale of the Coca-Cola investment: "Coca-Cola if you like legitimized the industry, the amount of money that was going into soccer . . . but I don't think ever quite realised the importance of their association and how it being abused enabled this club, this whole mafia going on within sport, to be really supported by them because they gave it all credibility". Dassler got Havelange to impress the Coca-Cola people, at the company's world headquarters in Atlanta, by flying in on his private plane to meet with them. Nally argues that the Coca-Cola connection gives sports organizations an aura of respectability, generated by the Coca-Cola global image of corporate cleanliness:

> [The federations] . . . are in some ways, because of Coca-Cola, beyond reproach. There's no government checking on them. There's no auditors checking them. Nobody's trying to see where the payment goes or what the individuals get so somehow the IOC and the IAAF and FIFA is totally beyond reproach. They have the same aura of credibility and pristine cleanness and Coca-Cola helps that and yet they can get away with blue murder . . . but if the can of worms ever really got open and people started challenging why these people have the ability to do what they do and why they are there and why do they get all these things – the club – then I think Coca-Cola are going to get a lot of stick from it and Coca-Cola's image is going to suffer immensely.

One outcome of this new political economy of world sport, an important effect of the innovative form of partnership at the heart of this political economy, was the elevation in status of positions in sports organizations:

> It's suddenly becoming an extremely important and powerful position to be in, the President of an International Federation that is rich because there is money flowing in from the Olympic Games and other things. Now, it means trips, it means travel, it means awards, air tickets, it certainly beats sweeping out the back of the garden at the weekend if you're flying first class everywhere to major international events.

How did Horst Dassler hold together an operation on this scale? Clearly, he provided lavish hospitality, the "compulsory Adidas dinner" at every international sports federation meeting at a time when the federations were relatively impoverished, and "Adidas was the only company that ever supported them"; his own residential and catering complex at Landersheim, Alsace; and mostly for Africans and Asians in Paris, his sports shop, and restaurant with other hospitality facilities in Montmartre. He retained useful individuals in unlikely capacities – the late Harry Cavan, Northern Irish football administrator and FIFA Vice-President, for instance, as "shoe consultant". And he made, and kept, commitments and promises that would catapult sport into a new phase of economically expanded and financially lucrative transnational practice.

Dassler was not completely secretive about his strategy and his means towards his ends. When approached in 1982 by Lord Howell, the eminent former Minister of Sport in Britain's 1970s Labour Government, on the issue of sponsorship in sport, "we had a pleasant and far-reaching discussion, and Dassler could not have been more forthcoming" (Howell, 1990, p. 352). The context of Howell's report on sport sponsorship (Central Council for Physical Recreation, 1983) was clear:

> An increasing cause of concern was the advent of international sports agencies who seemed to dominate sport and were negotiating contracts, both for performers and governing bodies, in order to get television exposure and to assume more and more power . . . the increasing dominance of the international agencies was a big source of concern and we spent a lot of time examining their influence and relationships within various sports and their interlocking financial interests. (Howell, 1990: pp. 348 and 352)

The committee received little cooperation from Mark McCormack of International Management Group (IMG), with whom Howell wanted to discuss issues around "possible conflicts of interest, highlighted by the fact that McCormack represents sponsors and sports bodies, creates events . . . negotiates television rights and even commentates on the event" (Howell, 1990, p. 353).

The Howell report concluded that "such a situation is pregnant with conflict of interests and cannot carry public confidence", and proposed that the British government should examine in depth IMG's relationship with UK-based sports events "to establish whether any monopoly situation exists" (CCPR, 1983; Howell, 1990, pp. 553). Howell and his committee also expressed some astonishment, whilst exploring the relationship between Adidas and FIFA, "to be told that Adidas had undertaken an extensive programme of education in Africa on behalf of FIFA, the most powerful governing body in world sport" (Howell, 1990; p. 352). The committee recommended that such initiatives should be monitored by bodies such as the General Association of International Sports Federations (GAISF), or the International Assembly of National Organizations of Sport. Such bodies, the Howell report concluded in its Recommendation 65, should:

> . . . consider the financial involvement of Adidas and its associates in respect of the Federation Internationale de Football Association, the International Olympic Committee and other international sports federations in order to ensure that such involvement is compatible with the interests of international sport. (CCPR, 1983, p. 110)

This recommendation was premised on the assumption that such bodies were independent: in actuality, these bodies, too, were to be brought into Dassler's extending network of tame and implicated organizations. Dassler promoted the creation of the Association of Summer Olympic International Federations (ASOIF), as a counter to the influence of the independent GAISF, and propelled Primo Nebiolo into its Presidency, and later into the Presidency of the International Amateur Athletics Federation (IAAF); and by 1986 the GAISF gained as its President the Korean Kim Un Yong (Mickey Kim), nine days after he became a member of the IOC itself. It has been reported that Nebiolo was rewarded by the organizers of the 1988 Seoul Olympics, for changing times of track and field events to suit the American broadcasters, NBC, having initially proposed schedules wholly inappropriate for a mass American television audience. The background of Dr Kim Un Yong, guardian of all of the world's sports federations, has been traced to dubious developments in international taekwondo politics, and to the Korean Central Intelligence Agency (Jennings, 1996; pp. 72 and 94). Lord Howell's referrals would have met with short shrift if they had ever been on the agenda of the networks and the club of the international sports leaders.

Howell believes that, in general terms, "the concern we expressed about ethical conduct and conflicts of interest has grown rather than diminished since we reported" (Howell, 1990, p. 349), despite some positive outcomes for sports development worldwide, in Africa and Asia in particular. He observes that the commercialization process has continued to race out of control: "I think that the finance of sport, professional sport particularly, has now become almost obscene, and is totally destroying the soul, what I call the soul of the game . . . people have been trying to buy the soul of the sport, and therefore corrupting it, with disastrous results" (interview with author, October 8, 1996).[3] Certainly, the Nally narrative of Dassler and Adidas's remarkable worldwide impact testifies to the accuracy of Howell's insights and warnings. Perhaps most important of all, Dassler collected information on the world of sports politics, and kept promises to individuals whose individual careers he could promote, constructing what was in effect an international intelligence system for the sports industry, and an institutional and interpersonal base for the brokerage of positions of power in world sports politics, as well as sports marketing rights.

Dassler did not deny the levels and scale of his involvement in world sports when he met with Howell, stating openly that "we exist to sell boots and shirts and wherever the action is we need to be there" (Howell, 1990, p. 352). He met with Howell after placating the Welsh Rugby Union, in the context of controversy over boot sponsorship of individual amateur players, by meeting with the Union and arranging a comprehensive team sponsorship deal. The administrators of the Welsh Union, in Lord Howell's words, "totally embraced Dassler and changed their attitude. He paid them for the right to supply boots and pay the players, and they totally changed the whole of the ethos of their sport" (interview with author, October 8, 1996). Clearly, Dassler's combination of personal dynamism and economic patronage could prove speedily effective. Howell and his committee were right to target him as a pivotal figure in the evolving pattern of the global sports economy:

> I started by asking a question such as "Can you give me any justification as to why a football boot manufacturer should wish to decide who should become the President of FIFA and control world football?" And his reply was that he had in his office a tremendous computer and records department which had every periodical and news letter issued by every sports body round the world and these were all tabulated. Therefore it was very natural that if anyone wanted to pursue a career like Havelange . . . they would come to him to get the names and addresses of all the contacts. That is what he supplied and the same facilities, he said, were available to Sir Stanley Rous, except Sir Stanley Rous didn't ask for them – and I don't suppose could have afforded to have made all these contacts around Africa and Asia, which enabled Havelange to get himself elected as President of FIFA. (interview with author, Birmingham, October 8, 1996)

The Howell Committee saw the question of the governing bodies' relationship to sponsorship income as an ethical issue. In its meeting of May 16 1983, on the theme of "International matters": "It was agreed that the role of the governing bodies in international sport should be discussed" in a chapter of the report on ethics and social issues; "also the fact that governing bodies were not equipped to deal with multi-nationals" was noted. The lesson was clearly learned that the power of an Adidas could come to dominate sports development, and Philippe Chartrier of the International Tennis Federation had stated such concerns to the Committee. But since the death of Dassler the federations themselves could assume more power, working within the networks of the rest of the world's federations and committees. As Nally saw it:

> . . . now it is more spread they can still do what Horst was doing individually, together. If Samaranch needs the Latin support from South America, then obviously he's got to stay close to an Havelange. If Havelange eventually doesn't want to allow total professionalism of soccer into the IOC because he feels it would dilute the World Cup, Samaranch will only go so far – but then agree to the Under-23 rule because he needs the support. All of them have become more developed but what it's done, it's rather put a structure together. To get real clean new people in, it's very difficult because the system is now established that all the people that have got there, have got there for being part of that tainted system.

Keeping It in the Family: The Birth of ISL

A major step in consolidating that "tainted system" was the setting up of ISL. Lord Howell learned of this as his report was at the printers, and telexed some questions to the former British athlete John Boulter at Adidas (Boulter had accompanied Dassler during the meeting with Howell and John Wheatley, director of The Sports Council (London)). Howell recalls his committee's main areas of concern:

> The danger I saw was the danger that if you had a company which is going to be solely responsible for the advertising and commercial promotion of sport at FIFA level, would that then lead to commercial control of the government of the sport? I have to say that I don't think it has. Perhaps I overstated the dangers. But because Horst Dassler's company Adidas was very much at the heart of that exercise I felt it was something which had to be very closely watched. (Interview with author, October 8, 1996.)

Lord Howell's concern was not shared by the Adidas representative. He "received a reply from Boulter telling me that he was becoming increasingly concerned about the nature of my enquiries' (Howell, 1990, p. 353). "When I raised" any questions or issues "critical of Dassler, Boulter was threatening me with actions' (interview with author, October 8, 1996). The formation of ISL was the masterstroke in Dassler's emerging monopoly of world sports marketing. Howell was unequivocally correct to express the concern that he did about such an initiative involving no process of open bidding or tendering; and Boulter was understandably nervous that such questions were being posed on the verge of what would be a major coup within the field of international sports marketing. International Sport and Leisure would also benefit from a low profile as a similar coup was being planned for the control of Olympic marketing rights.

The president of the IOC signed the contract for the marketing of the Olympics with what was in effect Dassler's ISL in May 1985. A month later, some IOC members expressed reservations about not having seen the contract, and ignorance of the company and the process whereby it had secured the contract (Whannel, 1992; Jennings, 1996, pp. 52–3). But ISL had been in the making for some years, and when Nally and Dassler's business relationship ended in 1982, Dassler established the company that was to dominate sports marketing in the boom years of global expansion. Wilson (1988), also citing Nally, describes this well:

> Dassler kept the rights to FIFA's events, setting up a company he called ISL, part owned by Adidas' Japanese partner Dentsu and run by his Adidas assistant Klaus Hempel, and Nally kept the rights for West Nally in athletic's [sic] first world championships in 1983 and their 1985 World Cup. ISL out-bid him two years later for the rights to the second championships. "Our presentation was the most sophisticated and meaningful but we didn't get in because Horst was offering a vast sum up front" . . . FIFA turned away an offer of 85 million Swiss Francs for the 1994 World Cup from the Monaco-based agency Telemundi. Havelange had rewarded Dassler's original support by promising him, before he died in March, 1987, that ISL would have all advertising and marketing rights for the 1994 and 1998 World Cups. (Wilson, 1988, p. 185)

The IOC's executive committee appointed ISL, in March 1983, to manage its new fund-raising programme (TOP, The Olympic Programme), one of ISL's advantages being that the strategy for contracts based upon exclusivity of marketing rights for selected global giants was proving successful in the world of football. By mid-1983, within a matter of months of its creation, ISL was handling merchandising rights and rights for stadium advertising for FIFA, UEFA and, embryonically at least, the IOC. By October 1983, the company had also signed to handle any of the Seoul Olympic Games Organizing Committee's merchandising, licensing, sponsorship and supplier contracts; and was publicizing, in a special supplement to *Time* magazine's European edition, its successes in attracting sponsors for its football marketing programme – not least, via advertising in the supplement reserved exclusively for the company's own regular clients such as Canon, Camel, JVC, Seiko, Fuji and Air France.

Globally ambitious companies such as Coca-Cola, Bata and Cinzano could quickly see the benefits of exclusive sponsor programmes, and ISL put these in place for its contracted clients for the 1984 European Football Championships in France. The main benefit was perimeter advertising in all of the stadia used during the tournament, guaranteeing worldwide television exposure. Exclusive franchising rights were also included in the package, and further exposure in event-based media. Sponsors also provided services to the media – a harried press person could loan photographic equipment from Canon, and photocopy on a Canon machine; take a refreshing drink of Coca-Cola; admire the ball-boy kit and opening ceremony equipment provided by Bata; check detail on television monitors provided by JVC; and check copy deadlines and match timings via the official timekeeper Seiko. With its system in place – and despite the problems of Sport Billy Productions continuing to claim its contracted ownership of the FIFA emblem, trademark and mascots – ISL dominated world football marketing in this formative phase of the industry, cultivating some of the world's top brand names in the consumer industries. At the five World Cups from 1986 to 1994 the sponsors were as follows:

Mexico, 1986: Anheuser-Busch; Bata; Canon; Coca-Cola; Cinzano; Fuji; Gilletttе; JVC; Opel; Philips; R.J. Reynolds (Camel); Seiko (twelve general sponsors with stadium advertising privileges). Two reserved sponsorship packages were granted to a selected group of Mexican firms to run local advertising; and to Arena Swimwear, as a result, it was claimed, of Anheuser Busch not taking up an option of supporting promotion measures. These extra deals certainly made sense to the main players: the man running the World Cup was Havelange's long-term ally, Mexican FIFA Vice-President Cañedo; Arena, of course, was an Adidas subsidiary.

Italy, 1990: Anheuser-Busch; Canon; Coca-Cola; Fuji; Gillette; JVC; Mars; Philips; Vini Italia (nine general sponsors with stadium advertising privileges). The sum raised from these sponsors was reported to be an estimated 100 million Swiss Francs, to be shared between FIFA, the Italian Organizing Committee and the participating teams. Two further categories were sold. "Official suppliers" were Alitalia, Fiat, Olivetti, the Italian Post Office, Italian Railways, the RAI state TV Company, and the INA insurance company. The title "official product" was sold to a range of companies, including Adidas, Seiko, Mastercard, Barilla (pasta), Sagit (ice-cream), and Garan Padano (cheese).

USA, 1994: Canon; Coca-Cola; Energizer; Fuji; General Motors; Gillette; JVC; Mastercard; McDonald's; Philips; Snickers (eleven general sponsors).

France, 1998: Adidas; Canon; Coca-Cola; Fujifilm; Gillette; JVC; Mastercard; McDonald's; Opel; Philips; Snickers (eleven official sponsors, though Anheuser Busch/Budweiser had to be taken off the list(s) due to the unanticipated enforcement of French national laws relating to the advertising of alcohol).

Japan/Korea, 2002: Adidas; Avaya; Budweiser; Coca-Cola; Fuji Xerox; Fujifilm; Gillette; Hyundai; JVC; KT-Korea/NTT-Japan; Mastercard; McDonald's; Philips; Toshiba, Yahoo (fifteen official, general sponsors, more than ever before, paying a total of £290 million for the privilege, ranging from £10 million to a little over £20 million each).

Fast foods and snacks, soft and alcoholic drinks, sports kit and clothing, cars, batteries, photographic equipment, electronic media and telecommunications, credit sources – and razors for the men – these are the items around which global sponsorship of football has been based, with their classic evocations of a predominantly masculinist realm of consumption: drinking, playing, snacking, shaving, driving. The marketing of the commodities throughout the regions of the world game has clearly been effective. If it were not, companies of this stature would have been unlikely to re-invest in ISL's recurrent Inter-Soccer programs, or the equivalent schemes of its rivals.

After Dassler's death, it was confirmed that FIFA had assigned all of the marketing and sponsorship rights for the 1994 and 1998 World Cup Finals to ISL, with an option included for the 2002 event, in a multi-million Swiss Francs contract that also included the merchandising rights for FIFA's logos, which at the time were still held by Sport Billy Productions up to 1990. Continuity was the order of the day. Dassler's long-time protégé, John Boulter, was installed as head of promotions at Adidas within a few months of Dassler's death. And the ISL operation worked prolifically and productively for FIFA, the IOC, the IAAF and other lucrative clients, wrapping up the global marketing of the world's highest profile sports. But power plays were under way in the boardrooms of Adidas and ISL. At the end of 1990, Horst Dassler's four sisters disposed of their 80 percent share of the Adidas company, and the husband of one of them took over as the president of the holding company that was the majority (51 percent) owner of ISL. Dassler's own two children became marginalized in this reshuffle. Within weeks, two key ISL personnel, Klaus Hempel and

Jürgen Lenz had all but stopped work with ISL. Dassler's sisters placed Jean Marie Weber in the Chief Executive's position, and by the Autumn of 1991, Hempel and Lenz had formed their own rival operation. Their Hempel-Lenz & Partner AG co-founded The Event Agency and Marketing AG (TEAM) – since renamed Television Event and Media Marketing AG – with backing from German industrialists. TEAM announced its aim "to set new standards in the field of sports and cultural sponsoring on the basis of innovative concepts and thus make sponsorship an innovative marketing element." Team Football Marketing AG was also established, and bids planned to UEFA and other sports bodies. TEAM's biggest success has been in many respects the marketing and the concomitant restructuring and expansion of the UEFA Champions' League, the idea for which stemmed from TEAM personnel, rather than football administrators in the European association/confederation. For FIFA, Dassler and ISL had established a base for an unprecedented growth in the marketing of football; and an accompanying growth in the number of marketing agencies seeking to profit from sport and football's new wealth.

Such lucrative commercial opportunities could hardly be kept in the family for ever, as ISL's split and then its dramatic collapse in 2001 demonstrated. The rewards have been so staggeringly high for the marketing gurus that internal schisms and rivalries would hardly be unexpected, fueled by a heady cocktail of power and greed. At the end of 1996, as the date loomed closer for FIFA's tender for marketing contracts for the 2002 and 2006 World Cup tournaments, three senior ISL executives resigned. Weber, still at the helm as ISL chairman, had announced a restructuring plan. The *Financial Times* picks up the story:

> The executives were key figures in ISL's successful SFr2.8bn* (£1.3bn) bid with the German media group Kirch for television rights outside the US to the 2002 and 2006 World Cups . . . Mr Weber has created a holding company called ISMM Investments and a group management board, which has him as president and includes three senior ISL executives. The three who quit were excluded from the new management structure, but had been offered continuing senior roles in ISL's TV, football and legal departments . . . an internal memorandum said the move followed "major philosophical differences" over management and strategy. (Burns, 1996b)

How to recoup £1.3 billion in auctioning the rights to the world's television companies would certainly have given ISL much to talk about, but Weber appears to have restricted the number of participants in such talks. Nevertheless, FIFA's traditional partner still looked to take world football into the new millennium on long-established confidence. When ISL won the marketing rights as well as the television rights, this would be the first time that both television and

*References to billions throughout this volume are American billions. One billion is thus 1,000,000,000.

marketing were in the hands of the same company. On December 3, 1997, the FIFA Executive Committee, in Marseilles for both its meeting and the World Cup 1998 draw, approved the ISL "marketing concept":

> Members of the Executive . . . declared themselves entirely satisfied with all the explanations provided with regard to the ISL concept, which has a total value of 420 million Swiss Francs for 2002 and SFR. 470m. for 2006, with profit sharing foreseen in excess of these figures. (FIFA Press/Communications Division, Marseilles, December 3, 1997)

This new contract covered not just the two World Cup tournaments, but also "all other FIFA events during the period", and was reported as an innovative new concept/agreement, which:

> provides for a more exclusive group of commercial partners, closer co-operation with the organizing committees of the FIFA events, the development of a FIFA brand, and a cohesive and on-going licensing programme. (FIFA Press/Communications Division, Zurich, December 15, 1997)

In short, more and more takings from and for fewer and fewer major players. What is more, Adidas had also come back fully into the frame, the sole sportswear company on the exclusive list of FIFA's World Cup sponsors (for the finals in France in 1998), warding off the challenges of North American giants Nike, and other challengers such as Reebok, and boasting in October 1996 that, in the words of chief executive Robert Louis-Dreyfus, "Adidas is proud to be the first sports equipment maker to join the circle of official sponsors of the soccer world championship" (Gilardi, 1996). The cost of these rights (paid to FIFA, and to Sony Corporation of Japan, the latter having the sole global merchandising rights to the event) was not made public, but commentators compared the cost of one-off Olympic event rights for global sponsors, which for the 1998 Winter Olympics in Nagano, Japan, were around US£40 million per sponsor. Adidas spokesman Peter Csanadi commented: "This is one sign that Adidas is back in the world market. It is a big honour for us to be a sponsor because we have a long history in soccer. But it is also an enormous business opportunity" (Gilardi, 1996). Adidas could now use the World Cup logo on its products – shirts, balls, and other sportswear items worth many millions in sales. It would also provide the uniforms for an estimated 12,000 World Cup helpers and staff. The company had already had a long-term role as supplier of official football and referee equipment for FIFA matches. There may have been splits in the family units over the years, but FIFA showed in this 1996 deal that the main branches of the extended FIFA family could be as reciprocally self-serving as ever.

Other agencies, including Rupert Murdoch's News Corporation/Sky Television, had considered entering the bidding process for the 2002 and 2006 television rights. Murdoch was reputed to have withdrawn due to "the widespread scepticism about the bidding process" (Burns, 1996a). Certainly, the EBU (European Broadcasting Union), holder of the rights for the 1990, 1994 and 1998 finals, must have shared such skepticism, worthless as its "provision for priority negotiations" for future contracts turned out to be. David Will, vice-president of FIFA, implied that ISL would certainly remain a front-runner for the marketing rights, as its competence, reliability, and familiarity – after so many years of working with FIFA – meant, realistically, that awarding the rights to any other agency would be a risk (interview with author, Brechin, Scotland, October 9, 1996). By the end of 1997, ISL had indeed been confirmed as FIFA's continuing partner.

Yet a little over three years later ISL collapsed into bankruptcy. Around April and May 2001, the time of the company's collapse, any sport marketing man with ISL experience would shuffle away if asked what happened, what went wrong at ISL. "Oh, I was only junior", I was repeatedly told in the conference rooms and lobbies of Switzerland and Lausanne's swankiest hotels. FIFA moved swiftly to bring the marketing brief inside the organization, securing a safe haven too for the closest colleagues from ISL itself. Blatter could hardly deny his intimate links to and within the ISL networks. Questioned in 2002 by a BBC television journalist, he wriggled visibly, twitching in his responses:

Interviewer: You called the ISL deal with FIFA, a sweetheart deal, like a Venetian night of love.

Mr Blatter: When was that?

Interviewer: I've read in the newspapers your quote, you said it was a sweetheart, the ISL FIFA relationship was sweetheart, like a Venetian night of love.

Mr Blatter: Perhaps I have said that when it was working well and when ISL was working well, not only for FIFA, they were working well for UEFA, they were working well for Africa and why they are not working well now, because instead of playing the game of football, they wanted to go to other sports, they wanted to go to tennis, they wanted to go to cars.

Interviewer: So it wasn't a sweetheart deal in the end?

Mr Blatter: At the end it is not a sweetheart, definitely not, but at the time when they also came in, in television it was a wonderful partnership for everybody and for the benefit of football, for the benefit of the associations of the confederations.

Interviewer: But not a sweetheart deal. What about the so called 'slush' fund, the secret Lichtenstein Bank Account into which money meant for FIFA was diverted?

Mr Blatter: Yes, but they have diverted this money.

Interviewer: But when did you find out about the so called slush fund?

Mr Blatter: When one of the television companies which has made this payment have alerted us in the year 2001, in the first month of 2001, when the difficulties of ISL started, they went to us, it was O Globo, they came here.

And then of course Blatter moved swiftly. He was not for nothing Dassler's star protégé.

Blatter had worked as head of public relations at the Swiss Association of Sport for two years, before going to Swiss Longines, "where I worked in marketing, equally sport, I mean the sports chronometer, and it was there that I entered into contact with the big names of the sports world, so the great name Adidas". Joining FIFA "it was an old house, there wasn't yet an office here, I went to Landersheim, to the French section of Adidas, and I worked there during the month of August until the month of December 1975" – Blatter was FIFA's technical director from 1975 to 1981, when he became general secretary:

> For six years, I was ambassador or itinerant missionary for football, I did the development programme Futuro which we did together with Coca Cola and Adidas. If we hadn't had Adidas and Coca Cola, who both supported us during this period, we would have never entered the world of football with such a fantastic programme of development . . . I will never forget Adidas because, I repeat, without Adidas we wouldn't have had this development programme. Without Adidas I think that FIFA would not be where she is today.

Horst Dassler, almost exactly the same age as Blatter – both born in as Blatter put it "the beautiful year of '36" – is recalled with passion by Blatter:

> He was an extraordinary man, a man of courage, of initiative, a visionary. He went at the age of 20 years, in '56, with a small suitcase, the first to try to make well-known athletes identify with the brand name Adidas, the father of sport sponsoring. One can never repeat this enough. It is he who said that one must associate the product, develop the product with the sport, and equally to increase sales of sports equipment.

Dassler was an obsessive workaholic, who slept little and showed few signs of tiredness. He was an exceptional motivator of people, with high expectations of all who worked for him, and calls on personal loyalty: "Each person was truly persuaded that he was part of the family and not just part of the company, and this was wonderful". Blatter sees Dassler as not only "a great salesman, but also a great diplomat", who would have solved all the problems in world sport, if he had lived: "he always knew how to fix things when there were differences".

Dassler the fixer was close to Blatter. They saw some problems but grasped the vast potential of football in the world's burgeoning global markets, and were effective salesmen pitching at the world's top companies. Guinness didn't bite, but that didn't deter them. Blatter knew some big bucks had to be found. Together they'd also approached food companies, bank and insurance companies, to fund FIFA's development programmes and so pay Havelange's debts. But Blatter concedes that it was almost by chance that FIFA fell in with the Coke empire: "By accident we found that we'd drunk Coca Cola with a bit of rum in Paris, I remember. I drank Coke, and he said one thing you should have is that, everyone drinks Coca Cola. That day in the same restaurant in a hotel in Paris there was a guy who worked for Coca Cola in England, and it was like that it began". Not quite the same account as Patrick Nally's, but Nally couldn't be everywhere.

Blatter talks of Adidas with the collective "we", of Dassler himself with filial awe. Recalling Adidas's dip in fortunes after Horst Dassler's death in 1987, it was because "we did not pay attention to the market, we didn't see the waves, and we sold this business for a morsel of bread". He sees in Adidas's new owner Dreyfus a strong man in the old Dassler mould, a man fit to re-establish and strengthen still further the close ties between FIFA and the company.

Blatter sounds angry when fielding questions concerning this close relation: "Those who make such reproaches are people who don't know the ethical and moral value of business and of sport". Blatter's morality means that Adidas gets preferred treatment, and that if it is outbid by another potential sports equipment sponsor, it is not the law of the free market that presides. Blatter makes sure that FIFA remembers its debts and honors old loyalties:

> I presented this report to the Finance Commission, to the executive committee, to tell them that the moral value of the Adidas company was worth more than the difference in the financial plan the American competitors were offering. If a journalist says that it was biased, it's not true. It is simply that it is necessary to think again that someone has made a particular effort over the years. Since I began they were really committed.

Of course they were. Blatter is an Adidas product, a Dassler disciple. Blatter draws upon a rhetoric of tradition and morality to account for this FIFA-Adidas cosy arrangement: "The wider family of football is everyone who is in football, including the economic partners like Adidas, Coca Cola, also all other manufacturers of sport articles, and the media. The media are just as much our economic partner, and also make up the family of football". From technical director of FIFA to the FIFA presidency, won in 1998, Blatter has been the lynchpin for the networks and structures that have elevated the corporate sponsor to a central role in contemporary sport. FIFA had become careless in its relation with an over-expanding ISL, as Dick Pound who took the IOC business away from the company in the mid 1990s has confirmed to me (interview, May 20, 2001, Lausanne). But Blatter had been in this business for close to thirty years. The ISL debacle could be swept under the carpet, the big sponsors sweetened. Thumbing through your FIFA 2002 World Cup Spectator Guide, coming to the center pages, you would find FIFA's most extreme capitulation to such partners:

> Through their financial and product support the Official Commercial Affiliates of the 2002 World Cup contribute greatly to the success of the event. However, other companies try to take advantage of the worldwide stage provided by the FIFA World Cup to promote their products and to gain a false association, but the fact is these "ambushing" companies don't invest one penny to support the event – they simply rip it off!
>
> Do not bring commercially-branded material (company names, logos, etc.) into the stadium such as flags, banners, hats, balloons, scarves. Please be aware that stadium security will be removing all such items at the stadium entrances.

It will be clothes next. Make sure that you don't turn up in your Nike shirt or Gucci underwear. Potentially invading and controlling the personal, individual body space of the sports fan, the corporate sponsor's assumptions and arrogance now reached new levels of influence and absurdity.

Conclusion: the Billion Dollar Game

Havelange's commitment to expand the World Cup catapulted FIFA into a new era of global expansion, fueled by a concomitant economic imperative. To achieve what he had pledged and committed, Havelange established new economic partnerships that were to become a template for the political economy of world sport. Critical in the brokerage of such deals and partnerships were opportunistic marketing figures such as Nally, most importantly the powerful and manipulative figure of Horst Dassler of Adidas, and the breed of sports marketing men that he established. FIFA's capacity to generate such deals was premised upon its supra-national status. As an INGO (international non-government organization) – a body with a global remit, but no accountability to any particular national government or governments (Waters, 1995, p. 113) – FIFA could offer the potential of worldwide markets to its commercial partners. And as an OFC (offshore financial centre) – "a centre that hosts financial activities that are separated from major regulating units (states) by geography and/or legislation" (Hampton, 1994, p. 237) – FIFA could assume a fiscal autonomy that could service a cosmopolitan and luxury lifestyle for its operatives and, crucially, broker distinctive deals for the marketing of the game. That the organization was based in Switzerland, such a prominent international center for OFC dealing, expedited the pace and the scale of such transformative transactions.

The success of FIFA's marketing strategy in the last quarter of the twentieth century might have achieved much for the previously disenfranchised football nations and regions of the world, in an expanded calendar of FIFA-promoted events, and important forms of technical and economic aid. The marketing monies that have poured into football have also made the top clubs in the wealthier footballing nations still wealthier. The tension between the needs of elite clubs and the demands of national associations recurs with predictable regularity, and in its calculating way the FIFA of Havelange and Blatter, knowing full well where the votes at Congress come from, will usually side with the case of the national body. Whatever the outcomes, though, they were not driven by any selfless sense of global equity within FIFA, more by the entrepreneurial motivation and machiavellian global networking of FIFA's bosses and their business allies; an effective dynamic that was to generate rival strategies developed by the likes of the European confederation and its thrusting commercial partners. FIFA would manoevre its way around the collapse of ISL, bringing those whose loyalty and silence it needed into the camp of its own new internal marketing department; and ruthlessly moving against those whom it saw as dispensable. As the headline flashed across the news services on November 12, 2002 – "Four former ISL executive arrested over FIFA complaint" – the words of Niccolo Machiavelli came to mind: "men ought either to be well-treated or crushed, because they can avenge themselves of lighter injuries, of more serious ones they cannot". In such contexts and circumstances, global markets for sports business and for major sponsors have expanded with little or no reference to the wider constituencies of sport, or to the ruling forum of individual sports organizations. Benefits may have accrued to under-resourced areas of the football world, but such expansion has been driven by the commercial interests of an incestuous network of sports leaders, administrators and commercial entrepreneurs. In the early 1980s, the critical juncture in this story, some sports administrators saw what was happening. Lord Howell's inquiry into sponsorship in sport approached the world governing bodies for their views, and Philippe Chartrier of the International Tennis Federation wrote back: "the control of sport could shift from the International Federations due to the pressure of money", he observed, and argued that the federations should be properly organized and given the means to do their job. Blanche duBois, in Tennessee

Williams' *A Streetcar Named Desire*, is led to her tragic fate by men she has never met, men in white coats, as she utters the great line "I have always depended upon the kindness of strangers". "I have always depended upon the kindness of sponsors" might be the epithet, indeed the epitaph, to sport's boom years, in which sport administrators were seduced by the men in business suits, blind to the real direction in which they would be led.

Acknowledgements

Some of the material in this chapter was also used in Chapters 1 and 4 of John Sugden and Alan Tomlinson (1998), *FIFA and the Contest for World Football – Who Rules the People's Game?* Cambridge: Polity Press), and in their other books (Sugden and Tomlinson, 1999, Chapter 5; 2003) on FIFA. I am grateful to the University of Brighton (Chelsea School Research Centre) for financial support towards the fieldwork and documentary materials upon which these publications are based. Thanks too to Dr Udo Merkel for some useful editorial advice between the conference presentation and the publication of the text of the presentation (see Note 1 below).

Notes

1. An earlier version of parts of this chapter was written by Alan Tomlinson, for presentation, (made by John Sugden), at a Leisure Studies Association conference, and adapted for publication as "FIFA and the Marketing of World Football", in Udo Merkel, Gill Lines, and Ian McDonald (eds) (1998), *Production and Consumption of Sport Cultures: Leisure, Culture and Commerce*, Leisure Studies Association Publication No. 62, Eastbourne: Leisure Studies Association, 1998.
2. Unless otherwise indicated, further Nally material and other unattributed sources are from the Nally transcripts, and other materials, in SCAIR, the Sports Cultures Archive for Investigative Research, University of Brighton.
3. Dr Kim's ambitions knew no bounds and, in July 2001, he was runner-up in the election for the presidency of the IOC, beating the Canadian Dick Pound into third place (in the final round, Dr Jacques Rogge won with 59 votes against Kim's 23, Pound's 22 and six for Pal Schmitt). That more than one-fifth of the IOC electorate could vote for him despite strong evidence as far back as August 1999 that he had

used Salt Lake City (Winter Olympics 2002) connections to secure his son a job was indicative of the hold that the Korean sustained over blocs of IOC members.

By January 2004, Kim had been suspended from all his Olympic responsibilities and duties, resigning on January 9, acknowledging that "he sometimes got careless" and "did things wrong". On January 13, melodramatic and scheming to the end, Kim collapsed and was hospitalized in Seoul, where he was treated for dizziness and high blood pressure. This gave him the possibility of evading arrest and prosecution, on medical grounds. In early January, Rogge had asked the IOC ethics commission to investigate the scandals of Kim's finances at his taekwondo federation. And when, on June 3, 2004, a South Korean court convicted Kim on charges of embezzling more than $3 million from the sports organizations under his control, and accepting $700,000 in bribes, the Korean fraudster was sentenced to two-and-a-half years in jail. His successor as head of the World Taekwondo Federation, Choue Chung-won, was the first competitively elected head in the federation's 31-year history. Dr Kim's fiefdom was truly exposed, his endemic corruption laid bare. The judge attributed the relatively short sentence to Kim's "life-long contribution to the global promotion of teakwondo, illness from age and repentance". Yet, self-deluding to the end, Kim said that he would appeal against the conviction. All that was left for the IOC to do at its full meeting on the eve of the Athens 2004 Summer Games was to expel its corrupt vice-president, and cover the embarrassment of those twenty-three members who had seen him as fit for the IOC presidency. See: http://news.bbc.co.uk/2/hi/asia-pacific/3771931.stm, updated June 3, 2004, retrieved August 12, 2004 ['IOC official jailed for corruption']; http://www.cbc.ca/story/olympics/national/2004/06/11/Sports/TKDprez040611.html, last updated June 11, 2004, retrieved August 12, 2004 ['Choue to replace Kim as World Taekwondo head']; http://sportsillustrated.cnn.com/2004/more/01/23/bc.eu.spt.oly.ioc.kimsu.ap/, posted/updated January 23, 2004, retrieved August 12, 2004 ['IOC bans Korean official in corruption probe']; http://www.canoe.ca/SlamOlympicScandalArchive/aug5_kim.html, August 5, 1999, retrieved August 12, 2004 ['Kim could face tougher punishment'].

Glossary

ASOIF	Association of Summer Olympic International Federations
CCPR	Central Council for Physical Recreation
EBU	European Broadcasting Union
FIFA	Fédération Internationale de Football Association
GAISF	General Assembly of International Sports Federations
IMG	International Management Group

ISL	International Sport and Leisure
INGO	International non-government organization
IAAF	International Amateur Athletic Federation
IOC	International Olympic Committee
ISL	International Sport and Leisure
NBC	National Broadcasting Corporation
OFC	offshore financial center
SCAIR.	Sports Cultures Archive for Investigative Research
SMPI	Société Monaquesque des Promotions Internationales
TEAM	Television Event and Media Marketing AG
TOP	The Olympic Programme
UEFA	Union Européenne de Football Association

Interviews with the Author

Lord Denis Howell, Birmingham, October 8, 1996.
Richard S. (Dick) Pound, Lausanne, May 20, 2001.
Guido Tognoni, Zurich, May 21, 1996.
David Will, Brechin, Scotland, October 9, 1996.
Sir Walter Winterbottom, Cranleigh, Surrey, November 24, 1996.

Archival Sources

Nally Tapes, FIFA Archive, SCAIR (Sports Cultures Archive for Investigative Research, Sport and Leisure Cultures, University of Brighton).

Papers of the Central Council of Physical Recreation's Committee of Enquiry into Sport Sponsorship (the Howell Report), SCAIR, University of Brighton.

Further (confidential/unattributable) documentary sources, copies of which are held by the author on tape or in transcript form.

References

Bernstein, A. (2002), Is it Time for a Victory Lap? Changes in the Media Coverage of Women in Sport, *International Review for the Sociology of Sport*, 37(3/4): 415–28.

Burns, J. (1996a) Murdoch quits race for World Cup TV, *Financial Times*, May 15.

Burns, J. (1996b), Marketing of World Cup at Risk as Three Quit ISL, *Financial Times*, November 26.

CCPR (Central Council of Physical Recreation) (1983), *Committee of Enquiry into Sports Sponsorship – The Howell Report*, London: Central Council of Physical Recreation.

FIFA News, FIFA, Zurich, various issues.

Gilardi, J. (1996), Adidas to Sponsor 98 Soccer World Cup, *Reuters Financial Report* (Wire Service), October 8.

Gruneau, R. (1984), The McDonaldization of the Olympics. In A. Tomlinson and G. Whannel (eds), *Five-Ring Circus – Money, Power and Politics at the Olympic Games*, London: Pluto Press.

Hampton, M. (1996), Where Currents Meet: The Offshore Interface between Corruption, Offshore Finance Centres and Economic Development. In B. Harriss-White and G. White (eds), *Liberalisation and the New Corruption: IDS Bulletin*, 27(2): 210–28.

Harris, J. and Clayton, B. (2002), Femininity, Masculinity, Physicality and the English Tabloid Press – The Case of Anna Kournikova, *International Review for the Sociology of Sport,* 37(3): 397–413.

Howell, D. (1990), *Made in Birmingham – The Memoirs of Denis Howell*, London: Macdonald/Queen Anne Press.

Huntington-Whiteley, J. (ed.) (1999), *The Book of British Sporting Heroes*, London: National Portrait Gallery.

Jackson, S.J., Batty, R. and Scherer, J. (2001), Transnational Sport Marketing at the Global/Local Nexus: The Adidasification of the New Zealand All Blacks, *International Journal of Sports Marketing and Sponsorship* 3(2): 185–201.

Jennings, A. (1996) *The New Lords of the Rings – Olympic Corruption and How to Buy Gold Medals*, London: Simon & Schuster.

Machiavelli, N. (undated) *The Prince* (translated by W.K. Marriott, with an introduction by J. Butterfield), London: JM Dent & Sons Ltd.

Rous, S. (1978), *Football Worlds – A Lifetime in Sport*, London: Faber & Faber.

Simson, V. and Jennings, A. (1992), *The Lords of the Rings – Power, Money and Drugs in the Modern Olympics*. London: Simon & Schuster.

Sugden, J. and Tomlinson, A. (1998), *FIFA and the Contest for World Football – Who Rules the People's Game?* Cambridge: Polity Press.

Sugden, J. and Tomlinson, A. (1999), *Great Balls of Fire – How Big Money is Hijacking World Football*, Edinburgh: Mainstream Publishing.

Sugden, J. and Tomlinson, A. (2003), *Badfellas – FIFA Family at War*, Edinburgh: Mainstream Publishing.

Tomlinson, A. (1994), FIFA and the World Cup: the Expanding Football Family. In J. Sugden and A. Tomlinson (eds), *Hosts and Champions: Soccer Cultures, National Identities and the USA World Cup*, Aldershot: Arena/Ashgate Publishing Limited.
Tomlinson, A. (2004), Olympic Survivals: The Olympic Games as a Global Phenomenon. In L. Allison (ed.), *The Global Politics of Sport*, London: Routledge.
Waters, M. (1995), *Globalisation*, London: Routledge.
Whannel, G. (1992), *Fields in Vision – Television Sport and Cultural Transformation*, London: Routledge.
Wilson, N. (1988), *The Sports Business*, London: Mandarin.

Internet sources

FIFA Press/Communications Division – releases on FIFA web site http:// www.fifa.com
Adidas website: http//: www.adidas.com – read on November 11, 2002.

4

Sport, Tribes and Technology: The New Zealand All Blacks *Haka* and the Politics of Identity

Steven J. Jackson and Brendan Hokowhitu

Globalization has emerged as one of the foremost discourses of our times. According to Anthony Giddens in his recent book *Runaway World: How Globalisation is Reshaping Our Lives* "globalisation is not incidental to our lives . . . . it is a shift in our very life circumstances. It is the way we now live" (Giddens, 2000, p. 19). Giddens' remark forms part of a mounting chorus of scholars, politicians, social activists, economists, transnational entrepreneurs and ordinary citizens who, despite not necessarily agreeing on the specific nature or consequences of globalization, understand that there have been dramatic changes in contemporary patterns of social existence (Appadurai, 1990; Featherstone, 1996; Herman and McChesney, 1997; Scott, 1997; De Mooij, 1998). Key forces in these changes are the new media technologies that enable distant events, people and processes to have a more powerful and immediate impact on our lives (Morley and Robins, 1995; Miller, 1998). Consequently, there has been considerable discussion and debate about the impact of globalization and, in particular, the influence of global forces on local cultures. The local has been defined and conceptualized in a variety of ways, including the nation state, but our focus is within the context of indigenous cultures.

This study examines how global forces are shaping local, indigenous cultures with a particular focus on the relationship between global capitalism, new media technologies, transnational advertising and *Mäori* culture and identity in Aotearoa/New Zealand. We outline a contemporary political debate surrounding indigenous culture and intellectual property rights as they relate to the appropriation of *Mäori* culture by transnational corporations. Specifically, we examine the politics of identity associated with global sport company Adidas and their use of the traditional New Zealand All Black *haka* as part of their global advertising campaign. Central to our discussion are the power, politics and contradictions of representation. We begin by briefly overviewing the changing position of New Zealand rugby within a global context. As the national sport, rugby is a key site for the representation of New Zealand national identity, including *Mäori* culture and identity.

New Zealand Rugby between the Global and the Local

Although it had operated for quite some time as a semi-professional sport, in 1995 New Zealand rugby experienced the most dramatic change in its 100-year plus history. Two rival international companies were attempting to turn the All Blacks, along with the Australian and South African national teams, into a global commodity. Throughout 1995, and particularly around the period of the third Rugby World Cup in South Africa, the World Rugby Corporation (WRC) and News Limited engaged in what FitzSimons (1996) described as the "Rugby War". Both sides attempted to sign players and major television contracts as part of a new global sporting competition. Eventually, Rupert Murdoch's News Limited emerged victorious with a 10-year, $NZ555 million deal signed with the three rugby unions. Most people agreed that a major television contract was essential for the financial stability of the New Zealand Rugby Football Union (hereafter NZRFU) particularly given its difficulties in retaining top-level players who were being lured away by lucrative overseas contracts. Yet, while Murdoch's millions may have provided a healthy injection, it could also be argued that the unprecedented changes to the national game in 1995 served as an awakening with respect to New Zealand's position within the global economy. Arguably, the national game was now, more than ever before, subject to foreign influences and control. The nature of the global/local dilemma in New Zealand as well as rugby's centrality within that debate is outlined by Laidlaw (1999, pp. 177–8):

> There is a real danger that control of the game in New Zealand will steadily be wrested away from New Zealand hands . . . . It is the bottom line of the national personality that is at stake and we are in danger of letting McWorld have it for a few pieces of silver. The massive deals that have been done with major sponsors were the only way of preserving that sovereignty.

Thus, on the one hand New Zealand rugby benefitted, perhaps even survived, by harnessing the resources and technologies made available by transnational corporations such as Rupert Murdoch's News Limited and, subsequently, Adidas. On the other hand there was a price to pay for going global given that both Murdoch and Adidas demanded various forms of control over the brand in which they had invested. Part of that brand is the history, tradition and culture of the All Blacks. Within a local context this means ownership of aspects of the New Zealand community and its collective memory. Thus, transnational investment in the national sport provides privileged access to the past, present and future meaning of not only the game, but also the nation.

In New Zealand, team sports, and in particular rugby, have been one of the few cultural sites where *Mäori* have achieved any sense of equality. According to Starr (1992, pp. 134–5) "Rugby is one of the too few spaces on TV, where *Mäori* people are given texts which show *Mäori* doing well . . . . Rugby is a Pakeha created game that has been adopted by *Mäori* men and used for enjoyment, mana, group spirit, and for a few, prestige and upward mobility in a Pakeha world." While *Mäori* have certainly excelled at rugby over the years and are clearly over-represented at the elite level, critics argue that this simply serves to justify Pakeha (white European) sentiments that a level cultural playing field exists.

It is rugby's mythical and popularized role in defining New Zealand identity and in uniting *Mäori* and Pakeha (cf. Phillips, 1987; Zavos, 1998; Maclean, 1999) that helps explain the significance of the *haka*. This may be because the *haka*, as one of New Zealand's most identifiable national sporting rituals, is performed and displayed during heightened moments of national significance, that is, when facing foreign opponents. It is during these key periods that a large segment of the population focuses its attention on fifteen men who, before entering the battlefield of sport, demonstrate a unity of passion, commitment and assertiveness that, although explicitly masculine and uniquely New Zealand, is expressed in *Mäori* terms.

The result, according to Starr (1992) is that the *haka*, as a powerful symbol of *Mäori* culture, has simply been colonized as a national rugby symbol in order to represent racial harmony despite the lack of *Mäori* material advances. Thus, the *haka* represents much more than a national sporting ritual. It is a contested terrain, perhaps the key site where *Mäori* culture gains more global exposure than any other aspect of their identity. Consequently, there are important implications associated with the appropriation of the *haka* both locally and globally. For example, there are crucial issues linked to intellectual property rights and the authority over the representation of one's cultural identity. According to Smith (1999, p. 89) people and their culture consisting of the material, the spiritual and, the exotic have become "the first truly global commercial enterprise: trading the *Other*". Here, we examine the trading of the *Other* within the context of indigenous culture, new media technologies and transnational sport advertising.

As an introduction we overview the historical origins and significance of the *Mäori haka* including its popularized, if bastardized, appropriation within sport. By providing a literal translation and locating the *haka* within its appropriate cultural context we explain why some critics feel its status is being exploited. Subsequently, we provide a description and analysis of the controversial 1999 Adidas All Black "*haka*" advertisement. It was use of *Mäori* imagery in the advertisement that contributed to recent challenges concerning the control and representation of *Mäori* cultural identity. Finally, we refer to recent legal challenges, largely centered on intellectual property rights related to the *haka*, being mounted by particular *Mäori* groups in their search for compensation from both the NZRFU and Adidas.

The Meaning and Mana[1] of the *Haka*

Although we will later elaborate more fully on the history, meaning and significance of the *haka*, it deserves at least a brief description here particularly for those unfamiliar with the sporting ritual. While there are vast arrays of different *hakas*, globally, the best known is the All Black "*Ka Mate*" *haka*. The New Zealand national rugby team performs this haka before it competes in international "test matches". While descriptions cannot do it justice it is important for readers to have some basic understanding of what the *haka* involves. In brief, prior to each game and immediately following the respective national anthems, the All Blacks, usually led by a senior *Mäori* player, form a semi-circle at midfield facing their opponents. At this point they collectively engage in the *haka,* which consists of about forty seconds of coordinated recitation of words and vigorous body movements that, in combination, tell a story. Arguably, the *haka* has become an essential part of any All Black sporting event serving as an expression (or as we argue misrepresentation) of cultural identity, an entertainment spectacle, and an attempt to motivate the players while intimidating the opposition. With the advent of globalization and new media technologies there is increasing exposure to, and interest in, New Zealand, rugby, the All Blacks, and the *haka*. This has led to a corresponding production and circulation of images and narratives about the *haka* that are further removed from *Mäori* control. As a consequence, there is greater potential for misunderstanding and exploitation. Below, we note some of the misinformed interpretations of the *haka*, and, in turn, identify its meaning and significance within a tribal context.

Whether one is examining Internet sites, watching All Black test matches or related television advertisements, or even discussing the meaning of the *haka* with everyday New Zealanders its popular, albeit mistaken, definition is one of a "war dance". According to Karetu (1993, p. 37) the *hakas* have been "Erroneously defined by generations of uninformed as 'war dances', the true 'war dances' are the *whakatü waewae*, the *tütü ngärahu* and the *peruperu*". Within *Mäori* culture *haka* is the generic name for all types of dance or ceremonial performance that involve movement. Historically, some were used solely for spiritual reasons; others were used for celebration, intimidation, or as a "psych-up" prior to battle (Black, personal communication, March 5, 2002).

New Zealand's sporting icons, the All Blacks, use a specific *haka* called "*Ka Mate*" composed in the 1820s by a famous chief of the Ngäti Toa tribe[2] – Te Rauparaha. Traditionally, the All Blacks leaped off the ground simultaneously to complete the *haka* an action reminiscent of movement particular to the *peruperu*, where warriors folded their legs underneath their bodies as they leapt off the ground. "The *peruperu* is the true war dance and is performed with weapons when the warriors come face to face with the enemy. . . (it) has the psychological purpose of demoralising the enemy by gestures" (Awatere, cited in Karetu, 1993, p. 37).

Karetu (1993) points out, however, that when "*Ka Mate*" was composed it was intended as a *ngeri*. *Ngeri*, "are short *haka* to stiffen the sinews, to summon up the blood, but unlike *haka taparahi*, have no set movements, thereby giving the performers free rein to express themselves as they deem appropriate" (p. 41). Karetu (1993) expresses his concern with the popularized version of "*Ka Mate*", which has: "become the most performed, the most maligned, the most abused of all *haka*. Jumping is not a feature of either *haka taparahi* or *ngeri* and it is these irritating perpetrations that lead to a lot of discord" (p. 68).

Another source of conflict and tension in relation to the haka is the fact that few people, including New Zealanders, understand and accept the story behind it, that is, its literal translation. Based on Karetu's (1993) translation, "*Ka Mate*" was composed by Chief Te Rauparaha while seeking refuge from his enemies at Chief Te Wharerangi's village. The story suggests that Te Rauraparah was concealed in a pit by Te Wharerangi's wife, Te Rangikoaea. She sat over the entrance of the pit to hide Te Rauparaha and to neutralize the chants performed by his pursuers in their quest to flush him out. Here, it is important to note that in *Mäori* culture it was believed that women's genitals could not only neutralize chants but embodied considerable power. In the pit Te Rauparaha hears the fluctuation of his fate in the discussion between his pursuers and the chief, and consequently mutters, *"Aha ha. Ka mate, ka mate. Ka ora, ka ora. Ka mate, ka mate*" – "I die, I die. I live, I live. I die, I die". Finally when he hears his pursuers leave, he exclaims, *"Ka ora, ka ora. Tenei te tangata puhurupuhuru nana nei i tiki mai whakawhiti te ra*" – "I live I live. For this is the hairy man who has fetched the sun and caused it to shine again." As he takes his first two steps out of the pit he says, "*Hupane, kaupane*" – "Spring up the terrace" and as he stands clear he shouts, "*Whiti te ra*" – "The sun shines".

There are many myths associated with the meaning of *"Ka Mate"*, in part linked to Pakeha efforts to interpret *Mäori* culture to suit their own beliefs and interests. For example, sportswriter Spiro Zavos discounts the former *Mäori* reading of *"Ka Mate"* because it makes reference to a woman's genitals ("the hairy man") and to the protection of men by women – a theme common to *Mäori* culture. Zavos's (1998) response is typical of *Pakeha* who believe they have a right to explain *Mäori* culture so that it conforms to their own cultural norms:

> . . . it does not ring true to *Mäori* tradition . . . *Mäori* culture is male hegemonic . . . It seems implausible that the All Blacks. . . would embrace a *haka* that had such embarrassing connotations . . . The hairy man in this *haka* is an archetype of strength, a figure of power, capable of bringing about the triumph of life over death . . . When the All Blacks chant their *haka* . . . they will lead their great team, and the nation that identifies with it, into the sun that shines. (Zaves, 1998, pp. 71–3)

Thus, a *Mäori* interpretation of the *"Ka Mate"* haka is rejected, not because it has been shown to be illegitimate but rather on the basis that it threatens male power and in particular white male power. However, few New Zealanders, *Mäori* and Pakeha alike, seem to know this literal translation of the *haka* within which a male chief acknowledges a woman's genitals because they are viewed to embody such power and strength. Understanding the literal meaning of the *haka* is important but it is also important to consider how a cultural tradition and ritual, which originally had nothing to do with sport, gained its popular, contemporary sporting identity.

In 1888, four years prior to the formal formation of the NZRFU, the first New Zealand team, referred to as the "New Zealand Native Football Representatives", toured Britain and Australia (Phillips, 1987; Ryan, 1993). For New Zealand it was an opportunity to demonstrate its sporting prowess against its colonial masters. One aspect of this demonstration was the performance of a *haka*. Notably, from its earliest sporting introduction, the *haka* performed a dual function: first, as an expression of cultural identity; and, second as part of an entertainment spectacle to attract British crowds. However, it was the tour of one of New Zealand's most famous teams that marked the first official use of the *"Ka Mate" haka* within a sporting context. The 1905 All Blacks, now referred to as "the Originals", are viewed as playing a key role in the formation and confirmation of New Zealand identity (cf. Phillips, 1987). Notably, the *haka* may have played a much more significant role in defining New Zealand's national identity than previously recognized. For example, Andrews (1996) notes that prior to the final game of the 1905 tour against Wales, the home team sang the Welsh national anthem "Hen Wlad Fy Nhadau" in response to the All Black haka. To this extent the performance of the *"Ka*

Mate" haka not only served as a symbol of New Zealand national identity – it may also have stimulated a burgeoning sense of Welsh identity. Inasmuch as identity, particularly national identity, is constructed out of difference the *haka* can be seen to play a pivotal role in defining New Zealand identity both domestically and abroad.

The place of the *haka* within New Zealand cultural identity has been a site of contradictions and resistance, both locally and globally. For example, foreign opponents, misinterpreting the meaning and purpose of the *haka*, often ignored or mocked it (Barlow, 1996; Revington, 1997). Yet, the real disrespect lies not in the opponents disregard but in the NZRFU's placement of the *haka* into an inappropriate arena. Increasingly, there are signs of criticism and resistance.

For example, the haka has been challenged for its role in contributing to the violent nature of sport particularly in New Zealand high schools ("Call to review sports haka", *The Dominion*, October 3, 1991). *The "Ka Mate" haka* has also been challenged because it is considered offensive to some members of the Maori tribe, Ngai Tahu, whose ancestors were slaughtered by Chief Te Rauraparah (Revington, 1997). There have also been a number of criticisms concerning the exploitation of the *haka* as it is linked to popular cultural spectacles such as the mock performance by the Spice Girls during a promotional tour of Bali in 1997 ("Spice Girls draw Maori anger for Mocking haka", *Dominion*, April 28, 1997, p. 1). Finally, with respect to the focus of this study there have been increasing concerns over the commodification and commercial exploitation of the *haka* within contemporary advertising. In recent years there have been numerous examples of *haka*-related imagery being used in advertising campaigns including: AMP Insurance, McDonald's, Lion Red beer, Steinlager beer, Lotto, Ford Motor Company, and most explicitly and recently, Adidas. Next, we outline the emergence of the new sponsorship relationship between Adidas and the NZRFU including the launch of the global advertising campaign featuring the All Black *haka* commercial. In turn, we examine the implications of the ad with respect to the politics of identity and subsequent *Mäori* challenges based on cultural insensitivity and intellectual property rights.

The Adidasification of the All Blacks

In July, 1999 the New Zealand All Blacks commenced their relationship with a new major sponsor, global sport company, Adidas. Arguably, the deal was timely for both sides. As previously noted the NZRFU had been struggling financially despite the substantial 1995 television contract deal signed with Rupert Murdoch's News Corporation. According to then chairman of the NZRFU, Rob Fisher "We believe this is the single largest and most strategically important decision ever made by the NZRFU" (*Otago Daily Times*, October 21, 1997,

p. 23). Adidas, on the other hand, was making significant progress in its plan to overtake Nike as the world's premier sport company. Adding the All Blacks, the premier global icon within the sport of rugby, would do wonders for its image, particularly in the lead-up to the 1999 Rugby World Cup. Yet, while rugby administrators rejoiced, there were concerns within certain sectors of New Zealand about how a foreign company was going to handle the nation's most treasured commodity, the All Blacks. Not only was Adidas displacing longstanding local sponsor, Canterbury, for control of the most famous and respected jersey in rugby but there were rumors that they might actually change its traditional design. Indeed, a new jersey was released but, judging by popular demand for the brand, the new sponsor was a huge success (Jackson et al., 2001).

Notably, the *haka* became a focal point for both the NZRFU and Adidas during 1999. The All Blacks sought advice from *Mäori* cultural leaders about how they could reinforce the power and mana of the *haka*. On July 10, 1999, New Zealand witnessed the performance of a rejuvenated All Black *haka* at Carisbrook Stadium in Dunedin complete with boom microphones that reverberated sound around the stadium like never before. Coincidentally, this was also the launch of the new Adidas brand and All Black jersey. Leading up to the 1999 Rugby World Cup Adidas, in conjunction with global advertising firm Saatchi, launched a dramatic, sixty second, black-and-white commercial featuring the All Black haka. The New Zealand-produced advertisement, which was a year in the making, was intended for a global audience of over forty countries (Admedia, 1999). In brief, the commercial begins with shots of bubbling mud pools, symbolic of the volcanic thermal hotsprings that are a key feature of the tourist hotspot, Rotorua, home to one of the largest tribes, Te Arawa. The scene then shifts back and forth between images of current All Black players performing the *haka* and of *Mäori* warriors of the past. The scantily clad warriors are portrayed as intense, angry fighters complete with moko, that is, traditional *Mäori* facial tattoos. The advertisement's concluding shots feature *Mäori* All Black Kees Meeuws staring back intensely at his opponents after completing the *haka*. A key feature of the ad was the dramatic sound. The audio track was created using 80 layers of sound beginning with the actual game *haka* but also including the voices of individual players through post synching. According to Howard Greive, Saatchi head of television, the concept "was always centered around the *haka* and a 'primal' sound design . . . we always wanted to create a sort of primal scary ad" (1999, p. 22). Further insights from the producers provide important information about the intentions of Adidas. The commercial was shot by a community of cinematographers, including two cameramen from the National Football League (NFL), during the first night game at Eden Park (Auckland). This was done in order to capture the dramatic atmosphere and to control the lighting. According to Howard Greive, Adidas was looking for something unique in order to brand its products and they believed they could capture this through the *haka*:

> You have to go back to: why did Adidas come in and pay all that money for the All Blacks? It's because the All Blacks can deliver something to their brand that no other team or individual can in sport. Which is they are playing a very, very physical game – it has been called the last warrior sport in the world. Not only that, but they play it with intensity and the easiest way to judge that intensity is through the *haka*. That is exactly what Adidas wanted in terms of what the All Blacks could bring to their brand. It introduced a gutsier, more primal element – as well as the sheer artistry of rugby. (*Admedia*, 1999, p. 22)

Greive's comments are revealing. First, although he does not explicitly refer to globalization he certainly alludes to the unique contribution that the All Blacks can make to the Adidas brand. However, it is Greive's statements about how the All Blacks can provide this that are most interesting. He suggests that it is the intensity and physical nature of their style that sets the All Blacks apart; a style characterized by a *primal*, warrior element that is best expressed through the *haka*. In an interview with *AdMedia* magazine Greive's (1999, p. 22) further notes that "One of the key words that Adidas were keen to go with was authenticity – so that's why we shot a game and that's why we shot the *haka* . . . . We knew that if we could just show people what it is actually like to be confronted by the *haka* and to watch the All Blacks play their game – then you don't have to manufacture anything. All you have to do is show it." One can only wonder if Greive sees the irony of his statements about authenticity in light of the extreme lengths to which his production team went in order to socially construct the powerful collage of signs that cumulatively constituted an Adidas advertisement.

The advertisement certainly received attention and Adidas ensured that it gained additional exposure beyond television through a synergy of media technologies. For example, the advertisement was featured on the Adidas WWW homepage where it could be downloaded and viewed. Moreover, corresponding poster and billboard campaigns were launched in conjunction with the television advertisement. One dramatic image revealed a huge black and white billboard in central London, featuring various All Blacks doing the *haka* with nine tribal warriors montaged into the background. Another billboard showed a huge moko-faced Maori warrior glaring angrily at all who gazed upon him with the Adidas trifoil logo and the NZRFU trademark silver fern subtly located on the left and right hand sides of the image respectively.

For ardent rugby fans or perhaps even those who had simply seen the full-length video advertisement the giant billboards may have served to reinforce the brand. However, it is not known what unsuspecting pedestrians must have thought about this compelling image. Perhaps it left a lasting impression about the Adidas brand, in which case it succeeded as a transnational marketing exercise. However, it is important to consider the implications with respect to the global image of *Mäori*. Could such representations reinforce global stereotypes of New Zealand's indigenous people as violent, noble savages or exotic others? For example, according to Wall (1997, p. 41) the ambivalent and contradictory signifiers and discourses made available through the media (and arguably via the Adidas television and billboard advertisements) reinforce stereotypes of *Mäori* as the: "Primitive savage warrior, the immoral sexual predator, the naïve comical simpleton, the spiritual/irrational environmentally-aware tribesperson". As a consequence the image produced and reproduced is what she describes as the "quintessential Maori" (Wall, 1997, p. 41). While we can only speculate, the Adidas quest to capture the authenticity of the All Blacks through the primal images and sounds embodied in the *haka*, suggests some attempt to seize, or more accurately manufacture, one particular aspect of *Mäori* culture.

Ultimately, stereotypes of *Mäori* are used as part of a transnational marketing campaign that is, in effect, exploiting indigenous culture. The exploitation occurs not only through the misappropriation of a ritual but also through the attempts to nostalgically forge a particular version of New Zealand's past. As a consequence the inequalities of history are erased, or at least ignored, while *Mäori*, as a racial/ethnic group, is repositioned into the stereotypical representations of the past. According to Fleras (1991) the use of racial/ethnic stereotypes works to sanitize majority perceptions such that indigenous minorities are "rendered less threatening by framing them in familiar and comforting terms; this, in turn, diminishes their impact as a threat to the social fabric. Stereotypes also reassure the audience that potentially troublesome constituents are still 'in their place'" (Fleras, 1991, p. 352). Arguably, stereotypes are an important issue with respect to *Mäori* culture and the performance of the *haka*. To perform the *haka* correctly requires intensity and strength that is displayed by, for example, dilation of the eyes and a protruding tongue. However, just like the earliest Europeans who encountered *Mäori*, those unfamiliar with the *haka* may view such rituals as uncivilized and confine "themselves to such epithets as 'grotesque', 'savage', and 'indecent'" (Karetu, 1993, p. 29). Yet, the stereotypes are truly in the eye of the beholder and only become stereotypes because *Mäori* culture has become decontextualized. For *Mäori* the expression in *haka* is a reflection of their culture, that is, "the eyes are the windows of the soul and . . . say much that the rest of the body can't . . . the tongue is the avenue whereby the thoughts of the mind is [sic] conveyed to the audience" (Karetu, 1993, pp. 29–30).

Control is a key issue in relation to the global circulation of indigenous rituals and images. Few familiar with rugby and the All Blacks would deny the intensity of their play, nor the symbolic power of the *haka*. Yet, given the vast array of new technologies and representations *Mäori* have less and less collective determination of how the *haka*, and other aspects of their culture are represented and distributed. For example, a cursory search of the World Wide Web using the key word "*haka*" reveals over twenty sites, in various languages and with different purposes. Largely, these sites focus on the sport of rugby and tend to celebrate the legend of the All Blacks. Notably, most at least attempt to provide an explanation about the meaning and significance of the *Mäori haka*. However, one must ponder the implications of a decontextualized American, German or Japanese-based Web site dedicated to explaining the meaning and significance of the haka particularly in relation to *Mäori* cultural history. Recently, there have been signs of resistance to the appropriation of *Mäori* culture, particularly the *haka*. We examine one of the most publicized challenges to date: the intellectual property rights case against Adidas and the NZRFU following the launch of the new global *haka* advertising campaign.

Resisting Commodification

Although the Adidas campaign was launched in July 1999, it was nearly a year later that a formal, consolidated protest emerged. On June 11, 2000 the front page of the *Sunday News* displayed the headline "$1.5m for *haka*". The accompanying article outlined claims by Ron Peters, a Northland lawyer, rugby administrator and brother of controversial NZ First political party leader Winston Peters, that "There are immense concerns out there among *Mäori* people". In part, these concerns center around the fact that some *Mäori* believe they "deserve a large slice of the $120 million adidas sponsorship of NZ rugby, because the sportswear giant uses *Mäori* imagery in its branding" (Reid, 2000, p. 1). However, the very next day the NZRFU, through its chief executive, David Rutherford, refused to recognize any such claim for compensation. According to Rutherford:

> We don't want the *haka* to be for sale and if it were we wouldn't be a willing buyer of it. I don't think anyone thinks the *haka* is performed for commercial purposes. If it was ever reduced to that I'm reasonably sure we wouldn't want to perform it. If the *haka* is for sale, what isn't? The *haka* is very special to New Zealand rugby and it has a very special place. It's a part of our game; we've defended the right to do it against attack from time to time. We've never had to pay for the privilege. To do so would demean the mana of it for us. ("No $1.5m *haka*", *Otago Daily Times*, June 12, 2000, p. 18)

Rutherford's comments are curious. On the one hand, he claims that the NZRFU "wouldn't be a willing buyer" of the *haka* but, in effect, they serve as the broker that sells the *haka* through television rights contracts to broadcast All Black games and, in the case of Adidas, through an advertising campaign. The use of All Black players under contract in the Adidas advertisement is a clear example of the commodification of the *haka*. Moreover, each instance in which the NZRFU is affiliated with corporations that use the *haka* in their advertisements, directly or indirectly, condones its use.

Approximately, one week after publication of the newspaper article the issue of ownership of the *haka* appeared in the media again. This time it was featured during a segment of *Backchat*, a Television One arts, culture and entertainment program. The show, hosted by Gordon Harcourt, featured three guests: copyright lawyer John Hackett, *Mäori* claims lawyer Maiu Solomon, and *Mäori* artist, designer and curator Julie Paama-Pengelly. Several segments of the discussion are worth noting in detail simply because they embody the most comprehensive public discussion of the issue to date. The segment begins with the perspective of copyright lawyer John Hackett. From a legal standpoint Hackett argued that there are two central issues with respect to Adidas' use of the *haka*: trademark and copyright. He immediately discounts the trademark issue and, in turn, rejects any claim of copyright because, Hackett claims, they aren't absolutely certain who created the *haka* and there is no written contract to verify ownership, making it part of the public domain. However, as Maiu Solomon points out, the very use of a colonial legal tradition to evaluate and judge cultural and intellectual property rights (IPR) is fraught with contradictions:

> I think what this whole debate highlights . . . is: (1) that the intellectual property rights system is totally inadequate to recognise and protect *Mäori* cultural values and cultural rights, for example, the IPR system was developed to protect private economic rights that came out of the Industrial revolution but when you talk about *Mäori* tanga cultural heritage rights these are collective; by nature so they don't belong to one individual, they belong to the whanau, the hapu or the iwi. What we are seeing happening now, increasingly, is that you've got major corporates who are drawing upon *Mäori* branding, *Mäori* imagery and *Mäori* icons to promote their products. Now if they're going to do that they've got to go to *Mäori* and make sure that they have the proper authority that they are doing the right thing, that they are using those images and icons in a culturally appropriate way. And if there is going to be a commercial return then what share of those benefits will *Mäori* get. (Maiu Solomon, *Backchat*, Television One, June 18, 2000)

The host of the program, Gordon Harcourt, probes in order to gain an understanding of what the real problem is:

> As a Pakeha New Zealander watching that ad, which . . . was an incredibly powerful branding campaign for the All Blacks, [to me] it creates a powerful image of New Zealand, it attaches enormous significance and heart to that *Mäori* imagery and that *Mäori* imagery then becomes an ambassador for New Zealand. What really at the end of the day is wrong with that? (*Backchat*, Television One, June 18, 2000)

In response, Julie Paama-Pengelly replied: "Well that's a great thing but *Mäori* aren't in control of how they're portrayed in their imagery. How do we know that that's how they want their moko to be seen because moko is not just about being warriors or champions" (*Backchat*, Television One, June 18, 2000). Here the moko, what we've previously described as *Mäori* facial tatoos, becomes the focus of discussion. Responding to Paama-Pengelly, the host notes that "It's a bit simplistic I know but there's a *Mäori* guy involved in that [ad] whose face had a digitally created moko on it. I'm not sure of the ins and outs of the making of that ad but its not just being done without anybody's say at all" (*Backchat*, Television One, June 18, 2000). In part, Harcourt makes the case that if a *Mäori* person consents to the use of the image then there shouldn't be a problem. However, as Maiu Solomon quickly points out, the moko, *haka* and other aspects of *Mäori* culture must be located and understood within an appropriate cultural framework:

> The tau moko is not just the individual lines on the face it tells a whole story of that person's heritage, of the marae of the tribe . . . its part of that collective right . . . the person carries all of that mana, all of that heritage, all of that tradition. So, it is wrong for me to go and try and copyright an ancestor figure that's been carved on a tree because I've got a company and I want to use it on a logo because that belongs to my collective, it belongs to my iwi. (Backchat, Television One, June 18, 2000)

The point being made is that in *Mäori* culture, like many other indigenous cultures, there is a different sense of history, ownership and community. Individuals are defined in relation to their family history and in *Mäori* culture this includes: family (immediate), whanau (extended family), hapu (subtribe), iwi (tribe) and waka (lineage based on the boat in which one's *Mäori* ancestors arrived in New Zealand). At this point the legal proceedings regarding the *haka* are in their very early stages. However, given the symbolic power of the *haka* in the cultural, ideological and commercial realms it is likely to remain a site of considerable tension and debate.

Conclusion

New global technologies appear to hold the potential to serve as both savior and enemy of indigenous culture. On the one hand new technologies such as the Internet and satellite television are enabling remote, often marginalized, tribes to communicate and gain a sense of solidarity with other global indigenous groups. Likewise, the media can play a significant role in drawing the world's attention to the serious plight of some groups thereby providing a stimulus for social change. However, these same technologies can, intentionally and unintentionally, contribute to the exploitation and perhaps even eradication of indigenous interests.

The implications of global capitalism, new media technologies and transnational advertising for indigenous cultures are immense. In 1996 the leading world advertising and broadcasting associations devised a single global standard for the purchase and production of television advertising (Ross, 1996, p. 3). Furthermore, predictions are that global advertising will have increased from $335 billion in 1995 to $2 trillion in 2020 (Coen, 1995). In combination, the consolidation of these major global political, economic and cultural power brokers is driving a new culture of enterprise that enlists the enterprise of culture (Harvey, 1989; Jameson, 1991). The implications of such a shift with respect to global advertising and indigenous culture are highlighted by Goldman and Papson (1996). They assert that as advertisers seek new signs and excavate fresh cultural territory "no meaning system is sacred, because the realm of culture has been turned into a giant mine" (Goldman and Papson, 1996, pp. v–vi). In light of such a forecast the outlook for maintaining authority over the representation of indigenous, and other, cultures will be increasingly difficult. According to Melucci (1989, p. 258) "the freedom to belong to an identity and to contribute to its definition presumes the freedom to be represented" (1989, p. 258). Therefore we need cultural spaces "which enable individuals and social groups to affirm themselves and be recognized for what they are or wish to be" (Melucci, 1989, p. 172).

The case of the (mis)appropriation of the *Mäori haka* by the NZRFU and Adidas is but one of many examples of the challenges faced by indigenous cultures. There are avenues and signs of resistance, but transnational corporations and their vast array of technologies continue to benefit from an expanding environment of national, commercial and legal deregulation. Consequently, within the context of global capitalism the struggle to maintain and protect cultural spaces where identities can be constructed and affirmed will become increasingly difficult.

Notes

1. In general terms mana refers to prestige and respect but often carries even more significance.
2. Tribe from the Wellington area.

References

Adidas Appointed to Outfit the All Blacks, *Otago Daily Times*, October 21, 1997, p. 23.

Andrews, D. (1996), Sport and the Masculine Hegemony of the Modern Nation: Welsh Rugby, Culture and Society, 1890–1914. In J. Nauright and T. Chandler (eds), *Making Men: Rugby and Masculine Identity*, London: Frank Cass, pp. 50–69.

Appadurai, A. (1990). Disjuncture and Difference in the Global Cultural Economy, *Theory, Culture and Society*, 7, 295–310.

Barlow, H. (1996), More to the Haka than Meets the Eye, *Dominion*, June 28, p. 9.

Call to Review Sports Haka, *The Dominion*, October 3, 1991, p. 3.

Coen, R. J. (1995), The Advertising Trends up to 2020, paper presented to Marketing 2020 conference, New York City, March 16, 1995.

De Mooij, M. (1998), *Global Marketing and Advertising: Understanding Cultural Paradoxes*, Thousand Oaks CA: Sage.

Featherstone, M. (1996), Localism, Globalism, and Cultural Identity. In R. Wilson and W. Dissanayake (eds), *Global/Local: Cultural Production and the Transnational Imaginary*, Durham NC: Duke University Press, pp. 46–77.

FitzSimons, P. (1996), *The Rugby War*, Sydney: HarperCollins Publishers.

Fleras, A. (1991). Beyond the Mosaic: Minorities and the Media in Multiracial/Multicultural society. In B. D. Singer (ed.), *Communications in Canadian Society*, Scarborough: Nelson Canada, pp. 344–67.

Giddens, A. (2000), *Runaway World: How Globalisation is Reshaping Our Lives*, London: Routledge.

Goldman, R. and Papson, S. (1996), *Sign Wars: The Cluttered Landscape of Advertising*, New York: Guilford Press, pp. 1–19.

Harvey, D. (1989), *The Condition of Postmodernity*, Oxford: Blackwell.

Herman, E. and McChesney, R. (1997), *The Global Media: The New Missionaries of Global Capitalism*, London: Cassell.

Jackson, S. J., Batty, R. and Scherer, J. (2001), Transnational Sport Marketing at the Global/Local Nexus: The Adidasification of the New Zealand All Blacks, *International Journal of Sports Marketing and Sponsorship*, 3(2): 185–201.

Jameson, F. (1991), *Postmodernism, or the Cultural Logic of Late Capitalism*, Durham NC: Duke University Press.

Karetu, T. (1993), *Haka – Dance of a Noble People*, Auckland: Reed Publishing.
Laidlaw, C. (1999), *Rights of Passage: Beyond the New Zealand Identity Crisis*, Auckland: Hodder Moa Beckett.
Maclean, M. (1999). Of Warriors and Blokes: The Problem of Maori rugby for Pakeha Identity in New Zealand. In T. Chandler and J. Nauright (eds), *Making the Rugby World: Race Gender and Commerce*, London: Frank Cass, pp. 1–26.
Melucci, A. (1989), *Nomads of the Present: Social Movements and Individual Needs in Contemporary Society*, London: Hutchinson Radius.
Miller, T. (1998), *Technologies of Truth: Cultural Citizenship and the Popular Media*, Minneapolis: University of Minnesota Press.
Morley, D. and Robins, K. (1995), *Spaces of Identity: Global Media, Electronic Landscapes and Cultural Boundaries*, London: Routledge.
No $1.5m Haka, *Otago Daily Times*, June 12, 2000, p. 18.
Phillips, J. (1987), *A Man's Country: The Image of the Pakeha Male, a History*, Auckland: Penguin.
Primal Team (1999), *Admedia*, 14(9): 22–3.
Reid, N. (2000), $1.5m for Haka *Sunday News*, June 11, p. 1.
Revington, M. (1997). Haka hooligans, *New Zealand Listener*, December 6, p. 22.
Ross, C. (1996), Global Rules are Proposed for Measuring TV, *Advertising Age*, August 12, p. 3.
Ryan, G. (1993), *Forerunners of the All Blacks: The 1888-89 New Zealand Native Football Team in Britain, Australia and New Zealand*, Christchurch: University of Canterbury Press.
Scott, A. (1997), *The Limits of Globalization: Cases and Arguments*, London: Routledge.
Smith, T. L. (1999), *Decolonising Methodologies: Research and Indigenous Peoples*, Dunedin: London Books.
Spice Girls Draw Maori Anger for Mocking Haka, *Dominion*, April 28, 1997, p. 1.
Starr, L. (1992), Undying Love, Resisting Pleasures: Women Watch Telerugby. In R. DuPlessis (ed.), *Feminist Voices: Women's Studies Text for Aotearoa/NZ* Auckland: Oxford University Press, pp. 124–40.
Wall, M. (1997), Stereotypical Constructions of the Maori "Race" in the Media. *New Zealand Geographer*, 53(2): 40–5.
Zavos, S. (1998), *Ka Mate! Ka Mate! New Zealand's Conquest of British Rugby*, Auckland: Viking.

5

Marketing Generosity: The Avon Worldwide Fund for Women's Health and the Reinvention of Global Corporate Citizenship

Samantha King

The observation that political, economic, and technological changes over the past two decades have removed barriers from markets that until recently were closed or highly regulated is by now familiar.[1] Although the specific effects of the end of the Cold War, the emergence of international trade blocs, the expanding influence of bodies such as the World Trade Organization, and the availability of new technologies are the subject of ongoing debate, it is generally acknowledged that corporations play a more central role in international relations of power than they did prior to this period and that new configurations of economic activity have profound implications for the territoriality and sovereignty of nation-states (Barber, 1995; Jameson and Miyoshi, 1998; Sassen 1998; Frank, 2000).

The economic and legal trajectories of the current global order have emerged in coincidence with a profusion of local, regional, and transnational NGOs and social movements that constitute in the eyes of some commentators a burgeoning global civil society. However, the extraordinary diversity of NGOs and social movements in existence, in conjunction with the multiple, often contradictory, meanings of civil society in circulation make coherent theoretical analyses of this phenomena decidedly difficult. Frederic Jameson's (1998) discussion of the two distinct levels at which the idea of civil society operates is useful in this respect. He points out that this term signifies both the political "freedom" of social groups to negotiate their political contract and the economic "freedom" of the marketplace as a dynamic space of innovation and production, distribution and consumption. Crucially, however, he notes that there is frequent slippage between the political and the economic as one level is "slyly" substituted for the other in "a kind of ideological prestidigitation" (p. xiii).

This chapter is concerned with analysing one particular site of such symbolic conjuring – the emergence of global strategic corporate philanthropy and community relations programs (GSCR).[2] In contrast to the mostly random, eclectic, and unscientific approach to corporate giving that dominated until recently, GSCR programs take a highly measured, profit-conscious approach to such activities. Businesses often explain their move to create GSCR programs both in terms of a need to "fill the breach" caused by a widespread reduction in the number and depth of government-provided welfare and healthcare services worldwide (although such explanations are usually couched in language that suggests that corporations themselves have played no part in this downsizing) and heightened public concern and expectations about corporate responsibility.[3] In addition, GSCR programs are one of a range of strategies by which transnational corporations seek to engage with "the local" in order to demonstrate that they enjoy more than a commercial connection to the multiple sites in which they conduct business and to recognize the differences – cultural, social, and so on – among them. While claims about "filling the breach" are not merely rhetorical maneuvers, a *conjuncture* of social, economic, and political forces not visible in the corporate account of this shift has provided the conditions out of which these programs emerged. Moreover, while the specific content of GSCR programs is often generated locally, and therefore varies across national borders, the analysis that follows will suggest that these programs are often superficial efforts that are probably more effective in presenting a positive company image to consumers in the North, than they are in tackling the specific issues they purport to address.

Thus, through a discussion of the conditions from which GSCR programs emerged – my sources include court records, Conference Board reports, corporate philanthropy handbooks, and business management literature – I seek to explore the social commitments that are enabled and constrained when "economic freedom" is pursued through the language and structures of global corporate philanthropy. While I acknowledge that GSCR programs have arisen as corporations have come to view themselves as responsible to new and diverse communities, the history presented here posits economic and managerial imperatives, as much as ethical considerations, as the spur to their creation. In other words, as corporations seek to produce and sell goods in an ever-expanding number of locations, philanthropy and community relations are increasingly deployed not merely to further some social good, but as techniques for market penetration and retention, both in the domestic market and abroad.

There are numerous examples of the turn toward GSCR programs among large sports apparel and equipment producers such as Nike and Reebok – the same corporations whose labor practices and strategies for growth have, of course, been the subject of major criticism and resistance among workers and activists (Enloe, 1995; Ballinger, 1998; Stabile, 2000). Reebok's sponsorship of Amnesty International's Human Rights Now! concert tour in 1988 developed into a long-term commitment to human rights causes. The company underwrites a Human Rights Award, established the Witness program (through which activists are given hand-held video cameras to record human rights abuses), and created a global grant-making program to support the human rights activities of nonprofit organizations. Nike also sponsors a range of philanthropic and community-relations initiatives in the countries in which it produces and sells goods. They support self-enterprise and continuing education programs in Indonesia and Vietnam, and a variety of community programs for youth in the US.

With the exception of C. L. Cole's (1996) analysis of Nike's PLAY campaign – a US-focused effort – such initiatives have not been the subject of academic research. This absence in the literature might be explained, in part, by an understandable commitment on the part of scholars to focus on the urgent issues raised by corporations' reliance on sweatshop labor. In addition, it is easy to dismiss corporate philanthropy as a transparent attempt on the part of the capitalist machine to veil or distract attention from its "evil doings". But, as I have already indicated, corporate philanthropy and community relations are being deployed, on a transnational scale, as an integral component of capitalist expansion and in this respect deserve to be taken seriously.

Here I have chosen the Avon corporation's GSCR programs as the specific example through which to make my case.[4] I draw on interviews with Avon employees, press releases, business news coverage, annual reports, and Internet and other publicity to explore the Avon WorldWide Fund for Women's Health, a global initiative launched in 1992 in which Avon operations around the world have been encouraged to develop a women's health program. In addition, I discuss the Avon Running Global Women's Circuit, an international network of 5k runs that aims to encourage competitive and recreational running and walking among women.

There are a number of reasons for focusing on Avon's programs. First, they are among the oldest and most extensive of contemporary GCSR initiatives. In addition to providing rich empirical evidence, their age allows for a historical analysis that is sensitive to the ways that changes in corporate strategy are reflected in approaches to community-relations programing. Second, discussions of the links between transnational capitalism and sport have tended to focus on the imbrication of men's interests, needs, and desires in global sport networks, often to the exclusion or tokenization of women's interests, needs, and desires. While the analysis presented here can claim to make only a modest intervention in this trend, it is my hope that it will provoke further probing of the gender of sport globalization. Finally, an analysis of Avon's GSCR programs allows for an exploration of the ways in which opportunities to participate in sport are used by non-sport related corporations as a form of strategic philanthropy and community relations. In other words, it enables a consideration of the ways in which the social meanings and valences of sport are produced, deployed, and consumed; how these meanings and valences might change – or not – as they travel on a transnational scale; and how they might help shape the meanings and values attached to global capitalism.

Global Corporate Philanthropy and Community Relations: A Short History

Corporate Philanthropy in the US: The Post-War Era

Programs by which to demonstrate corporate commitment to community relations and philanthropy are not new, although it was not until 1953 that the New Jersey Supreme Court gave broad legal sanction to corporate donations by US companies. Two years previously, the board of directors of A. P. Smith Manufacturing had donated $1,500 to Princeton University for general maintenance purposes. Several stockholders challenged the legitimacy of the gift in the New Jersey courts by charging that this was a misappropriation of corporate funds and went beyond corporate powers because the company's charter did not explicitly authorize such donations. The judge, however, ruled in favor of the company, whose president had argued that he considered his contribution to be sound because the public expects such philanthropy from corporations, because it would obtain goodwill for the company in the community, and because it would further the company's self-interest in assuring a continual flow of well-trained personnel for employment in the corporate world (A.P. Smith Manufacturing v. Barlow 13 N.J. 145 (1980) – available online at http://www.lexis-nexis.com/universe; Yankey, 1996; Muirhead, 1999). Such giving was also necessary, the Court argued, to ensure the survival of private educational institutions and thus of the "system of free enterprise". Significantly, the Court also suggested that with the transfer of wealth from individuals to corporations and with the "burdens of taxation resulting from increased state and federal aid", corporations were expected to assume the modern obligations of good citizenship just as individuals had in the past. In subsequent legal challenges, state courts ruled that corporations were free to give to charities whether or not they were related to the business of the company. These rulings opened the door for corporate support of charities and corporate funding in support of domestic arts and education, in particular, increased dramatically (Muirhead, 1999).

Although the development of government social welfare programs under the New Deal marked a turn toward social democracy, the development of the idea of an "associative state" was crucial to the institutionalization and expansion of corporate philanthropy in the years following World War II, which at this time remained very much targeted towards recipients within the US. Business leaders such as Frank Abrams of Standard Oil of New Jersey, Alfred P. Sloan of General Motors, and Arthur W. Page of AT&T created the Council for Aid to Education to encourage corporate support for higher education because they believed that by funding private universities, businesses might stem the growth of government-supported public education, and the expansion of government programs more generally, which had resulted from the war, the New Deal, and particularly the enactment of the GI Bill (Himmelstein, 1996).

Although these business leaders maintained an ambitious vision for the role of philanthropy, from the 1950s to the 1980s, corporate giving moved away from its position at the center of business activity to assume a more peripheral and independent role. While philanthropy was viewed as valuable insofar as it enhanced a corporation's reputation, it was not yet viewed as a tool that could be employed directly in the service of selling goods (Drucker, 1984; Dienhart, 1988; Zetlin, 1990; Yankey, 1996; Muirhead, 1999). This was to change, however, in the last two decades of the twentieth century, a period in which the philosophy and practice of corporate philanthropy has undergone rapid transformation.

Corporate Downsizing and Strategic Philanthropy

The early 1980s saw numerous US corporations move their manufacturing bases overseas and an intensification of the spate of deregulation-induced corporate diversification, restructuring, and downsizing that had begun in the late 1970s. As businesses merged and streamlined, corporate contributions, which had been propelled into public consciousness through the promotion of Ronald Reagan's 1981 Task Force on Private Sector Initiatives, became the focus of managers who were seeking to gain efficiency in an increasingly competitive marketplace. In the words of James P. Shannon (1996), a corporate philanthropy consultant and recognized proponent of the shift to strategic philanthropy, these changes "put the current managers of corporate philanthropy on notice that henceforth their departments would be evaluated by management against the same standards of performance, efficiency, production, and achievement as all other departments in their companies" (p. ix). As a result, some contributions programs disappeared, while others were streamlined. Barry Lastra, a public affairs consultant with the Chevron Corporation, describes the impact of the Chevron-Gulf merger on their corporate giving function as follows:

> In melding corporate contributions, one plus one seldom equals two. When Gulf's $10.2 million contributions budget was combined with Chevron's $20 million contributions budget there was an immediate 11% reduction to a combined program of $27 million . . . A merger forces an overall analytical review that is invaluable – my experience would suggest this type of critical review is in order even without the trauma of a corporate merger. (Lastra quoted in Muirhead, 1999, p. 41)

Lastra also articulates here the widespread belief in the need to streamline corporate contributions *in general*, even in times of relative economic stability – a belief that has been widely put into practice in the past fifteen years.

As pressure increased for efficiency and restraint in corporate contributions a key shift occurred. Staff in these areas began to look for ways to make philanthropic activities assist with profit-making and strategic giving emerged as the solution. A Conference Board report, for instance, describes how Kodak's community relations and contributions program, facing a decrease in its budget, strove to make "community relations a strategic resource in gaining revenue for the company" (Muirhead, 1999, p. 41). Kodak's new strategy involves partnerships between the contributions department and other units of the business so that these units learn "the value of investing in urban markets", "promote business-to-business relationships – not just philanthropic ones – with nonprofits", "leverage contributions to enhance sales opportunities," and "*make grants that enhance global access*" (emphasis added) (Muirhead, 1999, p. 41). Thus, Kodak's philanthropic and profit-making functions have become inextricably intertwined, as philanthropy is viewed as a possible route to gaining access to new markets at home and abroad, finding new partners with whom to do business, and enhancing sales.

Kodak's shift toward strategic philanthropy is typical of corporate America's move to "treat donations like investments" and thus to "expect some return from them" – a move that simultaneously represents a turn away from the understanding of philanthropy as a straightforward obligation of corporate citizenship (Dienhart, 1988, p. 64). By the 1990s, management guru Peter Drucker's (1984) argument that altruism cannot be the criterion by which corporate giving is evaluated had become a guiding assumption of contributions programs as businesses discharged their "social responsibilities" by converting them into "self-interest" and hence "business opportunities".

While there are instances in which corporations make financial contributions without reference to their markets or overall strategic plans, research by the Conference Board and others suggests that many corporations, particularly large multi-nationals, now employ a business driven approach to contributions as they seek to attach "value", "strategic vision", and "mission" to their charitable activities (Zetlin, 1990; Alperson, 1995; Kulik, 1999; Muirhead, 1999) This business-driven approach, referred to as "strategic giving" (Zetlin, 1990) or "charitable investing" (Dienhart, 1988), requires that every dollar given must mesh with the company's markets or employees and work as part of their overall strategic plan.

In order to make corporate philanthropy profitable, executives have also sought ways to make it more "scientific". Referring to the effect of demands for efficiency on corporate contributions departments, John Shannon writes, "The problem posed by these new standards is that until now many corporate giving programs have had no clear mission statement, no regular documentation of their effectiveness and no systematic way of measuring whether or how their work products complement the mission or the strategic plans of their parent companies" (Shannon, 1996, p. ix). Similarly, Craig Smith, president of Corporate Citizen (a corporate philanthropy consulting firm) and another leader in the move toward strategic philanthropy, calls for increased research in the field and argues that "if corporate philanthropy is to flourish or even survive, it will be at least in part because researchers have generated the theoretic [*sic*] framework, the methodologies, measurements, and data that show skeptical corporate executives how corporate philanthropy assists corporate competitive strategies" (Smith, 1996, p. 1).

From these developments, a new generation of philanthropic consultants trained in the principles of business administration has emerged. The role of these consultants is to develop appropriate strategies and research methods to decide how and where to distribute grants and other resources and to help corporations develop systems for tracking the effectiveness of their giving programs both in terms of impact on their designated social problems and profitability. Thus, instead of merely giving in reaction to appeals for charitable grants, the process has become proactive, with "sets of objectives, budgetary priorities, program planning, coordination, and accountability" (Smith, 1989, p. 335). In turn, it is these professionals who have been charged with inventing a vast array of tools, plans, strategies, and techniques for governing philanthropic activities. These include manuals detailing the components of a profitable contributions program (Shannon, 1991; Alperson, 1995; Muirhead, 1999); qualitative and quantitative methods to measure outcomes and performance (Scott and Rothman, 1992; Wood and Jones, 1996); the creation of new courses in philanthropy (such as the New York-based Rockefeller Foundation Course in Practical Philanthropy and the Boston-based Impact Project), which teach potential philanthropists and corporate contributions officials how to evaluate organizations for their financial responsibilities (Miller, 1997); and the publication of numerous new magazines such as *Guidestar* ("the Donor's Guide to the Nonprofit Universe"), *Who Cares: The Toolkit for Social Change, More than Money*, *The American Benefactor*, and *Build*, which have joined more established journals such as the *Chronicle of Philanthropy* and the *Nonprofit Times*.

In practice, the shift toward strategic philanthropy has meant that most large corporations have undertaken at least some of the following changes in their approach to philanthropy and community relations:

- Use of a narrow theme (for example, environmental protection, breast cancer) to maximize impact of giving and align contributions with business goals and brand characteristics.
- Support for programs that target beneficiaries who are or could become customers.
- Integration of company's giving program with marketing, public affairs, and government relations departments.
- Formation of partnerships with community groups, local governments, and other companies who share a common interest in a particular concern (for example, former President Clinton's drive to build "empowerment zones" in economically depressed communities through business, government, and nonprofit partnerships).
- Development of volunteer programs with awards, matching gifts, paid volunteer time, or other incentives to encourage employees to "serve their communities".
- Use of already existing company resources to enable noncash forms of contributions.
- Use of public relations campaigns that highlight company activities.
- Increased emphasis on the measurement of program results.
- Instigation of global volunteering or grant-making programs that emphasize and attain a "worldwide" presence.

The "Globalization" of Strategic Philanthropy and Community Relations

Despite frequent references to the growth of GSCR practices among US corporations in literature on corporate social responsibility, there is a paucity of empirical research on the global or transnational dimensions of strategic community relations (Tichy, McGill and St Clair, 1997). The claim most often made is that GSCR programs have become an important part of many companies' public relations strategies as corporate operations are increasingly globalized (Tillman, 2000). However, given its infancy relative to domestic community relations programming, as well as management and accounting complexities (in terms of whether a cash contribution, for instance, originates from local business operations outside or within the US), GCSR is difficult to track.

Despite these constraints, there is some limited information available. Anne Klepper of the Conference Board found that corporate executives most often cite improved personal and government relations, improved corporate image, and a boost in market penetration as the major advantages of global contributions programs (Klepper, 1993). In other words, global contributions are viewed by CEOs to function as strategic tools for multi-national corporations. The Conference Board has also recorded the contributions of US corporations to non-US beneficiaries since 1983 and it is possible to discern from these figures that the increasing internationalization of corporate operations has been accompanied by greater giving overseas (although the figures do not show if giving is greater relative to pre-tax profits). Thus, Tillman (1995) found that the median contribution of US corporations to non-US beneficiaries in 1983 was approximately $100,000, a figure that by 1988 had risen to approximately $175,000. By 1993, this figure had reached $600,000. Although the median contribution declined to a low of $350,000 in 1996, it had climbed back to $700,000 by 1998. Another Conference Board report ('Corp. Citizenship,' 2002), found that 42 percent of surveyed companies currently have an international giving program and 10 percent intend to implement a program in the next three years. Managers ranked North America, Europe, and Asia as the top three recipient regions. A visit to the Web site of any global corporation confirms these figures and the importance corporations place on their GCSR programs, with page upon page of high production value images and texts documenting their commitments made available to the online public.

The Avon Corporation is no exception and the company's Web site currently offers multi-page, multi-link descriptions of six different GCSR programs: the Avon WorldWide Fund For Women's Health, the Avon Breast Cancer Crusade, the Avon Walk for Breast Cancer, Avon Women of Enterprise (a program that honors top businesswomen for "entrepreneurial spirit and achievements"), the Avon Women's Survey (discussed below), and the Avon Foundation (which disburses funds raised through other Avon initiatives).

The Avon Corporation: A Case Study in Global Strategic Philanthropy and Community Relations

The History of Avon and the Politics of Gender

Founded in 1886 and recognized as a pioneer of door-to-door sales, Avon is currently the world's largest direct vendor of beauty products, with $6 billion in annual sales. In 2004 the Fortune 500 company produced over 600 million sales brochures in 25 languages and sold its products to women in 143 countries through 4 million representatives.

Despite its long history and sizeable market, business analysts have expressed skepticism about Avon's ability to survive as a direct-selling organization. Its image "had an aging grandmother feel to it" (Byrnes, 2003), and it continued to rely on the part-time labor and custom of "housewives" in an era in which increasing numbers of women are in paid employment (72.5 percent of direct salespeople in the US are women, and 90 percent of direct sales agents work part time, according to the Direct Sales Association, www.dsa.org) (Byrnes, 2000a, 2003; Rivituso, 2003). However, while sales in the US have been slow and sometimes stagnant since 1994, (sales grew 5 percent between 1990–2000 and profits by 4 percent; in 1999 sales grew by 1.5 percent), profits garnered overseas have continued to grow steadily and commentators point to Avon's success in the Latin American and Asian markets, in particular, as key to their survival.[5] Avon obtains two-thirds of its revenues from overseas transactions, and markets in Asia, Eastern Europe, and Latin America commonly post double-digit increases in sales and profits. Thirty-eight percent of its operating profit comes from Latin America alone, where the company commands 20 percent of the cosmetics market, four times it share in the US (Byrnes, 2000b). As such, the Avon Corporation is typical of the direct sales industry as a whole, which grew 269 percent between 1987 and 1997 and saw the number of salespeople increase by 336 percent during the same period (Bartlett, 1998).

Avon entered overseas markets early on, opening its first international office in Montreal in 1914. The company began selling in Venezuela in 1954, Japan in 1969, and China in 1990 (Byrnes, 2000b). Avon prides itself on its ability to adapt to local retailing cultures. For instance, in China, where door-to-door sales were made illegal in 1998, the company switched to distributing its products in boutiques and department stores. In the Philippines, orders are not mailed, but picked up at a central supermarket-style distribution facility and in Japan most business is done via mail order (Byrnes, 2000b).

While Avon's sales and marketing techniques are designed to mesh with "local" cultures, under the direction of CEO Andrea Jung, the company has moved away from regional branding and towards worldwide branding. A multitude of local products have been replaced by "global brands" such as Avon Color and the company launched its first international advertising campaign in 2000 at the cost of $100 million. Jung's vision for a new Avon is what she calls the "ultimate relationship marketer of products and services for women" (Byrnes, 2000a), and "the company that bests understands and satisfies the products, service, and self-fulfillment needs of women globally" (www.avon.com). While this move involves adding more products to the line, it also means that more attention is now paid to "ethical" relationships between brand, consumer, and salesperson through careful management of the meanings and values that Avon employees and customers attach to the products they sell and buy.

Avon is thus part of a broader trend in which brand management has moved from being little more than a corporate identity system – a logo and accompanying visuals built around the company name – "to something much broad, more professionally rewarding and, hopefully, more profitable for the company" according to Katherine Troy, Director of the Center for Performance Excellence (Troy quoted in Kulik, 1999, p. 7). Brand management now seeks to ensure that the brand and the corporation's philosophy of responsible citizenship share the same "territory" in the minds of all those who interact with the company or the product (employees, subcontractors, government officials, and consumers). Under this approach, brand is seen as a "veritable covenant with the customer" and as a way to align the vision of the corporation with its employees, so that the brand is "leveraged internally and externally with equal force" (Kulik, 1999, p. 7).

This concern is exemplified in the corporation's international slogan, "Avon: *The* company for women," and its move, in the face of shifting gender norms and relations across the globe, to position itself as a pro-woman corporation. Hence, Avon's US advertising makes repeated references to the company's self-proclaimed radical beginnings: "For more than a century Avon has provided women with economic opportunity and financial independence". "Avon provided one of the first opportunities for American women to be financially independent at a time when their place was traditionally at home"; and, "Women have sold Avon since 1886 – 34 years before they won the right to vote!" (http://www.avon.com/about/women/history/history.html). Avon's pro-women image thus helps to mediate the disjuncture between contemporary sensibilities about appropriate gender roles and Avon's arguably dated image as a company of and for "housewives" who sell products devoted to the maintenance of "normal" femininity.

The WorldWide Fund for Women's Health

This process of mediation is also enabled through Avon's entry into the world of women's health and fitness. In 1992, the company launched the Avon WorldWide Fund for Women's Health. Through the fund, the stated mission of which is to "break the barriers – social, cultural, financial and medical" to women's health, approximately $190 million has been raised to support programs for women's health issues in 34 countries. According to Avon, no other company has committed this much money to the cause of women's health ('2000 Avon', 2000).

The funds are raised primarily through cause-marketing programs, that is, by channeling a percentage of the sale price of a special product to the fund.

Table 5.1. *WorldWide Fund for Women's Health Programs*

Region/Country	*Program*	*Established*	*Cause*	*Raised*
Asia Pacific				
Australia	The Gift of Life – Breast Cancer Awareness Program	1996	Breast	$650,000
Indonesia	Women's Cancer Program	1995	Breast/cervical cancer	
Japan	Silver Age Support Campaign	1994	Support care-givers of the elderly; breast cancer	$1,200,000
Malaysia	Kesan Barah Awal (KEBAL) Cancer Early Detection	1994	Breast cancer	$128,000
New Zealand	The Gift of Life – Breast Cancer Awareness Program	1996	Breast cancer	
Philippines	Bigay Alam ay Bigay Buhay (Imparting Knowledge is Giving Life); Avon's Women's Cancer Crusade	1994	Breast and cervical cancer	$47,000
Taiwan	Foundation of Breast Cancer Prevention and Treatment	1999	Breast cancer	$872,720
Thailand	Women Running Against Breast Cancer. Avon Sue Rak . . . Pitak Suang (The Gift of Love from Avon . . . To Protect Your Breasts)	1998	Breast cancer	
Europe				
Czech Republic/ Slovakia	Kampan proti nadorovemu Ochoreniu prsnika (Project HOPE; Campaign Against Breast Cancer)	1998	Various women's health issues and breast cancer	

Table 5.1. *Continued*

Region/Country	*Program*	*Established*	*Cause*	*Raised*
Germany	Aktion: Bewubstein fur Brustkrebs (Action Awareness for Breast Cancer)	1999	Breast cancer	
	Mercure Day '96	1996	Muscular dystrophy	$32,700
Hungary	Multidiszciplinaris csoportok as eml rak ellen (Multidisciplinary Teams Against Breast Cancer)	1998	Breast cancer	
Ireland	Avon ARC Crusade Against Breast Cancer	1998	Breast cancer	
Italy	Italian League Against Cancer	1997	Women's cancers	
Poland	Wielka Kampania Życia – Avon Kontra Rak Piersi (The Great Campaign for Life – Avon Against Breast Cancer); Project Hope	1998	Breast cancer	
Portugal	Avon Breast Cancer Crusade	1999	Breast cancer	
Spain	Una Liamada de Esperanza Contra el Cancer (A Flame of Hope Against Cancer)	1994	Breast cancer	$659,000
Turkey	Meme Kanseri lle Mucadele Programi (Breast Cancer Charity Program)	1995	Breast cancer	$76,000
United Kingdom	Kiss Goodbye to Breast Cancer/The Avon Crusade Against Breast Cancer	1992	Breast cancer	$8,300,000

Table 5.1. *Continued*

Region/Country	*Program*	*Established*	*Cause*	*Raised*
Latin America				
Argentina	Un Lazo por la Vida (A Ribbon for Life)	1992	Breast cancer	
Brazil	Fashion Targets Breast Cancer; Running Against Breast Cancer; Breast Cancer Program	1995	Breast cancer	$2,000,000
Central America	Cruzada Avon Contra el Cancer en la Mujer (Avon Crusade Against Breast Cancer)	1995	Women's cancers	
Chile	Cruzada (Avon) Contra el Cancer de Mama(s) (Breast Cancer Crusade)	1997	Breast cancer	$205,000
Venezuela	Avon, Una Flor de Esperanza en la Laucha contra el Cancer (Avon, A Flower of Hope in the Fight Against Cancer)	1994	Breast cancer	$360,000
North America				
Canada	Avon Canada Flame Crusade Against Breast Cancer	1993	Breast cancer	$2,800,000
Puerto Rico	Avon Cruzada Contra el Cancer (Avon Crusade Against Cancer)	1993	Breast cancer	
United States	Avon Breast Cancer Crusade	1993	Breast cancer	$25,000,000
Mexico	Cruzada Nacional Avon Contra el Cancer en la Mujer (Avon National Crusade Against Breast Cancer)	1993	Women's cancers	$2,590,000

However, unlike most cause marketing programs in which the burden of donation falls on the consumer, Avon's programs often raise money through sales representatives forgoing their commissions. Sales representatives are also central to other aspects of Avon's community relations programming: One typical effort is "Give Information, Give Life" in the Philippines. Through this program, Avon sales teams are trained to give basic information on cancer to their clients, to demonstrate breast self-examinations, and to give referrals to community health centers and medical practitioners. In line with the philosophy of GSCR, this program constitutes sales representatives as grassroots healthcare workers at the same time that it helps solidify an intimate connection between the products they sell and the causes they promote.

As part of this same initiative, Avon conducts an international poll of women every two years to gather information on their "interests, issues, and challenges" ('Avon 2000', 2000). The 2000 Avon Global Women's Survey questioned 30,000 women in thirty-three countries via telephone and mail and found that access to quality health care is a leading issue for improving women's lives and that the top health concerns of women worldwide are "women's cancers" – especially breast cancer. Through programs such as Bigay Alam in the Philippines, Wielka Kampania Życia – Avon Kontra Rak Piersi (The Great Campaign for Life – Avon Against Breast Cancer) in Poland, O Câncer de Mama No Avlo da Moda in Brazil, and the Avon Breast Cancer Crusade in the US, Avon has made breast cancer its primary health "cause" – a choice that is of course legitimized by the survey's findings. Claiming that the results underscored the need for increased education, outreach and services, the survey also offered an opportunity for Avon to ensure its strategic community relations programs were reaching target markets. Thus, the survey asked participants not just about their health issues, but also about their beauty concerns. Questions attempted to ascertain, for instance, the relationship between outward appearance and self-esteem, women's ideal hair types, and "most desirable beauty product benefit". Press releases announcing the survey's findings also drew attention to the Avon Running Global Women's Circuit – an international series of women-only 10K runs and 5K walks launched in 1998.

Avon Running Global Women's Circuit

As an activity that is popularly associated with youth, freedom, and physical and emotional strength, sport in general, and running in particular, presents Avon with a perfect cause with which to associate. This is particularly the case given, as other critics have argued, that the 1980s and 1990s in the US have been constituted as a glorious era for women in sports – a period in which women have finally "made it" in a previously male-dominated domain (Cole and Hribar,

1997; Cole, 2000). Of course, this "glorious era" has not emerged through a process of natural evolution. Rather, on the heels of activist legislation such as Title IX – under which girls' and women's access to elite sports opportunities, in particular, has increased – sport has been taken up and deployed by numerous multi-nationals as an ideal site for the production of feel-good, corporate feminism.

Avon's interest in sport goes back further than most corporations, to the 1970s, when it assisted in the effort to create a platform for competitive women's running through the Avon International Running Circuit. These races proved popular and were largely responsible for securing the women's marathon as an Olympic event. Joan Benoit Samuelson, winner of the inaugural women's Olympic marathon in 1984, describes the political significance of the Circuit as follows: "The series nurtured and developed women's running at a time when it was felt that if a woman ran more than a mile, she would do herself bodily harm and would not be able to have children" (Samuelson quoted in *Avon Running*, 2000). This particular effort ended in 1985, when the company "refocused its marketing efforts" (*Avon Running*, 2000).

Avon returned to women's sport in the mid-1990s, when it was selected as the official cosmetics, fragrance, and skin-care sponsor of the 1996 Summer Olympic Games and the official cosmetic, beauty, and skin-care sponsor of the US Olympic synchronized swimming team. The company also sponsors the Olympic Woman Exhibition, a multi-media display that chronicled 100 years of women's advancement in the modern Olympic Games and the annual New York Mini Marathon (a women-only 5K race). The Avon Running Circuit differs from these other alliances, however, in that it is a physical activity program established *by* the corporation. Moreover, according to Katherine Switzer, program director of Avon Running, the new Avon Running Global Women's Circuit differs from its predecessor, the Avon Running Circuit: "Our mission then was acceptance. Our goal now is accessibility – to provide developmental activity and incentives to aspiring athletes, and to encourage the general fitness of women everywhere" (*Avon Running Global Women's Circuit: History*, 2000). The new objective is to "encourage women worldwide to the starting line of fitness through grassroots events that promote the positive rewards of a regular running or walking regimen" (*Avon Running Global Women's Circuit: History*, 2000).

In 2001, Avon Running events were held in nine cities across the US and in seventeen overseas locations.[6] The health education component of the circuit is focused on cardiovascular disease and breast cancer and circulates via publicity materials and "health and wellness villages" that are set up at each race. Avon also uses the villages to shape consumer desires in particular ways: new and existing products, particularly those that might be of interest to women committed to healthy lifestyles, are offered for testing.[7]

In the official words of the corporation, the circuit "empowers women of every age to take charge of their health". Through Avon Running, the corporation claims, women learn about the benefits of a regular running and walking regimen, which "provides a time-efficient, cost-effective and accessible exercise option for women, many of whom lead hectic, stressful lives and have difficulty making exercise a priority" (*2000 Avon Running*, 2000). In addition, they point to the community-building potential of the program: "a commitment to participation provides a fitness goal and the opportunity to meet and develop companionship with other fitness conscious women" (*2000 Avon Running*, 2000). To this end, Avon conducts training workshops in host cities prior to each race. Framed as "grassroots" education forums, these workshops provide information and guidance for beginning walkers and runners (*Avon Running Global Women's Circuit Launches its Third Year*, 2000).

While Avon running is marketed primarily as a program for introducing women to fitness training (in their words, "getting women to the starting line of fitness"), it is also sold as a strategy that brings women of all levels of interest and capability together: "Avon Running is the only global circuit of its kind that provides women the opportunity to pursue elite racing, moderate running or simple fitness in unified events" (*2000 Avon Running*, 2000). The opportunities the Circuit provides for elite runners are also narrativized through the language of feminist empowerment: "Even with the recent advancement of women's running as a sport, talented women have few avenues for training and development. Avon Running provides the serious runner the opportunity to set a competitive goal and win prize money and her way to the Avon Running Global Women's Championship" (*2000 Avon Running*, 2000).

In addition to the opportunities the races offer for women to participate in physical activity, a portion of each entry fee is donated to local charities in order to "give back" to the host cities. This aspect of the program reflects a trend in which participatory sports events are increasingly linked to charitable causes (King, 2000). The history of such events makes an interesting contribution to critical analyses of contemporary civil society: "thons" emerged in Western Europe and North America in the 1950s in response to the United Nations International Freedom from Hunger Campaign. National committees of the campaign launched the "Walk for Development" as a strategy to raise money and public awareness of poverty and malnutrition in developing countries, but, because they operated under a donor-choice format, the events soon evolved into forums that raised money for often controversial causes. In the US, the Walks became sites for training anti-Vietnam War activists and for public education that frequently took the form of radical critiques of structural inequality, racism, and colonialism. Funded causes included the National Welfare Rights and the American Indian Movement. Over the past two decades, however, thons have become increasingly professionalized and corporatized and events that were previously staged by nonprofit organizations with little, or any, sponsorship by corporations, are, in the case of Avon at least, being organized by corporations. Apart from undermining the potential of these events for radical critique, these changes have also meant that corporate agendas drive the decisions of where to donate money and that money raised is increasingly spent on the high overhead costs of these high-production value events. For these reasons, and because Avon made health insurance a prerequisite for participation, the Breast Cancer 3-Day, which has now transmogrified into the Avon Walk for Breast Cancer, came under particular scrutiny from breast cancer activist groups such as Breast Cancer Action in San Francisco and the Women's Community Cancer Project in Massachusetts (www.bcaction.org).

Avon: The Company for which *Women?*

Avon's philanthropic and community relations programing in aid of women's health raises numerous questions that cannot be addressed in the present essay. Who exactly are the women for whom Avon is concerned? How are their needs and desires constructed through GSCR programs? What gendered and racialized relations of power are concealed by the discourse of GSCR? What, in Avon's view, constitutes a barrier to women's health? How are health concerns best confronted? What are we to make of Avon's commitment when its GSCR programs operate only in those countries in which it sells its products? How exactly is the money Avon raises spent and who makes such decisions? Will GSCR programs be sustained in less prosperous periods for multi-national corporations?

For now, however, it does seem important to acknowledge, on the one hand, that the WorldWide Fund and Avon Running raise money for important causes, help elicit public awareness of the importance of women's health (however generally defined), and offer expanded opportunities for women to participate in physical activity. These are noble and worthwhile goals. Women's health concerns – apart from those that have to do with their reproductive capacities – have historically been neglected and increased attention to these concerns as well as greater opportunities to participate in health-related fitness represents some measure of progress. At the same time, the rather simplistic and universalizing nature of Avon's rhetoric leaves little space for consumers to think critically and complexly about what constitutes the "problem of women's health" on an international scale. Avon's stated goal – "to break the barriers – social, cultural, financial, and medical – to women's health" – sounds hopeful, but what exactly does that mean?

From their focus on running as a form of disease prevention, to the prominence given to mammograms/self-exams as ways to maintain good health, the general approach Avon assumes locates the factors that constitute women's health concerns, and the solutions to them, in individual behaviors. A consideration of the specific features of the company's breast cancer programs illustrates this point further. Bigay Alam, the Filipina breast health initiative, and the Breast Cancer Crusade, Avon's US-based program, are both marketed as efforts to prevent and eradicate cancer. But breast self examinations and funding for screening and detection-based research (the major target of the Crusade's fundraising efforts) – while necessary components of a complete response to the breast cancer epidemic – are not forms of cancer *prevention* and promise little in the way of eradication. The importance of this point goes beyond semantics. For Avon to raise questions of prevention, it would have to confront alternative and subjugated knowledges about the causes of breast cancer – those that question the search for causes in individual behaviors rather than exposures, for instance, or those that highlight environmental factors. These are difficult questions to address and attention to them would certainly detract from the optimistic, celebratory rhetoric through which Avon markets its strategic community relations programs.

The question of *which* women are the targets and beneficiaries of the WorldWide Fund for Women's Health and Avon Running also raises a number of difficult issues. Feminist theorists have long been concerned with the tendency to universalize women's experiences of oppression. To assume, that is, that all women experience gender relations and gender identity in exactly the same way. The problem with this assumption is that it elides the acute differences (based on, among other things, class, race, nationality and age) among women and has most often resulted in the experiences and desires of white, middle-class, Western women coming to stand in for the experiences and desires of *all* women. What we see in the rhetoric promoting the Avon Running Program and in analyses of the findings of the Global Women's Survey are precisely these kinds of elision. One interviewee at Avon was very aware that Avon Running did not serve the interests of all women – she spoke, for instance, of time, money, access to transport, and access to childcare as preconditions for women to take advantage of the program. But this insight does not surface in Avon's approach more broadly, as evidenced by the frequent reference to the accessibility and affordability of running "for women" and the more general lack of acknowledgement of the types of women that might actually be able to take advantage of the opportunities Avon provides.

Of course, as I have argued through the course of this chapter, these programs are clearly tied to company strategy. The WorldWide Fund for Women's Health collects and disburses money only in those countries in which Avon operates and Avon Running Global Women's Circuit events take place only in those countries in which Avon sells its products. The women who can afford to buy cosmetics are the same women who are going to be able to take advantage of opportunities to participate in a walking/running event. They are also most probably the same women who would have been questioned for the Global Women's Survey (a telephone and/or mail service being prerequisites for participation), which, it seems important to re-emphasize, asked participants not just about their health issues but also about their beauty concerns.

In this context, we might also think about how the marketing and consumption of Avon products link middle-class women in different national locations to one another. With new global brands sold through advertisements featuring uniformly light-skinned "multiracial" models (based on a survey of all those international Avon branches that have Web sites, the exact same images are used from country to country), Avon sells an image of cosmopolitan-yet-Americanized, bourgeois, femininity to those women that are able to participate in the global marketplace. In other words, it is not simply the case that Avon caters to the consumer aspirations of a transnational middle class. Rather, through projecting particular images in their advertisements, and selling products – skin lightening creams are among the most popular of their merchandise – that encourage women to aspire to a hegemonic "look," it could be argued that the company actually helps to produce that very class and the way that it appears.

At a more practical level, it is important to consider if and how strategic community relations programs fair in less prosperous periods for US-based multinationals. It is true that strategic community relations programs grew out of a drive for efficiency in a leaner economic moment. It is also true that the effect of this has been to create programs that are usually cost efficient. Cause-related marketing campaigns, for instance, while usually paid for out of public relations budgets, work as a form of subsidized advertising in terms of the tangible and intangible benefits that accrue to companies through such campaigns. Yet, as long as philanthropy and community relations programming are tied to market outcomes, there is a danger that corporations, faced with a downturn in the market or a decrease in the popularity of a particular cause, will abandon the programs they currently support.

Conclusion: The Many Guises of Neoliberalism

The story of the emergence of GSCR programs that I have told here highlights the ways in which previously eclectic and unscientific ventures have been transformed into highly measured strategies that are integral to the profit-making activities of business. It has also sought to trace how corporations, such as Avon, which are seeking to produce and sell goods in an ever-expanding number of locations, have increasingly deployed philanthropy and community relations not merely to further some social good, but as techniques for market penetration and retention.

What I want to suggest in conclusion is that Avon's GSCR practices must be understood not simply in the context of a shift in business culture, but also, and crucially, as part of a struggle over how and by whom socio-economic management on a transnational scale should be undertaken. Perry Anderson (2000, p. 11) has claimed that, "the Third Way is the best ideological shell of neo-liberalism today". The "Third Way" has been used to describe the ideology of the Clinton administration as well as Tony Blair's "stakeholder society" in Great Britain and in its ideal form represents a mode of governing that incorporates into a mostly neo-liberal approach, acknowledgement of the importance of at least some of the values of social democracy. Nikolas Rose (1999) suggests that the Third Way emerged from the realization that there was a need for strategies of government that acknowledged the limits of both social democracy and neo-liberalism, strategies that were freed from the "necessities to repeat the old battles between left and right" (Rose, 1999, p. 167).

There is much debate about the extent of the actual differences between the neo-liberal approaches of Reagan, Thatcher, and Bushes senior and junior and the Third Way of Blair and Clinton and thus whether or not Anderson's characterization is accurate. But I would like to suggest that there is at least one site for which his claim holds true. Among the most prominent manifestations of the Third Way as "neo-liberal shell" within the US, is a renewed emphasis on the social promise of volunteerism and philanthropy in the wake of the near blanket consensus that the era of welfare government should be at an end. Every administration since the election of Ronald Reagan in 1980 has told the American people that the state can no longer be relied upon to mitigate the social effects of capitalism and that America's spiritual and material prosperity depends upon the charitable works and voluntary financial commitments of individuals and corporations. This is a discourse, of course, that articulates quite neatly with the language and practice of structural adjustment and other manifestations of neoliberalism, as cutbacks in public sector services in many countries of "the South" and the former Eastern Bloc are replaced with private sector alternatives. As international lending agencies pave the way for corporations like Avon to continue to grow through such requirements, businesses themselves are taking the American version of generosity onto the world stage by underwriting "non-profit" ventures in the name of community renewal, grassroots participation, and a revitalized global civil society. While global strategic community relations programs are just one – often relatively small – part of any transnational corporation's overall business strategy, the chorus of corporate discourse on volunteerism, philanthropy, civic participation, and citizenship is growing ever louder. As such it should be taken seriously in struggles over what a global civil society might look like and how individuals and groups – within and across national borders – might negotiate the relationship between economic and political freedom.

Notes

1. I would like to thank Mike Silk and two anonymous reviewers for their feedback on earlier drafts of this chapter.
2. Before proceeding, a note on my decision to use the term "global strategic community relations" – instead of the more familiar "corporate social responsibility" or "corporate citizenship" – is in order. The precise meaning of the term "corporate social responsibility" (CSR) has been the subject of much debate (Wood and Jones, 1996). Broadly defined, CSR refers to the economic, legal, ethical, and discretionary responsibilities of businesses (Carroll, 1979; 1991). Literature on corporate social responsibility recognizes that corporations are responsible to numerous stakeholders, including customers, employees, suppliers, community groups, governments and stockholders. In addition, this literature suggests that corporations can demonstrate CSR through action in a variety of social arenas, including pollution abatement and other practices of environmental awareness, workplace diversity, corporate giving, product safety, and worker health and safety (Ulman, 1985; Wood and Jones, 1996; McWilliams and Siegel, 2001). The concern of this paper – international public relations programs that mesh community involvement (in this case, opportunities for women to participate in physical activity) with philanthropic activity – is with one particular aspect of corporate social responsibility, not with corporate social responsibility in general. Moreover, it proceeds on the assumption that corporate social responsibility cannot be demonstrated simply through the charitable giving and community relations programming. Giving might be one component of social responsibility but it is not a substitute for it. For these reasons, I have elected to use the term "global strategic community relations" (GSCR) to reference the phenomenon under consideration. I use the term "global" rather than "transnational," because this is term used by corporations to describe their transnational practices.
3. The more central role played by corporate concerns in international relations of power has been accompanied by – and, through the lending policies of bodies such

as the International Monetary Fund, helped shape – a downsizing of public sector services worldwide.

4. It is important to note here that Avon does not necessarily view the Avon Running Global Women's Circuit as a strategic community relations program and that this is a term I selected for its power to describe the phenomenon under consideration. I write "necessarily" here because there are conflicting representations of the program in circulation. Although in press releases it is sometimes described as part of a "marketing effort", one employee I spoke with was very concerned to separate the intent of the program from corporate strategy. More specifically, she insisted that the program not be represented as community relations but as something that is "really designed to bring awareness of health and fitness to women". Obviously aware of the instrumentalist connotation of community relations at the present time, the employee was at pains to emphasize her understanding that Avon does not gain anything from providing these opportunities for women. Although the intent of the program might not be strategic, the effect – to align, on a global basis, the Avon brand name with women's health and empowerment – certainly serves business strategy. The numerous press releases that publicize recent and forthcoming activities are just one illustration of this point.
5. It should be noted that, since the research for this project was completed, Avon's sales in the US have improved considerably. Under the leadership of Andrea Jung, the company has revamped its image and switched to a multilevel selling system that has helped increase the earning potential of its sales representatives (Byrnes, 2003).
6. Events in the United States were held in Anthem, Baltimore, Conway, Denver, Hartford, Kansas City, Minneapolis/St. Paul, Phoenix, and Tampa. Events outside the US were held in Bacolod, Bandung, Berlin, Bratislava, Budapest, Buenos Aries, Cagayan de Oro City, Concepción de Chile, Guatemala City, Kaula Lumpur, Manila, Mexico City, Milan, Rio de Janeiro, Santiago, Bangkok, and Santa Domingo.
7. As this chapter was going to press, an Avon employee informed me, in response to my query about the disappearance of information about Avon Running from the company's Web site, that Avon Running no longer exists in the US and is not therefore "foremost in corporate minds". According to my source, the program is "booming", however, in Italy, Germany, Brazil, Chile, Honduras, Guatemala, El Salvador, Dominican Republic, and Mexico.

References

Alperson, M. (1995), *Corporate Giving Strategies that Add Business Value*, New York: The Conference Board.

Anderson, P. (2000), Renewals, *New Left Review*, 2(1): p. 11.

Avon 2000, Global Women's Survey Finds Breast, Cervical, and Ovarian Cancers are Top Health Concerns for Women WorldWide (2000), Avon Products Inc. press release, October 10. Available: http://corporate-ir.net.

Avon Running Global Women's Circuit Launches Its Third Year (2000), Avon Products Inc. press release. Available: http://www.avon.com.

Avon Running Global Women's Circuit: History (2000), Avon Products Inc. press release. Available: http://www.avon.com.

Ballinger, J. (1998), Nike in Indonesia, *Dissent*, (Fall). 18–21.

Barber, B. (1995), *Jihad vs. McWorld*, New York: Times Books.

Bartlett, R. (1998), There is No Freedom without Free Enterprise, *Academic seminar on direct selling*, Sao Paulo, Brazil, October 6.

Byrnes, N. (2000a), Avon's New Calling, *Business Week*, September 18, p. 136.

Byrnes, N. (2000b), Panning for Global Gold in Local Markets, *Business Week*, (International Edition), September 18, p. 46.

Byrnes, N. (2003), *Avon is Calling Lots of New Reps Available*, http://businessweek.com/careers/content/june2003/ca2003064_2654_ca026.htm

Carroll, A. (1979), A Three-dimensional Conceptual Model of Corporate Social Performance, *Academy of Management Review*, 4: 497–505.

Carroll, A. (1991), Corporate Social Performance Measurement: A Commentary on Methods for Evaluating an Elusive Construct. In J. E. Post (ed.), *Research in Corporate Social Performance and Policy*, Greenwich: JAI, vol. 12, pp. 385–401.

Cole, C.L. (1996), American Jordan: P.L.A.Y., Consensus and Punishment, *Sociology of Sport Journal*, 13(4): 366–97.

Cole, C. (2000), The Year that Girls Ruled, *Journal of Sport and Social Issues*, 24(1): 3–7.

Cole, C. and Hribar, A. (1997), Celebrity Feminism: *Nike Style*, Post-Fordism, Transcendence, and Consumer Power. *Sociology of Sport*, 12: 347–69.

Corp. Citizenship Programs Gaining Attention (2002), Conference Board press release, August 13. Available: http://www.conference-board.org.

Dienhart, J. (1988), Charitable Investments: A Strategy for Improving the Business Environment, *Journal of Business Ethics*, 7(1–2): 63.

Drucker, P. (1984), The New Meaning of Corporate Social Responsibility, *California Management Review*, 26 (Winter): p. 59.

Enloe, C. (1995), The Globetrotting Sneaker, Ms (June/April): 10–15.

Frank, T. (2000), *One Market under God: Extreme Capitalism, Market Populism and the End of Economic Democracy*, New York: Doubleday.

Himmelstein, J. (1996), Corporate Philanthropy and Business Power. In D. Burlingame and D. Young (eds), *Corporate Philanthropy at the Crossroads*, Bloomington: Indiana University Press, pp. 144–57.

Jameson, F. (1998), Notes on Globalization as a Philosophical Issue. In F. Jameson and M. Miyoshi (eds), *The Cultures of Globalization*, Durham: Duke University Press, pp. 54–77.

Jameson, F. and Miyoshi, M. (1998), *The Cultures of Globalization*, Durham: Duke University Press.

King, S. (2000), *Civic Fitness: The Politics of Breast Cancer and the Problem of Generosity*. Unpublished doctoral dissertation. University of Illinois, Urbana-Champaign.

Klepper, A. (1993), *Global Contributions of US Corporations*, New York: The Conference Board.

Kulik, T. (1999), *The Expanding Parameters of Global Corporate Citizenship*, New York NY: The Conference Board.

McWilliams, A. and Siegel, D. (2001). Corporate Social Responsibility: A Theory of the Firm Perspective, *The Academy of Management Review*, 26(1): 117–27.

Miller, J. (1997). A Hands-on Generation Transforms the Landscape of Philanthropy, *The New York Times*, p. 8.

Muirhead, S. (1999), *Corporate contributions: The view from 50 years*, New York: The Conference Board.

Rivituso, M. (2003), *Avon's New Lipstick Available*, www.smartmoney.com/onthestreet/index.cfm?story=20031112

Rose, N. (1999), *Powers of freedom: Reframing Political Thought*, Cambridge UK: Cambridge University Press.

Sassen, S. (1998), *Globalization and its Discontents: Essays on the New Mobility of People and Money*, New York: New Press.

Scott, M. and Rothman, H. (1992), *Companies with a Conscience: Intimate Portraits of Twelve Firms that Make a Difference*, New Jersey: Carol Publishing Group.

Shannon, J. (1991), *The Corporate Contributions Handbook*, San Francisco CA: Jossey-Bass.

Shannon, J. (1996). Foreword. In D. Burlingame and D. Young (eds), *Corporate Philanthropy at the Crossroads*. Bloomington: Indiana University Press, pp. ix–xi.

Smith, C. (1996), Desperately Seeking Data: Why Research is Crucial to Corporate Philanthropy. In D. Burlingame and D. Young (eds), *Corporate philanthropy at the crossroads*, Bloomington: Indiana University Press.

Stabile, C. (2000). Nike, Social Responsibility, and the Hidden Abode of Production, *Critical Studies in Media Communication*, 17(2): 186–204.

Tichy, N., McGill, A., and St Clair, L. (1997), *Global corporate citizenship: Doing Business in the Public Eye*, San Francisco: New Lexington Press.

Tillman, A. (1995), *Corporate Contributions, 1994*, New York: The Conference Board.

Tillman, A. (2000), *Corporate contributions in 1999*, New York: The Conference Board.

Ulman, A. (1985), Data in Search of Theory: A Critical Examination of the Relationship among Social Performance, Social Disclosure, and Economic Performance, *Academy of Management Review*, 10: 540–77.

Wood, D., and Jones, R. (1996), *Research in Corporate Social Performance: What have we Learned?* In D. Burlingame and D. Young (eds), *Corporate Philanthropy at the Crossroads*, Bloomington IN: Indiana University Press, pp. 41–85.

Yankey, J. A. (1996). Corporate Support of Nonprofit Organizations. In D. F. Burlingame and D. Young (eds), *Corporate Philanthropy at the crossroads*, Indianapolis: Indiana University Press.

Zetlin, M. (1990), Companies Find Profit in Corporate Philanthropy, *Management Review*, 79(12): 10.

2000 Avon Running Global Women's Circuit At-A-Glance (2000), Avon Products Inc. press release. Available: http://www.avon.com.

6

All-American Girls? Corporatizing National Identity and Cultural Citizenship with/in the WUSA

Michael D. Giardina and Jennifer L. Metz

When a given symbolic national body signifies as normal – straight, white, middle-class, and heterosexual – hardly anyone asks critical questions about its representatives.

Lauren Berlant

Introduction

On February 15, 2000, the Women's United Soccer Association (WUSA) was officially formed with its stated goal of "launching the world's premiere women's professional soccer league" (WUSA Press Office). Lauded over as yet another positive step in the continued expansion of women's (professional) sporting endeavors and receiving national press coverage on par with the already-established Women's National Basketball Association (WNBA), the league and its players have not only become central to discourses of female athletic participation and empowerment but, equally as important, it has revealed itself as a key site from which to excavate the construction of "All-American" notions of family and identity in post-Reagan/Clinton America.[1] From league-wide community-relations initiatives centering on the family unit and its firm brokerage by such unapologetically American corporations as McDonald's and Sears to its breakthrough ownership matrix and corporate agenda, the WUSA thus stands as a practical exemplar of the rising incidence of the corporate capitalist fashioning of national consciousness. By this we mean that entities such as WUSA – as well as other transnational corporate capitalist enterprises operating on a global scale – are now more so than ever visibly in league with the State in defining the boundaries of "cultural citizenship" (Miller, 1998).

Using the WUSA as a representative case study, we interrogate the union between the State and corporate actors that has been facilitated by the rise and celebration of neo-liberalism as a defining feature for translating all dimensions of human life through economic rationality (Brown, 2003). Organizationally, we (a) contextualize the WUSA's structural formation; (b) articulate its family values entrenchment and celebration within the US to an emergent form of cultural citizenship; and (c) make visible the neoliberal imperatives governing contemporary American sport by unmasking the public-private investiture constituted by the WUSA and its sponsors. Such a relationship is illustrative of the various ways in which a conservatively positioned yet progressively framed set of family-value markers are understood within contemporary America. Specifically, it is our contention that the WUSA's iteration of the American family and its commitment to the (future) well being of the imagined nation (-state) in the global age raises salient questions concerning the nature of politics and the operation of power related to neoliberal corporate endeavors.

Contextualizing Women's Sports in Late-modern America

> The public self and its masks are increasingly defined by a media-oriented mass culture in which youth, health, and sexuality have taken on premium values.
>
> Norman K. Denzin

A scant thirty years ago, much of the US watched as Billie Jean King defeated Bobby Riggs in the now-legendary "Battle of the Sexes" tennis match that marked as concrete the changing cultural perceptions involving women in general and female athletes in specific. Fast-forwarding ahead through time we see the passage of Title IX, its general lack of enforcement, unending criticisms of sex-role behavior, the daunting challenge of raising funds for girls youth leagues, and so on. Today, however, female athletes are seen outfitted by Nike, drinking Coca-Cola, and driving American-made Sport Utility Vehicles (none of those Toyotas or BMWs for this group, thank you very much). This American (sporting) woman of the late-modern era is (allegedly) far-removed from her 1960s counterpart as she actively invests in, consumes, and is shaped by a long and winding road of multi-national corporations who have brought us the latest version of the empowered female.

Female sporting successes in the 1990s have not only marked a paradigmatic shift toward the active promotion and acceptance of such athletes but, more insidiously, have also become caught up in a globally organized, transnational matrix of corporate power designed to capitalize on the physical exploits and exploitations of this seemingly progressive cultural trend. Whether in the form of Nike's "Everyday Athletes" campaign, Gatorade's "Yes You Can!" message, the WNBA's "Be Active" initiative, or the US government's "Girl Power!" campaign, the image of the successful female (athlete) and her mythical heir apparent – the American daughter – has become a reified hieroglyph of progressive rhetoric within the landscape of American popular culture.[2] From the all-too-well-known image of Brandi Chastain revealing her (Nike) sports bra after scoring the cup-winning goal in the 1999 Women's World Cup Final to the NBA parading its female-counterpart WNBA athletes in front of the media spotlight as baby-toting, basketball dribbling, career-oriented superwomen, the "empowered female" has become the dominant national hieroglyph since the 1990s. As Berlant (1997, p. 104) comments, this national hieroglyph can be seen as being representative of "both the minimum and maximum of what the dominating cultures will sanction for circulation, exchange, and consumption". Such hieroglyphic markings of athletes such as Hamm, Chastain, the WNBA's Sheryl Swoopes, tennis player Martina Hingis and golfer Annika Sorenstam are meant to represent the achievement and progress of a still very sexist and racist country where many opportunities for women remain constricted, exploitative, and under-paid.

Embracing such corporeally embodied figurations thus articulates and makes noticeable the comfort zone of the American public with images and representations of female athletes, a category that has often been considered as "Other" throughout most (if not all) of American cultural history. Whereas the aggressive, empowered female athlete *on the field* is a sight the American public has become accustomed to seeing and supporting, the female (athlete) who maintains this empowerment *off the field* still conjures up feelings of discomfort for many individuals raised in and so entrenched within the hegemonic shoves of a white, male, patriarchal society. The resulting compromise enacted by both consumers and marketers, then, remains one that dictates the aggressive female athlete must invoke some level of hetero-social normativity and display feminine characteristics *when she is not engaged in sporting activity.*

Taken as a whole, the "success" – socially, culturally, politically, and/or economic – of the WNBA, WUSA, Women's Tennis Association, and female athletes in general allows the American public to engage in self-congratulatory rhetoric vis-à-vis the state of women's athletics, where admiring those individuals whose strong character, determination, and lifestyle contribute to such success is seen as a sign – symbolic or otherwise – that all is well in the world of male/female relations. This course of action is particularly enticing for many women for, as bell hooks (1999, p. 183) writes, "marginalized groups deemed Other, who have been ignored, rendered invisible, can be seduced by the emphasis on Otherness by its commodification, because it offers the promise of recognition and reconciliation". In other words, the seductive appeal of such seemingly "empowered females" works precisely because these athletes operate as *iconic* minority figures. As Berlant (1997, p. 104) cogently explicates

> these luminaries allow the hegemonic consuming public to feel that it has already achieved intimacy and equality with the marginal mass population; as minority exceptions, they represent heroic autonomy from their very "people"; as "impersonations" of minority identity, they embody the very ordinary conditions of subjective distortion that characterizes stereotypical marginality.

But wait! How is this (largely) white, (mostly) middle-class, (seemingly) heterosexual, (usually) ponytailed group a "minority?" Berlant (1997, p. 104) continues:

> the national minority stereotype makes exceptional the very person whose marginality, whose individual experience of collective cultural discrimination or difference is the motive for his/her circulation as an honorary icon in the first place.

It is this honorary iconicity that the WUSA specifically plays to in terms of its affiliations with adidas, Hyundai, McDonald's, Nike, the NBA and the whole host of multi-national and transnational corporations who have invested in, shaped, and benefited from women's sporting "success" (cf. Cole, 2000). While considerable focus has been paid to the WNBA and its location within the socio-political matrix of American sport (cf. Bannet-Weiser, 2000; McDonald, 2000), the WUSA remains a largely untapped site of cultural artifacts.[3] This paper attempts to fill that void.

WUSA, Inc.

> When corporate politics is cloaked in the image of innocence, there is more at stake than the danger of simple deception. There is the issue of cultural power and how it works to make claims on our understanding of the past, national coherence, and popular memory as a site of injustice, criticism, and renewal.
>
> Henry A. Giroux

Following the initial successes – both on and off the field – by Team USA's women's soccer team at the 1996 Olympic Games and 1999 Women's World Cup of Soccer, and coupled with the rise in sporting participation, coverage, and overall appeal of women's sports in general,[4] the feasibility of an (inter)national sporting organization comprised solely for the advancement of women's (professional) soccer interests began to take shape. Spearheaded by the efforts of John S. Hendricks, founder and CEO of Discovery Communications (Discovery Channel, Learning Channel, Animal Planet, and Travel Channel, among others), who contributed the initial startup fees of $8 million and organized the secondary influx of $56 million from an assemblage of cable giants composed of Cox Enterprises, Cox Communications, Comcast

Corporation, and AOL Time Warner Cable, the WUSA was from the outset positioned so as to realize fully its media(ted) potential. Where before the NBA first "went global" by mirroring the corporate philosophies of Disney and Time Warner (cf. Andrews, 1997), the WUSA has taken the proverbial next step by not only aligning itself with the largest media companies of the world, but by bringing such conglomerates directly into its full ownership spectrum. These communication entities now act as chief investors/team operators in relation to their strongest geographic positioning (Comcast, based in Philadelphia, is the chief operator of the Philadelphia team; Cox Enterprises, based in Atlanta, is the chief operator of the Atlanta team, and so forth). League-wide, AOL Time Warner has acted as the *de facto* broadcast partner, controlling national broadcasting rights to the league's twenty-two game national TV schedule and airing the games on Turner Network Television (TNT), and CNN/SI.[5]

Additionally, and populated by athletes hailing from such diverse locales as Brazil and Australia to China and Denmark, the WUSA has come to embody the literal realization of a transnational sporting enterprise that "has been fashioned into an explicitly American and [yet] increasingly global media(ted) institution" (Andrews, 1997, p. 77). While addressing itself as a global brand that "literally and digitally reaches the entire world" (Turner Sports, 2000) via the AOL Time Warner family of media outlets, the WUSA's marketing efforts work to explicitly locate it within a discourse of "All-American" family values and ideas. Says (now former) league CEO Barbara Allen, "This is an American, apple-pie story . . . we've got to appeal very broadly to families." It is this focus on "All-American family values" that reverberates most noticeably throughout the WUSA's origin story, legitimating it as a pure site of athletic achievement and cultural acceptance. At the same time, this marketing strategy is couched within and makes implicit overtures to its inherent global flavor and appeal, highlighted in part by an international television package that broadcasts league games in China, New Zealand, and Canada.

However, while the open commodification of women's sports over the last ten years has focused attention on the empowered female consumer, a subtle shift has occurred – generatively organized by the WUSA – that moves the discursive alignment regarding the future of American national identity to a new plane of effectivity, one predicated on and realized by constructing the traditional middle-class family[6] through a complex circuit of exchange and promotion that marks *as necessary* a public-private identification with "a postpolitical and postnational utopia of 'culture' [that] confus[es] the era of the present tense with an imminent yet obscure future" (Berlant, 1997, p. 30). That is to say, while the WUSA falls in line with it pseudo-sister WNBA in reaching out to attract family-oriented audiences and female athletes, it goes one step further, wrapping itself around a mantra of values and ideals that defines "All-Americanness" as being representative not of a 1980s faux traditionalism but rather of a faux *progressivism* of a fully integrated, multicultural, future-present. However, this imagined idea of what it means to embody these "All-American" values necessarily remains bound by an always already ideology of white male patriarchal hegemony that goes unchallenged by most (re)viewers.

In other words, and offering up in its totality a representational manifesto of what it means to "be American", the WUSA originary narrative (subconsciously) erases political and ethical considerations that mark history as a site of struggle, producing what Henry Giroux (1995, p. 57) calls "a filmic version of popular culture", one that effaces the everyday hardships and struggles of daily life in favor of a reformulated, faux progressive *Leave it to Beaver*-esque vision of race, gender, and class relations. In doing so, the term family values – itself a complex matrix of ideals with links between morality, sexuality, politics, and personal responsibility – becomes positioned as the always already site from which the league defines itself. As Mary G. McDonald (2001) argues, the phrase "family values" "suggests a nostalgic yearning for a yesteryear in which the traditional nuclear family – composed of the provider/father, stay at home nurturer/mother, and children – [is] the presumed cornerstone of the nation" (p. 167). As such, the active deployment of a fictionalized past drawn from traditional notions of Americana "becomes a vehicle for rationalizing the authoritarian, normalizing tendencies of the dominant culture that carry through to the present" (Giroux, 1995, p. 47). This type of normalizing practice, to borrow from Lawrence Grossberg (1992, p. 10), is clearly related to a number of important political and ideological struggles; among them, ". . . to (re)regulate sexual and gender roles . . . [and] . . . to monitor and even isolate particular segments of the population, especially various racial and ethnic minorities who, along with women and children, make up a vast majority of the poor". In order to best understand the WUSA neo-liberal positioning within the US market, we invoke and build on the work of Michel Foucault, applying his conception of governmentality to the mediated landscape and trans/national corporate environment within which the WUSA both resides in and performatively (re)creates.

Foucault, Governmentality and Cultural Citizenship

> A fully realized neo-liberal citizenry would be the opposite of public-minded, indeed, it would barely exist as a public. The body politic ceases to be a body but is, rather, a group of individual entrepreneurs and consumers.
>
> Wendy Brown, 2003, p. 5

As Michel Foucault (1991, p. 100) outlines, governmentality "has as its purpose not the action of government itself, but the welfare of the population, the improvement of its conditions, the increase of its wealth, longevity, health, etc." Although Roland Barthes (1973) – who originally coined the term "governmentality" in the 1950s – was concerned with economic imperatives, market variables, and the state's relationship to both, Foucault more fully developed the idea to account for "the way in which the modern state began to worry about individuals" (Foucault, 1991, p. 4). In his 1978 lecture on "Governmentality", Foucault (1991, p. 87) suggests that governmentality, or the art of government, concerns "how to govern oneself, how to be governed, how to govern others, by whom the people will accept being governed, how to become the best possible governor". Toby Miller, Geoffrey Lawrence, Jim McKay, and David Rowe (2001, p. 100) succinctly outline Foucault's threefold concept of governmentality that helps to explain modern life: "The first utilizes economics to mould the population into efficient and effective producers . . . [T]he second is the array of governmental apparatuses designed to create conditions for this productivity . . . [A]nd the third is the translation of methods between education and penology that modifies justice into human improvement."

Taken as a whole, the techniques of governmentality are employed, as Mitchell Dean (1999, p. 11) states, "for definite but shifting ends and with a diverse set of relatively unpredictable consequences, effects, and outcomes". However, the art of governing is not limited solely to State actors in the traditional sense (for example, elected officials, governmental agencies, and so forth). Rather, as Bratich, Packer and McCarthy (2003) stress in their cogent explication of the relevance of Foucault to cultural studies, the cultural realm – seen here in the deployment of the WUSA as a wholly American(ized) institution – is of paramount importance to Foucauldian understandings of governmentality. They state in part:

> [I]n the simplest terms, governmentality refers to the arts and rationalities of governing, where the conduct of conduct is the key activity. It is an attempt to reformulate the governor-governed relationship, one that does not make the relation dependent upon administrative machines, juridical institutions, or other apparatuses that usually get grouped under the rubric of the State. Rather . . . the conduct of conduct takes place at innumerable sites, through an array of techniques and programs that are usually defined as cultural. (Bratich, Packer and McCarthy, 2003, p. 4)

That is to say, "government" refers to the activities of all institutions concerned with the regulation, management, and manipulation of populations in general via technologies of containment, surveillance, and subjectification.

But how exactly is culture conceived of within this frame? For that, we can look to the most active proponent of integrating governmentality into cultural studies, Tony Bennett, whose (1992) essay "Putting policy into cultural studies" stands as a call for challenging what he sees as the Gramscian limitations of cultural studies' counter-hegemonic approach to understanding the "policing" of cultural citizens in modern nation-state formations. More specifically, Bennett's essay attempts to move cultural studies away from viewing culture primarily in terms of signifying practices. To this end, he foregoes Raymond Williams's (1961) oft-cited view of culture as a "whole way of life" – which has its own originary history within the British cultural studies tradition – in favor of Williams's less-cited but perhaps more revealing conceptualization of culture as the "generalized process of intellectual, spiritual, and aesthetic development" (Williams, quoted in Bennett, 1992, p. 25). This "other" view of "culture" makes evident that "culture" has been both the object and the instrument of government. Recuperating Williams and integrating Foucault thusly allows Bennett to suggest that "culture":

> is more cogently conceived . . . when thought of as a historically specific set of institutionally embedded relations of government in which the forms of thought and conduct of extended populations are target for transformation – in part via the extension through the social body of the forms, techniques, and regimens of aesthetic and intellectual culture. As such, its emergence is perhaps best though of as a part of that process of the increasing governmentalization of social life characteristic of the early modern period with Foucault and others have referred to by the notion of *police*. (Bennett, 1992, p. 26–7, emphasis in original)

Culture, in Bennett's view, is therefore an integral part of the policing process, whether in the sense of America's new mediated "war" on terrorism (Giroux, 2003); new "global strategic community relations" (see King, 2002) programs aimed at engendering consumer loyalty and affiliation to transnational corporations; or in the form of popular sporting representations such as Hollywood cinema perpetuating a white capitalist patriarchal hegemony in its demonition of African American youth (Cole and King, 1998; Giardina and McCarthy, in press).

In a similar vein, Lauren Berlant (1997, p. 226) has argued that "[T]he national knowledge industry has produced a specific modality of paramnesia, an incitement to forgetting that leaves simply the patriotic trace, for real and metaphorically infantilized citizens, that confirms that the nation exists and that we are in it". Caught up in an always already narrative of national fantasy (Berlant, 1991) that binds us to an allegorical "American Dream", positioning the WUSA as a positive – and, in fact, necessary – corporate neighbor reinforces the (a)historical necessity of neoliberalism. Moreover, interrogating the WUSA's "conduct of conduct" – the reformulation of public and private behavior as a public-private investment in the future-present wellbeing of the nation – reveals a changing dynamic in the multiplicitous modalations of ideal citizenship writ large. Expanding on Berlant's original supposition, Samantha J. King (2003, p. 297) reinforces the notion that a post-Reagan ideal of citizenship "demonstrates commitment to the nation-state by embracing bourgeois, humanistic values such as the need to perform organized, charitable works". However, this commitment is not so much about economic capitalization as it is about the "capacity to solidify the contemporary articulation of physical health to moral and civic fitness" (King, 2003, p. 298).

Drawing on King's (2003) Berlantian (re-)characterization of "ideal citizenship" allows us focus our investigation on the role in which "all-American" transnationals play in the "governing" of the future-present. Masked by and authored under the guise of neo-liberal doctrines such as "de-regulation" and "privatization", transnational capitalist corporations are increasingly entering into the discussion of so-called citizen-building practices "by developing and deploying a remolded view of the United States as a nation whose survival depends on publicly celebrated, personal acts of generosity mediated through – and within – consumer culture" (King, 2003, p. 297). Here we (re-)configure "personal acts of generosity" to similarly include a concomitant attachment to and identification with not only the symbolic wellbeing of the nation, but the future-present re-definition of such a (post-)national space, especially when considering its position in the growing global environment. As Michael Silk and David L. Andrews (2001) posit, "The transnational corporations that drive the global economy have clearly acknowledged, and indeed sought to capitalize on, the enduring cultural resonance of experience and *national* belonging within the various *national* markets they seek to penetrate" (Silk and Andrews, 2001, p. 186, emphasis ours). In other words, at the same time as the political and economic milieux head toward post-national identification, we are also witnessing a changing – although certainly not weakening – conception of the nation(al imaginary) under the aegis of transnational corporate capitalism (Silk and Andrews, 2001).

Expanding on Foucault's original assertion(s) with regard to governmentality – and considering the conception of ideal citizenship – the age of global expansion, popular mediation, and boundary-crossing subjectivities has led to a reconceptualization in the practical application of and benefits from techniques of governmentality. In both its mediated and live (that is, in person) form, consumption of the WUSA (be it at a social, cultural, political or economic level), instantiates a sense of national self-identification and "offer[s] to large groups of people the feeling that they can and do make a difference in shaping the organization, direction, aspirations, and ideals of the nation-state in which they live" (King, 2003, p. 297). However, while King's excellent analysis of so-called "cause-related marketing" reveals the linkage of physical health to moral fitness for the benefit of the State, our critique of the WUSA turns on the question of re-constructing and re-defining America's National Symbolic within the global popular; specifically, the way in which trans/national corporations seek to define the space of consumption and its relation to citizenship (Miller, 1998) in an age of multiplicity, hybridity, and difference such that the Corporate elides the State in formative relations of identity.[7]

"Marketing" the WUSA

> [T]he task is to formulate within this constituted frame a critique of the categories of identity that contemporary juridical structures engender, naturalize, and immobilize.
>
> Judith Butler

Specific to our project, and constituted through various power/knowledge relationships, this newly fashioned ethic of ideal corporate citizenship reveals itself through three inter-related sites of cultural production germane to the WUSA's marketing and "global strategic community relations" (King, 2002) initiatives: (1) its strategic involvement with the American Youth Soccer Organization (AYSO), which promotes health and wellbeing through soccer at the grassroots level; (2) its partnership with the American Legacy Foundation's Smoke-Free Kids program; and (3) its overall corporate sponsorship alignment with family-oriented institutions, a package of $15 million worth of accounts that features, among others, Coca-Cola, McDonald's, Johnson & Johnson, Hyundai, and Procter & Gamble. All function to legitimate and naturalize the WUSA as being a necessary, unquestioned piece of the National Symbolic.

Listed as a 501(c)(3) corporation (a non-profit organization), AYSO counts in its ranks 250,000 volunteers and 660,000 players, offering a ready-made stream of future consumers for the WUSA to reach out and influence. The alliance formed between the WUSA and the American Youth Soccer Association is revealing in that the AYSO's stated effort is to "promote health and well-being through soccer at the grassroots level" through the implementation of WUSA community programs (WUSA Press Office, 2001). AYSO Chief Marketing Officer Cathy Ferguson stresses the community-based interaction by stating: "We are proud to have WUSA members on our team to act as role models for our nation's youth" (Press Office).

This alliance between AYSO and the WUSA is couched in the belief that childhood participation in sport creates "healthy, fit" citizens. Given that a growing proportion of American youth is increasingly diagnosed as sedentary and/or overweight, and given that over 10 million children in the US are without viable healthcare, this public-private coupling appears at first glance to be a model for corporate responsibility within a grassroots setting. However, seeing that the demographic makeup of both the WUSA's fan base and the AYSO's female player population are generally white, middle-class, girls and young women, such a relationship is cause for question. Without suggesting that this forward-thinking agenda is anything less than genuine in its *intent*, there is room to speculate as to the potential economic benefit presented the WUSA: a ready-made demographic of so-called "tween consumers" – those individuals between 8 and 13 years old – who, while accounting for only 20 percent of consumerist audiences, wield overwhelming spending power with the family unit (Schetting, 2001, p. 19).[8] Thus, while WUSA utilizes its AYSO relationship to promote health and fitness to a growing "at risk" demographic, it similarly benefits from youthful AYSO participants by imbricating them into a specific ideological construct at an early and impressionable age.

Likewise, and playing off of the oft-criticized "Girl Power!" campaign implemented by the US Department of Health and Human Services in 1996,[9] the anti-tobacco group American Legacy (of the infamous "Truth" ad campaign) and the WUSA have come together in a grassroots effort to create a program titled "Kick Ash", the goal of which promotes healthy living and anti-smoking messages. Chosen for its ability to "deliver the audience [American Legacy] wants to target . . . soccer moms, kids, and family" (Klein, quoted in Cassidy, 2002), the WUSA's positioning within the socio-political matrix of contemporary consumer culture allows American Legacy to reach a population of young, image-conscious, (upper-)middle class girls and their hipster mothers, a core group oft-overlooked by traditional "at-risk"-themed public service announcements. Aired during the 2002 WUSA season, and featured in national women-centered magazines such as *Vogue*, *Glamour*, *Self*, *Vanity Fair*, and *Cosmopolitan*, the "women and smoking" campaign graphically depicts middle-aged and older women both taking responsibility for their "irresponsible lifestyle choice" while also demonizing the corporate demagogues of the tobacco industry for failing to be interested in and look out for their well-being. In each print advertisement, a solitary, black-and-white photograph (shot by world-renowned fashion photographer Richard Avedon) is accompanied by copy that takes the form of a death-bed letter to their loved ones. Calligraphed in their own handwritten script, the following text is indicative of the narrative style taken by each announcement:

> To my family, Smoking is taking years off my life. Years I should be spending with you. I'm sorry. My love for you will not go with me, it will grow inside you all.

> To my children, I don't want you to be sad! Remember me, and forgive me for leaving you so soon. When it's over, mom will just be sleeping.
>
> To the tobacco companies, My name is Desmonda. I have emphysema from smoking. You stole my dignity. You killed the spirit of a beautiful young woman. And the worst is yet to come. For that, you should be sorry.

This tripartite frame – apologizing to one's family, asking forgiveness of their children for having to "leave" them, and a condemnation of "Big Business" for failing *them* – thus reinforces a belief in personal agency and responsibility, while also highlighting that the WUSA and *its* relationship to "Big Business" is one of positive, consumer-directed, (self-)efficacy.

Finally, and drawing attention to the various corporate sponsors of the WUSA,[10] it becomes overwhelmingly apparent that each sponsor reveals a Clintonian understanding of popular conservatism, one that values family-oriented *narratives* based on utilitarian individualism (Bellah et al., 1985) while engendering an (imperial) neoliberal belief that civic volunteerism (King, 2003) and corporate-directed community welfare assistance are necessary stand-ins for the socio-political governing apparatuses of the Welfare State. This renarration of the Reaganite project invisions, to quote from Bill Clinton's first inaugural address, all Americans "tak[ing] more responsibility, not only for ourselves and our families but for our communities and our country" (Clinton, 1993, p. 2).

A prime example of alleged "good corporate citizenship" within the WUSA is found in two of its primary sponsors – Coca-Cola and McDonald's. Advancing the belief that "responsible corporate citizenship" is the defining characteristic of the Coca-Cola Corp., it sees itself – here aligned in tandem with McDonald's – as an active co-participant in contributing to "numerous philanthropies and organizations, and also regularly provid[ing] educational opportunities and scholarships to students in the US and around the world" (www.coca-cola.com). That the WUSA is seen by Coca-Cola as a philanthropic and educational opportunity to be capitalized on is representative of the way in which most if not all of WUSA's sponsors view the league. However, it is the consumerist narrative that – even in official press offerings – is emphasized over and against the physical wellbeing of America's youth. Says Julie Foudy, San Diego Spirit midfielder and player representative on the WUSA Board of Governors:

> To forge a relationship with two legendary companies like Coke and McDonald's is reflective of the impact this league can have on the consumer. Our main demographic is a perfect tie-in for Coke and McDonald's . . . They are the world leaders in their fields, as we are in ours, and together we can make a lot of young kids smile. (WUSA Press Office, 2002, our emphasis)

However, the repetitive, child-centered narrative advanced by the league and its sponsors does not at all mask its consumer-driven agenda, as one would assume. Rather, it celebrates the articulation between a happy childhood, a healthy body, and the (necessary) role corporate capitalist entities (must) play in the (neo-liberal) future-present.

Coda

> National identity provides, then, a translation of the historical subject into an "Imaginary" realm of identity and wholeness, where the subject becomes whole by being reconstituted as a collective subject, or citizen.
>
> Lauren Berlant

Sport, citizenship, and corporate America. As the new millennium unfolds, and the post-modern nation-state comes face-to-face with an increasingly hybridized population, deepening patterns of aestheticization in advertising (McCarthy, 2002), and the intensification of diasporic flows of cultural and economic capital, transnational capitalist entities are increasingly seeking to "represent national cultures in a manner designed to engage the nationalist sensibilities of local consumers" (Silk and Andrews, 2001, p. 186), while similarly offering a connection to the larger global popular. Further, and as Cameron McCarthy (2002, p. 20) cogently explicates, "The new consumer is the new citizen whose aesthetics of existence are now ever more deeply imbricated in a universalization of the entrepreneurial spirit and the propagation of the redemptive neo-liberal value of choice". From AYSO/WUSA partnerships revealing a ready-made consumer youth market to the strategic "women and smoking" campaign that shows an acceptance of responsibility for one's lifestyle choice to the ubiquitous celebration of corporate America's positioning within the neo-liberal future-present definition of the nation, we are witnessing a reconfigurement of the acceptable boundaries of corporate capitalist interaction within the modern Welfare State.

"Rather than being viewed as a commercial public sphere innocently distributing pleasure to young people", as Henry Giroux (1995) has argued with regard to global corporations such as Disney and Nike, the WUSA and its corporate armatures must likewise "be seen as a pedagogical and policy-making enterprise actively engaged in the cultural landscaping of national identity and the 'schooling' of the minds of young children" (Giroux, 1995, p. 65). While not to suggest that the WUSA alone operates on any scale near that of Disney, its circulation within the popular arena is necessarily linked to its relationship with megaconglomerates Coca-Cola, McDonald's, and AOL Time Warner, which amplifies its cultural significance within a core segment of the population:

white, middle-class, young female consumers. Such a configuration, then, operates in tandem with transnational corporations to produce, as Cameron McCarthy (2002, pp. 5–6) argues, "technologies of truth and identification that serve to transform concrete individuals into cultural citizens whose lines of loyalty and affiliation now exceed the territory and social geography of the nation-state". However, and given our previous discussion of governing practices within post-modern America, we must remain cognizant of the role transnational capitalist corporations are playing in the formation of our youth, our community, and our selves. It is only after we unmask such productive relations of power can we then begin to understand our *own* role in the governing of our selves.

Notes

1. Lauren Berlant (1997) characterizes the National Symbolic as a mythic archive of images and fictions that define a nation, suggesting that "the collective possession of these official texts – the flag, Uncle Sam, Mount Rushmore, [and] the Pledge of Allegiance . . . creates a nation 'public' that constantly renounces political knowledge where is exceeds intimate mythic national codes". Further, we "are already inextricably bound together by America . . . because we inhabit the *political* space of the nation, which is not merely juridical, territorial (*jus soli*), genetic (*jus sanguinis*), linguistic, or experiential, but some tangled cluster of these" (Berlant, 1991, p. 5, emphasis in original).
2. We have previously argued (Giardina and Metz, 2004) that America's fascination with, active involvement in, and widespread promotion of women's sports (and, with it, the not-so-subtle construction of a national and political landscape) reveals the complex intersections of sport, media, and social issues that assist in defining the acceptable boundaries of personal subjectivity.
3. With the exception of Mary McDonald, this volume.
4. While female athletic participation in the 1990s has shown a dramatic increase in overall participation rates, soccer has recorded the most dramatic of these increases, jumping an astounding 34 percent between the years 1991 and 1999, resulting in a record 7.5 million soccer playing females (Sporting Goods Manufacturer Association press release, 1999). On the collegiate level, 1998 saw 39 percent of all NCAA athletes as women 1998 saw 39 percent of all collegiate athletes as women, a staggering increase from 1972, when women accounted for only 2 percent of college athletes (Amateur Association of University Women press release, 2001).
5. After an inaugural season in which cable ratings for the WUSA hovered at 0.4 on Turner Sports, the league switched partners to PAX TV, a subsidiary of Paxson Communications Corp. Although the deal provided a definitive weekly broadcast

time slot (as well as $2 million in annual rights fees), ratings for the second season of WUSA drew only a 0.1 rating – approximately 300,000 fewer viewers than in season one (Glier, 2002, p. 8). Further, published reports say that the WUSA lost close to $40 million in its first season. Such figures are not yet available for Season Two (Umstead, 2001, p. 9).

6. Obviously, the term "middle class" is highly ambiguous, owing in no small measure its definition to those who choose to say they belong to such a class distinction. For our purposes, and following Rayna Rapp (1999, p. 190), we loosely accept the term to mean – in its broadest sense – the portion of the population that is "dependent on wages . . . [yet] lives at a level that is quite different from the wage level of the proletarian working class".
7. Understood within this context, power is seen as productive and not as an instrument of oppression, further operating not externally but rather internally, by inducing people to aim for a mode of self-improvement which *seems* voluntary. For more on the practical application of Foucault to contemporary society, see the excellent collection of essays in *Foucault, Cultural Studies, and Governmentality*, edited by Bratich, Packer, and McCarthy (2003).
8. A secondary WUSA demographic, those aged 12–17 – the so-called *Generation Y* crowd – spend $120 billion each year and influence their immediate family to spend another $150 billion annually (Drake, 2002, p. 2).
9. Launched in association with Bill Clinton's "President's Council on Physical Fitness and Sports," the stated aim of the alleged politically and socially forward thinking campaign is to "encourage and empower 9–14-year-old girls to make the most of their lives" (HHS/Girl Power! Official Website). See Giardina (2001); Giardina and Metz 2004 for more on the impact of "Girl Power!" on women's sport and American popular culture.
10. The following corporate entities sponsor[ed] the WUSA: Hyundai, Acuvue, Band-Aid, Reach Toothbrush, and Clean & Clear are "Charter Sponsors"; Maytag, Gillette Venus and Gillette Satin Care, McDonald's, Coca-Cola, AFLAC Supplemental Insurance, Gatorade, Sports Illustrated for Women, HealthSouth, PAX Television, MBNA America, American Youth Soccer Organization, and US Youth Soccer are "League Sponsors"; American Legacy is the official "League Cause" partner; and Select Sport, Kwik Goal, and Official Sports are "Equipment Sponsors" (http://www.wusa.com/sponsors/).

References

Anderson, B. (1983), *Imagined Communities: Reflections on the Origin and Spread of Nationalism*, London: Verso.

Andrews, D. L. (1997). The (Trans)National Basketball Association: American Commodity-sign Culture and Global-local Conjuncturalism. In A. Cvetkovich and D. Kellner (eds), *Articulating the Global and the Local: Globalization and Cultural Studies*, Boulder CO: Westview Press.

Banet-Weiser. S. (2001), Professional Basketball and the Politics of Race and Gender, *Journal of Sport and Social Issues*, 23(4): 403–20.

Bellah, R. N., Madsen, R., Sullivan, W. M., Swidler, A. and Tipton, S. M. (1985), *Habits of the Heart: Individualism and Commitment in American Life*, Berkeley: University of California Press.

Berlant, L. (1991), *The Anatomy of National Fantasy: Hawthorne, Utopia, and Everyday Life*, Chicago: University of Chicago Press.

Berlant, L. (1997), *The Queen of America Goes to Washington City: Essays on Sex and Citizenship*, Durham NC: Duke University Press.

Bratich, J. Z., Packer, J. and McCarthy, C. (2003), Governing the Present. In J. Z. Bratich, J. Packer, and C. McCarthy (eds), *Foucault, Cultural Studies, and Governmentality*, Albany NY: State University of New York Press, pp. 3–21.

Butler, J. (1990), *Gender Trouble: Feminism and the Subversion of Identity*, New York: Routledge.

Children's Defense Organization Press Office (2002), Available at: http://www.childrens defense.org/hs_chipmain.php.

Clinton, W. J. (1993), Inaugural Address, January 20, Public Papers of the Presidents of the United States: William J. Clinton, 1993, Washington DC: Government Printing Office, pp. 1–3.

Coca-Cola Press Office (2002), Corporate citizenship: Coca-Cola is a good neighbor. Available at: http://coca-colacareers.com/undergrad/why/corporate_citizenship.html

Cole, C. L. (2000), The Year that Girls Ruled, *Journal of Sport and Social Issues*, 24(1): 1–6.

Cole, C. L. & King, S. J. (1998), Representing Black Masculinity and Urban Possibilities: Racism, Realism and Hoop Dreams. In G. Rail (ed.), *Sport and Postmodern Times*, Albany, NY: State University of New York Press, pp. 49–86.

Dean, M. (1999), *Governmentality: Power and Rule in Modern Society*, London: Sage.

Denzin, N. K. (1991), *Images of Postmodern Society: Social Theory and Contemporary Cinema*, London: Sage Publications.

Drake, D. L. (2002), It's a Wise Marketer who Knows Your Child. *NJBiz*, 15(25): 2.

Foucault, M. (1991), Governmentality. In G. Burchill, C. Gordon and P. Miller (eds), *The Foucault Effect: Studies in Governmentality*, Chicago: University of Chicago Press, pp. 87–104.

Giardina, M. D. (2001), Global Hingis: Flexible Citizenship and the Transnational Celebrity. In D. L. Andrews and S. J. Jackson (eds), *Sport Stars: The Cultural Politics of Sporting Celebrity*, London: Routledge, pp. 201–17.

Giardina, M. D. and McCarthy, C. (in press), The Popular Racial Order of "Urban" America Sport, Identity, and the Politics of Culture, *Cultural Studies and Critical Methodologies*.

Giardina, M. D. and Metz, J. L. (2004), Women's Sports in Nike's America: Body Politics and the Corporo-empowerment of "Everyday Athletes." In S. J. Jackson and D. L. Andrews (eds), *Sport, Culture, and Advertising: Identities, Commodities, and the Politics of Representation*, Westport CT: Praeger Press.

Giroux, H.A. (1995), Innocence and pedagogy in Disney's world. In E. Bell, L. Haas and L. Sells (eds). *From Mouse to Mermaid: The Politics of Film, Gender, and Culture*, Bloomington IN: Indiana University Press, pp. 43–61.

Glier, R. (2002), WUSA Takes Wait-and-see Approach to Attendance Drop, *USA Today*, April 22, p. 8.

Grossberg, L. (1992). *We Gotta Get Out of this Place: Popular Conservatism and Postmodern Culture*, New York: Routledge.

King, S. J. (2002), Marketing Generosity: Avon's Women's Health Programs and New Trends in Global Community Relations, *International Journal of Sports Marketing and Sponsorship*.

King, S. J. (2003). Doing Good by Running Well: Breast Cancer, the Race for the Cure, and New Technologies of Ethical Citizenship. In J. Z. Bratich, J. Packer, and C. McCarthy (eds), *Foucault, Cultural Studies, and Governmentality*, Albany NY: State University of New York Press, pp. 295–316.

McCarthy, C. (2002). *Understanding the Work of Aesthetics in Modern Life: Thinking about the Cultural Studies of Education in a Time of Recession,* unpublished manuscript, Urbana IL: University of Illinois, Urbana-Champaign.

McDonald, M. G. (2000), The Marketing of the Women's National Basketball Association and the Making of Postfeminism, *International Review for the Sociology of Sport*, 35(1), 35–48.

McDonald, M. G. (2001), Safe sex symbol? Michael Jordan and the Politics of Representation. In D. L. Andrews (ed.), *Michael Jordan, Inc.: Corporate Sport, Media Culture, and Late Modern America*, Albany NY: State University of New York Press.

Miller, T. (1998). *Technologies of Truth: Cultural Citizenship and the Popular Media*, Minneapolis: University of Minnesota Press.

Miller, T., Lawrence, G., McKay, J. and Rowe, D. (2001), *Globalization and Sport: Playing the World*, London: Sage Publications.

Rapp, R. (1999), Family and Class in Contemporary American: Notes Toward an Understanding of Ideology. In S. Coontz, M. Parson and G. Raley (eds), *American Families: A Multicultural Reader*, New York: Routledge, pp. 180–96.

Rose, N. (1999), *Powers of Freedom: Reframing Political Thought*, Cambridge: Cambridge University Press.

Schetting, C. (2001): 'Tween shall meet,' *Broadcasting and Cable*, 131 (March 5): 19.

Silk, M. (2001), Together We're One? The "Place" of the Nation in Media Representations of the 1998 Kuala Lumpur Commonwealth Games, *Sociology of Sport Journal*, 18(3): 277–301.

Silk, M. and Andrews, D. L. (2001), Beyond a Boundary? Sport, Transnational Advertising, and the Reimagining of National Culture, *Journal of Sport and Social Issues*, 25(2): 180–201.

Sporting Goods Manufacturers Association Press Office. (1999), 'Female soccer participation at all-time high.' Available at: http://www.sgma.com/press/1999/press986503572-9968.html.

Stacey, J. (1993), Good Riddance to the "Family": A Response to David Popenoe, *Journal of Marriage and Family*, 55(3): 545.

Turner Sports (2000), Women's United Soccer Association Exclusive Multi-year Television Agreement, Official Press Release of Turner Sports, April 10. Available at http://sportsillustrated.cnn.com/turnersports/specials/news/2000/04/turner_

Umstead, R. T. (2001), WUSA, PAX Net TV Soccer Pact, *Multichannel News*, 22(52): 9.

Women's United Soccer Association Press Office (2001), Coke and McDonalds sign on as WUSA sponsors. Available at: http://www.wusa.com/press_room/292089.html.

7

Imagining Benevolence, Masculinity and Nation: Tragedy, Sport and the Transnational Marketplace

Mary G. McDonald

On September 11, 2001 three hijacked commercial airplanes intentionally crashed into the World Trade Center's (WTC) North and South Towers, and the US Pentagon igniting all three structures and a global media event. Immediate television coverage from the US was extended to many parts of the world transmitting horrific images of the death and devastation, as well as desperate, often heroic attempts by firefighters, police and other public safety officials to rescue survivors. These images and additional stories documenting the death toll of approximately 3,000 people, traumatic emotional aftermath on the part of victim's friends and families, the immediate negative economic impact (especially on New York City) and public mourning over the dead were subsequently rebroadcast innumerable times. While analogies in the US were drawn from public memory to December 7, 1941 when the Japanese military attacked Pearl Harbor, it soon became apparent that the recent attack within the US's geographical boundary was different. Aimed at the symbols of global corporate capitalism and the US's influential, often militarized contributions in its development, the offensive was not the work of a recognized nation-state but that of Al-Qaeda, a militia network with central operations in Afghanistan under the leadership of Osama bin Laden.

Worldwide and local US responses prior to, during and after September 11 were multi-faceted and multi-layered rearticulating conflicting and fractured geographic, political and economic sensibilities.[1] Additionally as a global media event, frames of meaning were constantly remade, so much so that events before, on and beyond September 11 are not simply mere representations of what happened, but rather forces that help to construct "the reality of the event that may or may not have preceded it" (Fiske, 1994, p. 4). Such diversity of these "glocal" responses and the politics of representation suggest that these divergent retorts including those produced within the world of sport are impossible to easily characterize. Yet according to Henry Giroux (2002), too often dominant US media accounts offered unquestioned support for the US governmental policy of waging a "war against terrorism" including military retaliation against bin Laden, the Taliban and Al-Qaeda in Afghanistan, and subsequent support for military intervention in Iraq, while providing very little attention to dissenting views.[2] For Giroux (2002) engaging dissent means rethinking and politicizing notions of nation, examining prior and existing policy decisions as well as seeking a broader dialogue to determine what exactly should constitute a just diplomatic response to the brutal acts of violence committed on September 11.[3]

While offering minimal attention to these and other dissenting views, the post-September 11 corporate-owned media mostly continue to legitimate state actions that in turn protect transnational capital expansion by envisioning the US as a righteous and benevolent nation whose cherished ideals and way of life are under attack by terrorists (Johnson, 2002). And while some initial commentary suggested the insignificance of sport amongst the tragic loss of life, sport proved to be a visible site for similar invoking of the nation and nationalism. *Sports Illustrated*'s romanticization of sport, the US and consumption in the immediate aftermath of the attacks is among the most hyperbolic in declaring "the ability to congregate each Sunday in ballparks (or at least in front of a game on TV) is one of our society's most sacred freedoms" (Hoffer, 2001, p. 30).

This chapter examines sport's place in constituting the US as both benevolent and masculine by critiquing and (re)contextualizing mediated responses of elite, commercial sport especially focusing on two sites: the debate over whether or not to postpone play in the aftermath of September 11 and the symbolism surrounding the 2001 Major League Baseball (MLB) World Series, the first major sporting event after the attacks. Almost immediately a debate ensued over whether or not to play or postpone major sporting events. Eventually, with the resumption of play and especially during the World Series, these sporting narratives assisted in reproducing a historically salient articulation that casts the nation in a masculine, paternal role in response to an external threat from a chaotic other. The official standpoint of the leagues, players and sponsors articulated to another persistent discourse urging a return to "business as usual", a response that legitimates the capitalist workplace, multi-national corporations and the consumer culture as stabilizing forces in uncertain times.

Rather than simply documenting professional sport's responses to the tragic attacks on the World Trade Center and Pentagon, then, this chapter supports the need to read sport critically – to produce counter stories and dissenting views by suggesting the ways sporting narratives work within larger complex and contradictory cultural, political, social and economic realms (McDonald and Birrell, 1999). In sum, this chapter offers cultural criticism by interrogating the linkages between dominant sporting discourses and those seeking to legitimate the neo-liberal transnational marketplace through a continuing attachment to masculinist ideologies and the very idea of nation.

Sport, National Fantasies and Fantasy Economics

Elaine Scarry's (1985) argument about wounded bodies as profound sites of sense making is an insight that can be applied to the suffering and emotionally salient discourses wrought in the wake of September 11, 2001. For Scarry (1985, p. 62) "the incontestable reality of the body – the body in pain, the body maimed, the body dead and hard to dispose of – is separated from its source and conferred on an ideology" that serves to anchor narratives and thus seemingly materialize otherwise abstract ideals including those of patriotism and nation (see also Detloff, 1999). Lauren Berlant (1991, p. 5) employs the term "national fantasy", to designate a related process of meaning making. "National fantasy", much like the conferring of nationalist meanings upon wounded bodies, also suggests a passionate and emotional process whereby "national culture becomes local – through the images, narratives, monuments and sites that circulate through personal/collective consciousness" (Berlant, 1991, p. 5). This notion of national fantasy suggests that there are neither essential meanings nor a fixed form to the nation, "but rather, many simultaneous 'literal' and 'metaphorical' meanings stated and unstated" (Berlant, 1991, p. 5). As Sheila Croucher (2003, p. 2) argues, an awareness of this contingent, performative and often ambiguous constitution of nations allows us "to locate in globalization both the conditions and mechanisms that support national imaginings". Given these unstable, emotive, often hierarchical global (re)imaginings, it is important to ascertain who is promoting what invocations of nation, for what purposes and with what consequences.

That elite, competitive, mediated sport would serve as one powerful site in the post-September 11 process of national imagining is not surprising given its historical relationship to narratives of nation. For within the mainstream, "sport is assumed to act as a vehicle for confirming a sense of citizenship, fostering a sense of social bonds and serving as an unashamed celebration of nationalism and patriotism. As such sport teams and even individual athletes are assumed to represent, and in many respects become extensions of our national identity" (Jackson, 1998, pp. 229–30). And since contemporary elite sport in the US is imbedded in commodity logic "intimately linked to the technological opportunities afforded by various media delivery forms (satellite, cable, webcast and microwave)", selected emotionally charged images of sport and nation are frequently transmitted globally (Miller et al., 2001, p. 24). Increasingly the marketing strategies of transnational corporations have mobilized locally resonating caricatures of nation and sport in an effort to secure brand identification and profit "thereby embracing the nation as a source of consumer identification" (Silk and Andrews, 2001, p. 199).

The violent acts of September 11 opened up possibilities for fresh imaginings of nation both within the world of sport and beyond. For example, the events potentially heightened the awareness of the American people that the US is part of a globalized system, the effects of which cannot be completely controlled (Giroux, 2002, p. 1,138). Other narratives politicized the nation noting the ways in which US foreign policy and economic interests might be assessed and changed for partially aiding in the rise of new forms of terrorism and fundamentalisms around the globe. More often, however, within US borders a sense of unanimity "organized not only around flag-waving displays of patriotism but also around collective fears and an ongoing militarization of visual culture and public space" ensued (Giroux, 2002, p. 1,138). That many of these latter expressions took place within a commercial context was also apparent in the months after September 11, when events like the World Series between the Arizona Diamondbacks and the New York Yankees and later the 2002 Super Bowl and Olympics in Salt Lake City merged symbolic displays of militarism, patriotism, national unity and consumption.

In the days immediately after September 11 professional and elite college sport provided important locations where the tensions and contradictions between the interests of the nation imaginary and capitalist entertainment industries were illustrated as administrators and corporate sponsors "wrestled with this need to honor a country's grief and the requirement to do business, the need to entertain" (Hoffer, 2001, p. 31). Debates arose within the sporting world on how best to proceed. Officials wondered whether to "cancel out of sympathy for the victims? Play to show strength and defiance? Postpone to do both?" (Weisman, 2001, p. 1C). Promoters ultimately negotiated the tensions and contradictions by constructing elite commercial sport as having the ability to demonstrate proper respect for the dead while ensuring fan security and thus enhancing corporate profitability. Eventually, questions of whether or not to postpone Division I college and professional sporting events (including those of MLB, the National Football League and others)[4] often merged with similar efforts to project a vision of a good, caring nation.

Fox Sport television executives were among those involved in initial discussion over how to respond. The Rupert Murdoch-owned and controlled transnational corporation had a six-year $2.5 billion rights fee investment "to televise Major League Baseball, including provisions to produce so-called 'virtual advertising,' including a number of promotions for Fox shows during the World Series" (Shapiro, 2001, p. D2). This virtual advertising would allow both Fox and MLB transnational corporate sponsors like Nextel, Gatorade, Radio Shack and MasterCard to project advertisements on ballpark walls and fences that would only be visible to television viewers at home (Shapiro, 2001). In the days immediately following September 11 Fox television, MLB along with its corporate and advertising sponsors including Anheuser-Busch International, Pepsi-Cola, John Hancock, Post Cereals, Adidas and Nike thus feared that cancellation would mean another type of loss – the loss of profit with "players expecting to get paid, stadium rental payments, agreements with vendors", refunds to season ticket holders and loss of media exposure (Weisman, 2001, p. 1C). However, continuation of play might suggest insensitivity generating a backlash that also might erode sponsorship and capital accumulation. After all, during the previous year, over "$9.5 billion was spent in North America on sponsorship. . . and over 69 percent was deployed in sports" (Tays, 2001, p. 1B).

Intersecting with fears that professional sport and its transnational corporate sponsors not "suffer" undue loss of profit in the days immediately following September 11, discussions took place about the potential national psychological benefits of either playing or suspending play. While most elite and professional sports leagues eventually temporarily suspended play, on one side of these deliberatations were those who argued, "don't let the terrorists control us", whereas others insisted that that play should be suspended as sport is not significant since "the nation must have time to grieve" (P. King, 2001, p. 60). No matter what the response – either for the continuation or the suspension of play – the very framing of the best way to respond frequently produced incomplete responses with homogenized visions of the US largely devoid of global connections, historical contexts and disparate economic relationships.

Those arguing for the continuation of play often did so as testimony to American uniqueness and masculine resolve. A continued schedule would "demonstrate the stiffness of America's spine. What more magnificent insult to terrorists than to show up in packed stadiums, which after all are the real symbols of our culture, and sound our defiance with a loud and lusty national anthem?" (Hoffer, 2001, p. 30). This imagining of the nation is consistent with the imagery used in speeches given by President George Bush and British Prime Minister Tony Blair, notions that idealize their respective nations as strong, benevolent and unified "by invoking ways of living and by powerfully intervening in them" (Johnson, 2002, p. 211). According to Rosalind Petchesky (2002,

p. 318) frequently "acquisitiveness, whether individual or corporate, also lurks behind" arguments that freedom, resolve and "our way of life" need to be celebrated and fiercely protected. Furthermore, echoing throughout the speeches of Bush and Blair as well as numerous sporting discourses arguing for the continuation of play is the conviction that "these ways of living are not expected to change. Rather they are to be defended because they are under threat externally" (Johnson, 2002, p. 213). Or in the hyper-masculine policy statements of Bush, the "only way to defeat terrorism as a threat to our way of life is to stop it, eliminate it, and destroy it where it grows" (Bush, 2001a).

Those arguing for the suspension of play did so suggesting the need for inward reflection while citing the insignificance of sport. For example, according to NFL Player's Association Representative Gene Upshaw: "I don't buy into this 'If we don't play, they win' . . . This isn't about the terrorists. It's about us – the people who are here, the firemen and rescue workers, the victims and their families and friends. Do you really think the terrorists care if we play?" (cited in Weisman, 2002, p. 1C). In many similar arguments the figure of the terrorist serves as an imagined other from which to project a particular vision of unity and a good caring nation.[5] And as with any binary system of meaning, the unified, caring "us" is produced against projections of an undifferentiated "them" where in both cases alleged internal sameness helps obscure class, ethnic, gender, political, economic, historical and other differences.

Sports writer Frank Deford's (2001, p. 63) words reflects the role of sport as a key contributor to this type of national fantasy creation and presumed national belonging through suggestions that post-September 11 contests could and would eventually provide stadium space "crucial for a democratic society because it's where all classes and types of people come together, mix and share in a common public space". This "opportunity for that precious and comforting assembly" means that sport could serve as a potential cathartic vehicle:

> For, in times of sorrow and fear, the chance for Americans to gather in any huge stadium, to stand together, bound together, provides a powerful – even patriotic – nectar. To look around at friends and strangers, Americans all, is to draw strength and find resolve; it is to catch a glimpse, in that congregation, of happier times and a brighter America ahead. Only a stadium offers that potential for vision . . . In a way we all, in the great crowd form an American flag, a people proudly hailing for the world to see . . . (Deford, 2001, p. 63)

Not to disparage or dismiss expressions of grief and sadness,[6] yet this particular sentimental rendering of national, racial and class harmony and homogeneity offered by Frank Deford and others remake a reductive connection between identity and belonging assuming that only those who identify as Americans are sport fans while also overstating the ability of poor and disenfranchised groups to purchase their way into stadiums in the first place, Similar framings elide elite US sport's role in celebrating mythologies of social class accord, personal initiative, benevolence, freedom and choice – which are also hallmarks of the liberal transnational marketplace seeking to legitimate local and global economies of inequality. It is therefore important to point out the consequences of similar "massive deployment of therapeutic discourses that ask people to understand the impact of the events of September 11 and their aftermath solely as (American) 'trauma'" (Transnational Feminists, 2002, p. 61). This overwhelming emphasis on the therapeutic dimensions including those celebrated through sport "tends to reinforce individualistic interpretations" . . . that further obscure "the complex nexus of history and geopolitics that has brought about" the events of September 11 (Transnational Feminists, 2002, p. 61).

What has been largely absent from mainstream US media, popular, and governmental discourses is any sort of sustained attempt to critique particular pre- and post-September 11 notions of the nation linked to popular culture forms like sport as well as US domestic, foreign and military policies that continue to support transnational capitalist expansion, which in turn perpetuates global inequalities. Indeed, while mostly advertising the nation as united including imagining accord and benevolence in sporting and popular discourses very little information provided by the corporate-owned media challenges linkages to prior US foreign policy and a new emerging form of militarized capitalism (Giroux, 2002). For example, the "war on terrorism" and the 1991 Gulf War both enforce the "Carter doctrine", a policy designed by then US President Jimmy Carter in the 1970s to maintain "stability" in the Persian Gulf and "Middle East" in order to sustain the flow of oil from the region (Klare, 2002). As cultural critic Richard Johnson (2002, p. 228) argues this "oil lubricates the ways of living" while bolstering American economic and political hegemony in helping to fuel the consumer culture providing profits for transnational corporations at a considerable cost to others. "Oil stands for and enables many excesses from prodigal uses of space to the poisonous wastes of plastics and the wasteful corporate branding and packaging. Levels of production, consumption and trade in and for the 'developed' societies pollute the earth and atmosphere, and exploit the poor in large parts of the world" (Johnson, 2002, p. 228).

Masculine Resolve and Commodified Patriotism

Several scholars have noted that when the recipient of a violent attack the nation is often feminized, conceived of as weak and in need of protection. Given contemporary gender norms particular "gendered tropes associate weakness and victimization with both femaleness and inadequate masculinity conveying the message" of national lacking especially in the absence of a similarly violent retort (Ehrenreich, 2002, p. 45). In the immediate aftermath of September 11, this process was also linked to fears about the "future of capitalist economy" (Johnson, 2002, p. 214). Indeed "on both sides of the Atlantic a loss of confidence was feared, a catastrophic decline of purchasing power and a full-scale economic crises on top of a recession was already evident (and soon to be officially recognized) in the United States" (Johnson, 2002, p. 214). Dominant narratives suggested that both US and the economy had been dealt a devastating blow that must be overcome for the rhetoric of violent conflict as with the rhetoric of sport and business is "all about how defeat feminizes and humiliates the defeated – and how it must be revenged by victory" (Ehrenrich, 2002, p. 46). In response particular individual (mostly White male) bodies displaying extraordinary fortitude are often made to take on great importance for the national body. Bodies from within the government, military, business, and popular culture including sport ideologically declare the country's potency and are frequently used to rally support for impending war, economic plans and dominant policy positions (Tickner, 2001). In the aftermath of September 11 American (capitalist) resilience was reasserted in the mainstream media's constant focus on the (typically White male) bodies of firefighters and rescue workers at "ground zero", the former site of the WTC as well as those of soldiers in Afghanistan as exemplary of American heroism and bravery (Lorber, 2002).[7]

Eventually within sport the dominant narrative gradually shifted away from narratives of grief, mourning and insignificance to narratives arguing that sporting figures and events such as the World Series offered particular importance for economic recovery and expressions of masculine resolve. That sport and (mostly male) athletic bodies would emerge as a symbolic site for the (re)visioning of American determination is consistent with Trujillo's (2000, p. 17) contention that "perhaps no single institution in American culture has influenced our sense of masculinity more than sport. Throughout our history, dominant groups have successfully persuaded many Americans to believe that sport builds manly character, develops physical fitness, realizes order, promotes justice and even prepares young men for war." Indeed upon the resumption of play after a six day suspension, MLB Commissioner Bud Selig suggested his ballplayers served as symbolic soldiers who could potentially play a part in "providing some stability" toward "helping bring this country back" (cited in Curry, 2001, p. 15). Later the New York Yankees were not only expected to be "lifting their game" against the Arizona Diamondbacks for the World Series title, but were expected to bolster a sense of national belonging by "lifting their citizens" (Lee, 2001, p 1).

The conjoining of hegemonic (heterosexual) masculinity with nationalism and a type of sporting militarism was readily apparent with the resumption of play. Amongst extra security and amidst what one reporter describes as "the red, white and blue that blanketed each ballpark" as "chants of 'U-S-A, U-S-A!' rang out from stadium to stadium" (Curry, 2001, p. 15) the bodies of athletes reflected new related national import. American flags were placed on uniforms, caps and helmets while at many major league ballparks "God Bless America" was played in "conjunction with the national anthem before the game or instead of "Take Me Out to the Ballgame" (Curry, 2001, p. 15). Another story suggested that sports like baseball "helped a nation escape, focus, heal. They gave us places to unite, sing and wear red, white and blue. They helped us carry on when the concept seemed too fuzzy and confusing" (Marriotti, 2002, p. 127). During game three of the World Series played at Yankee stadium in New York City, one commentator argued that the hometown New York Yankees served as emblematic combatants "playing for the city and the country and for freedom" (cited in Lee, 2001, p. 1). Baseball was helping "to draw people back out of their houses and into the economy, getting them to spend money again", according to Keith Law, co-author of the annual Baseball Prospectus (King, D. 2001, p. 1C). In a similar way the World Series was seen as lifting the nation from its emotional and economic woes including "restoring some normalcy to troubled Madison Avenue" (McCarthy, 2001, p. 3B).

President Bush's instantaneous outlining of the new war against terrorism where the righteous American and coalition forces would work to "smoke out the terrorists from their hiding places" in order to protect the American borders and (an imagined) way of life follows a similar formula. To the extent that a president stands for a nation, representations of Bush's post-September 11 "hard-bodied" rhetoric and actions much like those echoing throughout the world of sport seek to remasculinize America.[8] In 2004, well after the attacks on the WTC and especially while commenting on the subsequent war in Iraq Bush continues to use vivid language and imagery to portray himself and by extension the nation as capable of decisive and swift action in response to external threats to the American way of life.[9] In late 2004, this idealized way of life continues to be a highly selective one that now includes an emphasis on homeland security, the need to spread democracy worldwide as well as achieving economic recovery and prosperity for transnational corporations and their stockholders. Here profit and security are held in esteem in ways that universal health care, establishing a living wage, civil liberties, the eradication of global poverty, as well as provisions for adequate housing, nutrition and education are not. Rather according to Bush the promise of American recovery is best achieved through both a strengthened military and a continuation of his economic policies of privatization (except for security and military purposes), tax cuts for the wealthy and reinvigorated consumption. The latter would be best achieved according to Bush

(2001b) as Americans "go about our business of going to World Series games or shopping or traveling to Washington, D.C." In this instance, much like advertisers, Bush conceives of the nation within the realm of consumer identification.

Embodying his advice for recovery in 2001 while clad in a Fire Department of New York windbreaker, the former owner of the Texas Rangers baseball club "his jaw firmly set, strode to the Yankee stadium mound before game 3 and from the crest of the hill fired a hard, true strike with the ceremonial first pitch" (Verducci, 2001, p. 117). Here Bush seeks to emerge "as the national hero who expresses the hurt the folks are feeling, but who stands up with them, their pugilist, their world player, their pitcher too" (Johnson, 2002, p. 217).

One writer scripted the subsequent conflation of World Series imagery, the "business as usual" mantra with state power as:

> Three F-14 fighter jets roared overhead and a gigantic American flag was brought on to the field by 60 West Point military cadets. As if all that were not enough, a bald eagle, another symbol of American nationalism, flew down to the pitcher's mound after it was released from a perch on the main scoreboard. A banner draped by fans from one of the upper terraces declared: "America fears nobody – play ball". (Usborne, 2001, p. 9)

Rudolph Giuliani, then the mayor of New York City further endorsed this mixture of Darwinian economics and unreflexive patriotism suggested that Bush's visit showed "we're not afraid, we're undeterred and that life is moving on the way it should" (Usborne, 2001, p. 9). The next day Tim Brosna, an executive vice president of Major League Baseball in New York was quoted as suggesting advances had been made toward recovery as "baseball is getting back to normal. And advertising is getting back to normal" (McCarthy, 2001). Howard Bloom, publisher of the online *Sports Business News*, made explicit the underlying assumptions of similar arguments about a return to normalcy: "Sports is a multibillion-dollar industry, and business needs to go on" (cited in D. King, 2001, p. 1C).

Concluding Thoughts

Without a doubt the events of September 11 and beyond raised questions about our world suggesting linkages "between choices of war and peace", the limitations for most of the world's population of "capitalist political economies, the deepening risk to the bio-sphere and the deep moral ambiguity and ultimate indefensibility of the most privileged ways of life" (Johnson, 2002, p. 228). While many continue to work to ensure more equitable ways of living, within mainstream US élite sporting discourses including MLB, the proliferation of therapeutic discourses, appeals to a "caring nation" and masculine discourses promising a return to "business as usual" help mute these larger global concerns while serving as advertisements and endorsements for policies that largely protect the interests and profits of transnational corporations. The cumulative result is that these particular sporting narratives combine with other dominant framings to obscure competing interpretations sensitive to "intersecting systems of meanings and fragmented identities" as well as the conditions of crisscrossed economic disparities produced through transnational capitalism (Behdad, 2000, p. 398). Still, given the unstable process of these imaginings, it is premature to suggest that these latter constructions are inevitable and indeed one goal of this analysis is to contribute to the practice of identifying and challenging hegemonic interests as the struggle for alternative ways of living continues.

Notes

1. Two examples from the worldwide media responses demonstrate this specificity. For instance, for the first time in recent Iranian history the mantra of "down with the USA" was not spoken during the Friday Prayer out of empathy with pain and suffering wrought by the assaults on the American people (Entezari and Rad, 2002). Malaysian newspaper coverage reflected similar sympathies toward Americans and yet it was also peppered with criticisms directed at recent US economic, military and foreign policy in the "Middle East". Citing the uneven, often disastrous economic and anti-democratic consequences of previous US political and military intervention in the region many commentators not only implored US President George Bush to proceed with caution in responding to bin Laden, but also urged "the US and its allies to deal with the injustice towards the Muslims, Palestinians, Lebanese and Iraqis" (Badarudin, 2002, p. 12). In the US, alternative publications such as the *Nation* (see Heuvel, 2002) offered frequent critiques of US policy initiatives both prior to and after September 11. See Hawthorn and Winter (2002) for examples of feminist critiques.
2. The Internet continues to serve as a transnational site of dissent providing information not often disseminated by the corporate-owned media and Bush administration. One such site is Foreign Policy in Focus (www.foreignpolicy-infocus.org/index.html), For lists of similar URL addresses see George (2002).
3. While I am interested in exploring narratives from the US context, see Lincoln (2002) for an interesting comparison of rhetoric of George Bush and Osama bin Laden. While not suggesting equivalence, Petchesky (2002) offers an analysis of the overlapping posturing between those supporting terrorist networks and those supporting global capitalism.

4. According to (Weisman, 2001), Major League Baseball, the National Football League, Major League Soccer, the Professional Golf Association, the National Hockey League and the U.S. Women's Soccer World Cup Doubleheader (between US and Japan, and Germany and China) all postponed or cancelled play. Some major college conferences postponed events while others played.
5. Additionally, within the US context, this exploitation of a false unity of "we the people", "we the American (sporting) nation" is frequently positioned as White and superior to a socially and psychologically different (typically dark-skinned) other. The latest example of the "terrorists" resonates with a stereotypical vision of a (typically) "dark skinned" other-enemy that is not just replicated in popular culture including countless Hollywood war and action films but also played out in US foreign policy as the "'real life' wars the US has seen fit to fight since World War II have been against nations of color: Korea, Vietnam, Grenada, Iraq and now Afghanistan" (Ehrenreich, 2002, p. 47).
6. Expressions of grief, anger and flag-waving patriotism might also suggest the "need to experience some sense of community and higher purpose in a society where we are so atomized and isolated from one another and the world" according to Petchesky (2002, p. 321).
7. Judith Lorber (2002) argues that media accounts and US governmental rhetoric reproduced binary understandings of gender by repeatedly lauding actions of heroism performed by male rescue workers and decrying the victimization of the women in Afghanistan by the Taliban. Lorber offers evidence that micro-politics of individual actors were much more complicated than these accounts pointing to examples of bravery exemplified by female rescue workers at the World Trade Center and noting collective and personal acts of resistance on the part of Afghani women against the Taliban.
8. Susan Jeffords' (1994) work demonstrates historical antecedents of this process through an investigation of the masculine imagery deployed by then President Ronald Reagan in the 1980s. In this case the "hard body" masculinity promoted by Reagan served to elevate his policies of militarism, individualism and capital expansion in apparent contrast to the soft, liberal, and "weak" ideals of the welfare state and Carter administration. Jeffords also demonstrates the way that this sensibility permeated notable Hollywood films of the era through a celebration of military force, masculine resolve and individualism.
9. One obvious example of similar hard-bodied masculinity is the May 1, 2003, jet landing of Bush on an aircraft carrier thirty-nine miles from San Diego so that in his own words, Bush could "thank our troops". Democrats such as Senator Robert Byrd of West Virginia immediately criticized the President arguing that the event was a publicity stunt designed to launch Bush's re-election bid while costing the American taxpayers approximately one million dollars. Reporter Bob Deans (2003, p. 3A) described the events on the *USS Abraham Lincoln* in this way:

A former fighter pilot in the Texas Air National Guard, Bush donned a flight suit and helmet to fly in the co-pilot's seat of a Navy S-3B Viking, a four-seat jet. The event was carried live on national television, with many stations showing extended footage of Bush swaggering across the flight deck, shaking hands with scores of crew members. Bush addressed the nation from the deck, declaring the Iraq war over.

References

Badarudin, N. B. (2002), *Who's Under Attack? An Analysis of News Presentation of September 11 by Malaysian News Networks.* Paper presented at the twenty-third International Association for Media and Communication Research (IAMCR) Conference, Barcelona, Spain.

Behdad, A. (2000), Global Disjunctures, Diasporic Differences, and the New World (Dis)order. In H. Schwarz and R. Sangeeta (eds), *A Companion to Postcolonial Studies*, Oxford: Blackwell, pp. 396–409.

Berlant, L. (1991), *The Anatomy of National Fantasy: Hawthorne, Utopia and Everyday Life*, Chicago: University of Chicago.

Bush, G. (2001a), Address to the Joint Session of Congress and the American People. Available at www.whitehouse.gov/news/releases.

Bush, G. (2001b), President Calls for Economic Stimulus (National Association of Manufacturers). Available at www.whitehouse.gov/news/releases.

Croucher, S. (2003), Perpetual Imagining: Nationhood in a Global Era. *International Studies Review*, 5, 1–24.

Curry, J. (2001). Flags, songs and tears, and heightened security. *New York Times*, September 18, p. 15.

Deans, B. (2003). Bush Shrugs off Criticism of Trip. *The Atlanta Journal Constitution*, May 8, p. 3A.

Deford, F. (2001). Delay of Games. *Sports Illustrated*, September 24, pp. 62–3.

Detloff, M. (1999), Thinking Peace into Existence. The Spectacle of History in between the Acts, *Women's Studies*, 28, 403–33.

Ehrenreich, N. (2002), Masculinity and American Militarism. *Tikkun*, 17(6), 45–8.

Entezari, A. and Rad, M. M. (2002), *Intercultural Communication Aspects in Iranian Press Caricatures about September 11th and the Related Events*, Paper presented at the twenty-third International Association for Media and Communication Research (IAMCR) Conference, Barcelona, Spain.

Fiske, J. (1994), *Media Matters: Everyday Culture and Political Change*, Minneapolis MN: University of Minnesota.

George, L. (2002), The Pharmacotic War on Terrorism: Cure or Poison for the US Body Politic? *Theory, Culture & Society*, 19(4), 161–86.

Giroux, H. (2002), Democracy, Freedom, and Justice after September 11th: Rethinking the Role of Educators and the Politics of Schooling, *Teachers College Record*, 104(6): 1138–62.

Hawthorne, S. and Winter, B. (eds) (2002), *September 11, 2001: Feminist Perspectives*, North Melbourne: Spinifex.

Hoffer, R. (2001), Play Suspended, *Sports Illustrated*, September 24, pp. 30–1.

Heuvel, K. V. (eds.), *A Just Response: The Nation on Terrorism, Democracy, and September 11, 2001*, New York: Thunder's Mouth/National Books.

Jackson, S. (1998), Life in the (Mediated) Faust lane: Ben Johnson, National Affect and the 1988 Crises of Canadian Identity, *International Review for the Sociology of Sport*, 33(3): 227–238.

Jeffords, S. (1994), *Hard Bodies: Hollywood Masculinity in the Reagan Era*, New Brunswick NJ: Rutgers University.

Johnson, R. (2002), Defending Ways of Life: The (Anti-)terrorist Rhetorics of Bush and Blair. *Theory, Culture & Society*, 19(4): 211–31.

King, D. (2001), History Lesson: Baseball Speeds Recovery for Many during a War, *San Antonio Express-News*, September 19, 1C.

King, P. (2001), *Sports Illustrated*, September 24, pp. 56–61.

Klare, M. The Geopolitics of War. In K. V. Heuvel (eds), *A Just Response: The Nation on Terrorism, Democracy, and September 11, 2001*. New York: Thunder's Mouth/ National Books.

Lee, A. (2001), Laboring Yankees still the Apple of New York's Eye. *The Times (London)*, October 30, p. 1.

Lincoln, B. (2002), *Holy Terrors: Thinking about Religion after September 11*, Chicago: University of Chicago.

Lorber, J. (2002), Heroes, Warriors, and Burqas: A Feminist Sociologist's Reflections on September 11. *Sociological Forum*, 17(3): 377–96.

Mariotti, J. (2002), A Poignant Does of Reality, *Chicago Sun Times*, September 11, p. 127.

McCarthy, M. (2001). Advertisers Quit being Serious for World Series, *USA Today*, November 1, p. 3B.

McDonald, M. G. and Birrell, S. (1999), Reading Sport Critically: A Methodology for Interrogating Power, *Sociology of Sport Journal*, 16: 283–300.

Miller, T., Lawrence, G., McKay, J. and Rowe, D. (2001), *Globalization and Sport: Playing the World*, Thousand Oaks: Sage.

Petchesky, R. (2002), Phantom Towers: Feminist Reflections on the Battle Between Global Capitalism and Fundamental Terrorism. In S. Hawthorne and B. Winter (eds), *September 11, 2001: Feminist Perspectives*, North Melbourne: Spinifex, pp. 58–63.

Scarry, E. (1985), *The Body in Pain: The Making and Unmaking of the World*, New York: Oxford University.

Shapiro, L. (2001), Put Corporate Logo Here; "Virtual Advertising" Draws Eyes, Ire at World Series, *Washington Post*, October 24, p. D2.

Silk, M. and Andrews, D. (2001), Beyond a Boundary? Sport, Transnational Advertising and the Reimagining of National Culture, *Journal of Sport and Social Issues*, 25(2): 180–201.

Tays, A. (2001). Sports Fighting to Bear Market, *The Palm Beach Post*, October 7, p. 1B.

Tickner, J. A. (2001), *Gendering World Politics: Issues and Approaches in the Post-cold War Era*, New York: Columbia University.

Transnational Feminists (2002), Transnational Feminist Practices Against War. In S. Hawthorne and B. Winter (eds), *September 11, 2001: Feminist Perspectives*, North Melbourne: Spinifex, pp. 58–63.

Trujillo, N. (2000), Hegemonic Masculinity on the Mound: Media Representations of Nolan Ryan and American Sport Culture. In S. Birrell and M. McDonald (eds), *Reading Sport: Critical Essays on Power and Representation*, Boston: Northeastern, pp. 14–39.

Usborne, D. (2001), Campaign Against Terrorism: New York – Symbolic Pitch of Baseball Helps a Nation's Healing. *The Independent (London)*, November 1, p. 9.

Verducci, T. (2001), Near, Yet so Far, *Sports Illustrated*, September 24, p. 36.

Weisman, G. (2001), To Play or Not to Play, *USA Today*, September 13, p. 1C.

8

Beyond Sport: Imaging and Re-imaging a Transnational Brand

John Amis

As discussion has intensified over recent years with respect to the impact that various global processes have on our daily lives, so it has become increasingly recognized that we exist in a new global political economy. This has become characterized, and conceptualized, by wide-ranging debates regarding distributions of power and the role of the nation-state, the (co)existence of national and global cultures, the changing nature of local, regional and global economic systems, and an increasingly connected and interdependent network of state and private enterprises. This has led at least one prominent commentator to note that globalization is not incidental to our lives, but a driving force of our time (Giddens, 2002).

A prominent feature of much of this discourse has been the rise in importance of transnational corporations (TNCs). The increasing influence that TNCs can have on the economic stability of countries in all parts of the world becomes apparent when one considers that firms such as Mitsubishi, Mitsui and General Motors regularly report sales figures greater than the gross domestic products of nations such as Denmark, Saudi Arabia and South Africa (Morgan, 1997). Furthermore, it has been estimated that TNCs account for 70 percent of world trade (Perraton et al., 1997). With such firms able to engage in strategies of rapid relocation to search out cheap work forces, favorable trading regulations, and beneficial exchange rates, the political and economic power that they can exert on even highly developed countries can be pronounced.

A further characteristic of the new global economy, characterized by the existence of multiple and highly complex networks of institutions and organizations (Castells, 1996) is the control of information by technology companies, most notably Microsoft, and the influence that media companies such as News Corporation can exert through a seemingly limitless appetite for vertical and horizontal expansion (see, for example, McGaughey and Liesch, 2002). The accompanying heightened managerial complexity is exacerbated when one considers that much of this expansion is occurring at a time when other large firms are reportedly engaging in more flexible forms of accumulation characterized by vertical *dis*integration through processes such as outsourcing and sub-contracting (Harvey, 1989). Consequently, understanding the role of strategic managers within TNCs in general, and for the purposes of this book, in the cultural and sporting industries in particular, has become necessary for any individual interested in global flows of capital, people and political influence.

What makes an understanding of some of the processes that shape global commerce so challenging is the rapidity with which such apparently complex changes are unfurling in political, economic and technological systems around the world. While Ohmae's (1995) prediction of the end of the nation-state appears unfounded, the context of the nation as a location for commercial activity has clearly changed. The extent to which corporations engaged in international trade need to take into account the local environments in which they operate has been a topic of debate, and a point of great contestation, in the international business literature for the last forty years or so. Clearly, though, as the confluence of technologies, systems of political regulation and personal mobility has become more pronounced, so the interest in, and impact of, global commerce has increased.

However, as Parker (1999, p. 235) has noted, while the impact of globalization may be revolutionary, our understanding of it proceeds in a more evolutionary manner:

> those who manage organizations under conditions of globalization also recognize the multiplicity, variety and complexity of issues associated with it, but many are too busy coping with change to either document or explain it. Consequently, descriptions of the practices associated with these revolutionary changes are more anecdotal than organized.

Perhaps as a consequence, the empirical evidence regarding the impact of international diversification on firm profitability is decidedly mixed (Hitt, et al., 1997; Vermeulen and Barkema, 2002). While there are a number of well known TNCs that are able to straddle the globe and operate highly successfully (from a shareholder standpoint!), there are numerous others that have succumbed to the vagaries and complexities associated with competing in a global marketplace.

Consequently, the purpose of this chapter is to add to our understanding of the operation of TNCs and some of the associated global processes that affect strategic decision-making through an analysis of the Guinness brand. In particular, in keeping with the theme of this book, the intent is to examine the role of cultural intermediaries responsible for the development and implementation of brand positioning in different locales, and the ways in which sport is used to deliver particular brand messages in Guinness' three major markets, Ireland, Great Britain and Africa. This is particularly apposite because, whereas the brand management of Guinness has recently become highly centralized, there is a realization that the firm must also remain sensitive to the idiosyncrasies of its various local marketplaces. Thus, Guinness presents an example of a brand that has to wrestle with the at times seemingly paradoxical complexities of engaging with global processes intensified by the technologically induced compressions of time and space while retaining the traditional appeal upon which the brand has been constructed. In the next sections, I explore some of these processes in more detail before going on to an empirical examination of the strategies employed to market what has become a highly distinctive and well known global brand.

The Rise of the Transnational Corporation

While writers may disagree about the impact of globalization, when it began, or what it means, there is little doubt that private firms have been engaged in systematic cross-border trade for several hundred years. The precursor for the modern TNC can be traced back to the Industrial Revolution, which precipitated large-scale production practices and a subsequent spread of international trade, particularly by British-based firms (Hirst and Thompson, 1999). However, it was during the second half of the twentieth century that a combination of technological advances and favorable legislation led to opportunities for an unprecedented number of firms to engage in international trade and the subsequent rise in influence of what have become widely, and often loosely, termed "transnational corporations".[1] The widespread use of the term "transnational" has resulted in a somewhat nebulous conception of a monolith that operates with impunity across temporal and spatial dimensions. It is a term that, as globalization, is at once widely used, ill-defined, contested and often poorly understood. The need for definition is thus important and beyond semantics. A useful starting point for such a definition is the highly influential work of Bartlett and Ghoshal (1989).

In assessing the structures, strategies and operating practices of nine firms engaged in international business, Bartlett and Ghoshal (1989) uncovered three distinctive models that they felt were indicative of large organizations engaged in cross-border trade. The *multi-national form* was seen to derive its competitive advantage by "building strong local presence through sensitivity and responsiveness to national differences" (p. 15); the *global form* sought to "build cost advantages through centralized global–scale operations" (p. 15); the *international form* was seen to derive its advantages from "exploiting parent company knowledge and capabilities through worldwide diffusion and adaptation" (p. 15). Bartlett and Ghoshal (1989) noted that while each of these forms had worked well in the past, operating environments characterized by increasing levels of competitive activity, heightened volatility and rapid rates of change, pointed to the need for a different strategic approach. In this new global arena, successful firms would be required to develop global efficiencies, multi-national flexibility and worldwide learning capabilities simultaneously. While Bartlett and Ghoshal (1989) termed this the *transnational solution*, and saw it as a changed management mentality rather than a distinctive form in its own right, we can develop this line of thought to define a *transnational corporation* as a firm that is structured and operated in such a way that it takes advantage of certain efficiencies of scale and scope by operating internationally; details products or services to meet local requirements; and has the capability of operating flexibly and quickly in response to, or in anticipation of, rapid changes in its operating environment, be they competitive, technological, economic or political in origin.

This final point normally requires that organizations be able to develop and implement a system of global organizational learning whereby advances made in one part of the organization can be rapidly transmitted elsewhere. In this way, actual and potential problems can be quickly recognized and dealt with in an efficient manner. Thus, implementing an efficient mechanism of global learning is a feature of true TNCs. While there have been questions as to the applicability of knowledge generated in one country being transferred elsewhere (Delios and Beamish, 2001), this clearly depends on the nature of the organization and the knowledge being transferred. Most commentators agree that promoting interdependence, rather than dependence or independence, among sub-units enhances flows of knowledge, intelligence, ideas and resources that can in turn make each sub-unit stronger than, in particular, local national competitors (Bartlett and Ghoshal, 1987). As Bartlett and Ghoshal (1989, p. 12) pointed out, managers of successful TNCs "see that they can gain competitive advantage by sensing needs in one country, responding with capabilities located in a second, and diffusing the resulting innovation to markets around the world."

Of course, while a TNC needs to have the capability of simultaneously meeting the demands laid out above, it does not need to do so across all of its operations at the same time. For example, a TNC may have opportunities to derive a competitive advantage from purchasing, manufacturing, packaging, distribution, marketing, customer service, research and design, software development or some other aspect of the firm's business. It may be possible to gain from economic scale advantages in critical functions such as research and design, amortize investments in areas such as brand development over a broader base, exploit market imperfections, or exhibit greater bargaining power over influential institutions (Hitt, Hoskisson and Kim, 1997). Thus, there may be opportunities for efficiencies from standardized operations and scale economies in some activities, opportunities for increased innovation from economies of scope in other activities, and specializations to meet local needs where necessary elsewhere (Segal-Horn and Faulkner, 1999). This strategic approach has been exemplified in the past by firms such as Sony, Matsushita, IKEA, PepsiCo, Procter & Gamble and McDonald's. In other words, we can conceive of TNCs as functioning within fundamentally changed operating parameters of time, space, and culture, and thus having a much wider array of available strategic options than has previously been the case.

National Identity and Local Resonance

Much of the debate regarding the opportunities and outcomes of global strategizing intensified following Levitt's (1983) prediction of the convergence of markets as a result of increasing economic and socio-political interdependencies. In particular, Levitt argued that new communications technologies would lead to an increasing homogenization of markets and a concomitant reduction in social, economic and cultural differences. While much of Levitt's (1983) theorizing has been dismissed as an overly extreme representation of the impact of global forces, it is undeniable that national identities have been heavily affected by the permeability of markets to cultural carriers. Tomlinson (1999), for example, has argued that the place of habitation is no longer the main pillar of identity. Parker (1999, p. 244) similarly suggested: "in a globalizing world, the nation-state is not necessarily the main source of culturally acceptable behaviours or beliefs as behaviours, norms, assumptions and values emerge from outside national boundaries. In this sense, culture becomes 'boundaryless' as business activities transcend national borders."

Of course, a major reason for this has been the technological advances that have resulted in a compression of time and space, and that in turn have served to extend the range and quicken the pace of commercial interactions of all types. In fact, Harvey (1989) has suggested that time and space have disappeared as meaningful dimensions when it comes to considering human thought and actions. Technologies such as the Internet, satellite television, personal digital assistants (PDAs) and even electronic banking and stock market transactions were in a nascent state when Ohmae (1990) presented his conception of a 'borderless world', but a decade on technological advances have resulted in seemingly instant access to a multitude of activities and information, whether work- or entertainment-related, at almost anytime of our choosing, irrespective of where we are in the world.

One outcome of this has been the ways in which satellite television is able to "collapse world spaces" into a series of televisual images (Harvey, 1989). In this way, events, people and processes from around the world can be almost instantly communicated and have an immediate influence (Morley and Robins, 1995; Miller, 1998). Satellite television networks such as BSkyB and Star TV, along with more specialized providers such as MTV and Eurosport, can instantly and simultaneously transmit popular culture, and associated advertising, beyond international boundaries. This is exemplified, according to Parker (1999), by the spread of English as a global language, and the proliferation of common consumer goods and services, from cola to jeans, television entertainment to music, films to clothes. It is thus apposite to consider the extent to which the nation-state is being transformed (Mann, 1997) and the impact that this may have on TNC marketing.

Building on the work of Kahn (1995) and Robertson (1995), Parker (1999, p. 235) argued that, rather than increasing cultural homogeneity, "as boundaries dissolve, as barriers are permeated, as the world compresses, as we become interdependent, we become more aware of cultural *difference* and diversity" (emphasis in original). Consequently, the nation retains its importance as a point of identity and differentiation (Silk and Andrews, 2001).

If we consider national identity to be something of an anchor that plays on the psyche of local consumers, then it becomes incumbent upon TNCs to play to local sensibilities rather than seeking some homogenous global appeal. It is therefore of little surprise that many global marketers are keen to draw on elements of local culture and nostalgia (Morley and Robins, 1995). Sport can be particularly effective in accomplishing this, hence the massive investment of TNCs such as Coca-Cola, Nike, Adidas, and McDonald's in local sports teams and competitions around the globe. In this respect, the nation, far from being obsolete as Ohmae (1995) predicted, appears to be a highly important signifier of place, identity and culture. Resonating with these abstract axioms appears to be a necessary component of any TNC's strategic positioning.

Managerial Complexity

The foregoing discussion illustrates that a TNC must try to function in such a way that it allows the firm to realize certain economies that should be available when following a multi-national strategy, it must be able to respond to local idiosyncrasies, and it should be able to apply learning that takes place in one part of the organization to other parts spread around the world. Further, geographic dispersion of sub-units, varying government regulations, trade laws, currency fluctuations, cultural diversity, social costs, and country differences in access to raw materials and skilled labor all work to increase transaction costs and managerial processing demands (Bartlett and Ghoshal, 1989; Hitt et al., 1994, 1997; Vermeulen and Barkema, 2002). In effect, managers have to engage in individual local relationships, such as negotiating with workers and local suppliers, while coordinating the global flow of capital (Castells, 1996).

The consequence of this is that strategic management in a TNC is highly complex. While this may be something of a truism, it bears saying because of the inherently simplistic approach that many analysts and managers have adopted in trying to comprehend the ways in which such firms are operated. In carrying out 250 interviews with managers from nine of the (then) biggest multi-nationals in the world, Bartlett and Ghoshal (1987) reported that when faced with complexity, managers largely reduced strategic decisions to a series of dichotomous choices, such as national responsiveness or global integration; centralized or decentralized allocation of assets and resources; central control or subsidiary autonomy. Yip (1989) similarly reduced his discussion of global forces to a consideration of either a "pure multi-domestic" or a "pure global" strategy. Finally, Hitt et al. (1997) reported that the complexity of governance often exceeds managerial capabilities and thus executives may shift from an emphasis on strategic controls that require an in-depth understanding of each sub-unit's operations and markets and significant coordination between business- and corporate-level managers to one that gives priority to more easily understood financial measures. This search for simplifying measures, by managers and academics, highlights a lack of understanding as to how strategic managers work to meet the demands of operating in a TNC. The remainder of this paper seeks to shed some light on this through an exploration of the activities of those cultural intermediaries responsible for the worldwide positioning of the Guinness brand.

'Believe!' The Transnational Positioning of the Guinness Brand[2]

The Guinness brand dates back to 1759 when founder Arthur Guinness paid £100 for a 9,000 year lease on St James's Gate Brewery in Dublin. Originally a brewer of traditional ale, Guinness became intrigued by a distinctive black beer imported from England known as porter. Guinness decided that the future of his company lay with porter rather than ale, and thus by the end of the eighteenth century he was brewing only the black beer that would make the firm famous. Extensive expansion over the course of the nineteenth century resulted in Guinness, by 1886, becoming the largest brewery in the world with an annual production of 1.2 million barrels and established markets in North and South America, Africa, the Far East and Australia (Brand Map, 2001).

The twentieth century saw continued expansion, largely as a result of a series of technical innovations that radically improved product quality and allowed casked, canned and bottled beer to be sold all over the world. Consequently, by 2001 Guinness had developed three major variants packaged in eight different ways (Guinness Global Strategy Presentation, 2001). Despite the steady global expansion that had resulted in Guinness becoming one of the most recognized brands in the world, the end of the twentieth century found Guinness with a fragmented marketing approach and some indifferent financial results (Brand Map, 2001). Along with this, a series of mergers and takeovers ultimately resulted in Guinness becoming a "premium global brand" in the Diageo stable rather than a standalone company. The time was thus appropriate to reconsider the strategy that underpinned brand positioning across the globe.

The global brand director (GBD) informed me that, at the start of the twenty-first century, Guinness was moving from a strategy of "growth, growth, growth" to one that was underpinned by the philosophy that "it's not only about pure growth, it's about how you grow". Central to this has been the transnational positioning of the brand. Three key themes emerged from the data as underpinning this revised approach: a pronounced policy of organizational learning, a desire to benefit from the advantages available to a firm that trades globally, and a realization that such a global strategy must be implemented in a way that retains a local resonance with disparate populations. Clearly these are not discrete; in fact their coherent integration is a necessary feature of an effective transnational strategy. An analysis of the implementation of these three strategic initiatives forms the balance of this chapter.

"Share and Spin": The Implementation of Organizational Learning

Effective systems of organizational learning that allow dispersed sub-units to benefit from each others' advances are seen as a vital component of TNCs (Bartlett and Ghoshal, 1989). This is seen as particularly important in overcoming national brands that often have some "home field" advantages, such as increased understanding of local idiosyncrasies, long-standing labor or resource agreements, or an established cultural tradition and reputation. Recognition of this within Guinness has resulted in the development of a formal program, known as "Share & Spin". Under this program, each market, with the assistance of the global brand team (GBT), is expected to draw on initiatives that have been successfully implemented elsewhere, adapt them as necessary, and introduce them to the local market. As outlined in an internal 'Guinness Global Strategy Presentation' (2001, p. 8), the GBT is expected to track the return on investment of different sub-units and come up with a listing of low-performing "Dogs" and high-performing "Stars", and "share and spin proven 'stars'". It is intended for a "model to be developed for each activity of principles and deployment guidelines so [good practice] can be adapted and adopted across markets". Mann

(1997) has suggested that the global is a complex mix of the local, the national, the "inter-national" and the transnational. It is through processes of organizational learning that managers are able to determine the various components of this mix, something that is particularly necessary if growth is to be attained by TNCs in highly competitive markets. The assistant brand manager for Ireland (ABM – Ireland) informed me that out of a total of 3.6 million inhabitants, just over one million are of legal drinking age. As he suggested, the most attractive segment of this market are those that are thirty-five and under: "there must be thirty major drink brands that are targeting them because they are the ones with, as you can probably imagine, the disposable income, the leisure time, social time, and it's a highly, highly competitive market." Such intense competition, present not just in Ireland but worldwide, highlights the need for an effective learning process.

The implementation of "Share and Spin" is carried out in a number of ways: "Open and frequent communication between markets, the GBE [Global Brand Executive], and the GBT; sharing ideas and trading information via the quarterly Team Guinness newsletter; cross-market peer group work on key initiatives" (Guinness Global Strategy Presentation, 2001, p. 9). A major component of this involves extensive meetings held between members of the GBT and those in local markets. A member of the GBT will travel to each major market at least once a month with the GBD himself travelling to most major markets two or three times a year (see Figure 8.1). According to the GBD, this is seen as a two-way process whereby the GBT can act as a conduit of learning, bringing ideas that have proved useful in other markets and also collating information that may have utility elsewhere. This was confirmed by the brand director for Africa (BD-Africa), suggesting that the GBT play "a consultation role in terms of sharing best practice, what is happening in Great Britain, what is happening in Ireland, and sharing best practice to us and supporting us in areas where possibly we may not have the specialized capability that is required." The BD-Africa carries out a similar role, working with his regional team to disseminate learning among, in particular, the five most prominent African markets of Nigeria, Cameroon, Ghana, Kenya, and Ivory Coast.

While organizational learning has been widely recognized as a mechanism to improve performance in competitive markets, there are those who have urged a degree of caution in its implementation. Vermeulen and Barkema (2002), for example, have suggested that any form of expansion in building TNCs is subject to time compression diseconomies whereby rates of return are diminished as complexity of the organization increases. Thus, initiatives that are designed to spread operating practices from one country to another must be introduced at a rate that does not negatively impact the cognitive processing abilities of

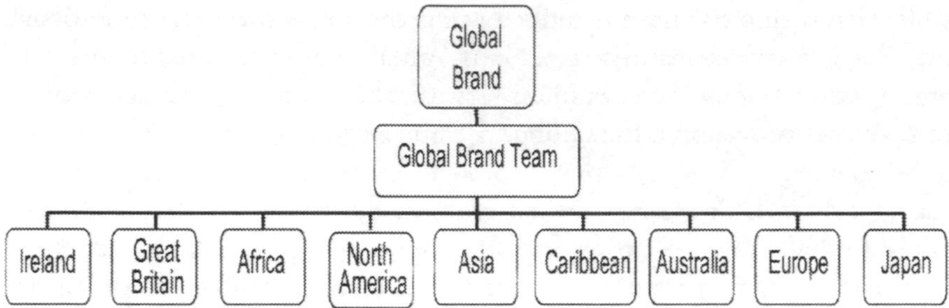

Figure 8.1. *Guinness Global Management Team.*

sub-unit managers. As Eisenhardt and Martin (2000) pointed out, experience that comes too rapidly can be overwhelming and consequently not allow managers to transform new experiences into "meaningful learning". Notwithstanding that proviso, organizational learning is undeniably important in developing or maintaining a competitive advantage.

Two major ways in which organizational learning has become manifest at Guinness are the implementation of a "global study" and the development of a common advertisement for transmission across multiple markets. The global study was carried out over 2000 and 2001 in Guinness' major markets with the intent of uncovering a single "Key Brand Benefit" (KBB), intended to provide a common focal point for virtually all brand development initiatives across the world. The representatives that I spoke to from Africa and Ireland claimed that their markets had been particularly influential in coming up with the KBB: Guinness reflects my inner strength. According to the BD-Africa:

> There was a global study, around the whole world, trying to get out a key brand benefit. And inner strength, which is a key brand benefit in Africa, came out tops. So globally that key brand benefit has been accepted . . . What we've done is that our own key brand benefit which we have developed has now become a global one and the global ads are therefore driving the same key brand benefits.

In other words, "best-practices" had been accumulated by the GBT from Africa and other markets, collated and distributed back to other local teams, primarily in the form of the KBB.

The development of the KBB has been accompanied by the creation of the global "Believe!" advertising campaign. The first advertisement created in this campaign, "Free In", is set at the end of a hurling match and was thus seen, particularly by the Irish brand team, as being a natural progression from the sponsorship in Ireland of the "Guinness All-Ireland Hurling Championship".

This sponsorship has been described as the most effective sport sponsorship in Ireland (*Sponsorship Strategies*, 2000). A reason for this, cited by the head of sponsorship for Guinness in Ireland (HS-Ireland), is the close match between the values that underpin the Guinness brand and the sport.

> We looked at the DNA of both hurling and Guinness and they are so remarkably similar . . . it's 9.9 out of 10. It's so, so perfect. So when we saw or heard the concept behind the new 'Believe!' campaign was going to be around hurling, we said sure, it's so obvious. We've tested it, and it's proven over the last eight years to be a perfect fit.

Thus there is further evidence of organizational learning occurring as the GBT seek to build on what has been successful in one market and utilize that elsewhere.

It has been suggested that knowledge and capabilities developed in one country may have limited applicability when transferred across borders (Madhok, 1997; Delios and Beamish, 2001). However, this is mitigated here by the length of time that Guinness has had a presence in most of its major foreign markets. It has a history of transferring technological and other advances from one location to another (Simmons and Griffiths, 2001) that has been incorporated over time into Guinness' "administrative heritage" (Bartlett and Ghoshal, 1989). This combination of time and experience has been shown to offset some of the difficulties that TNCs may encounter when seeking to adapt assets from one country to allow exploitation in another (Delios and Beamish, 2001). Thus, Guinness would seem to be well positioned to benefit from a common KBB and the "Believe!" hurling campaign, something to which I now turn in greater detail.

"Inner Strength": Realizing a Common Global Initiative

According to the GBD, the marketing of Guinness is now carried out in a much more centralized and coherent way than it was at the turn of 2000. As he explained in an interview in August 2001:

> I suppose in the past we were a quite decentralized business. Certainly 18 months ago we had seven advertising agencies; we had seven different key brand benefits around the world. There was very little central marketing. And we've moved away from that. We are now probably much more centralized. And we do believe that Guinness is a global brand . . . The benefits of a global brand strategy leverage off commonalities that lead to consumer benefits.

The rationale for the shift to just two advertising agencies, BBDO and Saatchi & Saatchi, and a single KBB was summed up in the Guinness Global Strategy Presentation (2001, p. 7) referred to earlier: "Multiple communication platforms fragment our message, confuse the consumer, and reduce the impact of our marketing, whereas focussed communication builds strong, powerful brands." The reasons for this increased fragmentation was outlined by the brand manager for Great Britain (BM-GB), and centered upon the various technological advances that have altered the time-space dynamic in which Guinness competes.

> From a parochial point of view, for myself in Great Britain, was every time we showed an ad on satellite TV over here, that ad was also shown to everyone in Ireland who was watching satellite TV at the time, which is a fair audience. And when Ireland and ourselves had very different styles of advertising, which was only say a year ago, then that was becoming more and more of a problem: that consumers would be watching satellite one minute, see one completely different ad with a different strap line and a different idea behind it, to when they switched on to their terrestrial TV. And there are more examples of that, of media starting to cross more countries. Also, the fact that, whether or not it was just consumers in one country or consumers moving around from country to country, they would see a slightly schizophrenic brand because in different countries you would see such a different type of positioning around it. And then thirdly, also an element of cost efficiency by the fact that ultimately we can reach the stage where we can show the same advert in different countries.

Thus, while there is a desire to realize efficiencies that a global advertising strategy can deliver (Hitt et al., 1997), it is the collapsing of time and space precipitated by technological advancements and the increasing flow of people around the world for work or leisure reasons that has been a determining factor on the decision to reposition Guinness as a brand with a common global strategy. Of course, central to this has been the development of the KBB that underpins all brand communications for each of the different variants (see Figure 8.2). Following the 'global study' referred to above, Guinness announced "we have a powerful global consumer insight on which we are building our vision: In a world of increasing speed, disconnection and uncertainty, young men need to draw on their 'innate' inner strength" (Guinness Global Strategy Presentation, 2001, p. 2). Crucially, the KBB was seen as a message that would resonate across the brand's global markets, a testimony to the organizational learning that had precipitated its emergence. Thus, irrespective of where the young men who constitute the brand's target market were located, the notion of "Guinness reflects my inner strength" was perceived by the cultural intermediaries who settled on the slogan as having an immediate worldwide affinity and appeal. As the GBD pointed out, "we know that our brand fulfils this need of inner strength. So whichever market you go into, Africa, the UK, Ireland, Guinness brings out my inner strength . . . is a commonly held belief and a very motivating belief." Thus, while the KBB is common to all markets, it is felt that the widely resonant nature of the message will overcome the type of disjuncture that Appadurai (1990) noted as a common problem when it comes to realizing global

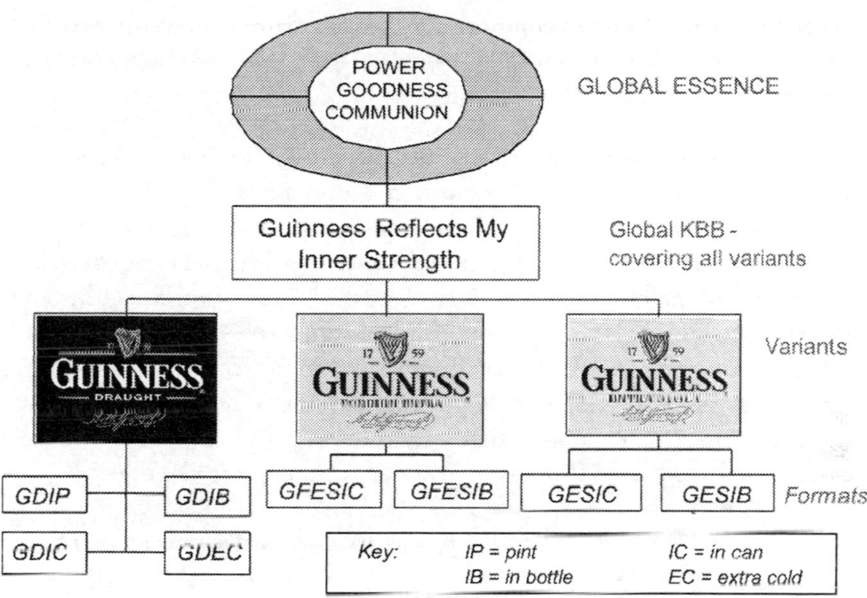

Figure 8.2. *Guinness Brand architecture. Adapted from Guinness Brand Strategy (2001).*

processes in local cultures. It was also felt that the KBB could be communicated as being underpinned by the brand values, or brand essence, of power, goodness and communion, as illustrated in Figure 8.2, that to varying degrees had long featured in the brand's marketing. Thus the history and tradition that the GBD and ABM-Ireland informed me are felt so keenly by all those involved with Guinness could still be drawn upon.

The first transnational manifestation of the KBB is the "Believe!" campaign that highlights the ways in which young men can draw on their inner strength, articulated as self-belief, to achieve challenging objectives. Central to this is the use of sporting analogies to deliver the KBB, most notably the "Free In" hurling advertisement referred to earlier. The narrative from the advertisement vividly depicts the unfurling scenario (Guinness, 2002).

> Just one minute of injury time left in a knife-edge match and a vicious foul creates a chance. Over the bar and the game is tied, but into the goal and the game is won. Stepping up to take the free as the crowd go wild, our man's mind spins out of control. His doubts turn the opposition into gladiators bristling with steel in an impossibly distant goal – Gunmen and bared-teeth primates loom menacingly on the sidelines. The sliother [ball] and hurley [stick] shape-shift . . . With a deep breath the player looks down. He sees himself and the coveted

> silver cup held aloft on the shoulders of exuberant fans, victoriously sipping a well-earned pint of creamy Guinness stout. Inspired by the vision of success he whips the ball up off the ground. If you want it, you've got to believe!

This advertisement was launched in Great Britain in February 2002 and was subsequently rolled out across Guinness' major markets.

The reason for using hurling, a little known Irish sport that appears to be a combination of field hockey and lacrosse played on a field that is approximately the size of a football[3] pitch with hybrid football and rugby goals at either end, was articulated by the BM-GB. He noted that during trials, the advertisement's storyline was consumer tested using football and rugby scenarios. It was found that football was simply not seen as a good fit for Guinness in the highly important British market, and that while rugby was seen as fitting well with the Guinness brand, it held no appeal for those consumers who did not like rugby.

> What hurling gave was a generic sport that people didn't necessarily know exactly the rules, but they got the idea that it was a last-minute free-kick [sic], and were therefore able to take out the point of the bloke needing self-belief to score.

This point was further reinforced by the decision to utilize a nameless, unknown figure as the central character, seemingly something of an anomaly in an age of global celebrities (Andrews and Jackson, 2001; Wong and Trumper, 2002). The desire is clearly that the KBB should not be overshadowed by the sport or the characters within it. This point was further emphasized by the HS-Ireland:

> The concept behind the hurling ad is nothing to do with hurling as such. That's just the execution. The idea behind it is that here is a guy who is calling on his inner-most strength to achieve something in life that is worth doing. . .. And that doesn't really make an awful lot of difference whether it is hurling or anything else. Hurling [just] demonstrates it very, very well.

It also, of course, carries a distinctly Irish theme that promotes the heritage of the brand in a manner that will resonate with different segments of the population, albeit in different ways. Consequently, whereas the advertisement employs common imagery that *may* be differentially interpreted, it effectively carries the generic KBB, "Guinness reflects my inner strength". Thus, in a world characterized by an interweaving of simulacra into daily life in a manner that brings different worlds into the same time and space (Harvey, 1989), Guinness becomes overtly attached to, and works to (re)create a heritage as an Irish sporting brand. In this respect, Guinness is working towards creating a global campaign that seeks to draw affiliations with particular lifestyles and values rather than distinct national territories (Silk and Andrews, 2001). While it is too early to perceive any noticeable impact on sales, market testing certainly suggested that the hurling advertisement will have the desired effect of linking the brand with the KBB.

Of course, this use of sport in an advertisement is just one way in which firms try to associate their brands with specific properties. The ways in which Guinness has attempted to do this in different markets is discussed below, with particular emphasis accorded to the ways in which the firm tries to use sport to resonate with local populations.

The Place of the Nation: Local Resonance

Sport has long enjoyed a prominence within Guinness' marketing initiatives, particularly at the local level. The 1999 Rugby World Cup did allow Guinness to engage with a major sport property on something of a global scale, and indeed was regarded as very successful in several key markets (Rines, 2001). However, while the GBD expressed his desire to attain a sporting property that could be exploited across different markets, he has yet to be able to find an appropriate property that is both available and priced at an acceptable level. Nevertheless, within national markets sport is perceived to deliver the KBB in a distinctive manner that resonates with the local population. This is important because, while the global hurling advertisement may have utility at prompting awareness of a particular brand benefit, advertising assets have traditionally been seen to be less fungible than most organization resources and thus most in need of local adaptation (Anand and Delios, 2002). Thus, a local component that resonates with national sensibilities appears to be a necessary feature of any transnational marketing campaign. The BD-Africa articulated how this unfolds within certain African markets:

> I am saying the need for self-belief, the need for inner strength is particularly relevant in Africa. The reason for this is that Africans see themselves as coming from a disadvantage. In every way of life, Africa is behind the world. Again Africans believe, because we are Africans we can overcome all of those obstacles and we can achieve things almost of world standard. It comes through in football and we've leveraged it, so one good example will be where we begin to say . . . if you believe in yourself and your ability you can overcome your obstacles and your disadvantages and perform at a first world class. We have leveraged that during the [football] World Cup with the football ad, where we have shown Africans training on sub-standard pitches, without sports equipment and saying 'Well, because we are what we are, because we believe in ourselves, we can overcome' and then we lead on from that showing national teams, African national teams, that have played in the World Cup and have performed well. So again,

> it is tying that need of Africans to believe that in spite of our disadvantages we can still be reckoned with at the global stage, and tying that to the brand benefit of inner strength, that it reflects your inner strength.

It clearly emerged from the data that there are three ways in which Guinness makes use of sport to promote the KBB; and as every participant informed me and several electronic and more traditional documents reinforced, every marketing initiative, sport related or otherwise, has to build towards the KBB, with the exception of some product promotions built around St. Patrick's Day. The first of these is direct sponsorship. In all three markets that I examined, Guinness sponsored several different properties. In Africa, this mainly revolved around football, such as the local Guinness marketing team in Cameroon sponsoring the national team in the African Cup of Nations, a tournament that the team won. Each local marketing team was encouraged to develop a football sponsorship program that supported their national teams, particularly those that qualified for the 2002 World Cup Finals in Japan and Korea. In Great Britain, Guinness currently sponsors, among others, London Irish Rugby Football Club, a professional team that plays in the highest division of professional rugby in England. It also sponsors the Cheltenham Horseracing Festival, noted for its prominent Irish theme and the fact that thousands of Irish racing supporters travel over from Ireland to attend the week's races. In Ireland, among the multitude of sponsorships that include golf and horseracing, the most notable is the "Guinness All-Ireland Hurling Championship". This event has been supported by Guinness for over eight years, and is seen as being a flagship sponsorship by the Irish brand team. In each of these cases, the cultural intermediaries at Guinness seek to use a direct sporting affiliation to prominently place the brand within the various nations' identities. In this way sport is used to exploit the cultural differences referred to by Parker (1999) in a way that draws out, and resonates with, key elements of local culture and nostalgia (Morley and Robins, 1995).

The second major way in which Guinness uses sport is through in-house promotions tied to televised sporting events. In Ireland, there is a carefully orchestrated series of events that tie in with the All-Ireland Hurling Championship, and work to encourage Irish people to get together with their friends to watch the televised games in local pubs. Quiz nights, musical entertainment and local talent competitions are all used to encourage individuals to drink Guinness in their local pub while the games are being played (Not Men, but Giants, 2001). In England, the brand director for Great Britain (BD-GB) informed me that Guinness had spent £2 million on promotions around the 2002 Football World Cup Finals and £500,000 on the 2002 Six Nations Rugby Championship. Thus, even though no money had been spent on official sponsorships, the brand had been closely tied to both high-profile competitions. The move towards football is something that is new within Great Britain, but one that members of the brand team in Great Britain informed me has become more relevant and more acceptable to consumers. The resonance of the promotion was explained by the BD-GB with reference to England captain David Beckham's goals that first ensured that England qualified for the World Cup Finals and second resulted in a decisive win against one of the pre-tournament favorites, Argentina:

> David Beckham scoring a free kick in the last minute against Greece in the World Cup qualifiers; scoring a penalty against Argentina in the World Cup. Just look at his face as he goes to take it, and he controls his breathing and he settles himself and it's all about self-belief. We believe that there are a huge amount of self-belief moments in sport and in some ways the fans in the pub need a bit of self-belief when they're watching the matches as well!

Third, Guinness uses sport as a theme in many of its television advertisements. The hurling "Believe!" advertisement referred to above is one obvious example. Here, although the sport may not resonate with local consumers, for example in a British market, the message and imagery certainly do, particularly as they have been reinforced by other initiatives promoting the same KBB. Sports that play well with local sensibilities are, of course, also used. In Africa, there have been several television advertising campaigns that have featured the fictitious Michael Power, a character adept at getting people out of uncomfortable situations. The BD-Africa explained the development of the Michael Power character, and how football is used to make the advertisements more relevant to consumers:

> He is like a brand icon and we have run three minute ads, which are what we call dramas, stories about the role of this character. And basically, the positions we have placed him have been in difficult situations. When people are in difficult situations, Michael Power arrives and he sorts it out. And he sorts it out using, not brute strength, but his intelligence, quick thinking and strength of character. And we have various stories about this, so much so that Michael Power now is well rooted in the minds of our consumers. What we've now done in the second phase is we are saying, apart from Michael Power being a James Bond kind of character, how do we bring him more into the day to day life of Nigerians, or of Africans in a way that drives affinity with the brand? So what we've done is said "What are the key things that Africans value of their lifestyle?" We have said, one, we know there's a big passion for football and football is one part of, one way of life that Africans also excel in. And what we've then done is to use the same Michael Power character to cut a 45 second advert which is all about the power of African football. And there he is talking to Africans and we are showing football cuts in it,

> and he is talking to Africans about, that if you believe, you can achieve it and in spite of your obstacles and your disadvantages, with hard work and perseverance that you will, that we will excel. And he is saying this against the Guinness branding, and the Guinness brand actually is properly integrated in that. And the thing for the consumers is that one, that Guinness recognizes our passion for football and supports it. And both Guinness and Michael Power are therefore getting more affinity with the brand.

In this way, Guinness provides what Harvey (1989) called "an image, a simulacrum, a pastiche" to create artificially a tradition that ties the brand and prominent local sport teams, events or hyperreal characters together in an evocative manner.

No matter what the mode of delivery, direct sponsorship, in-house promotion, or television advertisements, sport clearly plays an important role in delivering the KBB to consumers in a locally sensitive and male-oriented way. Further, they are also articulated in a way that promotes the underlying global brand essence (see Figure 8.2). The nature of the sports that are associated with the brand, such as football, rugby, hurling and horseracing exemplify the use of controlled "Power" in competitive situations. The gathering together of fans, in what the Irish brand team term tribalism, exemplifies "Communion". The notion that sport is there to be enjoyed and that Guinness is working to enhance that experience through various promotions or sponsorships highlights the traditional notion of "Goodness", long associated with the Guinness brand. The ways in which these various sporting associations contribute to the manifestation of Guinness' image and reputation, while beyond the scope of this chapter, are explored in Amis (2003).

The HS-Ireland further suggested "the values that are associated with the Guinness brand and the values that you would associate with Ireland are very similar." Depictions of Ireland typically revolve around Celtic traditions imbued with mystery and spiritualism, the rugged west coast, friendly people, traditional farms, small, historic towns and of course rural pubs. The notions of power, goodness and communion are easily associated with such images, and thus, as the GBD explained, the Irish heritage of the brand is heavily emphasized in some markets, notably those that are home to the Irish diaspora. "In some markets where it exists, like Great Britain, Ireland obviously, the USA, Australia, it tends to be our draught markets [the Irish heritage of the brand is exploited]; in Africa and Asia, it means nothing." Thus, the Guinness brand is positioned in a way that maximizes its resonance with different national markets, and further than that of course, with particular segments of those markets, be they young Nigerian males of legal drinking age interested in football, English rugby fans, or followers of hurling in Ireland. Andrews and Cole (2002, p. 123) pointed out, "the 'nation' remains a virulent force in everyday lived experience". This is certainly recognized and exploited at Guinness.

Conclusion

It is quite apparent that cultural intermediaries, as with managers of TNCs generally, have to cope with tremendous complexity when devising a brand positioning strategy that encompasses multiple national markets. First, there is a need for systematic programs of organizational learning that allow firms to take advantages of advances in brand development and global efficiencies. Second, cultural intermediaries must demonstrate an ability to not only cope with compressions of time and space that have radically altered the ways in which consumers receive and perceive advertising texts, but to profit from this changed global environment. Third, there is a requirement that advertising messages are presented in a way that plays to local sensibilities. Finally, and perhaps most importantly, each of these requirements must be met in a coordinated and coherent manner if brand messages are not to become fragmented and confused. Despite these requirements being central characteristics to TNCs (Bartlett and Ghoshal, 1989), our understanding as to how managers deal with these complexities remains underdeveloped.

As we have seen here, cultural intermediaries at Guinness have not only recognized the need to embrace organizational learning to take advantage of global flows and processes while retaining national resonance, they have put together a coherent strategy that takes advantage of central coordination and local interpretation. This local interpretation can take many forms, not just in terms of the sports and events that utilized, or the media through which advertising messages are communicated, but also the ontological perspective on the position of the brand. For example, despite the long history of Guinness in Africa, it is still viewed relatively simply as a brand of beer. Football is used because it is seen as a way of forming an attachment between Guinness and local consumers in a way that promotes the KBB. In Ireland, the brand is viewed by the Guinness advertising managers to whom I spoke as being embedded in Irish culture in much the same way as the shamrock, hurling, the Ceílí and set dancing. Consequently, there is a widely held belief that brand managers have a responsibility to safeguard an icon of national import: the use of sport in any marketing initiatives must reflect this. Thus, while I agree with Silk and Andrews (2001) that advertisers use sport to depict a gendered and inevitably superficial simulacra of a particular society, it must also be noted that this defining and redefining of the nation to fit a particular desired brand image can have differing levels of resonance. These may vary from a simplistic presentation of national characteristics that are superficially consumed in local and foreign markets to a perceived widespread impacting on a national psyche. In this respect, the representations generated and the messages relayed can be problematic from the point of view of cultural representation, explored more fully elsewhere in this book. The need to account for this multi-level interpretation also adds to the inherent complexity of managing TNCs.

Dealing with this complexity requires a comprehensive array of integration devices (Lawrence and Lorsch, 1967). Integration at Guinness is achieved primarily by the establishment of highly functional communication mechanisms. While these embrace electronic, telephonic and video technologies, the most important method of integration involves face-to-face meetings. The GBD and members of his team travel regularly to meet with local marketing teams in their own countries. In addition to the spread of organizational knowledge discussed above, this personal interaction promotes an understanding of local idiosyncrasies that can be accounted for within a more global brand positioning strategy. This type of understanding is important because, while the anticipated merits of international expansion are well documented, the accompanying increased complexity among geographically diverse sub-units frequently outweighs any benefits that may accrue (Hitt et al., 1997). Thus, the need to understand TNC management practices that combine learning opportunities, global coordination and national flexibility remains pronounced.

Transnational corporations are exposed to a multitude of pressures. They are expected to become ever-more efficient and "business-like" while being socially responsible; they must variously accommodate homogeneity and heterogeneity across different functional areas; they must reduce inequities while maintaining profitability. Consequently, strategic initiatives must account not just for economic shareholder expectations, but also for the political, legal, and social responsibilities to which they are increasingly held accountable (Parker, 1999). This requires a reconceptualization of business practices that allow managers to enmesh traditional competitive practices with an understanding of what is required to operate effectively in a post-modern political economy with its accompanying emphases on rapid technological transformation, interdependent global networks, a changing and perhaps ephemeral nation-state, and altered patterns of consumption. While we have seen how one transnational brand is positioned to cope with a fundamentally changed operating environment, we require more in-depth analyses of managerial practices that allow the multiple and complex realities of the strategy making processes within TNCs to be better understood.

Notes

1. While I agree with Hirst and Thompson's (1999) contention that such "global forces" have been with us since at least the nineteenth century, the pace and scope of changes to traditional modes of operating massively increased during the second half of the twentieth century, and thus opened up global markets to many more firms than had previously been the case.
2. This chapter is drawn from a larger study into the strategic management of the Guinness brand. Data were collected from interviews with senior managers, company documents, internal presentations, academic, popular press and industry publications, electronic training materials, and promotional videos. Further details are available in Amis (2003).
3. I use football here rather than soccer to maintain consistency with the terminology used by the participants in the study.

References

Amis, J. (2003), "Good Things Come to Those Who Wait": The Strategic Management of Image and Reputation at Guinness, *European Sport Management Quarterly*, 3: 189–214.

Anand, J. and Delios, A. (2002), Absolute and Relative Resources as Determinants of international acquisitions. *Strategic Management Journal*, 23, 119–34.

Andrews, D. and Jackson, S. (2001), Introduction: Sport Celebrities, Public Culture, and Private Experience. In D. Andrews and S. Jackson (eds), *Sport Stars: The Cultural Politics of Sporting Celebrity*, New York: Routledge, pp. 1–19.

Andrews, D. L. and Cole, C. L. (2002), The Nation Reconsidered, *Journal of Sport and Social Issues*, 26, 123–4.

Appadurai, A. (1990), Disjuncture and Difference in the Global Cultural Economy, *Theory, Culture and Society*, 7, 295–310.

Bartlett, C. A. and Ghoshal, S. (1987), Managing Across Borders; New Organizational Responses, *Sloan Management Review*, 29(1): 45–53.

Bartlett, C. A and Ghoshal, S. (1989), *Managing Across Borders: The Transnational Solution*, Boston MA: Harvard Business School Press.

Brand Map (2001), Internal Guinness 2-cd-rom set.

Castells, M. (1996), *The Information Age*, volume 1: *The Rise of the Network Society*, Oxford: Blackwell.

Delios, A. and Beamish, P. W. (2001), Survival and Profitability: The Roles of Experience and Intangible Assets in Foreign Subsidiary Performance, *Academy of Management Journal*, 44: 1028–38.

Eisenhardt, K. M. and Martin, J. A. (2000), Dynamic Capabilities: What are They? *Strategic Management Journal*, 21 (special issue, 10–11): 1105–22.

Giddens, A. (2002), *Runaway World: How Globalisation is Reshaping Our Lives*, second edition, London: Routledge.

Guinness (2002) http://www.guinness.com/guinness/en_GB/seeing/ads/ad/0,6438,125495_125898,00. Accessed December 7, 2002.

Guinness Global Strategy Presentation (2001), internal company presentation.

Harvey, D. (1989), *The Condition of Postmodernity: An Enquiry into the Origins of Cultural Change*, Oxford: Blackwell.

Hirst, P. and Thompson, G. (1999), *Globalization in Question*, second edition, Cambridge: Polity Press.

Hitt, M. A., Hoskisson, R. E. and Ireland, R. D. (1994), A Mid-range Theory of the Interactive Effects of International and Product Diversification on Innovation and Performance, *Journal of Management*, 20: 297–326.

Hitt, M. A., Hoskisson, R. E. and Kim, H. (1997) International Diversification: Effects on Innovation and Firm Performance in Product-diversified Firms, *Academy of Management Journal*, 40: 767–98.

Kahn, J. S. (1995), *Culture, Multiculture and Postculture*, Beverley Hills CA: Sage.

Lawrence, P. R. and Lorsch, J. W. (1967) *Organization and Environment*, Boston MA: Harvard Business School.

Levitt, T. (1983), The Globalization of Markets, *Harvard Business Review*, May–June, pp. 92–102.

Madhok, A. (1997), Cost, Value and Foreign Market Entry Mode: The Transaction and the Firm. *Strategic Management Journal*, 18: 39–61.

Mann, M. (1997), Has Globalization Ended the Rise and Rise of the Nation-state? *Review of International Political Economy*, 4: 472–96.

McGaughey, S. L. and Liesch, P. W. (2002) The Global Sports-media Nexus: Reflections on the "Super League saga" in Australia, *Journal of Management Studies*, 39: 383–416.

Miller, T. (1998), *Technologies of Truth: Cultural Citizenship and the Popular Media*, Minneapolis: University of Minnesota Press.

Morgan, G. (1997), *Images of Organization*, Thousand Oaks CA: Sage.

Morley, D. and Robins, K. (1995), *Spaces of Identity: Global Media, Electronic Landscapes and Cultural Boundaries*, London: Routledge.

Not Men but Giants (2001), Internal Guinness promotional video.

Ohmae, K. (1990), *The Borderless World*, New York: Harper Business.

Ohmae, K. (1995), *The End of the Nation State*, New York: Free Press.

Parker, B. (1999) Evolution and revolution: From international business to globalization. In S.R. Clegg, C. Hardy and W.R. Nord (eds) *Managing Organizations: Current Issues*, Thousand Oaks CA: Sage, pp. 234–56.

Perraton, J., Goldblatt, D., Held, D. and McGrew, A. (1997), The Globalization of Economic Activity, *New Political Economy*, 2(2): 257–77.

Rines, S. (2001), Guinness Rugby World Cup Sponsorship: A Global Platform for Meeting Business Objectives, *International Journal of Sports Marketing and Sponsorship*, 3: 449–65.

Robertson, R. (1995), Glocalization: Time-space and Homogeneity-heterogeneity. In M. Featherstone, S. Lash and R. Robertson (eds), *Global Modernities*, London: Sage, pp. 25–44.

Segal-Horn, S. and Faulkner, D. (1999), *The Dynamics of International Strategy*, London: International Thomson Business Press.

Silk, M. and Andrews, D. L. (2001), Beyond a Boundary? Sport, Transnational Advertising, and the Reimagining of National Culture, *Journal of Sport and Social Issues*, 25: 180–201.

Simmons, J. and Griffiths, M. (2001), *Believe: Six Turning Points for Guinness that Hinged on Inner Strength*, London: Guinness UDV.

Sponsorship Strategies (2000), Dublin: Amárach Consulting.

Tomlinson, J. (1999), *Globalization and Culture*, Cambridge: Polity.

Vermeulen, F. and Barkema, H. (2002), Pace, Rhythm, and Scope: Process Dependence in Building a Profitable Multinational Corporation, *Strategic Management Journal*, 23: 637–53.

Wong, L.L. and Trumper, R. (2002), Global Celebrity Athletes and Nationalism: *Fútbol*, Hockey, and the Representation of Nation, *Journal of Sport and Social Issues*, 26: 168–94.

Yip, G. (1989), Global Strategy . . . in a World of Nations, *Sloan Management Review*, 3(1): 29–41.

9

SEGA Dreamcast: National Football Cultures and the New Europeanism

Philip Rosson

Commercial sponsorships have become an important element in most sports. This is certainly true in English football where, since the early 1980s, shirt and kit sponsorships have generated important revenues for clubs at all levels. Companies increasingly view sponsorships as an effective way to promote their corporate and/or product brands. This chapter presents a case study of SEGA Europe's use of a football shirt sponsorship in the launch of its new video gaming console and brand (the Dreamcast) in the UK market. The sponsorship sought to capitalize on the popularity of football among the prime market segment for its product and to benefit from television and other media exposure. The case study outlines the circumstances that led SEGA Europe and Arsenal FC to partner with each other, as well as subsequent developments. It was prepared using secondary sources and interviews with key informants in football organizations, sports marketing firms, and football researchers.[1]

Introduction

SEGA Enterprises, a Tokyo-based video game company, launched its new Dreamcast console in the Japanese market on November 27, 1998. North American and European introductions were planned for September 1999. SEGA expected that the Dreamcast console would challenge Sony's PlayStation for market leadership. Management at SEGA's European subsidiary was considering football shirt sponsorships as one element in its launch and market development plans. Why football? Because it was the number one sport in Europe and its fans' demographics increasingly mirrored those for video gamers. In addition, television was broadcasting more and more football games – often on a pan-European basis – providing valuable exposure for companies and their brands. Therefore, football seemed ideally suited to communicating with those most interested in buying the Dreamcast. This was particularly the case in the UK, where football was a national passion and video gaming was also a favorite pastime. Consequently, in late 1998 SEGA Europe management was giving active consideration to partnering with a top English football club. There was about a six-month window before a sponsorship deal would come into effect, and the Dreamcast launch was nine months away. In other words, there was some pressure for a decision to be made.

London's Arsenal FC was a logical football club for SEGA to consider as a sponsorship partner. Arsenal has had a long and rich history. Founded as the Royal Arsenal FC in Woolwich, Kent, in 1886, the club moved to its present location at Highbury in North London in 1913 (Soar and Tyler, 1989). It is one of a handful of English football teams that is well known and supported around the world and in the last decade, after Manchester United, has had the single best record of English clubs. In December 1998, it was announced that Japanese electronics giant JVC would end its long-standing shirt sponsorship with Arsenal, effective June 30, 1999. This meant that Arsenal would have to seek another shirt sponsor for the 1999–2000 season, which kicked-off in late August.

The case study that follows examines SEGA and Arsenal in turn. The industry environment of each organization is described, then the shirt sponsorship factors are outlined, followed by details of the shirt sponsorship deal that was struck, as well as subsequent developments. A number of final comments bring the chapter to a close.

The Video Gaming Industry

In the late 1990s, three Japanese companies fought for dominance of the global video game industry. Despite its late entrance, Sony was the market leader. Nintendo and SEGA had at various times occupied the top spot but these long-standing rivals currently trailed in Sony's wake. SEGA's new entry – the Dreamcast video console – was launched in Japan late in 1998, and North American and European introductions were planned for September 1999. Nintendo was rumored to be launching a new product. As a result, both companies expected to gain substantial ground on Sony and its extremely successful PlayStation. However, Sony itself would be launching a new product – the PlayStation 2 – in 2000. Product and game technology, market timing, and marketing flair were all critical to company success in this industry.

History

The video game industry started in the 1980s and has gone through several cycles of boom and bust, with shakeouts of marginal companies and the arrival of newcomers. The industry grew in the late 1980s when Nintendo and SEGA used sixteen-bit technology to develop much faster and more sophisticated games. A period of depressed sales occurred in the early 1990s when PC technology played leapfrog and drew users away from video game companies. In late 1994, video gaming broke back when Sony introduced its innovative PlayStation. This development changed the industry dramatically. The quality of images and sounds made possible by the technology meant that the industry was seen as selling something more than a toy. For the first time, large numbers of adult users were attracted to video gaming. Nintendo launched the N64 in 1997 in an attempt to regain some ground. In late 1998, all eyes were watching as the once preeminent SEGA launched its own innovative Dreamcast game system in Japan, based on 128-bit technology. The games industry is substantial. By the end of 1999, it was forecast that the installed base would number more than 100 million Sony PlayStations, Nintendo N64s, and SEGA Saturns and Dreamcasts globally. Household penetration levels were high and the value of industry sales (consoles and games) was about US$20 billion in 1999 (£12.2 billion)[2] – larger than Hollywood box-office revenues for the first time (Business, 1999).

SEGA Competitors

Sony was the competitor to beat, dominating almost everywhere with market shares in the 60 percent to 70 percent range. The PlayStation had proven to be a star product for Sony. It was estimated that 50 million homes owned the gaming console in 1999, and that in the fourth quarter of 1998, it provided 16 percent of Sony's sales and 44 percent of profits (Fulford, 1999). However, after four years of booming PlayStation sales, volumes were down (Sony warns, 1999). Sony was planning to introduce its PlayStation 2 to the Japanese market in time for Christmas 1999. Early reports suggested the new console would be a formidable competitor. Technically, the console would be able to outperform PCs and workstations and would be "backwards compatible" – old game libraries would not be made obsolete by the console. This was a benefit for users, software producers and resellers alike.

Nintendo was second in most countries, accounting for much of the rest of the market. It entered video gaming in 1983 and the eight-bit Nintendo Entertainment System (NES) dominated the second-generation of consoles. Nintendo also pioneered hand-held games and still leads that market with the GameBoy. Its success with the NES made it slow to develop a successor and the sixteen-bit Super NES (and later N64) failed to meet profit expectations. Although it had not publicly announced plans for a successor to the N64, Nintendo was rumoured to be working on a console to be launched in Japan in time for the important Christmas 2000 holiday.

Convergence in entertainment

Video gaming was fast becoming a "mainstream activity," appealing to a more mature user. In the early 1990s, eight- to sixteen-year-old males primarily owned video consoles. Following the release of the PlayStation, consoles sold across a wider age range (eight to twenty-nine years), with the average owner being seventeen years old (Littlewood, 1999). The broadening in the appeal of video gaming meant that close parallels existed between the prime market segments for gaming products and football.

Given the size and continued growth prospects, it was rumoured that Microsoft had designs on the US$15 billion (£9.1 billion) global video-game market. Another factor was the advanced graphics capabilities of the new consoles, which were seen as challenging the future of PC-gaming and, more broadly, interactive entertainment, including the Internet and digital TV. Microsoft could not allow these markets to move away from its domination (Ward and Chang, 1999).

SEGA and the Dreamcast

SEGA had seen its share of world markets slide dramatically since 1992. Its sixteen-bit MegaDrive console, launched in 1989 as the Genesis in North America, was the dominant third-generation gaming machine. However, SEGA was unable to make the transition to the next generation of player (using CD-ROM disks). The Saturn console, launched the same year as Sony's PlayStation, never met corporate objectives (Schofield, 1999). Consequently, SEGA's share had gone from about 50 percent in the early 1990s to stand at little more than 1 percent in the US market in 1998. In the UK, SEGA's market share was in the 4 percent to 5 percent range.

SEGA's market decline created difficulties. Smaller volumes of business meant there was less interest on the part of software developers in producing games and less money for marketing and advertising. Because of lower spending, sales plunged further and so the spiral continued. These difficulties affected SEGA's corporate performance. Gross sales fell from US$3.5 billion (£2.1 billion) in 1996, to US$2.5 billion (£1.6 billion) in the year ended March 1998 (Edwards, 1999).

A New Start

SEGA had what it believed would be a winning combination: the newest gaming console backed by an aggressive marketing strategy. SEGA was determined to win back a leadership position in the video game market. The Dreamcast was the first gaming system to be designed around 128-bit technology and, it was claimed, this enabled SEGA to offer a system that ran three times as fast as the latest arcade game and fifteen-times as fast as Sony's PlayStation.

Launched in Japan late in 1998, the debut of Dreamcast in North America was set for September 9, 1999. The European launch was planned for September 23, 1999. Being first to market had proven important in the video game market and SEGA expected to have a lead of at least one-year over Sony and Nintendo with its "next generation" console. The Japanese launch had gone well, with 900,000 units sold by March 1999. The console was priced at the equivalent of US$250 (about £150). Initially, nine games were available for use on the console and SEGA had signed software licenses with fifty companies (Edwards, 1999).

The president of SEGA Enterprises spoke of the Dreamcast capturing half the global market for gaming consoles. However, industry observers were skeptical that SEGA could achieve at this level, noting Sony's dominance, SEGA's lost momentum, and reduced interest by software developers as obstacles that lay in its way (Littlewood, 1999).

European Plans

In preparation for the European launch of the Dreamcast, London-based SEGA Europe made a number of management and organizational changes. The senior managers appointed had experience in the music and TV businesses. Others had backgrounds in video games, software and advertising. The plan was to centralize activities so as to take control of advertising and marketing.

SEGA then set about planning the £50 million to £60 million marketing campaign to launch the Dreamcast in Europe. Two advertising agencies were signed to assist the company: Bartle Boyle Hegarty, to deal with brand advertising, and M&C Saatchi, which was to handle other activities, including sponsorship, direct and digital marketing, and sales promotion. Industry members knew that the Dreamcast launch would determine SEGA's future in gaming. As one games analyst put it, "SEGA has to make this work; it has no contingency plans. It is heavily into debt to fund the marketing" (Littlewood, 1999).

The company's marketing approach was signaled when the European Marketing Director said "We are here to launch a brand [Dreamcast] first, a console second." SEGA clearly wished to reverse the lingering view that the company and its brands were not "cool". The key was to make Dreamcast "famous" by linking the brand with activities and personalities that are popular with, and appeal to youths and young adults. An early indicator of SEGA's plans was provided by the March 1999 European-wide sponsorship of the premiere of the futuristic thriller film eXistenZ (Littlewood, 1999). Pan-European promotional plans also involved cinema advertisements at all venues showing the new Star Wars movie *The Phantom Menace*, to be followed by TV advertisements until Christmas. Because the Dreamcast console was the first to provide Internet access, these advertisements would stress the possibility of multi-player gaming online. SEGA also planned to install the new consoles in 50 cinema complexes throughout the UK for consumer trial, as well as at train stations and other urban locations on the launch day (Campbell, 1999).

Football Sponsorship

Another marketing vehicle that was seriously considered by SEGA was the sponsorship of football teams in major European markets. Commercial sponsorship of football events, teams and players was growing quickly and this fact had not escaped SEGA Europe management, who saw big possibilities for capitalizing on the popularity and drama of the game. Commercial sponsorship is different from advertising and has been defined as ". . . the purchase (in cash or kind) of an association with a team, event, etc. in return for the exploitable commercial potential linked to that activity" (Meenaghan, 1983).

High profile brands adorned the shirts of most leading English football teams. These included global brands, such as Packard Bell (Leeds) and national brands, like Newcastle Brown Ale (Newcastle United). With increasing levels of TV coverage of big league and cup games in England, as well as European competitions involving top English clubs, considerable exposure was possible. Further, as one sponsorship consultant put it "Sport is a universal language that crosses boundaries and elicits a lot of passion. Companies want to associate their brand with such powerful passions, and sponsorship can deliver this" (Bell and Campbell, 1999).

The Launch

It was expected that the Dreamcast would be launched at a retail price of £199 in the UK, compared to street prices of £99.99 for both the PlayStation and N64. Some ten games were expected to be available for the European Dreamcast launch and a further twenty games were expected in time for Christmas 1999 (Littlewood, 1999). Whether Sony and Nintendo would engage in price cutting was unclear.

SEGA's plans elicited varying responses. Some industry observers anticipated that the Dreamcast would sell well up to Christmas but that sales would then fall away because European consumers would be prepared to wait for the new machines Sony and Nintendo would introduce late in 2000. Other observers were more critical: they did not see a long-term place for SEGA in the industry and argued that the company should focus on its strengths in software development and write for other platforms (Killgren, 1998). SEGA Europe's CEO's response was that that the Dreamcast was a reality whereas PlayStation 2 and Nintendo's new console were "just theory." SEGA forecast that European sales would total one million units in the first year and that by Christmas 2000, it expected to "have sold 1.5 million units and to have more than 100 games. We will have a great advantage" (Edwards, 1999).

Football in England

Football had seen a resurgence of interest in England. Through the 1980s, attendance at games had declined quite sharply. A combination of factors explained this situation: an economic recession in the early part of the decade; hooliganism at grounds, and on the way to and from games; and crowded and antiquated spectator facilities. From 1987 on, the situation changed. First, a consumer boom following the recession increased leisure spending. Second, government and clubs alike took action to deal with football violence and so make football a safe spectator sport once again. Third, following the death of ninety-six fans at a game in Sheffield as a result of policing and stadium problems, the Taylor Report made sweeping recommendations about safety and comfort within grounds.

Television

The increased popularity of English football was also a result of TV developments. The advent of satellite and cable pay TV brought new companies into the industry, which broke the cartel of the established channels and resulted in larger contracts for the right to televise more football. Sports programming delivered large numbers of viewers to the TV channels, which, in turn, permitted the selling of prime-time advertising slots. But TV companies were not the only winners. Clubs benefited from TV in two ways: first, substantial revenues flowed from new TV contracts; and second, the greater number of games aired at prime time fuelled fan interest and participation.

Revenue Sources

Football teams generate revenues through a variety of activities. Historically, the major source of revenue was gate receipts. Over time, the combination of more diversified operations and lucrative TV contracts had reduced the importance of ticket sales. Table 9.1 shows that gate receipts still accounted for the largest stream of football club revenues – 36 percent of total revenues in 1998–9, but TV was growing in importance (up from 21 percent of total revenues in 1996–7, to 26 percent in 1997–98).

British football clubs were at the forefront in "off-the-field" developments that have produced new revenue streams. The resurgence in football's popularity (and, to some extent, its move upmarket) has attracted numerous sponsoring corporations. One type is the so-called shirt sponsor, while another is the kit sponsor. Shirt sponsors are sometimes referred to as club sponsors because their presence is very obvious at the club in question. As well as appearing on the

Table 9.1. *Premier League sources of revenue**

	Percent	
Main revenue streams	*1996–97*	*1997–98*
Gate receipts	37	36
Television	21	26
Retail/merchandising	21	17
Other commercial activities	21	21

*Average data based on information from nine Premier clubs.
Source: Deloitte & Touche (1999, p. 12)

team's shirts,[3] the sponsor's name/logo was usually very much in evidence at the stadium, on match programs and tickets, Web sites and so forth. Manufacturers of sports clothing such as Adidas, Nike, Umbro and Reebok had kit sponsorship arrangements with leading football clubs. As well as supplying free kit, sponsors paid clubs a base fee and a portion of replica kit sales (the latter essentially being licensing fees). There was a strong market for replica kits. Children and teenagers wore the kit when playing football and as casual wear. Some adults also wore replica shirts at home, as well as to matches. Typically, about 22.5 percent of the retail shirt price would flow to the manufacturer and 8 percent to the club (Szymanski and Kuypers, 1999).

In addition to replica kits,[4] most Premier clubs offered a full range of sports and leisure wear, as well as books, videos, jewelry and other items, sold via club shops or through catalog operations. Sales also took place through independently owned sports shops and chains. Accordingly, retail and merchandising operations had become significant revenue streams.

Football as Business

Interest in football was rekindled and large amounts of TV and sponsorship money flowed into the game in the late 1980s and the 1990s. Whereas clubs had been largely owned and run as a hobby or as a service to the community, they were increasingly viewed as "for-profit" businesses in the 1990s.[5] It was felt that some teams could break out of their traditional local areas and, in these cases, become national or even global brands.[6] Top teams already had a fan base around the world and with increased coverage of English Premier games on local TV networks these supporters were able to follow their team and favorite players. Geographical market expansion developments such as these opened up major possibilities for merchandising and sponsorship growth.

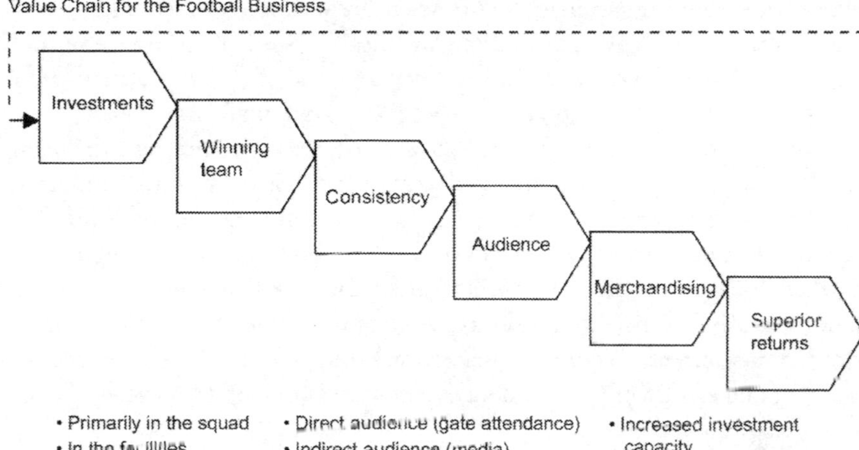

Figure 9.1. *Value chain for football business.*
Source: Salomon Brothers Inc. (1997, p. 67).

Considerable amounts of money were being spent to attract world-class players to top English clubs. There existed a strong positive link between a team's performance on the field and the club's profitability as a business, so clubs attempted to assemble the best possible squad of players (see Figure 9.1).

Arsenal Football Club

Arsenal Finances

Mirroring developments at other top clubs, Arsenal's revenue streams had grown and diversified in recent years. Home games were invariably played to a capacity crowd of 38,000 fans – a mix of season and regular ticket holders. Arsenal was considering a number of options for increasing gate receipts. The options included expanding its present ground at Highbury or building a new stadium. Arsenal generated about 40 percent of its total revenues from ticket sales.

Arsenal had been a major beneficiary of the TV contract in recent years. It received £9.7 million as its share of the domestic TV payments in 1997–8 (Deloitte & Touche, 1999). The eighteen-year shirt sponsorship deal with JVC was said to have been worth about £20 million to Arsenal since 1981 (JVC ends, 1998). Arsenal's kit sponsor is Nike, which had expanding interests in football and had established relationships with top clubs in several leagues in Europe, such as Barcelona and Inter Milan. One report stated that Nike's kit sponsorship of Arsenal was worth £40 million over seven years (Fry, 1997).

On the merchandising front, 350,000 Arsenal replica shirts were sold in 1996–7 at a price of about £40 each. Although replica kits were the major items sold, other merchandise was sold through two Arsenal shops and a mail order operation. Arsenal's mail order catalogue filled more than sixty pages.

Like other major teams, Arsenal had invested heavily to improve the team. In 1998–9, there were about thirty players in the first-team squad, almost all of whom had represented their country at a junior or senior level. The cosmopolitan nature of the Arsenal team was reflected by the fact that it included six Frenchmen, two from the Netherlands, and one from each of six other nations. The balance of the squad was British and included four current English international players. Arsenal's finances were sound. In terms of revenues and profits, it ranked fifth or higher among Premier League clubs. However challenges were ever-present.

The Relationship with JVC

In December 1998, it was announced that Japanese electronics giant JVC would end its long-standing shirt sponsorship with Arsenal, effective June 30, 1999. At the time of the announcement, Arsenal's vice chairman said: "There is no animosity. JVC have decided to channel their energies elsewhere. It has been a marvellous relationship over 18 years and we have both wished each other well" (JVC drops, 1998). The Arsenal sponsorship arrangement was with JVC's British subsidiary. The subsidiary's trade marketing manager stated "the sponsorship has certainly done the job for us in brand awareness." However, management had decided to move the budget into mainstream activities so as to bolster JVC Great Britain's modest current advertising budget (estimated to be about £200,000 in 1997).

Sponsorship Research

Although sponsorship was big business in football, the commercial nature of the agreements meant that detailed information on the terms struck between the parties, as well as the results achieved over the life of an agreement, were not publicly available. Three independent research studies provide some general insights. According to one market research company, football sponsorships provided a way of reaching one in two British males, with a fairly even distribution by age and social class. When asked to provide names of companies sponsoring football teams or leagues, on average between 5 percent and 10 percent of males sampled were able to do so correctly. When prompted with a company name, the level of correct response rose to 12 percent to 35 percent. One conclusion reached was that sponsorship could provide considerable exposure for a company, especially via TV (Wright, 1988).

A second study concerned electronics companies and their involvement in sports sponsorships around the world. Initially, companies were found to use sports as a new and different form of advertising, and one that was less manifestly "commercial". In a second stage, sponsorships were used less as an alternative to advertising in awareness building and more as a public relations tool to improve, change or maintain the image of a company's brand or products. Most of the companies sampled chose to sponsor events or sport associations rather than individuals or teams. Events were often preferred because they received a lot of attention for a short period of time and, because they are often televised internationally, they lent themselves to the pursuit of high-level marketing goals, such as regional or global image enhancement (Armstrong, 1988).

Another study focused on shirt sponsors for teams in the top two divisions of English football and reported that for 61 percent of sponsors, outcomes exceeded their expectations, and that 77 percent indicated their past experience pre-disposed them towards future involvement. The two leading success factors were "clear objectives and a professional approach" (32 percent) and "good communications" (28 percent). Three other factors were each endorsed by 12 percent of the sponsors: "high profile club", "full use of the sponsorship package" and "success on the field". Although sponsors were positive about their experience, they generally failed to employ the full range of accepted sponsorship techniques, particularly with regard to setting objectives, gaining leverage, conducting evaluations and integrating the activity with other elements of the communications mix (Thwaites, 1995).

Shirt Sponsorship: Costs and Benefits

With sports playing an increasingly central role in corporate marketing strategies, sponsorship costs were spiralling and concerns were voiced about value-for-money (Fry, 1997). Some insiders saw sponsorships as having only a limited influence on the public's awareness or image of a company. According to one experienced manager "Sponsorship should be judged (and researched) as a reinforcing or catalytic factor, rather than as an initiating or 'locomotive' factor" (Otker, 1988).

Football shirt sponsorship agreements varied in cost and duration. A number of recent shirt sponsorship deals are shown in Table 9.2. England's top-performing club was Manchester United and, as would be expected, its arrangement with Sharp was both long-standing and the most lucrative in England. At the other extreme, teams that had struggled to remain in the Premier League (such as Nottingham Forest and Derby) commanded arrangements of shorter duration and/or lower amounts of money.

Table 9.2. *Premier League recent shirt sponsorship deals*

Club	*Sponsor*	*Industry*	*Deal* (amount and time)*		*Annual amount*
			£m	*Years*	*£m*
Aston Villa	AST	Computers	6	5	1.2
Chelsea	Autoglass	Car components	6	4	1.5
Coventry City	Subaru	Cars	2	3	0.7
Derby County	EDS	Computers	0.5	1	0.5
Everton	One 2 One	Mobile phones	2	3	0.7
Leeds United	Packard Bell	Computers	4	4	1
Liverpool	Carlsberg	Brewing	4	4	1
Manchester United	Sharp	Electronics	4.8	2	2.4
Newcastle United	Newcastle Brown Ale	Brewing	4	3	1.3
Nottingham Forest	Pinnacle Insurance	Insurance	2	3	0.7
Tottenham Hotspur	Hewlett-Packard	Computers	4	4	1
West Ham United	Dr. Martens	Shoes	3	3	1
Wimbledon	Elonex	Computers	3	3	1

* Estimates only since details are seldom made public. Ultimate value may also depend on team performance, attendance levels and crowd behavior.
Source: Miles (1999); Szymanski and Kuypers (1999)

Despite the various costs, many companies saw considerable value from the exposure their brands would receive at the stadium, as well as through TV (and print) coverage of games involving the sponsored club. The more games played and televised, the greater the exposure and benefit. In this respect, teaming with a top club made sense because it was likely to receive more TV coverage. Further, because cup competitions took place on a knockout basis, the stronger teams more often reached the final rounds and hence, played more games. Top clubs played in national cup tournaments as well as those that took place on a European-wide basis, such as the Champions League. Again, this was important for companies such as SEGA that had pan-European interests.

It was difficult to compute the benefit sponsors realized from exposure of their brand on football shirts. Two calculations were often made. First, companies estimated how much TV advertising could be purchased for different levels of sponsorship spending. For example, instead of spending (say) £2 million annually on a shirt sponsorship deal, a company could run about forty TV commercials in the UK.[7] Second, research organizations evaluated how much time a sponsor's name was visible during a televised game, and worked out the amount of money such exposure would cost through advertisements.[8] As well as the exposure gained through the company/product name on the team shirt, sponsors often expected other benefits such as advertising and promotional rights at games, signage, use of the club stadium, film and photography rights, player endorsements and services, hospitality, use of club mark, and product sampling.

To Partner or Not?

SEGA and Arsenal were separately considering the matter of shirt sponsorships by the end of 1998. SEGA had nine months before the Dreamcast would be launched in Europe, whereas Arsenal needed to finalize a new shirt sponsor in time for the start of the 1999–2000 season. Management at Arsenal felt the club was in a strong position to select a new partner. Arsenal was one of England's most prestigious clubs, it had an excellent recent performance record, was located in the lucrative London market, and was the only Premier club that Nike had chosen for kit sponsorship purposes.

SEGA executives were aware that Arsenal was the prime shirt sponsorship available to meet the timing of the Dreamcast launch. In many ways, an arrangement with Arsenal would meet SEGA's objectives. Arsenal's history, location, fan support, squad profile, and recent performance, made the club a desirable "property". A shirt sponsorship would mean that the Dreamcast brand would enjoy good exposure in league and cup games. Another attraction for SEGA was that, at the half way point in the 1998–9 season, Arsenal seemed well positioned to fill one of the 1999–2000 Champions League places available for English clubs. This meant that should SEGA become Arsenal's shirt sponsors, the company would gain even broader exposure in England, continental Europe, and around the world, through TV coverage of Champions League games.

It is not clear when SEGA Europe and Arsenal FC first began to discuss a potential partnership. It is assumed that SEGA management had first committed to the idea of a football shirt sponsorship, and then was concerned to select the best club. The first indication that a deal was under consideration surfaced a few days after the termination of the JVC sponsorship was made public. One month later (January 24, 1999), it was reported that SEGA and Arsenal were in "advance negotiations." The speed with which the negotiations proceeded came as a blow to Sony and Nintendo; apparently SEGA's key rivals had both been approached about a sponsorship (Draper, 1999).

The SEGA-Arsenal Partnership

SEGA and Arsenal announced a shirt sponsorship agreement on April 22, 1999. For the 1999–2000 season, Arsenal's red and white shirts would bear the "Dreamcast" brand name whereas the SEGA corporate name was to feature on the change shirt (yellow with blue trim). The precise details of the sponsorship were not released. However, it was widely reported to be a four-year deal worth £10 million. Whatever the case, it was believed to be a record amount.

The CEO of SEGA Europe, explained the Arsenal deal as follows:

> There are two reasons why we made a deliberate choice to become involved with Arsenal FC . . . they are a European club with European players . . . This was an opportunity we could not miss. The chance to be associated with one of the best clubs in the world . . . The main Arsenal fan profile is ages 16–30 and this matches SEGA Europe's customer base. Together with Arsenal we will launch our new Dreamcast product in the UK and throughout Europe. (SEGA Europe, 1999)

Two months later, SEGA entered into shirt sponsorship deals with football teams in France (AS Saint-Etienne) and Italy (UC Sampdoria). A year later, SEGA announced a shirt sponsorship deal with RC Deportivo de La Coruna, the 1999–2000 Spanish champions.

Sequel

SEGA Dreamcast Performance

The European launch of the Dreamcast was very successful, building on positive pre-launch reviews and pent-up demand for new video game technology. In the first two months after the launch, SEGA Europe reported sales of over 500,000 Dreamcast consoles with a retail value of £225 m. Over 150,000 online Internet registrations were made, with 40 percent of customers using the Dreamcast online capability. The Dreamcast sold in the UK for £200. Sony and Nintendo reduced prices to £80 and £65 respectively in an attempt to neutralize SEGA's launch. SEGA's early success was not sustained. Between April and December 2000 some 2.32 million units were sold, which was 44 percent below company forecasts. Sales were particularly disappointing during the Christmas 2000 season. Sony launched its PlayStation 2 in Japan in March 2000 and made an immediate impression, shipping one million units in the first week and 500,000 in subsequent weeks. The disappointing market performance of SEGA led to it to announce that it would end production of its Dreamcast game console on March 31, 2001, and restructure the company to focus solely on videogame content. The company stated "SEGA will be significantly broadening its market of consumer purchasers, while dramatically expanding its revenue possibilities" (SEGA scraps, 2001). SEGA planned to sell software to its former rivals Sony and Nintendo, was in talks to provide software to Microsoft's Xbox, and would deliver SEGA games to Palm handheld computers and Motorola mobile phones.

By mid-2002, Sony had sold 30 million PlayStation 2 consoles. Nintendo's GameCube and Microsoft's Xbox were both brought to market in November 2001. In the first nine months, these new entries each sold about 4.5 million units. Competition between Sony, Nintendo and Microsoft is fierce, with console prices slashed to the point where they are sold at a loss, with profits secured from licence fees on the games sold for each platform (Business: Console wars, 2002).

Arsenal Performance

Arsenal experienced considerable success on and off the football field. In the 1999–2000 season, the team finished second in the Premier League and was beaten in the final of a second-level European competition (the UEFA Cup). In 2000–1, they once again finished second in the Premier League, were beaten in the FA Cup Final, and reached the quarter final of the Champions League. In 2001–2, they did "the double", winning the Premier League and FA Cup Final, and reached the second stage in the Champions League. Consequently, the Dreamcast brand received significant exposure through the sponsorship arrangement.

In September 2000, Granada Media Group spent £27 million to acquire a 5 percent shareholding in the club. Granada also invested £20 million in a new company, AFC Broadband to exploit new media rights. Arsenal saw these investments as assisting the club in meeting its two key objectives – building a world-class team and stadium, and developing the Arsenal brand on a global basis. In 2002, planning approval was given for the club to proceed with construction of a new 60,000-seat stadium close to Highbury.

The Future

Initially, it was not clear what effect SEGA's withdrawal from the video console business would have on its football shirt sponsorships. One view was that nothing would really change since the Dreamcast brand would be migrated to the new software offerings (SEGA Pull, 2001). The situation was clarified in January 2002, when SEGA Europe radically scaled back its central marketing activity and decided not to renew the shirt sponsorship of Arsenal (Kleinman, 2002). This meant that Arsenal had to search for a new shirt sponsor.

On April 19, 2002, it was announced that O2, a major provider of mobile communications in Europe, would fill the void. The arrangement was said to be worth between £6 million and £10 million, over a two-year period. The contract was, however, to run for four years with an option for the parties to review the partnership after two years (Kollewe, 2002). The deal comprised a sponsorship fee and a share of network revenue from jointly branded high-speed mobile data and audio services for the club's international fan base with "real-time" up-to-the-minute information (New Sponsor, 2002). Just as it had been for SEGA, the sponsorship of Arsenal was seen as an important element in the launch of O2 (also known as mmO2). Previously trading under the name BT Cellnet, O2 had operations in the UK, Germany, the Netherlands and Ireland, with more than 17 million customers.

Conclusions

The SEGA-Arsenal case study provides a full description of a partnership arrangement between two organizations. An attempt was made to describe the industry context of each organization, rather than focusing narrowly on the negotiation of a football shirt sponsorship arrangement. It is believed that an appreciation of industry context is important in understanding the strategies pursued by individual organizations.

The case study provides summary information on the performance of SEGA and Arsenal over the three-year sponsorship arrangement. It could be said that SEGA's poor sales results and the decision to stop producing gaming consoles casts a negative light on football sponsorships. That would be too harsh a judgement: industry experts had questioned SEGA's position in video gaming for some time. How well did football sponsorships work for SEGA? For several reasons we will probably never know the answer to the question. First, the data are proprietary and thus not available. Second, even if the data were revealed, without knowledge of the circumstances (objectives, activities, personalities), it would be difficult to know why the results occurred. Third, experts say that it is difficult to isolate the effect of sponsorships, particularly in large companies that are involved in many forms of promotion. This is not to say that sponsorship is a promotional "black hole". Expertise is available to help answer these questions, but companies should expect to spend 2 percent to 5 percent of their sponsorship costs annually on research. Few actually commit in this way and so sponsorship remains an art rather than a science.

In conclusion, it should be recognized that the case study presented above focused on a shirt sponsorship agreement at the highest level. Two prestigious organizations were involved and clearly what is true for SEGA and Arsenal is probably not the same for companies that do not have global business interests and deep pockets, or clubs that cannot offer sponsors exposure at the highest levels of football. Nevertheless, even for organizations such as these, orchestrating a major sponsorship deal is no small matter. Organizations must consider and resolve a variety of strategic and operational factors in a relatively brief period of time, while at the same time recognizing that they will live with the consequences of the sponsorship decision for some time.

Acknowledgements

The research for this chapter was made possible through the financial support of the Asia-Pacific Foundation of Canada. The author benefitted from the insights of several individuals during the interview phase in England.

Notes

1. SEGA Europe and Arsenal FC declined interviews, stating that information on the shirt sponsorship arrangement was proprietary and could not be disclosed.
2. Currency conversions are shown at the prevailing rates for January 1, 1999.
3. The Football Association regulated the placing of company or product names and logos on football shirts as follows "Such advertising may occupy an area no greater than 200 square centimetres to be calculated by measuring around the outline of the advertising . . ." (FA Handbook, 1999, p. 226).
4. Since their names were on the replica shirts, such sales provided additional exposure for shirt sponsors.
5. In fact, some eighteen English clubs became public companies in the same period. Arsenal remained a limited and closely held company.
6. Manchester United announced in May 1997 that it was in talks with licensees to open up to fifty club outlets in Asia.
7. A 30-second, prime-time television commercial cost approximately £50,000 in the UK (Zenith Media, 1999).
8. Calculations also included print media coverage of games and the prominence of company brands in the stories and photos.

References

Armstrong, C. (1988), Sports Sponsorship: A Case-study Approach to Measuring its Effectiveness, *European Research*, May, pp. 97–101.

Bell, E. and Campbell, D. (1999), For the Love of Money, *Guardian*, May 23.

Business: Playing with the Big Boys (1999), *The Economist*, May 15, pp. 65–6.

Business: Console Wars; Video Games (2002), *The Economist*, June 22, pp. 57–8.

Campbell, L. (1999), Thomas Lands Top Role for Dreamcast Launch, *Marketing*, July 22, p. 3.

Deloitte & Touche (1999), *England's Premier Clubs: A Review of 1998 Results*, Manchester: Deloitte & Touche.

Draper, R. (1999), Arsenal on Brink of £10m SEGA Deal. Retrieved January 25, 1999 from: www.soccernet.com/english/news/ENG-AFC – 5531-02499.htm.

Edwards, P. (1999), SEGA Plots Attack on Game Giants, *Marketing Week*, July 2, pp. 18–19.

FA Handbook (1999), *Rules of the Association and Laws of the Game. Season 1999–2000.* London: Football Association.

Fry, A. (1997), Sponsors Play to Win, *Marketing*, August 7, pp. 16–17.

Fulford, B. (1999), Killer Sequel, *Forbes*, April 5, pp. 52–3.

JVC Drops Sponsorship of Arsenal (1998). Retrieved October 4, 1998 from: www.wspsoccer.com.

JVC Ends Gunners' Sponsorship (1998). Retrieved December 14, 1998 from: www.fa-premier.com.

Killgren, L. (1998) SEGA Makes a Play to Win Back Top UK Slot, *Marketing Week*, January 22, p. 21.

Kleinman, M. (2002), SEGA Downsizes Marketing as Top Euro Post is Axed, *Marketing*, January 24, p. 1.

Kollewe, J. (2002), MM02 will Replace SEGA as Arsenal's Main Sponsor. Retrieved April 19, 2002 from: www.Bloomberg.co.uk.

Littlewood, F. (1999), SEGA Gearing Up for the Final Fight, *Marketing*, May 27, pp. 28–9.

Meenaghan, T. (1983), Commercial Sponsorship, *European Journal of Marketing*, special issue, pp. 1–73.

Miles, L. (1999), *Successful Sports Sponsorships: Lessons from Football*, London: The International Forum on Sponsorship.

New Sponsor: mmo2 Anyone? (2002). Retrieved June 2, 2002 from: www.arsenal-world.net/news/0202/060202b.htm.

Otker, T. (1988), Exploitation: The Key to Sponsorship Success, *European Research*, May, pp. 77–86.

Salomon Brothers Inc. (1997), *Football Values*. London, November 19.

Schofield, J. (1999), Consoles of War. Retrieved January 5, 2000 from: www.guardian unlimited.co.uk/Archive/Article/0,4273.3834940,00.htm.

SEGA Europe Strikes Record Sponsorship Deal with Arsenal FC (1999), SEGA Europe, press release, April 22.

SEGA pull plug on Dreamcast. (2001). Retrieved February 1, 2001 from: www.arseweb.com/cgi-bin/newsreel.pl?8:327.

SEGA scraps the Dreamcast (2001). Retrieved February 1, 2001 from: http://news.bbc.co.uk/hi/ English/business/newsid_1145000/1145936.stm.

Soar, P. and Tyler, M. (1989), *Arsenal: Official History*, fourth edition, London: Hamlyn.

Sony Warns of Fall in PlayStation Sales (1999) *National Post*, Toronto, April 28, p. C11.

Szymanski, S. and Kuypers, T. (1999), *Winners and Losers: The Business Strategy of Football*, London: Viking.

Thwaites, D. (1995), Professional Football Sponsorship – Profitable or Profligate? *International Journal of Advertising*, 14, pp. 149–64.

Ward, D. and Chang, G. (1999). Microsoft, Intel May Team Up on Video Games, *National Post*, Toronto, September 7.

Wright, R. (1988), Measuring Awareness of British Football Sponsorship, *European Research*, May, pp. 104–8.

Zenith Media (1999), *1999 European Market and Media Facts*. London.

10

"Resisting" the Global Media Oligopoly? The Canada Inc. Response

Jean Harvey and Alan Law

Introduction

Allegedly in order to help prospected new viewers to follow the puck better, Fox Sports introduced the FoxTrax glow puck for its telecast of the 1996 NHL All Star game. The device was strongly criticized by most hockey fans and journalists, especially in Canada, where the initiative has been widely perceived as yet another American cultural imperialist invasion of Canada's game.[1] This American "innovation" by one of the global media conglomerates is one of many signs of the ongoing clash between American-inspired global mass sport culture versus national traditions. One of the major battlefields where the future of national mass sport culture is being fought is undoubtedly at the infra-structural level. Indeed, the current consolidation and concentration of the global media oligopoly and the increasing inclusion of sport in it (see Law et al., 2002), has profound implications for all national mass media landscapes and the mass mediatization of sport culture. These implications have a tremendous impact, as national telecommunication industries become linked increasingly with the global mass media oligopoly through cross-ownership and joint ventures.

This chapter discusses the tension between the emerging commodified global sport mass culture, the development of which is fueled by the global media oligopoly. Through the Canadian example this chapter will address the issue of so-called national "resistance" to the global media oligopoly. The "resistance" we wish to focus on is not about the creation of grass roots based alternatives to commodified sport culture, neither a "re-appropriation" of dominant cultural forms. Rather, we wish to document how, in order to "protect" Canadian culture and identity, Canadian telecommunication corporations reacted to the emergence of the global media conglomerates in ways that modified substantially traditional regulation policy, thus facilitating replication of the global model of competition through corporate structure. Canada is a telling example for the study of the global versus the national. Telecommunication policy has always been at the core of a Canadian cultural policy that must be deployed in a multicultural environment, imbedded in the constitution and diffused throughout all sectors. Different imagined nations constantly confront each in negotiation of bordered identity. In such a context, communications policy carries very high stakes for all political arenas. Canada's model of mixed private and public telecommunications interests makes it a particularly poignant case for the examination of strategies to edify a new and integrated media oligopoly that places sport at center stage.

The 1990s were the years of the boom in communication and new information technologies. Guided by the sirens "convergence" and "synergy" the world of media witnessed the growth and expansion of a global media oligopoly built through a flurry of company mergers and assets acquisitions. Major players in this oligopoly include News Corp., Time Warner, Disney, Vivendi Universal, Berthelsman and Viacom (Law et al., 2002). In retrospect, the strategy of the major corporate players in order to become part of leading global media conglomerates has been clear and relatively simple. In short, the strategy they all adopted was, on the one hand, to acquire or develop assets in the broadest possible range of communication platforms, virtually the pipes through which content is distributed. These include assets in general TV stations, cable networks, newspapers, book publishing companies, telecommunication satellites, Internet infrastructure, wireless communication networks, and so forth. On the other hand, the strategy was to acquire or develop as much and as diverse as possible, content production capacity to distribute through those pipes. Content includes film and TV production, Web sites, Internet portals, specialty TV, radio and satellite channels focusing on the broadest ranges of themes, including sport. It also includes ownership of professional sport team franchises and/or the acquisition of exclusive broadcasting rights of premier sport events.

It is through the interconnection of distribution platforms and content production capacities within a large conglomerate that both "convergence" and "synergy" are produced. "Convergence" is the process through which otherwise different and independent communication platforms and content production assets become integrated "to provide an expanded range of delivery and merchandising services to a broadening range of consumers" (Stoddart, 1997, p. 93). For example, convergence is created when a single conglomerate simultaneously broadcasts NHL hockey game through its general TV network across different regional cable networks in the US and Canada, as well as across Europe, Asia and Latin America, through its satellite television outlets, while at the same time it broadcasts the game on one of its pay-per-view Web sites (webcast). "Synergy" is that process through which different parts of a conglomerate come together to create added value to a given initiative. Synergies are derived through cross promotion of commodities and achievable through corporate integration. Corporate integration enables "product lines" to promote each other through mutual association (Alger, 1998; Whitson, 1998; Andrews 2001). In this context, sports teams and in some cases, such as in Australia and Britain, entire leagues, supply content that is used to promote other contents such as television shows or other commodities, which also act to promote sports. Whitson refers to these as "circuits of promotion" (Whitson, 1998), a function of conglomerate structure, as one of the more compelling reasons pushing the rise of media corporation ownership of sports teams and indeed the price of exclusive broadcasting rights to colossal levels.

The 2002 burst of the speculative bubble in the telecommunication industry partly resulted from the failure of the Internet to deliver expected revenues, and subsequent high corporate debt. Relatively risk-conscious and cash-strapped corporations have examined the financial performance of sport team assets in their own right against the potential but less tangible benefits of "synergy" through equity participation. Recent sales and announcements of intention to sell sport teams, potentially herald a shift from the centrality of "synergy" via vertical integration through equity ownership of teams. Sport teams continue to make appearances in corporate umbrellas, particularly that of News Corp. However, it seems that contribution to profitability is demanded more directly than in the frenzy years as corporations seem to be sobering over direct losses and relevance to central business functions.

However, synergy in general remains an important element of structural strategy. For example, on October 1, 2002, a new major transaction was being made public. News Corp. purchased Telepiu, an Italian-based pay TV multi-channel service, from Vivendi Universal for $893 Euros (AP, 2002). The result of this transaction was yet another redistribution of a myriad of communication assets among some of the bigger players within the oligopoly.

The edification of the global media oligopoly has raised several concerns about its overall impact. For several, global media has become a threat to nation-state cultural sovereignty, to the existence of national cultures and, a menace to the world's sport cultural heritage. Some argue that athletes, teams, leagues and even nations have lost control of their own sport, now known in media circles as mere "software", in the process of its commodification, increasing in intensity along with the vertical integration of sports product media distribution conglomerates. Carrington et al. (1999, p. 7) refer to this dynamic as "highjacking" of sovereignty. Maguire (1999) argues that the interdependencies between the key groups making up the global sports media complex (sports teams, marketing companies and transnational corporations) have placed sports teams in dependent positions, where they no longer have control over the nature and form in which their sport is televised, reported and covered.

The present analysis underscores the point that national cultural policy now follows global competitive practice. Reaction to the globalization of media and the spread of global mass culture has been in the form of pushing concentrations of national media in the hands of the national bourgeoisie for the sake of keeping a Canadian national voice alive. This contradiction, a bigger concentration of media as a strategy to protect Canadian culture, is at the core of a key issue in the current context of globalization: the absence of international protection of cultural diversity as a counterweight to homogenization trends in global sport mass culture. Our analysis is pursued over three main steps. First we present and discuss the emergence of three of the largest transnational media conglomerates in an effort to establish the type of corporate structure at the heart of global competitive strategy with particular emphasis on the role of sport. Next, we present a sketch of the Canadian balance of private and public broadcasting in a discussion of the importance of such a system to pursue deeply embedded cultural politics. This is followed by an explication of Canadian corporate structures that have followed the global model with several types of state support. The role played by the Caisse de dépôt et placement of Québec is highlighted to underscore the state's effort to keep alive a Québec power house on the Canadian scene – configured to global demands. We conclude with a broader discussion of the impact of the last decade of changes in the Canadian media landscape as a case in point of national versus global culture in the context of current global mass media oligopoly. In this discussion, we wish to point out how "shareholders" interests are increasingly replacing "citizens" interests in the current political debate on media.

The Global Media Oligopoly and Sport[2]

According to Alger (1998), five dimensions of media conglomerate structures allow us to characterize and compare them. First, *horizontal integration*, concerns concentration in one medium. For example, multiple newspapers may be held by the same corporation. Second, *vertical integration*, refers to the degree of ownership of the entire supply chain from product development to consumer delivery. For example, one conglomerate might possess assets in film, from the production studio to the cinema theatre. The third dimension looks at *product and service extension* from one medium into other media realms. For example, extension from newspapers to broadcast to cable. The fourth one points out to *geographic market extension*. The focus here is on how one corporation has connections from one locality to another, between nations, across nations, and so forth. Finally, Alger's fifth dimension is concerned with *industrial-media conglomerate structure*, associated with financial links to previously unaligned businesses for the purpose of asset acquisition. The following sub-sections set out and discuss the corporate maps of three non-Canadian and global conglomerates presented here as case studies: News Corporation, Disney and AOL/Time Warner. Each case is presented in a simplified visual map and verbally presented according to Alger's dimensions.

News Corporation

As of June 30, 2002, News Corp. had total assets of US$37.1 billion and had achieved annual revenues of roughly US$16.3 billion (News Corp. 2002), making it one of the most diversified global media entertainment corporations. As can be readily seen in Figure 10.1, News Corp. exhibits high degrees of *horizontal integration* in delivery platforms including print media, television broadcasting, cable television and Internet.

News Corp. *product and service extension* is initially based in media properties and extends to sports oriented "products" for distribution. News Corp was initially capitalized from print media and aggressively expanded on a global scale into the mid-1980s. Following the massive expansion of the print empire, CEO Rupert Murdoch acquired delivery platforms, primarily through takeovers, progressively to expand his share of consumers' attention – translatable to advertising revenue. According to Murdoch, sport, with a particular emphasis on football, has been his "battering ram" to establish the competitive success of his media properties. For him sport provides entry into new markets because of the audience share delivered.

Among the major global media conglomerates, News Corp. is by far the one in which *vertical integration* is dominated by sport products – controlled through global and local broadcasting rights as well as different forms and levels of equity interest. News Corp. assumed control of the Los Angeles Dodgers in 1998 at the cost of US$310 millions. In early 2003, however, Murdoch was contemplating the opportunity to sell the club (allegedly for US$650) in order to raise money for the purchase of an asset he has been trying to acquire for several years, US-based satellite broadcaster Direct TV (*Evening Standard*, 2003). On October 10, 2003, the Fox Entertainment Group sent out a press release announcing an agreement for the sale of the Dodgers with the McCourt Company, a Boston-based real-estate corporation. News Corp. also has interests in Madison Square Garden, the New York Rangers and Knicks, as well as WNBA's Liberty through a joint venture with Rainbow Media, a Cablevision subsidiary. News Corp. also has a 40 percent interest in the $300 million US Staples Center, home to the Los Angeles Kings, Lakers and Clippers. Further

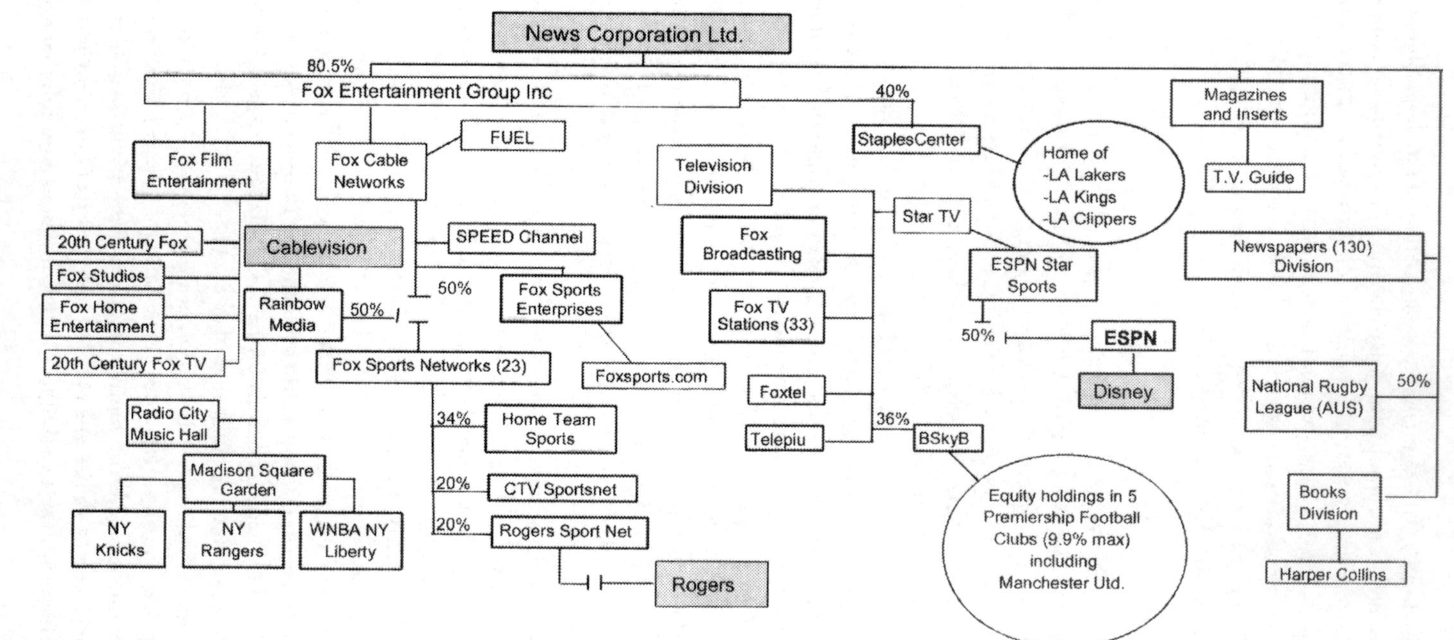

Figure 10.1. *News Corp corporate holdings (simplified). Note: Unless otherwise shown, holdings represent 100% ownership.*
Sources: Corporate Web site, Business Wire, Hoovers Online and annual reports. Updated from: Harvey et al., 2001, p. 444.

equity holdings include 9.9 percent (the most allowable) of Chelsea, Manchester United and Manchester City football clubs, 5 percent of Sunderland and 9.1 percent of Leeds (*Guardian*, 2000). Finally, News Corp. owns the British Rugby League as well as 50 percent of the Australian National Rugby League formed through merger with Super League and the Australian Rugby League in 1997.

These equity interests provide enhanced access to content material for its expanding delivery. However, broadcast rights continue to play a dominant role in sport products acquisition. The importance of the right to broadcast American football (NFL) is underscored by the $395 million increase over the previous contract (Landreth, 2000) with a provision that the league cannot renegotiate the deal before its fifth year, out of eight. Further, seventy-one of the seventy-six teams in the American big four leagues have agreements with Fox Sports Regional Networks (Andrews, 2001) for local broadcast. Exclusive broadcasting rights are held by News Corp. for the Super Bowl, NHL games, the MLB World Series, as well as the World Cup of Cricket and English Premiership Football.

News Corp.'s *geographic market extension* makes it a truly transnational corporation. Holdings that distribute across borders include virtually all media whereas those contained within borders include mostly national papers and domestic radio and television news programing. In addition to presence in Europe, North America and the Antipodes, recent years have seen expansion into India, Latin America and China. In early 2003, News Corp. acquired a licence to broadcast STAR TV, a Chinese-language entertainment channel, in China. (Associated Press, 2003). One important characteristic of News Corp.'s expansion has been its skill at creatively following national regulations. For example, News Corp. was able to follow British regulations that no newspaper proprietor should own more than 20 percent of a TV company (in this case BSkyB) by claiming that its broadcast actually emanated from Luxembourg, where the satellite network it operated with was based. Initial market failure, no matter how colossal, is little deterrent. The $1.2 billion that BSkyB lost between 1989 and 1992 was absorbed as a short-term cost of market expansion (APTN, 2000, p. 6). Football was leveraged as a cultural product that would inevitably attract domestic and international paying customers to News Corp.'s satellite services. Here we can see News Corp. using vertical integration for its geographic market extension strategy.

News Corp's *industry inter-relationships* are numerous. News Corp. has extensive and critical linkages with major global competitors including AOL Time Warner, Disney, and Vivendi Universal through joint venture investments, namely Rainbow Media (American) and ESPN Star Sports (American and Asian networks). ESPN Star Sports is a 50-50 owned Asian-based network that expand each conglomerate's series of global networks and subsequent consumer audiences. In 2002 News Corp. purchased Vivendi's 75 percent ownership of Italian pay-TV operator, Telepiu, taking effective control of the operator. Such strategic alliances and ventures of a profoundly global magnitude enable News Corp. to reach approximately three-quarters of the wired world (Baker, 1998).

Disney

Disney, the second largest media conglomerate, stems from entertainment products that are rooted in American values and tradition. Examination of Disney's corporate structure reveals different but related dynamics in comparison to those of News Corp. In contrast with News Corp.'s vertical structure, which has almost always been rooted in the use of content product to boost the profitability of existing distribution networks, Disney *began* with content product and simultaneously expanded both product and distribution networks.

Horizontal integration is substantial for Disney across entertainment product and distribution divisions, readily discernible from its corporate map. Founded on film and television production, Disney has ventured into the Internet and the world of sport substantially since the mid 1990s. Of particular interest is the density of retail involvement at both the product and distribution channel ends of the supply chain. This feature in particular adds a cross-promotional dimension not included in News Corp.'s empire.

As mentioned above, Disney's roots in image production have meant the emergence of multiple lines of *vertical integration* connecting product with audience. Sport is only one among several quite dense product lines. We are able to observe an array of sport rights, properties and related distribution channels, similar in structure to News Corp. Consider Disney's two major North American franchise teams: the NHL's Mighty Ducks and MLB's Anaheim Angels. The Angels were sold for US$183.5 million in May 2003 to Arturo Moreno, a Mexican-American who made a fortune in billboard advertising. There is also Disney's broadcasting portfolio, flowing through ESPN and ABC networks. ABC holds rights to over US$6 billion worth of sports coverage in college football, PGA Golf, the NHL, NFL and Major League Soccer over eight years. ESPN extends this trend with no less than four major broadcast agreements. Two of these (Major League Soccer and the PGA) are shared with the sister ABC network, but the NFL and MLB contracts stand alone at US$4.8 billion for eight years and US$440 million for four years respectively (Landreth, 2000).

Disney's Internet activities use sport to distribute Disney symbols. ESPN formed an agreement with the NFL in 1996 to co-produce the league's site in return for shared revenue and the opportunity to use the site for promoting other Disney interests, namely ESPN and its various media properties. A similar

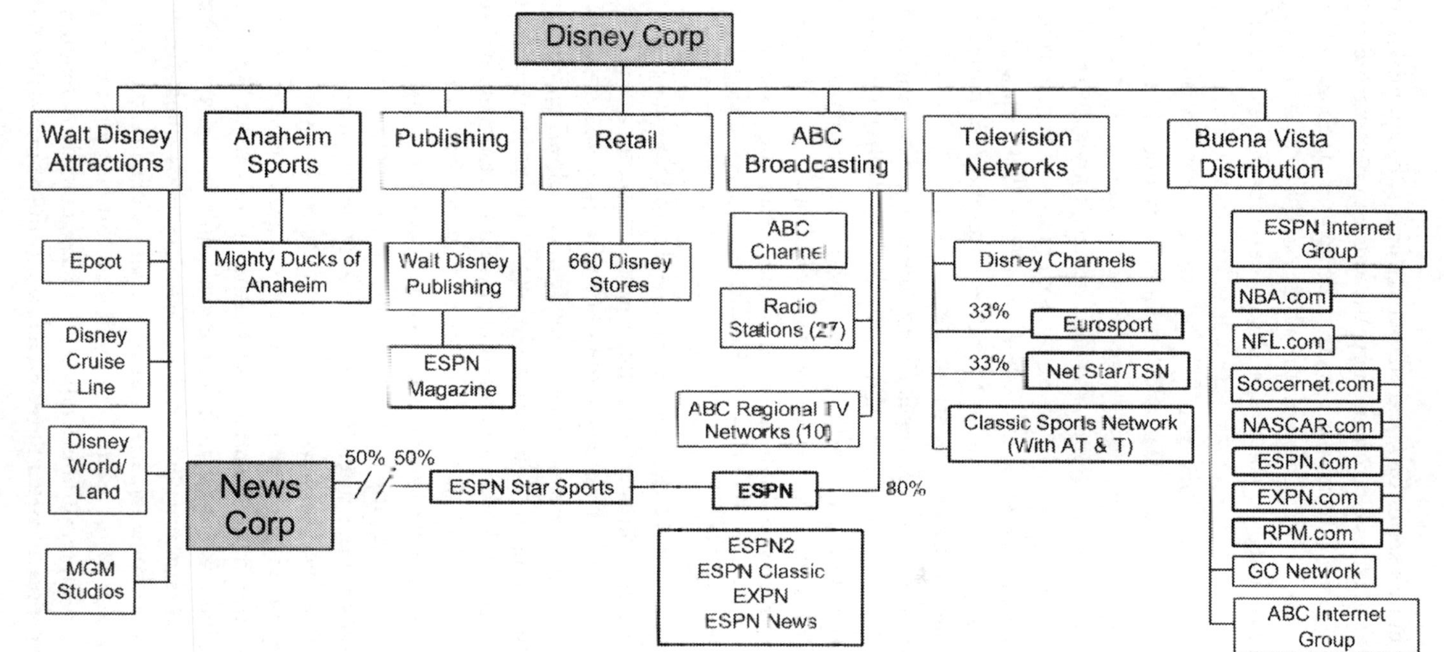

Figure 10.2. *Disney Corp. corporate holdings (simplified). Note: Unless otherwise shown, holdings represent 100% ownership.*
Sources: Corporate Web sites, Hoovers Online and annual reports.

arrangement is in place with both the NBA and NASCAR. Infoseek and the other Disney Web ventures all cross-promote the league sites of the NBA, NHL and NASCAR. Thus an alliance has been formed between these groups along with ABC.com, ABCNEWS.com and the Disney and ESPN sites.

The cross-promotional capabilities of Disney's empire that characterize its product and *service extension strategy* are substantial to say the least. Disney distributes, promotes and buys its own products. As much as possible, the conglomerate keeps manufacturing and production "in house", enabling the twenty-three internal divisions to work together and for one another. Organized under three main umbrellas, theme parks and resorts, filmed entertainment, and consumer products, Disney's assets are categorized most distinctly compared to other conglomerate exemplars. Interestingly, coherence of business lines does not result in corporate "silos"; rather, it enables clear and easy movement of overarching Disney symbols to be distributed.

Figure 10.2 shows substantial *inter-industry relationships*, even with traditional competitors. Perhaps the most important of these is the 50-50 joint ownership of ESPN with News Corp., created in November of 1996, extending Disney's reach to over 45 million homes throughout India, Taiwan, the Philippines, China, Thailand, Malaysia and a number of other Asian and Pacific nations.

Time Warner

Time Warner is considered the largest global media conglomerate, although it lost up to 75 percent of its market value in the first six month of 2002, as one of the most severely hit victims of the stock market bubble still retaining an accumulated debt in excess of US$800 millions. That blow prompted major restructuring, including AOL (America OnLine) demotion to the status of subdivision into the corporate structure (Vogt, 2002), and taken out of the umbrella name in October 2003. Time Warner is a conglomerate built from three historically distinct components, representing the merged interests of four corporations and making for highly dense *horizontal integration* in media production and distribution interests. Figure 10.3 shows the clustering of sport content production and broadcasting within the Turner Broadcasting group, now a subdivision of the Entertainment and Networks group, which also includes assets in cinema, and music production and distribution (HBO, Warner Bros. Warner Music, New Line Cinema). Under the media and communications group are now regrouped magazines (within the Time Inc. group), books (under the AOL Time Warner Group) cable distribution (Time Warner Cable), and most interestingly, the suite of "blue chip" components of the electronic distribution system within the America Online subdivision. Interestingly enough, not all the Internet properties are under the AOL umbrella. CNNSI.com, the Internet

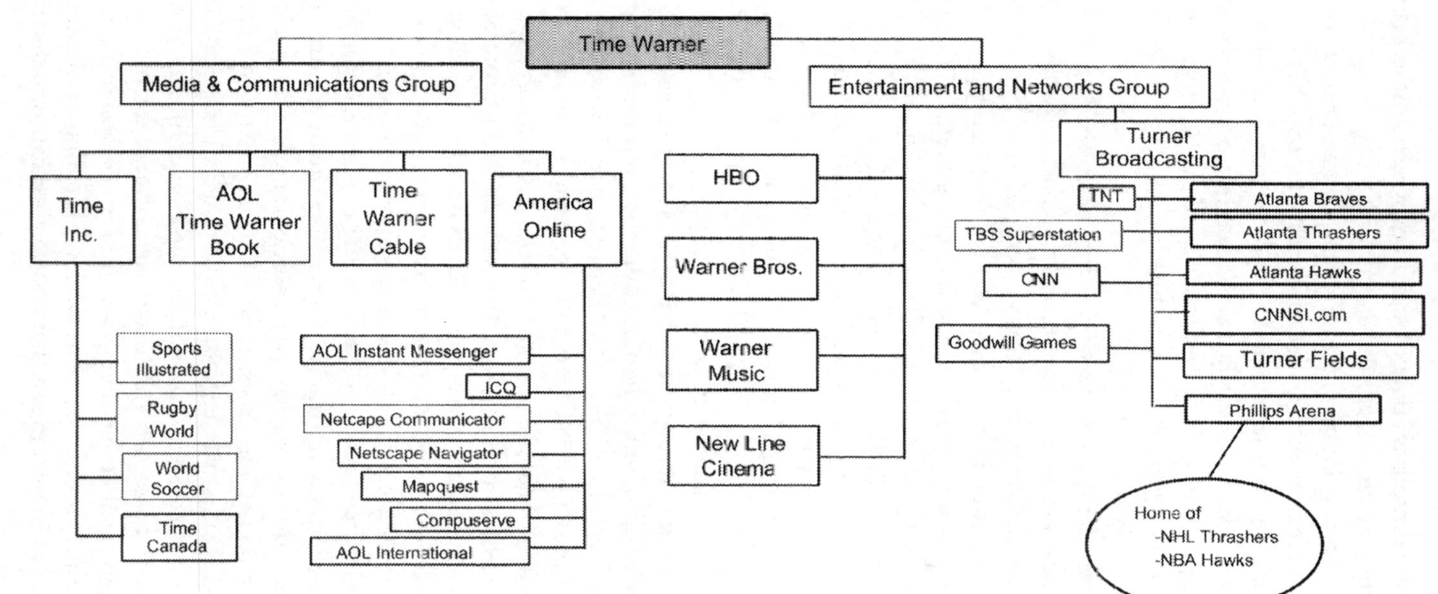

Figure 10.3. *Time Warner corporate holdings (simplified).*
Sources: Hoovers, corporate web site, Business Wire.

sport portal, falls under the roof of Turner Broadcasting where most sport content production properties are regrouped.

Before the recent restructuring, with the exception of Time, *vertical integration* has been a growth strategy of each independent corporation (that is AOL on the one side and the Time Warner group on the other side) and substantially amplified through *the product and service extension* strategy achieved by merger. There is not enough room here to retrace the growth strategies of each corporation in detail; however, each will be briefly canvassed to illustrate the point made here.

Time magazine, was founded as the world's first news weekly in 1923 and shortly expanded sideways with *Life*, *Fortune* and then *Sports Illustrated*. Warner Brothers Motion Picture Company was also incorporated in 1923. However, over the course of the twentieth century Warner Brothers expanded both horizontally and vertically into television and film production and distribution along with music labels in over seventy countries. Turner Broadcasting Systems joined the conglomerate in 1996. It should be noted that the purchase of the Turner properties was directly aimed at adding branded material to the existing holdings of Time Warner so that content could be distributed across a greater number of platforms and cross-promotional strategy could be extended (*The Economist*, 2000, p. 22). Turner brought to the table the Home Box Office network (HBO), CNN (arguably the world's first global news gathering and disseminating broadcaster although recently overtaken in terms of audience by News Corp's Fox News) and other cable and entertainment properties including the Atlanta Braves, Atlanta Thrashers, Atlanta Hawks, the Phillips Arena, Turner Fields, the Goodwill Games and World Championship Wrestling. In September 2003, 85 percent of equity and 100 percent of management rights in The Hawks, Thrashers and Phillips Arena were sold to Atlanta Spirit an Atlanta-based consortium. Associated press releases reported the sale as in the interests to "improve our financial ratios and increase our financial flexibility". This shift is probably the result of AOL's failure and development of a more narrow "bottom line" perspective, subordinating the less tangible asset of "synergy" to operating cash and financial leverage needs. The latter two properties represent Turner's attempt to create his own sport content, avoiding expensive broadcast rights and scheduling issues.

In January 2000, AOL joined the group. AOL began in 1985 with 500,000 subscribers. In 2000, it had over 17 million. Acquisition of Instant Messenger added 35 million users. (Krigel, 1999). The addition of Netscape Communicator and Navigator enabled AOL to capture a substantial proportion of the Internet access market. In addition to its primary service, providing consumers with access to the Internet, AOL went to great pains to keep the user within its "walled garden" of content in order to attract the consumer to its line of e-products and services (*The Economist*, 2000).

The merger between Time Warner and AOL was an attempt to combine brand name media, entertainment, news and broadband delivery systems with the extensive array of AOL Internet franchises and the infrastructure itself that reaches a large online consumer audience. By its magnitude and the extent of telecommunication and media properties involved, this merger struck the imagination of the industry. As a result, for many, that deal was the one that sparked the frenzy of millennium mega media, including for example the flamboyant deals leading to the now fragile Vivendi Universal consortium (see Law et al., 2002). Indeed, the potentially achievable cross-promotional strategy appeared vastly superior to other members of the global media oligopoly as no other company had access to such a large Internet infrastructure. However, the 2002 events demonstrated the extent of overestimated internet revenue and arguably had an impact of re-examining the concrete benefits to be derived "synergy" through combined vertical and horizontal integration corporate structural strategies.

Consolidation of "branding" is perhaps best illustrated in reference to sport with the joining of the CNN news reputation and the success of *Sports Illustrated* magazine. Here, the two have been merged for a sports news cable network (CNNSI was launched in December 1996) and a Web site devoted to sports news (CNNSI.com launched in July, 1997) (CNNSI.com, 1997). Such cross-promotional activity seems a key ingredient in the synergy of such new and old media. However, one might speculate about what is left of that strategy now that *Sports Illustrated* and CNNSI are in different divisions of the conglomerate.

In terms of *geographic and market extension*, although Time Warner's properties are mainly North American based and aimed at North American markets (especially their sport-based properties), some of their most high profile holdings are very much global in scope. The emergence of CNN as an international news gathering and disseminating source epitomizes their eagerness to be a transnational company. International AOL alliances with other members of the oligopoly exist. For example, AOL received a $75 million payment from Bertelsmann as part of an agreement to expand the two companies' online service in Europe via the Compuserve platform. This agreement dictates Bertelsmann's online presence in Europe (Compuserve Europe), but also extends AOL Time Warner's consumer reach. Finally, the Time Inc. group, through its some 140 periodicals, reaches sport consumers from all regions of the world through its vast selection of sport magazines dedicated to rugby, soccer, golf, ski, surf, cycling, BMX, yachting, and a wide variety of other sports.

The Canadian Mass Media Complex

In this section we will present and discuss maps of key Canadian private media corporations to show Canadian corporate response to global pressures pursued by the above corporations among others. However, before presenting and discussing Canadian corporate growth strategies it is useful to place these in normative context. Following a brief description of how Canadians approach their private/public media balance, we will also briefly discuss two recent controversies that highlight debates in Canada on the impact of "telecomedia" conglomerate growth. The first (*La Soirée du hockey*) highlights impacts of commodifying cultural policy by relegating cultural values to small market commodities within corporate structure. The second (*Gazette*) highlights effects of media concentration – an outcome of horizontal integration strategies.

The history of the Canadian mass media complex is complicated to say the least. It is only through the lenses of that history that one can understand what is at stake the current conjuncture. At the core of this history is a struggle between two major camps in an ideological war that started at the very beginning of radio broadcasting in Canada in 1920. Indeed, in the 1920s the advocates of public telecommunications, the "cultural nationalists", lobbied for a strong state control of media, motivated as they were by the fear of a US takeover of Canadian airwaves. They fought for Canada to create its own state-controlled "public broadcasting space", as a tool for public education and for the promotion of a Canadian culture distinct from American culture. In their view what Canada needed was a system that would provide quality, educational, high culture and some quality entertainment to Canadians. Radio and TV were public goods that were to be put at the service of the promotion of Canadian culture; they were to reflect Canadian values (Nash, 2001). For the "cultural nationalists" the mass media and cultural industries in general do not sell an innocent product. Rather, they produce cultural texts that affect society's values, beliefs, the way citizens see themselves and debate about society, culture, politics and sport. In other words, mass mediated culture is a significant part of what forms or constructs national identity. On this, their vision was not dissimilar to those prevailing in other industrial countries like Britain and France for example. Influential nationalists were in fact pushing for a Canadian BBC-style system. The state decision to create a Crown society, CBC/Radio-Canada, in 1936 was a partial victory for the "cultural nationalists".

On the other side of the fence are the "media barons" who always fought to develop media empires modeled on the US entertainment media enterprises. The media entrepreneurs counter-attacked the lobby of "cultural nationalists". What they wanted was to provide popular, as well as profitable, entertainment for Canadians. For them, "public service broadcasting have been forcing Canadians into programming meant to be 'good for you' at best or at worst straight propaganda for the government" (Nash, 2001, p. 15). For them, Canadians had the right to choose and they were there to provide them mostly American entertainment that was not available through the CBC. Freedom of speech was also used as a justification against a State monopoly of the airwaves (Vipond, 2000; Nash, 2001). The telecommunications war has been fought on several fronts: Royal Commissions struck by the federal government, legislation in Parliament, media licensing and obviously through the airwaves themselves, the media barons not shying away from using their own media outlets to undermine the legitimacy of the CBC.

As mentioned earlier, the creation of CBC/Radio-Canada in the 1930s was a partial victory for the "cultural nationalists". It was partial because, contrary to what was expected by them, the legislation did not provide for the public institution to regulate the airwaves, nor did it give CBC/Radio-Canada the monopoly they were looking for. As a result Canada's telecommunications and broadcasting system is a mix system of public and corporate corporations in which wars are constantly fought for their respective interests. Three main pieces of legislation regulate this system: the Telecommunication Act (1993, c. 38), the Broadcasting Act (1991, c. 11) and the Canadian Radio-television and Telecommunications Commission Act (1986, c. 22). For the purpose of this chapter the most salient points are the following. The legislation stipulates that telecommunication and broadcasting corporation shall be effectively owned and controlled by Canadians (c.11, p. 3(a)). More precisely, in order to obtain a licence, eighty per cent of the board members of a corporation must be Canadians and 80 percent of the corporation shares must be owned by Canadians (c.38, p. 16(3)a). Moreover, strict rules are applied to broadcasters in terms of Canadian content, cross ownership of media outlets, and so forth, that are determined and monitored by the Canadian Radio-television and Telecommunications Commission (CRTC), the state regulating body. Moreover, The Broadcasting Act list of objectives of the broacasting policy for Canada includes the requirement that the system, should ". . . serve to safeguard, enrich and strenghten the cultural, political, social and economic fabric of Canada" (c.11, p. 3(1)d).

That entire system has been challenged again by the private "media barons" during Canada's media consolidation frenzy of the 1990s. The chairman of the CBC/Radio-Canada describes what is at stake in the current context for the CBC and the CRTC in the following terms: "With the continuing trend toward globalisation and increased competitiveness in the Canadian marketplace, all these tools will come under pressure. Ensuring they remain effectively equipped to complement the activities of private broadcasters in boosting Canadian culture is very important" (Canadian Issues, 2002, p. 7).

What is at stake here is the kind of sport programming to be broadcast by particular types of corporations, following particular kinds of objectives. For the CBC, *Hockey Night in Canada* has always been a key Canadian content component of its programing. At the same time it has represented for white Anglo-Canadians (mostly males) a prime element of national identity, and continues as one of the few coherent national symbols (Gruneau and Whitson, 1993). For French-Canadians and Radio-Canada the equivalent show was *La soirée du hockey.* The following controversy over the near demise of the French-Canadian show is instructive of the continuing importance and relevance of public broadcasting to the oft precarious balance of constitutionally embedded multi-cultural national interests. Further, the controversy illustrates the marginal place of small market audience share within multi-platform conglomerates. Cultural politics is not only relegated to a matter of mere scale, it becomes subject to corporate strategies driven by global competitive pressures of convergence and synergy. Here some symbols proliferate – others rattle around in niches available only to those who can afford, or even find them.

La Soirée du hockey

For Quebecers, *La Soirée du hockey* has been sacred for more than fifty years. This tradition started well before the advent of the television, with radio presentation of Montreal Canadiens games. The first match, opposing the Boston Bruins to the then Montreal Maroons, was broadcast in early November 1937. The following week, the Canadiens played their first historical match against the Detroit Red Wings. This radio tradition continued through to May 1997 (Radio-Canada, 2003). Televised transmission of matches started on October 1952, again with the Canadiens playing against the Red Wings, on Radio-Canada. At that time, because of team managers' concerns that people would stop attending matches in the Forum, the program was only on air from 9:30 p.m. This proved wrong, however, and the program was allowed to start sooner until it coincided with the beginning of the match. In 1956, *La Soirée du hockey* had the highest rate of viewers in the Montreal area, with an average ranging from 300,000 to 350,000 people each night (Radio-Canada, 2003).

New technologies developed in the 1960s permitted viewers to watch repeats, then slow motion, and finally color broadcasting, which began in 1967. *La Soirée du hockey* broadened its horizons by presenting international events, such as the famous Canada-URSS Series in 1972, followed by the first Confrontation Series between the NHL and European hockey teams. This resulted in the number of viewers throughout the French Radio-Canada network reaching

557,000 homes in 1973, and the average of viewers for the Stanley Cup finals between the Montreal Canadiens and the New York Rangers in 1979 increased to 1,884,000 people (Radio-Canada, 2003).

The love story between the Canadiens and their fans is evidenced by the nightmare programers at Radio-Canada went through, especially in Quebec, when the NHL allowed US sports networks to decide the schedule of playoff games according to their needs. Daniel Gourd, Radio-Canada's director of programming, summarized the situation in those words: "The difference is that francophones really only care about one team, the Canadiens. When they are out of the playoffs, viewership drops dramatically. People in English Canada, on the other hand, will cheer for Montreal, Edmonton, Ottawa or Toronto" (Curran, 2001). In May 2002, Radio-Canada announced that the broadcasting deal it had with the NHL would expire at the end of the 2001–2 hockey season because tentative talks with the Réseau des Sports (RDS), a BCE subsidiary had failed (Reuters, 2002). In fact, RDS had concluded in March a four-year deal with the NHL, the Montreal Canadiens and the Ottawa Senators for the broadcasting rights over a minimum of thirty regular games and playoff games up to the conference finals (Réseau des Sports, 2002).

This would have meant the end of the legendary *Soirée du hockey*. Was one of the most sacred symbols of Canadian nationalism (for French Canadians) going to be sacrificed on the altar of BCE's corporate strategy? The announcement provoked substantial controversy not only among fans but throughout Canadian cultural political arenas. French-speaking inside and outside of Quebec would either have to watch Hockey Night in Canada or subscribe to cable or satellite television.

The Federal Heritage Minister Sheila Copps, responsible for national unity, sports and the CBC, expressed concerns about the fact that (freely translated) "throughout Canada, the French-speaking public would not have any more access to Canadiens games on La Soirée du hockey" (Canadian Press, 2002a). After parties appeared before the House of Commons Standing Joint Committee on Official Languages to look at this issue, RDS and the hockey team began new negotiations with Radio-Canada (Canadian Press, 2002b). Soon after, Radio-Canada concluded a three-year deal with RDS, which allowed the Crown corporation to broadcast between twenty and twenty-five matches on Saturday nights, as well as Canadiens off-season games (Radio-Canada, 2002).

Gazette Controversy

Concentration of ownership in print can raise important questions about the lack of diversity of views. CanWest Global Communications, under the control of the Asper family from Winnipeg, owns twenty-seven daily newspapers grouped together in the Southam News chain, which is estimated to represent 40 percent of the English-language daily newspaper circulation in Canada (CanWest, 2001). In December 2001, CanWest issued a new policy requiring local newspapers from publishing, once a week, an editorial distributed by the corporate headquarters on key national and international issues. Moreover, the newspapers were prohibited to publish, in unsigned editorial columns, opinions diverging from those contained in the chain-wide articles (Canadian Journalists, 2002).

An enormous controversy spurred from that decision. Freedom-of-expression advocates expressed concern about the owners' interference in their newspapers' content and about the initiative's impact on the potential loss of distinctive regional editorial voices. In an open letter, seventy-seven employees of *The Gazette*, the only English-language metropolitan daily newspaper in the province of Quebec, clearly protested against CanWest's centralizing policy by saying, in part, that "Without question, this decision will undermine the independence and diversity of each newspaper's editorial board and thereby give Canadians a greatly reduced variety of opinion, debate and editorial discussion . . ." (*The Gazette*, 2001).

Currently the Canadian private media landscape is dominated by the following power houses: BCE, Shaw, Canwest, Rogers, Quebecor and Torstar. In this chapter, we will focus on BCE, Rogers, Canwest and Quebecor.

BCE

BCE is Canada's largest communications company, offering a wide array of products and services. It was formed in 1983 by Bell Canada as a parent company and to separate Bell Canada's unregulated businesses from the regulated telephone service carriers (Jones, n.d.). With 24 million residential and business customer connections, BCE provides wireline, wireless, data, Internet and satellite entertainment services, principally under the Bell brand (BCE, 2002a). As of January 2003, BCE's product and service extension covers three main sectors – telephony or more recently "connectivity"; media (primarily television and Internet); and Commercial services – e-commerce, consulting and data services. These three sectors correspond to BCE's three Cs at the core of its convergence strategy: connectivity, content, commerce (Pitts, 2002). Each is horizontally integrated to a certain extent. The "connectivity arm" of BCE operates the largest telecommunications network in Canada through its Bell Canada segment. BCE owns 37.5 percent of Aliant, an Atlantic Canada phone provider, and Bell Canada has a 22 percent stake in Manitoba Telecom (CRTC, 2002a). Other holdings include Northwest Tel Inc. Bell Nordiq, Bell Mobility, its cell phone subsidiary.

BCE's *vertical integration vis-à-vis* content, flows primarily through its Globemedia division where cultural products circulates in satellite direct,

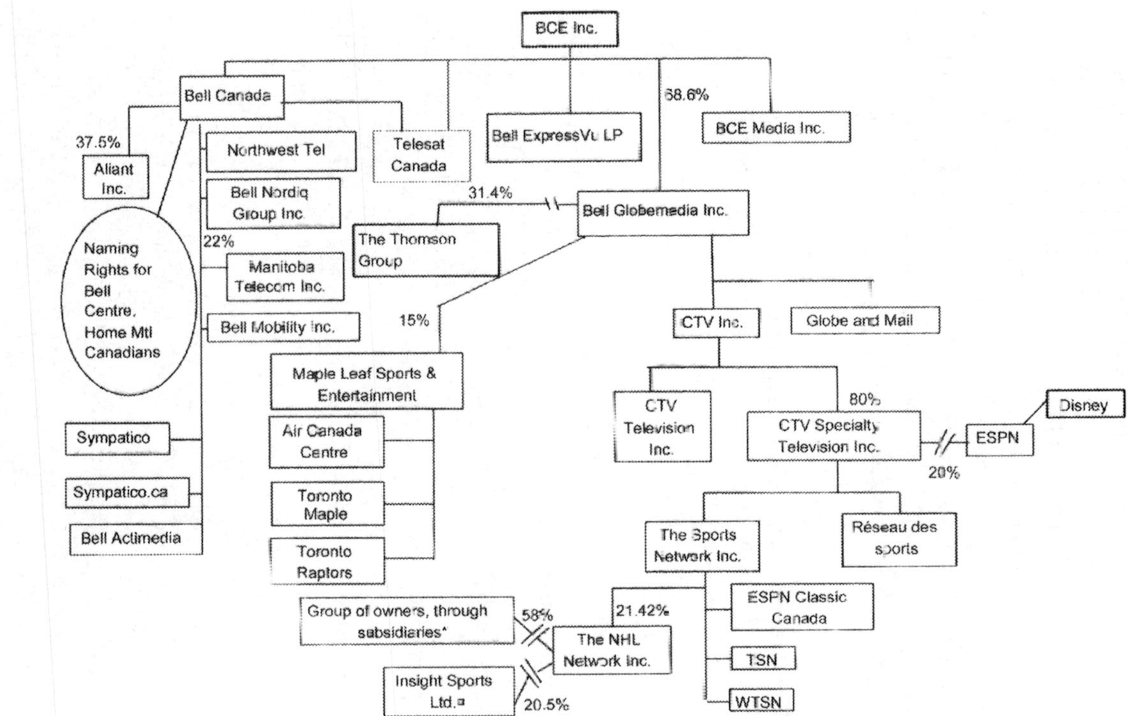

Figure 10.4. *BCE Inc. corporate holdings (simplified). *Including Ottawa Senators Hockey Club Corp., NHL Enterprises Canada LP, Edmonton Investors Group Ltd. and Calgary Flames LP. ¤ Insight Productions Company Ltd., MWI Nominee Company Ltd., Ignite Communications Inc. and Kilmer Enterprises Inc.*

Sources: Corporate Web sites, CRTC Web site, Hoover's Online.

broadcast, cable and Internet channels. For Monty, former CEO of BCE, in terms of real value, the type of content BCE was running after, namely for the Internet sector, are "news first, finance, sport, travel, and comedy" (Pitts, 2002, p. 132). On February 25, 2000, BCE made an unsolicited offer of $2.3 billion in order to acquire CTV Inc., one of Canada's pre-eminent broadcast communications companies. According to Pitts (2002), it is precisely this takeover of CTV that initiated the 2000 frenzy of mergers and acquisitions within the Canadian media landscape. Through its television operations, including the acquisition on September 2001 of CF Television Inc., the leading English-language television station in Montreal (Quebec), CTV reaches 99 percent of English-speaking households, offering a wide range of quality news, sports, information and entertainment programming. Monty, stated the following:

> Ownership of CTV significantly enhances BCE's consumer strategy of providing our customers with integrated information, communications and entertainment (ICE) services. The strength of the CTV brand, its strong programming line-up, and its award-winning expertise in the areas of news and sports will squarely place BCE as a leading player in the converging broadcasting and new media industries. (BCE, 2000)

BCE, which already had within its realm communications and information, has completed the convergence triad with this acquisition of CTV's entertainment content to display. In an attempt to become a major player in the world's communication market, BCE gained all twenty-five CTV affiliates as well as CTV's 68 percent (now 80 percent) stake (through CTV Specialty Television Inc.) in The Sports Network (TSN), the Canadian specialty channel (TSN, 2001); in RDS, the world's only 24-hour French language all-sports network (Bell Globemedia, 2002c); and later in ESPN Classic Canada and The NHL Network (Bell Globemedia, 2002d). It is interesting to note that the remaining 20 percent interest in CTV Specialty Television Inc. is held by ESPN (CRTC, 2002b), which is in turn a 80 percent-owned Disney subsidiary.

In February, 2002 Bell Canada acquired the naming rights for the Molson Centre, which was to become the Bell Centre. The Molson Centre, inaugurated in 1996, is the most important sports, cultural and business center in the province of Quebec. Every year, the home of the Montréal Canadiens attracts close to 850,000 spectators for its hockey games, while 650,000 people walk through its doors to watch some 120 shows, for a total of 1.5 million spectators. This business agreement between Bell, Molson and the Montréal Canadiens was intended to enable Bell to expand its community involvement and develop business synergy with the Canadiens and Molson, as expressed by Jean Monty:

> By associating our name with one of Québec's foremost venues, Bell hopes to reinforce its commitment to the cultural and sporting life of Quebecers [. . .] Wireless, high-speed Internet and satellite television facilities make the Molson Centre the most connected building in the city. The Bell Centre's visibility will contribute significantly to positioning the Bell brand and will enable spectators to enjoy an even more diversified Bell experience. (Bell Canada, 2002a)

In February 2003, the BCE acquisition of Maple Leafs Sports and Entertainment Ltd (MLSE) sent a shock wave into Canada's mass media and professional landscape. MLSE owns NHL's Toronto Maple Leafs and NBA's Toronto Raptors, their arena, the Air Canada Centre, as well as two specialty digital TV channels for the teams. With this acquisition, Bell Globemedia obtained a 15 percent share of MLSE the most valuable Canadian sport property. More importantly, what this transaction means is that, under BCE, direct or indirect control fall the two most important Canadian NHL franchises, The Canadiens and the Maple Leafs, as well, eventually the two prime Canadian professional sport telecast, *La soirée du hockey* discussed earlier and *Hockey Night in Canada*. Indeed, Bell Globemedia will be in the driver's seat when the TV rights for the broadcast of Maple Leafs and Raptors game will be renegotiated. It may happen that the TV rights of the Maple Leafs games move from the CBC, to BCE's CTV, TSN and RDS. In other words, for Canadian hockey fans, that deal may mark the end of fifty years of coast-to-coast, "free access" to *Hockey Night in Canada* on CBC, replicating the *Soirée du hockey* saga and therefore achieving the total privatization of hockey on Canadian airwaves.

One of BCE's overall strategic objectives is to leverage its unrivalled customer connections and its unique combination of wireline, wireless, broadband IP data and video assets with compelling content and e-commerce applications. This strategy will be reinforced through BCE's decision to return to 100 percent ownership of its core asset, Bell Canada, by early December 2002 (BCE 2002b). With its powerful national brands and customer connections, BCE is now focused on crafting solutions for consumers that enable "anytime-and-anywhere" access to information and entertainment; and solutions for business that enhance productivity and competitive edge (Bell Canada, 2002b). Bell Canada has access to the computer age via Sympatico Inc. Sympatico is a Canadian Web communications, commerce and media company that owns and operates a network of national and local Canadian Internet media properties. In a 1999 collaboration with Lycos, Sympatico launched Sympatico-Lycos, the most visited Canadian Web portal that gives access to online city sites, news, sports and entertainment. Bell Globemedia recently announced that it was acquiring 100 percent in the Sympatico-Lycos joint venture relationship (Bell Globemedia, 2002b). Bell Globemedia also owns the *Globe and Mail*, Canada's leading national newspaper.

Additionally, the company`s Bell ExpressVu allows more than one million consumers to have direct-to-home satellite entertainment services (Bell ExpressVu, 2001).

BCE's geographic market extension is primarily limited to Canada as its international presence is fading. Through a 1999 alliance with MCI WorldCom, BCE gained access to global networks worldwide (BCE, 1999), whereas Bell Canada International (BCI) (74 percent share) gave telephone, wireless, and cable television privileges to 4.5 million of cellular subscribers in Brazil (BCI, 2002a) and many others in China, Colombia, India, Korea, Mexico and Taiwan (*Hoover's Online*, 2002b). Financial difficulties led BCI to have a plan of arrangement approved by the court (BCI, 2002b) under which it sold its interest in Telecom Americas and will be distributing its remaining assets in the near future (BCI, 2002c). BCE's market extension is limited to Canada, but for its Canadian competitors its penetration of the Canadian market makes it a feared rival, a "Fortress Canada business" (Pitts, 2002, p. 125).

The stock-exchange bubble-burst in 2002 lead BCE towards large losses, as other similar business. Officially at least, BCE's convergence strategy is now a thing of the past according to its new CEO. BCE's Industrial Media conglomerate structure is reasonably well connected to multiple interests including Disney through ESPN.

CanWest

Founded in the early 1970s when Canadian Tax and Corporate lawyer I.H. Asper launched a new television station in Winnipeg, CanWest Global Communications Corp. is now Canada's largest integrated media company (CanWest, 2001a). A few years later, Global Television, which provided programing to the television station, suffered serious financial difficulties, and CanWest jumped on the occasion to acquire it progressively, up to 100 percent in 1989 (CanWest, 2002b). Due to its numerous acquisitions, CanWest's assets more than doubled to $6.3 billion between August 2000 and August 2001. The company seems to still be in expansion, as it generated revenues of $1.9 billion for the 2001 fiscal year, an increase of 166 percent from the same period in 2000 (Industry Canada, 2002).

CanWest is reasonably well horizontally integrated across it's main distribution channels and content production capabilities, which combined, also demonstrate a good degree of product and service extension in areas including television, Internet, print media and direct content production. Throughout the 1980s and 1990s, CanWest's television broadcasting division made the acquisition of several other television stations in Vancouver, Halifax and in Quebec. The recent and important purchase, approved in July of 2000, of the conventional

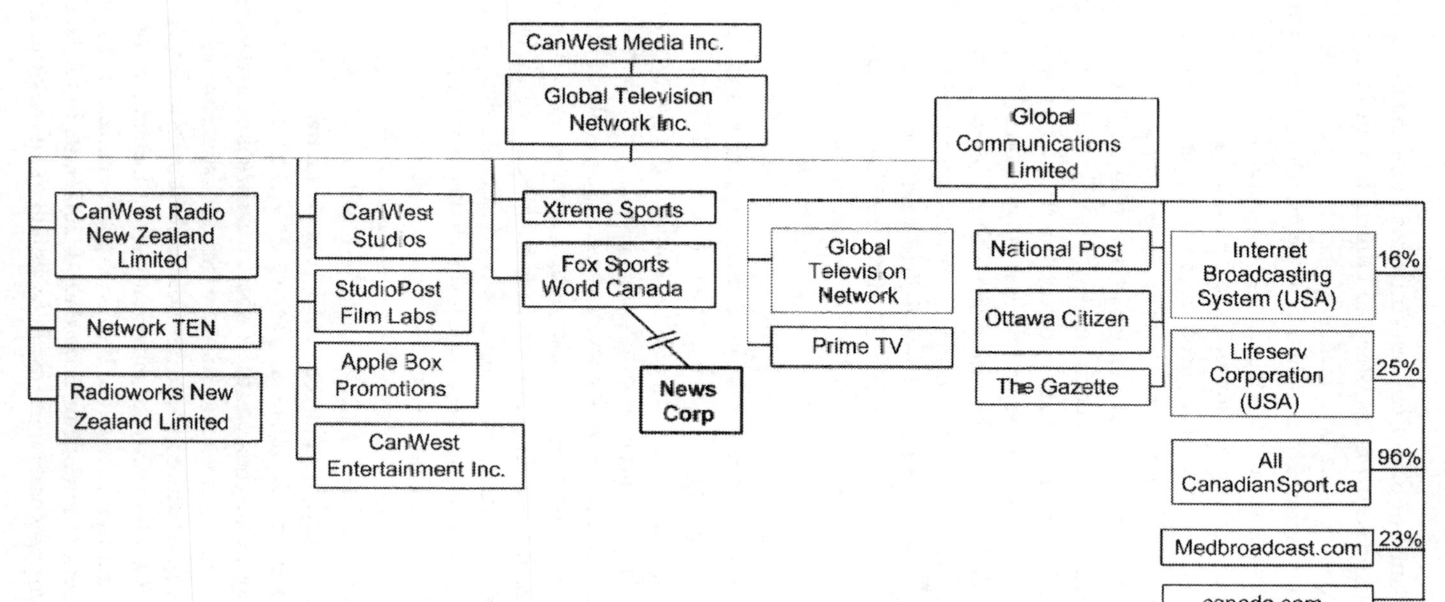

Figure 10.5. *CanWest corporate holdings (simplified).*
Sources: Corporate Web sites, CRTC Web site.

assets of Western International Communications Ltd., situated in British Columbia, Alberta and Ontario, transformed Global Television into a truly national network with a presence from Halifax to Vancouver (CanWest, 2002b). Global Television now broadcasts over-the-air via eleven television stations that reach 94 percent of the English-speaking Canadian population. CanWest also owns three independent television stations and two CBC affiliated ones.

It is only in 2000 that CanWest entered into the print publication industry with CanWest notable purchase of Hollinger's assets. The acquisition of the National Post (100 percent in 2001), along with fourteen major metropolitan daily papers, over 120 daily and weekly newspapers in smaller communities across Canada and a magazine group, resulted in a strong business, making CanWest Canada's largest publisher of daily newspapers (CanWest, 2002b). Referred to as the Hollinger deal, this impressive US$2.2 billion purchase produces an overlapping of television and newspaper coverage in twenty-five of its twenty-six markets, with an estimated overall 35 percent share of the Canadian advertising market (Ketupa.net, 2002). The same year, CanWest entered the out-of-home advertising business with the acquisition of Australia's second largest out-of-home advertising company, present in outdoor signage as well as in airports and shopping centres. CanWest also operates canada.com, Canada's most comprehensive Internet network and portal. Personalized information, news, sports and business from across Canada and the world is given to its 3 million monthly unique users for an average of 115 million page views (CanWest, 2002c) under the umbrella of canada.com, which also includes the hockey site Faceoff.com. In August 2000, CanWest also bought a controlling interest in All Sport Ventures, which operates All CanadianSport.ca, a provider of software, information and services for amateur sport in Canada (CanWest, 2002c).

CanWest's geographic market extension is truly Global with multidirectional distribution between several countries, which simultaneously support vertical integration through sports broadcast rights as well as direct production. Several television stations are owned in whole or part in Australia, New Zealand and Ireland, as well as commercial radio networks in New Zealand (Industry Canada, 2002). CanWest launched in the fall of 2001 six new digital cable specialty channels that add to Prime TV, in operation since 1997. The specialty channels owned by Global Television related to the sport industry are Xtreme Sports, an extreme sports events channel, and Fox Sportsworld Canada, which features international sporting news and events, as well as the broadcasting of soccer and cricket games (CanWest, 2002b). Fox Sportsworld Canada is a branch of Fox Sports World, which is part of the Fox Entertainment Group 85 percent owned by News Corporation (News Corporation, 2002). In 1999, "to ensure its place in the emerging world of new media technologies" (CanWest, 2002b),

CanWest launched its electronic publishing arm, CanWest Interactive, which operations consumer Web sites as well as the creation and sale of financial data, text, photographs and video (CanWest, 2002c). It consisted at the time of investments in Lifeserv Corporation and in Internet Broadcasting Systems, another US-based Internet content provider specializing in developing Web sites for local television stations in several American cities. Moreover, CanWest bought a stake, today of 23 percent, in Medbroadcast Corp, Canada's source of health information on the Web (CRTC, 2002c). Another of CanWest's operating divisions is centered squarely on production. In May 1998, CanWest made the acquisition of Fireworks Entertainment Inc, a leading Canadian independent film and television production company. A year later, CanWest Entertainment expanded its operations in London and Los Angeles (CanWest, 2002b). Not surprisingly, CanWest Entertainment, which produces a wide range of programming for Canadian as well as international broadcasters, is CanWest Global's primary content provider (Industry Canada, 2002).

CanWest's Industrial Media conglomerate structure is well linked into the web of relationships through jointly owned properties with corporations such as News Corp's Fox Entertainment.

Rogers

Rogers Communications Inc. is "a national communications company which is engaged in cable television, high-speed internet access, video retailing, wireless communications, radio and television broadcasting and publishing" (Rogers, 2002a). Ted Rogers established one television station as well as FM radio stations in Canada in the early 1960s and has leveraged its infrastructure and cashflow to become a substantial Canadian telecommunications provider (Ketupa.net, 2002).

Rogers is well horizontally integrated in three sectors including wireless communications, radio and television as well content production indicating a reasonable degree of product and service extension. Rogers Communications had to evolve quickly. Its wireless component, Rogers Cantel Inc., commenced service in 1985 to operate a national cellular telephone network in Canada that would compete with the established telephone companies. Rogers Communications now owns 51 percent of the public company Rogers AT&T Wireless (previously Rogers Cantel Mobile Communications Inc.) (CRTC, 2002d). Operating offices in Canadian cities from coast to coast, it is Canada's largest wireless communications service provider with almost 3.5 million wireless customers (Rogers, 2002a). Rogers AT&T Wireless provides a complete range of wireless solutions including Digital PCS, cellular, paging, two-way messaging, and wireless data services.

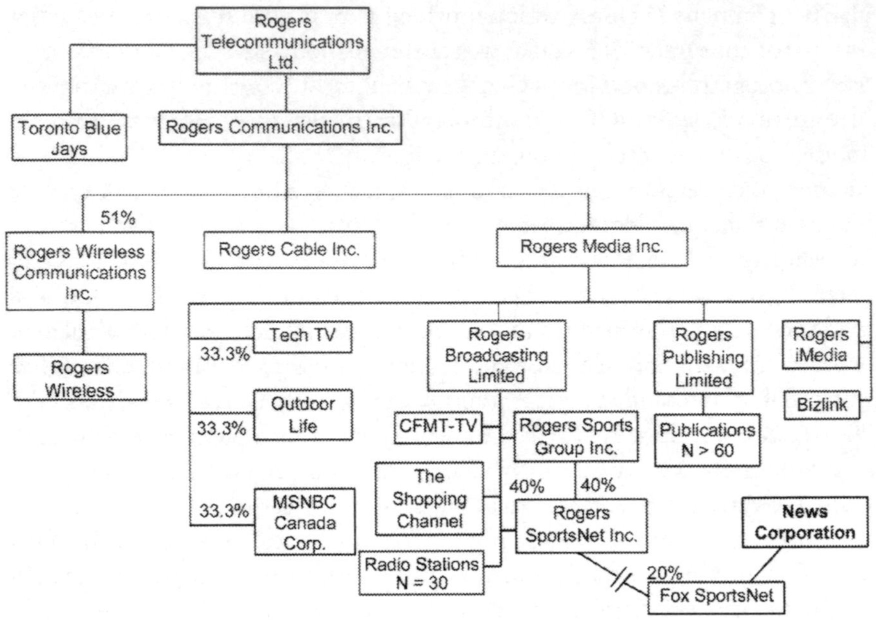

Figure 10.6. *Rogers corporate holdings (simplified).*
Sources: Corporate Web sites, CRTC Web site, Hoover's Online Web site.

The cable distribution segment is the second most important for the company with 37 percent of its 2001 revenues (Rogers, 2001b). In 1974, Rogers became the first cable company to expand past twelve television channels. It eventually specialized by adding more programing choice, in particular with multi-cultural television, thanks primarily to two important acquisitions. In 1979, Mr Rogers' company, Rogers Cable TV Limited, acquired control of Canadian Cablesystems Limited through a reverse takeover, and in 1980, Rogers purchased Premier Communications Limited (Rogers, 2002b). These transactions almost doubled Rogers' cable subscribers. The company also expanded the acquisition and building of cable television systems in the US during the years 1979 to 1982, and was able to sell those interests in March for a cash value of CDN $1.581 billion (Rogers, 2002b). Today, Rogers is the largest cable television company in Canada with over 2.3 million customers (Rogers, 2002a).

Rogers is using its cable networks efficiently to provide high-speed Internet access for residential subscribers through cable modems. The high-speed Internet service is one of Rogers' fastest-growing services, with more than 600,000 subscribers (Rogers, 2002a). Due to the bankruptcy of the American-based

Internet company @Home which provided Rogers with high-speed Internet backbone services, Rogers had to transfer its high-speed customers from @home.com to a @rogers.com e-mail suffix in early 2002 and move to a high-speed network operated in conjunction with Teleglobe Inc. (Industry Canada, 2002).

Currently, Rogers Broadcasting consists of 43 AM and FM radio properties across Canada, including THE FAN 590 in Toronto, an all-sports radio station. Another Rogers Media's asset is The Shopping Channel, Canada's only televised home shopping network (Rogers, 2001). Like competitors such as BCE and CanWest, Rogers has expanded into publishing and sports. On March 31, 1994, Rogers Communications Inc. successfully completed the acquisition of the shares of Maclean Hunter Limited for $3.1 billion (Rogers, 2002b). Rogers Publishing now has a catalog comprising more than sixty consumer magazines and business and professional publications.

In 2000, Rogers' $5.6 billion takeover bid for Videotron cable network was aborted, but in the same year it bought a 80 percent interest in the Toronto Blue Jays Major League Baseball team and a majority interest in the Toronto Phantoms Football Club, indicating vertical integration via equity interests in franchise sport. Rogers tries to advertise the fact that it owns professional sport assets by using its Web site to sell Blue Jays sporting merchandise. Industrial media conglomerate structure is substantial with multiple shared interests with "competitors". In 2001, again in the pursuit of an integrated sports-media alliance, Rogers acquired from BCE an additional 40 percent stake in Rogers SportsNet, of which the American company Fox Sports owns a 20 percent interest (Industry Canada, 2002). According to Pitts (2002), this transaction was made possible through yet another CRTC deregulation move in 2001, allowing cable operators to own specialty and pay channels. That new ruling made it possible for Rogers to put in place its sport convergence strategy. There are obvious synergies to be gained from this purchase, because Rogers, with its 80 percent share, can use SportsNet as the principal carrier of Blue Jay games. The idea behind securing the controlling interest of SportsNet is that "at a time when technology can now enable commercial messages to be skipped by viewers with personal video recorders, live sports is one of the few mediums where advertisers are guaranteed effective promotion" (Rogers, 2001b). However, unlike Canwest, geographic market extension is primarily limited to Canada.

Through this diversity of properties, Rogers' goal for the future is to "take advantage of the natural convergence opportunities across its assets: cross-promotion; cross-selling; product bundling; customer loyalty programs; shared channels; shared distribution; and shared infrastructure" (Rogers, 2001b).

Quebecor

Quebecor Inc. started in 1950 with a small neighborhood newspaper, which Pierre Péladeau resuscitated (Quebecor, 2003a). The company, which has expanded to become a communication leader, is now divided into two major subsidiaries: Quebecor World, the world's largest commercial printer, and Quebecor Media, a media company with over 15,000 employees, concentrated in Quebec and the rest of Canada but with operations elsewhere in North America and around the world (Quebecor, 2003b).

Quebecor is highly horizontally integrated across the most diverse range of divisions – topping the Canadian list in terms of product and service extension. Quebecor Media's major operations are in broadcasting through TVA, the top general-interest network in Quebec, and in newspapers with Sun Media, the second-largest newspaper group in Canada, eight metropolitan dailies in Canada and over 180 community newspapers and other publications across Canada and in Florida (Quebecor, 2003b). Quebecor also now owns Internet portals (Netgraphe and Canoe) and is involved in Web integration (Nurun), Business Telecommunications (Vidéotron Telecom) and in the distribution and retail of music and videos (Groupe Archambault and Le SuperClub Vidéotron) (Quebecor, 2003c). Vertical integration is not as dense as Rogers, and geographic market extension is low, but Quebecor's most interesting structural feature is its equity relationship at the parent level with the Quebec state. This feature of its inter-industry relationships, and the story of its creation underscores the importance of telecommunications corporate structures to Canadian cultural politics and locates the state as far more than a benign facilitator of global competition.

In February 2000, Rogers and Videotron Group Ltd., then Canada's third cable television company and an Internet service provider in the province of Quebec jointly announced an agreement to merge their activities (CBC, 2000). At the time, Ted Rogers had said that the motivation behind the deal was the huge AOL-Time Warner merger the month before and the need to compete with industry giants from the US. "These two companies are large in Canadian terms, but we're becoming more and more insignificant in North American terms," said Rogers (CBC, 2000). Moreover, the two companies thought the move would give them a strong position against Bell Canada, "one of the best-run phone companies in North America" (CBC, 2002).

On March 23, 2000, Rogers and Shaw Communications announced that they had agreed to swap Rogers' existing cable operations in British Columbia in exchange for Shaw's cable operations in southern Ontario and New Brunswick (Shaw, 2000). Commenting on the transaction, Ted Rogers said, "These

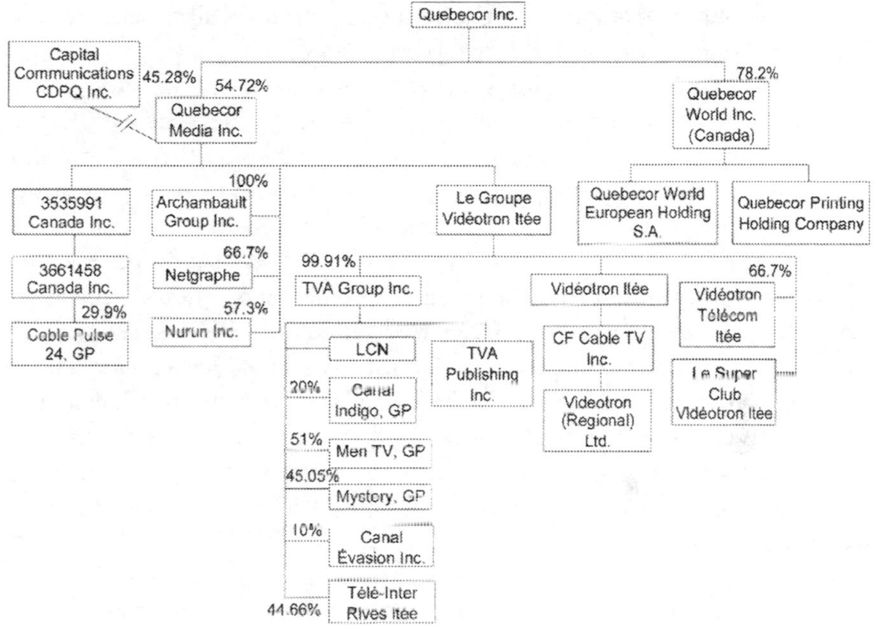

Figure 10.7. *Quebecor corporate holdings (simplified).*
Sources: Corporate Web site, CRTC Web site, Hoover's Online Web site.

transactions will continue our clustering strategy in Central and Eastern Canada. When combined with our proposed merger with Videotron, this will create a super-cluster of approximately 3.5 million customers in Ontario and Quebec all interconnected with fibre" (Shaw, 2000).

The day after, however, Rogers' expansion plans would become almost non-existent when Quebecor in turn announced its intention to make an alternative proposal to acquire all outstanding shares of Videotron, including shares of TVA Group (Quebecor, 2003d). At the same time, that is three days before the special meeting planned to present Rogers' proposition to Videotron's shareholders, Quebecor turned to the courts and obtained an injunction to prevent them, including majority owner André Chagnon, from voting on Rogers' offer (Canoe, 2000). For the transaction, Quebecor was financially backed by a subsidiary of the Caisse de dépôt et placement du Québec (CDPQ), a State owned corporation whose mandate is to yield profit from Quebec citizens' pension money. The CDPQ would own 45.3 percent of the $5.4 billion purchase of Videotron (CDPQ, 2000). After some court plays, Quebecor was able to mail its last offer to Videotron's shareholders in September, and in October,

2000, it announced that it had completed the acquisition of all the outstanding shares of Group Videotron Ltd (Quebecor, 2003d).

English-Canada media and investors were quick to criticize the intervention of the CDPQ, which was seen as another manifestation of the so-called "Quebec Inc" mentality whereby the Quebec government was seen as trying to avoid the loss of a headquarters in Quebec to the profit of a Toronto-based company. Moreover, the deal was perceived as a direct Quebec province intervention to keep the cable industry in the hands of Quebecers for the sake of the preservation of Quebec's French culture, if not the eventual promotion of Quebec's separation from Canada. The *Globe and Mail* reported that the CDPQ had reached the threshold of the intolerable, "becoming not just an agent of Quebec nationalism, but effectively a nationalizer itself" (as quoted by David, 2000). Whereas the CDPQ was claiming its right to block the Rogers transaction under its own agreement with the Chagnon family, a private shareholders' pact tied to an investment dating back twenty years (Friends of Canadian Broadcasting, 2000). As an analyst with the European Business School said, it would seem that the CDPQ's real rationale for being Quebecor's partner was to "maximise its long-term invesment in Videotron and avoid that only the Chagnon family benefit from the original deal" (Charette, 2001).

Clearly, the above description of the current largest Canadian media conglomerates demonstrate that in the recent past a truly Canadian oligopoly has developed that lead to a high degree of concentration of media ownership. Opponents to that trend also saw the realization of some of their worst nightmares, as illustrated in *La soirée du hockey* and *The Gazette* controversies discussed earlier in this chapter.

Discussion and Conclusion

Comparison across corporate structures of all seven conglomerates discussed reveals several glaring similarities. First, all are highly dense in product and service extension, canvassing print, broadcast and closed system electronic media, with the US-based Disney and Canadian-based BCE and Rogers demonstrating strong presence in other business sectors such as movie production, resort ownership and telecommunications infrastructure. All are vertically integrated, with only two (Quebecor and Canwest) showing no equity ownership in sport franchise assets. All are truly global in scope, through direct participation in international enterprise and/or joint holdings. Law, Harvey and Kemp (2002) argued that the strength and scope of inter-corporate linkages through jointly held assets indicates a "web"-like competitive structure wherein holdings occupied interconnected "zones of profitability" through which revenue generating activity flowed. Comparison of the seven corporations shown above underscores this interpretation with recognition of ubiquitous inter-corporate linkages, which in one way or another connect them all. Further, the timing and indeed discourses of corporate growth spurts read from the biographies presented reveals the central role of corporate structure in competitive pressure. From the early 1990s onward, serious competition has not been about readership between one newspaper versus another, nor about TV audience share in restricted areas. Rather equity presence across media and ownership of the supply chain within which media have traditionally been merely the "middle men" are standard competitive practices. No corporation is a mirror image of any other. However, the point made strongly here is that national policy about cross-sectoral holdings, concentration of media and foreign ownership have all been placed under pressure by the threat of competition from corporations that face no such regulatory constraints.

The race to expand distribution platforms and content production capability during the 1990s somewhat faltered due to .com overcapitalization. However, the logic of pursuing corporate expansion to consolidate positions in the web of now globally competitive marketplaces continues. On one hand, immediate impetus for expansion of corporate structures has come from both the emergence of new technologies and the strategic leads of those initiating multifaceted market reach. On the other, telecommunications and media interests have arguably been eyeing each other's markets and positions in the information supply chain for a long time. Recent moves on the part of several nation states such as Canada to allow cross sectoral competition can be seen as attempts to enable the kind of corporate consolidation necessary for domestic interests to compete globally.

The above analysis of three of the largest global media conglomerates suggests that the age of professional sport in "convergence" and "synergy" is reshuffling. News Corp. sold the Dodgers, Disney is actively looking for buyers for its two major league franchises and found one in Arturo Moreno (Hoover's Online 2003a), Time Warner sold 87 percent of its equity in its team sport franchises and, finally, the 2002 bankruptcy of Adelphia Communications, the holding company of the NHL Buffalo Sabres, seems to indicate that professional sport ownership might not ubiquitously accelerate profitability in "circuits of promotion". However, the sale of the Dodgers does not alter the fact that News Corp. is the conglomerate with sport as it's central pillar of its content strategy, with equity interests currently intact in non-North American jurisdictions. Similarly, in the case of Disney, the corporation still claims the importance of major league sport in its strategy through acquisition of broadcasting rights. On the other hand, Canadian corporations continue to expand their occupation of equity in sport franchise properties. Divestiture of sport franchises, immediately saleable, are likely the result of dot com cashflow demands, which have pushed major conglomerates toward "hard synergies" directly transferable through multiple platforms. The push toward convergence continues, albeit in new forms. Most recently, deregulation of investment restrictions including quantity of market presence has occupied a good deal of conglomerate attention. Further, as devalued Internet assets change hands at a time of high structural fluidity, the exact flow of cross-ownership benefits is shifting. The trajectory of deregulation, however, promotes the same "bulking-up" logic: larger, more diverse conglomerates in a race for audience reach. A decrease in proportionate national ownership of course furthers the probability of product homogenization.

Despite a much less flamboyant of not pessimist discourse about the financial prospects of "convergence" and "synergy", we are indeed at the eve of a new wave of mergers and takeovers that will result in yet another phase in the concentration and consolidation of the global media oligopoly. The most significant sign in early 2003 is undoubtedly the potentially forthcoming deregulation of media ownership in the US, a prospect already under way in other countries like Canada.

The changes would:

> . . . abolish rules that restricted a newspaper from owning a television station in the same city, or prevent a media conglomerate from owning two television networks. Current laws prohibit a network form owning stations that broadcast to more than 35 percent of the nation's homes. They also restrict a broadcaster from owning two television stations in the same market unless they are at least eight other competitors, and they prohibit a cable company from owning more than 30% of the national market. (Hoover's Online, 2003b)

Canadian electronic media are regulated by the CRTC, which has a legislated mandate simultaneously to protect and promote Canadian cultural expression (a citizenship function) as well as foster competition in electronic media delivery systems, under the belief that more competition will bring better service, prices and product quality (a consumer function). Winsek (1998) uses the term "*re*convergence" to describe late twentieth century moves *back* toward corporate participation in multiple platforms, which had been regulated against in the early part of the century in order to break up or prevent monopolies from dominating all forms of electronic communications at the national level. Moves in the 1990s to allow the entry of corporations previously distinguished as either broadcasters or electronic message carriers into each other's domain has been aimed at broadening competition in both telecommunications and broadcasting services. To a certain extent these moves have been prompted by the advent of digital technologies deliverable through a number of methods that have effectively collapsed distinctions between broadcast and point-to-point telecommunication to "information".

While mid-late 1990s regulatory changes that cleared the way for the Canadian platform converges shown above might be technologically enabled, they should not be taken as technologically *determined*. Rather, expansion of access to markets provides incentive to invest heavily in development of the high-speed digital infrastructure in Canada to keep pace with investment levels in other parts of the world. The CRTC has retained regulatory powers over percentage of domestic equity ownership as well as media content distributable through electronic means, and simultaneously potentially expanded funds available to boost domestic content production through additional contributions from telocs, in their broadcaster roles. However, the continuity of corporate investment in market expansion depends on overall growth in consumption, which has not occurred at the rate anticipated by those betting on returns from high debt loads.

Recent Canadian government discussions have centered on the possible raising of foreign equity ownership levels on the premise that overall national wealth (shareholder benefit) will be enhanced by new and intensive foreign investment. This not only introduces the possibility of higher degrees of non-Canadian control over Canadian content due to the extent of platform convergence, but also introduces a new type of citizen implied in the discourse of benefit. The 'Shareholder citizen' must articulate governance argumentation in terms of return on investment rather than cultural values – themselves hotly and politically contested in an intensely multicultural society. The shareholder citizen sits well with the consumer citizen protected through competitive relations. However, corporate consolidation combined with further growth enabled by non-national funds could push Canadian cultural content toward forms consumable by the mainstream of global infotainment audiences. Although promises of enhancing diversity and domestic expression are approached with market driven export arguments and indeed further injections of support for domestic "product", shareholder and consumer citizens combine to further the commodifcation of cultural politics.

The evolution of the global media oligopoly has direct impacts on national "mediascapes". This has been clearly demonstrated here through the Canadian example. The last decade of mega-mergers and consolidation of the global media oligopoly, at least in the Canadian case, resulted in the concentration of the media into a national oligopoly, already linked, namely through sport, to the global oligopoly. This evolution has been made possible through the progressive diminution of state regulation over media ownership, as well as over media concentration in local markets. The rapid edification of the Canadian global oligopoly has challenged the Canadian traditional mix telecommunications system. Indeed, the legitimacy behind the formation of the Canadian oligopoly was the need to build strong Canadian corporations able to compete with the global conglomerates and therefore make possible the presence of a Canadian voice. Paradoxically, the need for a strong Canadian voice was also justified through an attack on the public media corporations, namely CBC/Radio-Canada. The continuous demise of the "public broadcasting space" backed by the cultural nationalists made it even easier for the Canadian media barons to impose their model of a Canadian-controlled "mediated entertainment" model. Although media complex executives claim that corporate culture is really the driver of censorship levels and techniques, most critics agree that corporate structure delivers the muscle to refine programming, and circulate combinations of images capable of washing out distinctive nuance. Even the "local" merely becomes a quaint "placeless" place for the increasingly distributed audiences necessary to sustain the technology through which 'efficient' delivery occurs.

For professional sport consumers it has resulted in a decreased availability of their entertainment through basic services. Increasingly, to watch the Toronto Blue Jays, the Raptors, the Maple Leafs on CBC *Hockey Night in Canada*, and for French Canadians, *La soirée du hockey,* consumers are forced either to obtain cable (at the second tier level, or satellite television. Moreover, a concentrated press means also less diversified sport journalism reporting and an increased focus of the media on commodified sport forms. Moreover, the so-called need for a national entertainment media model meant that less important room has been left for broadcasting non commodified sport events. Instead of being centered around a national citizenship model, the universal right to access to quality broadcasting, the Canadian media system is now catering to the rights of the "shareholder citizen". The recent changes in the Canadian system has set the stage for the global circulation of commodified sport, disconnecting audiences from traditional forms of cultural affiliation based on locality and more concretely tying sporting imagery to the images of products.

The integration of sport content product within the global media complex is far from being over, despite recent .com events. Indeed, commodified sport remains a prime content product to circulate and cross promote in the global media market. As for national communication systems, they are now ready for: a new phase of consolidation (as demonstrated above the lobbying in that sense is well engaged), renewed attacks to the public service, most probably through challenges before the WTO for unfair competition, and consequently an increasing integration within the global media oligopoly. For Canadians, the forecast is that more "incidents" liked the "privatization" of *La soirée du hockey* and eventually *Hockey Night in Canada* (moving from the public service to a private media holding) and the infamous "Foxtrax glow puck" (Mason, 2002) will keep eroding what is left of a Canadian sport broadcasting heritage in favor of a global/US products-driven system.

In one sense, "telecomedia" remains one of the last bastions from which to consciously negotiate the terms of Canadian globalization. Corporate mergers, even among the hallowed financial institutions, were the great flag fall of global competition during the 1990s. Proponents of deregulation argue for the necessity of foreign infusion to keep up with technological investment (somewhat discounted given recent events), which is, of course, being driven by concentrated capital – and so on. The obvious contradiction promoted by the state is that concentration and foreign ownership are somehow good for competition (of the global kind) and that this promotes our national values. The shareholder citizen, like the corporate citizen only has values to the extent that these do not interfere witht the generation of wealth. Nations should not become known simply as "small markets". Cities should not be stripped of all characteristics but that of generating audience reach. Borders should not be erased in favor of new borders that depend on aquisition of dividends, or consumption of inhouse product. Conscious political negotiation of cultural diversity must prevail against the vagiaries of shareholder returns.

Notes

1. For a more elaborate account of this saga, see Mason (2002).
2. This section is a significantly revised and updated version of a discussion published earlier in Law et al. 2002.

References

Alger, D. (1998), *Megamedia.* Lanham MD: Rowman & Littlefield.

Andrews, D. L. (2001), Sport. In R. Maxwell (ed.), *Culture Works: Essays on the Political Economy of Culture*, Minneapolis: University of Minnesota Press.

Asia Pacific Technology Network (2000), *A Multimedia Global Empire: Changing Technology, Politics and Commercial Strategy in the Globalization of Murdoch's Newscorporation.* Retrieved September 29, from http://www.aptn.org/ibis/newscorps.htm.

Associated Press (2002). News Corp achète Telepiu, *Le Devoir*, p. B3. October 2, 2002.

Associated Press (2003), China Approves Nationwide Broadcasts of STAR TV Entertainment. Retrieved January 29, 2003, from http://hoovnews.hoovers.com. . .04

Baker, R. (1998). Murdoch's Mean Machine, *Columbia Journalism Review*. Retrieved January 5, 2000 from http://www.cjr.org/98/3/murdoch.

BCE (1999), *Bell Canada and MCI WorldCom in Strategic Alliance*. Retrieved November 13, 2002, from http://bce.ca/en/news/releases/bce/1999/03/03/4180.html.

BCE (2000), *BCE Offers to Buy CTV for $2.3 Billion in Cash*. Retrieved November 13, 2002, from http://www.bce.ca/en/news/webcasts/2000/20000225b/release.html.

BCE (2002a), *Simplify Communications for Greater Freedom*. Retrieved November 13, 2002, from http://www.bce.ca/en/about/business/bellcanada/.

BCE (2002b), *BCE to Complete Purchase of 100 per cent of Bell Canada*. Retrieved November 13, 2002, from http://www.bce.ca/en/news/releases/bce/2002/11/11/69512.html.

BCE Emergis (2002), *Making Business More Productive with E-commerce*. Retrieved November 13, 2002, from http://bce.ca/en/about/business/emergis/.

BCI (2002a), *BCI Announces the Sale of its Interest in Telecom Americas*. Retrieved November 13, 2002, from http://bce.ca/en/news/releases/bci/2002/06/03/69117.html.

BCI (2002b), *BCI Announces Approval by Court of Plan of Arrangement*. Retrieved November 13, 2002, from http://bce.ca/en/news/releases/bci/2002/07/17/69131.html.

BCI (2002c), *BCI Announces Third Quarter Results*. Retrieved November 13, 2002, from http://bce.ca/en/news/releases/bci/2002/10/31/69493.html.

Bell Canada (2002a), *Molson Center to Become the Bell Center in September*. Retrieved November 13, 2002, from http://www.bce.ca/en/news/releases/bc/2002/02/26/6834.html.

Bell Canada (2002b), *Bell Canada is Canada's Leading Integrated Communications Company*. Retrieved November 13, 2002, from http://www.bce.ca/en/about/business/bellcanada/.

Bell ExpressVu (2001), *Bell ExpressVu Reaches One Million Customers*. Retrieved November 13, 2002, from http://www.bce.ca/en/news/releases/bev/2001/11/27/6590.html.

Bell Globemedia (2002a), *Canada's Premier Multimedia Company*. Retrieved November 13, 2002, from http://www.bce.ca/en/about/business/globemedia/.

Bell Globemedia (2002b), *Bell Globemedia and Lycos Restructure Relationship*. Retrieved November 13, 2002, from http://www.bce.ca/en/news/releases/bg/2002/09/13/69308.html.

Bell Globemedia (2002c), *RDS Welcomes CRTC Decision on Videotron*. Retrieved November 19, 2002, from http://www.bce.ca/en/news/releases/bg/2002/08/29/69272.html.

Bell Globemedia (2002d), *NetStar Renamed CTV Specialty*. Retrieved November 15, 2002, from http://www.bce.ca/en/news/releases/bg/2002/05/31/69027.html.

Bellamy, R. (1998), The Evolving Television Sports Marketplace. In L. Wenner (ed.), *Media Sport*, New York: Routledge.

Canadian Issues (2002), An interview with Robert Rabinovitch, *Canadian Issues*, June, pp. 4–7.

Canadian Press (2002a), *L'avenir de la Soirée du Hockey à la SRC est assuré pour trois saisons*. Retrieved January 16, 2003, from http://cf.sports.yahoo.com/020723/1/7ko6.html.

Canadian Press (2002b), *La survie de la Soirée du hockey à la SRC sera discutée au Parlement*. Retrieved January 16, 2003, from http://cf.sports.yahoo.com/020531/1/77ml.html.

Canadian Radio-television and Telecommunications Commission (CRTC) (2002c), *CanWest Corporate Structure*. Retrieved November 20, 2002, from http://www.crtc.gc.ca/ownership/cht14.pdf.

Canadian Radio-television and Telecommunications Commission (CRTC) (2002d), *Rogers Corporate Structure*. Retrieved November 20, 2002, from http://www.crtc.gc.ca/ownership/cht27.pdf

Canadian Radio-television and Telecommunications Commission (CRTC) (2002a), *BCE Corporate Structure*. Retrieved November 13, 2002, from http://www.crtc.gc.ca/ownership/cht143.pdf.

Canadian Ratio-television and Telecommunications Commission (2002b), *BCE Specialty Services*. Retrieved November 20, 2002, from http://www.crtc.gc.ca/ownership/cht143f.pdf.

Canwest (2001).

CanWest Global Communications Corp (2002a), *Fast Facts*. Retrieved November 22, 2002, from http://www.canwestglobal.com/fastfacts.html.

CanWest Global Communications Corp. (2002b), *CanWest Timeline*. Retrieved November 22, 2002, from http://www.canwestglobal.com/canwesttimeline.html.

CanWest Global Communications Corp. (2002c), *Interactive*. Retrieved December 3, 2002, from http://www.canwestglobal.com/interactive.html.

Carrington, B., Sugden, J. and Tomlinson, A. (1999), Network Football: Transnational Capital and the Incorporation of World Football. Paper presented at the annual conference of the NASSS, Cleveland, Ohio, 3-6 November.

CBC (2000), *Rogers taking over Videotron*. Retrieved January 23, 2003, from http://cbc.ca/cgi-bin/templates/view.cgi?/news/2000/02/07/rogers000207.

Charette, J.F. (2001), *The Videotron Ltd take-over by Quebecor Inc and La Caisse de Depots et placements du Quebec*. Retrieved January 24, 2003, from http://jfcharette.com/videotron.html.

CNNSI.com (1997), CNN and Sports Illustrated Deliver Sports News with Immediacy and Depth, *CNN Sports Illustrated*. Retrieved February 21, 2000 from http://www.cnnsi.com/about_us/index.html.

Curran, P. (2001), Rad-Can Hot on Partnerships, not Hockey, *The Gazette*, August 22, Retrieved January 16, 2003, from http://friendscb.ca/articles/MontrealGazette/gazette010822.htm.

David, M. (2000), English Media Seem to see Separatists Under the Bed in Caisse-Quebecor Deal to Buy Out Videotron, *The Gazette*, Montreal, August 25.

Evening Standard (2003), News Corp May Sell Dodgers Soon, Retrieved January 29, 2003 from http://hoovnews.hovers.com/. . .074

Friends of Canadian Broadcasting (2000), *Rogers Says Videotron Deal in Danger*. Retrieved January 22, 2003, from http://friendscb.ca/articles/NationalPost/np000405.htm.

Guardian. (Marsh 3, 2000), 'BskyB's Grip on Premiership Tightens.' Retrieved September 29, 2000 from http://www.guardian.co.uk.

Gruneau , R. and Whitson, D. (2001), Upmarket Continentalism: Major League Sport, Promotional Culture, and Corporate Integration. In V. Mosco and D. Schiller (eds) *Continental Order? Integrating North America for Cybercapitalism*, Lanham MD: Rowman & Littlefield.

Gruneau, R and Whitson, D. (1993), *Hockey Night in Canada*, Toronto: Garamond.

Harvey, J, Law, A. and Cantelon, M. (2001), North American Professional Sport Franchises Ownership Patterns and Global Entertainment Conglomerates, *Sociology of Sport Journal*, 18(4): 435–57.

Hoover's Online (2002a), *Aliant Inc*. Retrieved November 13, 2002, from http://www.hoovers.com/co/capsule/6/0,2163,60046,00.html.

Hoover's Online (2002b), *Bell Canada International Inc*. Retrieved November 13, 2002, from http://www.hoovers.com/co/capsule/1/0,2163,54691,00.html.

Hoover's Online (2003a), California Businessman, Baseball Fan Makes New Pitch for Major League Team. Retrieved, January 29, 2003, from http://hoovnews.hoovers.com.

Hoover's Online (2003b), Change in FCC Rules Could Bring Media-Buying Spree in Orlando, Fla.' Retrieved January, 29, 2003, from http://hoovnews.hoovers.com. . .81.

Industry Canada (2002), *Telecommunications Service in Canada*. Retrieved November 20, 2002, from http://strategis.ic.gc.ca/SSG/sf05656e.html.

Jones Telecommunications & Multimedia Encyclopedia (n.d.), *Bell Canada International Inc*. Retrieved November 13, 2002, from http://www.digitalcentury.com/encyclo/update/bci.html.

Ketupa.net (2002), *Ketupa.net media profiles – Rogers*. Retrieved November 19, 2002, from http://www.ketupa.net/rogers.htm.

Krigel, B.L. (1999), *Microsoft Plays Catch-up with Instant Messenger*, July 19. Retrieved September 28, 2000 from http://www.canada.cnet.com/news/0-1005-200-345065.html.

LaFeber, W. (1999), *Michael Jordan and the New Global Capitalism*, London: Norton.

Landreth, N. (2000), *Broadcast Rights*. Retrieved January 28, 2000 from http://www.foxsports.com/business/resources/broadcast.

Law, A., Harvey, J. and Kemp, S. (2002), The Global Sport Mass Media Oligopoly: The Three Suspects and More, *International Review for the Sociology of Sport*, 37(3–4).

Maguire, J. (1999), *Global Sport*, Cambridge: Polity Press.

Mason, D. (2002), "Get the Puck Outta Here": Media Transnationalism and Corporate Identity, *Journal of Sport and Social Issues*, 26(2): 140–67.

Morley, D., and Robins, K. (1995), *Spaces of Identity: Global Media, Electronic Landscapes, and Cultural Boundaries*, London: Routledge.

New, B. and Le Grand, J. (1999), Monopoly in Sports Broadcasting, *Policy Studies*, 20(1): 23–36.

News Corporation (2002), 2002 Annual information to ADR holders, Sydney, Australia: Ernst & Young.

Pitts, G. (2002), *Kings of Convergence*, Toronto: Doubleday Canada.

Quebecor (2003a), *History*. Retrieved January 22, 2003, from http://www.quebecor.com/htmen/0_0/0_3.asp.

Quebecor (2003b), *Quebecor at a Glance*. Retrieved January 22, 2003, from http://www.quebecor.com/htmen/0_0/0_1.asp.

Quebecor (2003c). *Vast Market Reach*. Retrieved January 22, 2003, from http://www.quebecor.com/htmen/0_0/0_2.asp.

Quebecor (2003d), *The Videotron Transaction*. Retrieved January 23, 2003, from http://www.quebecor.com/htmen/0_0/0_1_4.asp.

Radio-Canada (2003), *La Soirée du hockey à Radio-Canada*. Retrieved January 15, 2003, from http://www.rogers.com/english/aboutrogers/historyofrogers/index.html.

Réseau des Sports (2002), *La LNH à RDS pour 4 ans*. Retrieved January 16, 2003, from http://www.rds.ca/information/fr.corp.communique.hockey.html.

Reuters (2002), *Fin de la légendaire Soirée du hockey à Radio-Canada*. Retrieved January 16, 2003, from http://cf.sports.yahoo.com/020530/3/77am.html.

Shaw (2000), *Rogers and Shaw Announce Major Swap of Cable Assets and Strategic Alliances in Internet Properties*. Retrieved January 23, 2003, from http://www.shaw.ca/Tmplt2.asp?PageID=244.

Stoddart, B. (1997), Convergence: "Sport in the Information Superhighway", *Journal of Sport and Social Issues*, 21(1): 93–102.

The Economist (2000), The Net Gets Real, *The Economist*, 354(8153): 22–4.

TSN (2001), *TSN and RDS Step to the Plate with Montreal Expos*. Retrieved November 19, 2002, from http://www.bce.ca/en/news/releases/tsn/2001/01/09/69215.html.

Vipond, M. (2000), *The Mass Media in Canada*, Toronto: Lorimer.

Vivendi (2000), *Vivendi-Universal Merger Press Release*. Retrieved June 21, 2000 from http://www.vivendi.com.

Vogt (2002), AOL Time Warner.

Whitson, D. (1998), Circuits of Promotion: Media, Marketing and the Globalization of Sport. In L. Wenner (ed.), *Media Sport*, New York: Routledge.

Winsek, D. (1998), Pursuing the Holy Grail: Information Highways and Media Reconvergence in Britain and Canada, *European Journal of Communication*, 13(3): 337–74.

11

From SBC Park to the Tokyo Dome: Baseball and (Inter)Nationalism

Jeremy W. Howell

Preface

In July 2001 I participated in a two-day professional meeting in Tokyo, Japan that focused on the possible development of a US/Japan-based executive educational program for sports management professionals within the Japanese sports industry. We were there at the invitation of Jack Sakazaki, one of the countries most prominent sports business leaders and owner of The JSM Group.[1] As part of our visit, we attended a professional Japanese baseball game between the Nippon Ham Fighters and the Kintetsu Buffaloes at the Tokyo Dome. There, I found myself seated next to Jean Afterman, an associate of Sakazaki and ex-legal counsel of Don Nomura, the sports agent representing many of the Japanese players who were currently playing in Major League Baseball (MLB).[2]

As one might imagine, this was an intriguing time to be discussing international sport management education while watching a baseball game in Japan, particularly as Ichiro Suzuki, the first Japanese-born position player to play in the Major Leagues, had just received 3,373,035 votes to become the top vote-getter award at the 2001 MLB All-Star game.[3] Ichiro, as we now know, was to go on and win Rookie of the Year and Most Valuable Player (MVP) honors in the American League. As for the actual seventy-second Midsummer Classic All-Star game itself, it was played in Safeco Field, the home of Ichiro's Seattle Mariner's, a team owned by the Nintendo Corporation. Hailed by MLB Commissioner Bud Selig as "An International Celebration of Baseball", the festivities highlighted the thirty nations represented in Minor and Major League Baseball.[4]

It was also the first ever MLB telecast widely distributed in High Digital Television (HDTV), the result of a unique partnership between MLB and Nippon Hoso Kyokai (NHK), the public broadcasting company of Japan. The

HDTV telecast was sent directly to Japan, while a standard definition signal of the All-Star Game was distributed in twelve languages to more than 205 countries worldwide (MLBI to Broadcast, 2001).

Four months after our Tokyo meetings I would again find myself watching a professional baseball game with Jean Afterman. But this time we were the guests of Jack Bair, Senior Vice President and General Counsel to the San Francisco Giants, and one of the key people responsible for the building of Pac Bell Park, the team's $319 million privately funded, brick-faced, open-air park. We were there to discuss some of the executive educational opportunities for management professionals working in the sports industry, but this time specifically in San Francisco, Los Angeles and San Diego.[5] As in Japan, this was an interesting time to discuss MLB business practices while watching a ball game, particularly given the fact that Commissioner Selig had openly discussed his intent to contract MLB's national number by dissolving two teams by the 2003 season.[6] Now the fact that some teams, according to Commissioner Selig, could not produce enough local revenues from their local markets to survive in the League (Major League Baseball Votes, 2001) may appear somewhat ironic given our surroundings in a capacity filled, brand new, privately built ballpark located in a rapidly gentrifying post-industrial neighborhood near downtown San Francisco. It may also appear ironic given our experiences in Japan and the clear attempts by MLB at international expansion.

I begin this chapter with these visits to the Tokyo Dome and SBC Park because, despite the thousands of miles distance, I think they shine light on some of the dramatic social, technological and global forces that are morphing the business structure of MLB from an *economic national champion* into a *global enterprise network*.

Baseball as a National Champion

Sports historians have told us that during baseball's period of early commercialism and professionalism, the game grew at an extraordinary rate. Many of the early teams were drawn from workplaces and played in the many industrial leagues of the time. Similarly, the emergence of crowds at local club games, due to the newly defined and heavily commercialized emergence of "free" time, led many of the new entrepreneurs of industrial capitalism to use sport as a vehicle to promote both their leading citizen status and patronage of their shops, restaurants, and saloons (Ingham et al., 1987; Schimmel et al., 1993; Hannigan, 1998). And, as one might expect given this twighlight period of industrial capitalism, the vast majority of teams went out of business within a few years of existence.

The National Association of Professional Base Ball Players, formed in March 1871, was the game's first professional league. Its bylaws allowed any professional or semi-pro club to enter the National Association pennant race by paying a $10 registration fee. The National Association was riddled with problems from the outset. Indeed, during its five years of existence, eight to thirteen clubs began each season, but each year one to six clubs failed to finish. Of the twenty-three clubs that competed in the National Association, only the Mutuals of New York, Athletics of Philadelphia and the Boston Red Stockings played all five years (Melville, 2001). For many, Boston's winning was due to its practice of enticing other teams' stars to sign with them, thus creating a "revolving door" labor pool. In this way, the National Association was really a loose association of clubs run by owners that were more concerned with their own profits (utility maximization) than they were with the welfare of a league (joint profit maximization). Any existing market inefficiency or chaos was to be resolved by the entrance of coal baron William Hulbert into the fray. On February 2, 1876, a select group of baseball owners met at the New York Grand Central Hotel to create what we today know as the National League. Led by Hulbert, owner of the Chicago White Stockings club and a respected member of the City's Board of Trade, the 1876 meeting was an attempt by a prestige set of owners to stratify the marketplace. These early "merchants of leisure" (Hannigan, 1998, p. 17) realized that the baseball industry had to be tutored and this could only occur with the formation of a single major league.[7]

Publicly, the formation of the National League was a "self-transformation" (Melville, 2001, p. 80) undertaken by the National Association's larger professionally run clubs to ensure better competitive cooperation, moral standards (for example anti-gambling and drunkenness initiatives) and financial success. But what the 1876 reformation movement actually did was put into place the two key structures that went on to define the economic structure of MLB for over a century (Schimmel et al., 1993; Howell, 2002).

First, monopolistic practices in the marketplace would guarantee a limited number of the most economically viable teams entry into the prestige league. Moreover, the same prestige set of owners would decide what firms would be allowed to enter the league and what territory they would be exclusively allocated. Thus, each charter team of the National League was situated in cities with populations of at least 75,000 potential consumers. Additionally, league rules would prohibit more than one team per city, thus guaranteeing the territorial integrity of each "franchise". Put a little differently, a small number of large firms, recognizing their oligopolistic interdependence, succeeded in tutoring the marketplace in a way that a profit-maximizing monopolist (single firm) might have done. And, to ensure fair play among the "cartel", a central league office was established to maintain records, set individual team schedules, designate standardized ticket pricing, make rule changes, manage umpires and adjudicate disagreements.

Secondly, monopsonic practices concerning inter-team competition for athletic labor would ensure teams having the exclusive right to enter into a contract with a player and to reserve the rights to that player via a perpetually renewable contract. The reserve clause meant that while a player could be traded to another team, that same player could not choose to play for another team or effectively campaign for a salary raise. Players would be tied to their team indefinitely, thus preventing inter-team bidding on labor. By 1887, the reserve clause was written into the standard player's contract, where it would remain until 1975.

Of course, there was resistance to such an artificial construction of market scarcity. The American Association of Baseball Players was founded in 1881, immediately threatening the National League restrictions on players. With a similar basic organizational structure, the American Association proved to be a viable threat. Within two years, in an attempt to prevent inter-league bidding on labor, a "national agreement" was enacted between the two leagues. While the National League and American Association would remain competitively independent, they agreed to respect the reservation of players by their respective individual clubs, thus keeping the reserve clause intact.

Hoping to capitalize on ongoing player dissatisfaction with the reserve clause, The Union Association was formed in September 1883. It folded within one year but not before its top team was given entry to the prestige league.[8] Similarly, in 1885 players organized the Brotherhood of National League Players arguing that the reserve clause could not be used to bind a player while his salary was being cut. Despite apparent National League support, owners would subsequently enact a labor classification plan that established a fixed payment scale for a player's ability. The most a player could make, regardless of ability or the team's success, was $2,500 a season. In response, the players formed a Players League to directly compete with the National League season. Many of the best players from the American Association and National League joined and indications are that the league actually outdrew the National League in attendance and income. Nevertheless, due to pressure tactics, media manipulation and the bribery of a couple of owners to sell out, the Player's League lasted only one season.[9] In 1892, when four of the top leagues were merged into an expanded National league, the American Association was to be overwhelmed.

This strategic amalgamation of teams as a preemptive move was often repeated in future threats to the "cartel", most noticeable with the 1901 formation of the American League. Several National League teams had folded by 1901, allowing the American League to set up teams in stronghold cities of Boston, Washington and Philadelphia. Due to better labor agreements, over 60 percent of American League players were from ex-National League teams. As in previous practice, the National League reached a new "national agreement" with the American League in 1903, creating an umbrella organization called Major League Baseball (McGuire and Kou, 1997). Today, the American and National League continue as MLB's two conferences with the winner of each playing for the World Series each year.

If Hulbert was largely responsible for the monopolistic and monopsonic economic practices that were to tutor the marketplace in new and innovative ways, it was his successor, Albert Goodwill Spalding, that is credited with developing the ideological practices that helped ensure that "a" form of organizational baseball became "the" legitimate, traditional, and national game. When Hulbert died in 1882, Spalding, a former Boston Red Stockings and Chicago White Stockings pitcher, served as president of the Chicago team until 1891. A powerful figure,[10] Spalding immediately sought to protect the cartelized format that Hulbert had put into practice. Using both his business and sporting acumen, Spalding took advantage of his Chicago sporting goods business,[11] which was to emerge as the dominant sporting-goods firm of the era, to promote the game. Besides producing the official National League ball, Spalding and Bros. also had the exclusive contract for the "official league book", which outlined the game's rules and regulations. In 1878 he also began publishing *Spalding's Official Baseball Guide*, an annual collection of team and individual records that also featured articles advocating Spalding's views on many baseball issues.

Spalding was unyielding in his promotion of cartelized baseball as the national pastime. For instance, he described the Brotherhood as "hot headed anarchists", led "by a few enthusiastic long chance capitalists whose only possible interest . . . is the amount of money they hope to realize out of it" (cited in Voigt, 1983, p. 163). As for the Player's League, he accused them of employing "terrorism peculiar to revolutionary movements" (cited in Voigt, 1983, p. 164). In each instance, Spalding saw his role as maintaining the "purity" of his national pastime.

This belief in the American "national pastime" is nowhere more evident than in his 1903 formation of the Mills Commission. Recommended by Spalding, and headed by the former National League president A.G. Mills, the Commission was given the arduous task of determining the origins of baseball. In so doing, it was clear that the Commission was to debunk the popular belief that baseball owed its origins to the British children's game of "rounders", an argument promoted by Henry Chadwick, Spalding's own editor who, as a long time reporter, had already played a critical role in popularizing the game. Spurred on by Spalding, documentation that favored the American origin of the game was uncritically accepted. And when the Mills Commission, on December 30, 1907, decreed that baseball was indeed invented by Abner Doubleday, a civil war hero, in the idyllic, rural American town of Cooperstown, baseball's tradition was well on its way to being written in stone.[12] This nostalgic rendition of history was an important ideological moment for Spalding. It ensured a baseball tradition full of mythical American lore, albeit a magical recapturing of a past that never truly existed. As he went on to write in his 1911 treatise, *Baseball: America's National Game*: "Base Ball owes its prestige as our National Game to the fact that as no other form of sport it is the exponent of American Courage, Confidence, Combativeness; American Dash, Discipline, Determination; American Pluck, Persistency, Performance; American Spirit, Sagacity, Success; American Vim, Vigor, Virility" (Al Spalding, n.d.).

That Spalding should promote a nationalistic "America" is hardly surprising. As he had indicated in his earlier battles with the Player's League: "The genius of our institution is democratic; Baseball is a democratic game" (cited in Goldstein, 1989, p. 150).

Of course, democracy always has a context. It is worth remembering that this was a radical period in industrial and urban development. For instance, between 1860–1910 the number of American cities with populations over 100,000 grew from nine to fifty. In 1860 Chicago had 109,260 inhabitants; by 1910 it had 2.2 million people. Similarly, the population of Boston grew from 177,840 to 560,892 between 1860 and 1910 (see Sage, 1990). Moreover, while there were 280,000 immigrants arriving in the US annually in the 1870s, by 1900 that figure had risen to over 2 million (see Reich, 1992). At the beginning of the nineteenth century, over 90 percent of the population was economically independent. By 1840, 20 percent of the labor force was in waged labor; in 1870 it was 52 percent and by 1910 that figure had risen to an astonishing 72 percent. And, while in 1870 less than 8 percent of the population was engaged in manufacturing, that number had risen to over 30 percent by 1910 with over half the population living in burgeoning cities (see Reich, 1992).

Like the other industrial "national champions" (Reich, 1992) of the time, perhaps it is not too surprising that the baseball industry would involve the reduction of domestic competition by consolidating production within a few large nationally based corporations. After all, it is in this context that such giants of American enterprise as American Sugar Refining, American Telephone and Telegraph, American Rubber, General Electric, General Motors, American Tobacco, American Woolen, Carnegie Steel, Standard Oil, and U.S. Steel were formed (Reich, 1992, p. 36). The latter corporation was founded by some of America's most legendary businessmen, including Andrew Carnegie, J.P. Morgan and Charles Schwab. It had an astonishing authorized capitalization of $1.4

billion and in its first year, with massive government protection via subsidies and tariffs, made 67 percent of all the steel produced in America (http://www.ussteel.com/corp/about.htm). Similarly, the Union Pacific and Central Pacific railroads were also granted an huge government subsidy of $65 million to build a single railroad connecting the east and west coasts of America (Reich, 1992, p. 23). As Reich (1992, p. 34) continues, this was the dawning of "economic nationalism: The well-being of the citizens was linked to the success of the national economy, which depended in turn on the success of its giant corporations".

As we now know, the rise of economic nationalism, fueled by the engine rooms of the major national champions, brought with it the real fear of manufacturers organizing into oligopolistic groups to coordinate investments, share financial capital, jointly purchase raw materials, jointly market their goods, and fix prices. To counteract this, the US Congress passed the 1890 Sherman Anti Trust Act prohibiting price fixing and market dividing "agreements." Standard Oil, founded in 1870 by John D. Rockefeller, was the subject of numerous suits accusing the company of anti trust violations. Estimated to be twenty times larger than any competitor and in control of 90 percent of the petroleum industry (Sage, 1990), the Supreme Court in 1908 ordered the corporation dismantled into thirty different companies.[13]

Despite the fact that Hulbert and Spalding may have appeared as baseball's version of Vanderbilt, Carnegie, Morgan, and Rockefeller, the "national agreement" would continue relatively unchallenged until the early 1920s, when a baseball team from Baltimore sued the National League over what it saw as monopolistic practices. The case, "Federal Baseball Club of Baltimore, Inc. v. National League of Professional Baseball Clubs et al.", reached the Supreme Court in 1922. Although the Baltimore lawyers demonstrated several monopolistic practices prohibited by the 1890 Sherman Anti-Trust act, including that the "defendants destroyed the Federal League by buying up some of the constituent clubs and in one way or another inducing all those clubs except the plaintiff to leave their League," (Federal Club, 1922) a unanimous Supreme Court ruled in favor of baseball. Chief Justice Oliver Wendell Holmes wrote in the court's opinion that baseball failed to meet the definition of interstate commerce because the transportation of player's across state line was "a mere incident, not the essential thing. That to which it is incident, the exhibition, although made for money would not be called trade of commerce in the commonly accepted use of those words" (Federal Club, 1922). Thus, the Court argued that the game was not subject to anti-trust. The implication was that baseball was not a business but rather a game.

Throughout the mid-twentieth century, baseball, like many national champions, continued to adapt to market and legislative forces. Just as America's core corporations came to be identified with the American economy as a whole, so did baseball continue to be identified as the "national pastime". And, just as the core corporations were the "champions of the national economy", in that "their successes were its successes" (Reich, 1992, p. 47), so too was baseball the great American game. Like other national champions, it too continued to receive much government protectionism, albeit in rather unique ways. Thus, when the Supreme Court exemption was challenged in 1953 by George Toolsen, a New York Yankee minor league pitcher who sued over the reserve clause, it is hardly surprising that the great "tradition" of baseball would be left intact. Although the Supreme Court did not deny that baseball was not interstate commerce, it ruled that the "business has thus been left for thirty years to develop, on the understanding that it was not subject to existing antitrust legislation" and "if there are evils in this field which now warrant application to it of the antitrust laws it should be by legislation . . . Congress had no intention of including the business of baseball within the scope of the federal antitrust laws" (Toolsen v. New York Yankees, 1953).

Despite Congressional inaction, the Supreme Court in 1972 would, for the third time in fifty years, again be asked to rule that professional baseball's reserve system was within the reach of the federal antitrust laws. Curt Flood, an all-star outfielder with the St. Louis Cardinals, refused to accept a trade to Philadelphia in 1969 leading him to sue MLB Commissioner Bowie Kuhn to be a free agent, arguing that the reserve clause was a restraint of trade under the Sherman Anti-trust act. Despite overwhelming evidence of collusion, the Supreme Court, citing baseball's treatment as an established anomaly, again ruled that it was up to Congress to change baseball's antitrust exemption.[14]

More explicitly, though, in delivering the rendition of the Court, Justice Blackman never mentioned Commissioner Kuhn, instead referring to "The Game". Blackman, writing in a manner that would make Albert Spalding proud, noted that "the ardent follower and the student of baseball knows of General Abner Doubleday; the formation of the National League in 1876; Chicago's supremacy in the first year's competition under the leadership of Al Spalding and with Cap Anson at third base; the formation of the American Association and then of the Union Association in the 1880's [sic] . . ." Blackman continued by naming numerous celebrated players "that have sparked the diamond and its environs and that have provided tinder for recaptured thrills, for reminiscence and comparisons, and for conversation and anticipation in-season and off-season". Finally, he waxed lyrically about baseballs great mythic place in American popular culture referring to "the World Serious", attributed to Ring Lardner, Sir Ernest L. Thayer's "Casey at the Bat"; the ring of "Tinker Evers to Chance"; and all the other happenings, habits, and superstitions about and around baseball that made it the "national pastime" or, depending upon the point of view, "the great American tragedy" (Flood vs. Kuhn, 1972).

While some of the owners celebrated, most realized a defeat for Flood only slightly postponed the inevitable. Three years later, after ongoing collective bargaining, an arbitrator struck down the reserve clause for good.[15] Nevertheless, it would not be until 1998 that Congress passed the Curt Flood Act, which said challenges to league rules that restrict player movement or compensation would be subject to antitrust laws. But the change may mean little as the Supreme Court ruled two years earlier, in Brown et al. vs. Pro Football Inc. (1998), that unionized employees may not file antitrust suits. This means that the players' association would have to decertify before players could challenge owners on antitrust grounds.

Of course, today's franchises continue to collude by artificially constructing market scarcity. When the League sees it in its own self-interest to grow and tap into newly emerging market (media) territories, it might grant an expansion franchise to a new set of prestige owners invited into the cartel. Similarly, MLB continues to restrict teams from moving to other cities and continues to have the right to fold teams at will, even if another market is a viable one. Conversely, should a market territory no longer be economically viable, the cartel may decide to contract its number of firms.[16] But, while collusion and competition remain the name of the game, MLB hardly operates under the auspices of economic nationalism in ways that it once did.

Baseball as a Global Enterprise Network

Nowhere is this more evident than in the ownership changes within the cartel itself. In 1992, Hiroshi Yamauchi, President of Nintendo Inc, became MLB's first foreign-born majority owner when he purchased the Seattle Mariner's franchise.[17] Seattle is home of Nintendo of America. Yamauchi received much criticism for attempting to infiltrate America's game of baseball. As Jay Greene and Ken Belsen were to put it in a *Business Week* article:

> Japanese carmakers were continuing their march on Detroit, U.S. landmarks such as New York's Rockefeller Center and California's Pebble Beach had fallen into Japanese hands, and just two days before the Mariners bid was announced, Japan's Prime Minister Kiichi Miyazawa criticized American workers as "too lazy." Baseball bluebloods railed about selling out America's pastime to the Japanese, and Philadelphia Phillies owner Bill Giles declared his opposition, saying: "It's a patriotic issue for me." (Greene and Belsen, 2001, para. 4)

To counteract these concerns, MLB team owners, in an act of national protectionism[18] that would eventually be revoked in 1996, agreed to Yamauchi receiving 60 percent ownership, but limited his voting interest to 49 percent.

An Asian business magnate owning such a sacred piece of American culture and heritage appeared unthinkable.[19]

Today the Japanese connection is applauded and encouraged, particularly given the success of Seattle's Ichiro Suzuki. Yamauchi, who followed Ichiro's rise to fame in Japan, believed Ichiro's popularity could translate into revenues in America. He was both astute and prescient. In Ichiro's first two years with the club, the team drew more than 6.6 million fans to Safeco Field, including a club record and American League-leading 3.5 million in 2002. The club netted an overall profit of nearly $15 million in 2001, which made the Mariners the second most profitable team in baseball (Mariner's Report, 2001). Ichiro's successful migration to the Major Leagues resulted in four major Japanese companies, Nintendo, Konami, Ajinomoto, and Nissan, purchasing a significant advertising presence at Safeco Field. Given the team's international TV exposure, the signs behind home plate target both American and Japanese audiences. Nintendo even has rotational signage in Kanji (Japanese script) behind home plate (Rovell, 2002). As the Mariners' CEO Howard Lincoln now admits: "I don't think any one of us Americans at the Mariners really understood the impact his one guy could have. We just didn't get it" (Greene and Belsen, 2001, para. 7).

Today, they clearly do. Only a few years ago, baseball fans in Japan could watch fifty major-league games over the course of a season. By 2002, with eleven Japanese players on the rosters of seven major-league teams, Japanese viewers could catch about 350 games a season. With three Japanese players on their roster in the 2002 season, all eighty-one of the Mariners' home games were broadcast on high-definition television in Japan. The Mariner's are now only one of many franchises reaching outside of the US to sign talent. Indeed, over 26 percent of the Major League rosters are now filled with foreign-born labor. That total goes to close to 50 percent when the Minor Leagues are included (Selig, 2003).

However, this transition did not happen overnight. The cartel, in an attempt to increase shared earnings, formed Major League Baseball International (MLBI) in 1990 to focus on the "worldwide growth of baseball through game development, broadcasting, special events, sponsorship and licensing" (MLBI Business Plan, 2001, p. 3). To satisfy these goals, the division had spent an estimated $75 million to $100 million in international market development by 2001 (King, 2001). Today, international youth programs such as Pitch, Hit and Run, PlayBall, and the Envoy Program introduce the game to kids in Australia, Germany, Italy, Mexico, South Africa, and the United Kingdom (Market Development, 2001). By the beginning of the 2002 season, MLB had worldwide sponsorship deals with Adidas (shoes/apparel), Franklin (equipment),

Majestic (apparel), MasterCard (credit card), New Era (headwear), Nike (shoes/ apparel), Rawlings (equipment) and Wilson (equipment). Major global brands also added international rights to their domestic sponsorship. Gillette and Pepsi-Cola added Central and South America, Gatorade added Canada, Anheuser Busch and Radio Shack added Puerto Rico. Agreements were also made with national brands; for example, Aeon, am/pm, Kirin, Mizuno, Nikko Cordial, Suntory, and Sato Pharmaceutical acquired international rights to Japan; Maltin Polar, Polar and Telcel for Venezuela; Cracker Jack and MBNA for Canada; Acclaim, Fox Sports, Qantas and Sizzler for Australia (By the Numbers, 2003).

Technological breakthroughs in allowing capital and information to flow freely around the globe, along with the deregulation of national protective economic policies leading to the enormous increase in distribution channels, have clearly aided in the expansion of the game. MLBI has extended television rights to Televen (Venezuela), Teleonce (Puerto Rico), Televisa (Mexico) and ESPNSTAR (Pan Asia) while also signing new agreements with MBC in Korea and ESPN Classic in Canada. By the end of 2001, MLBI had agreements with more than fifty broadcasters transmitting games to 224 countries and territories around the globe ("MLBI Business Plan, 2001).

MLB Advanced Media (MLBAM), the interactive media and Internet arm of MLB, offered live video webcasts of as many as 1,000 out-of market games during the 2003 season exclusively on MLB.com. MLB.TV allows baseball fans around the globe the ability to watch live full-game broadcasts online of forty-five out-of-market games each week. As Bob Bowman, CEO of MLBAM states: "Each new medium, from print, to radio, to TV, to cable TV, to satellite TV has contributed to the promotion and expansion of baseball around the world and we expect this new product will have the same effect. The unquestionable importance of the Internet as a communications tool and the rapid growth of broadband, should make this product attractive to fans around the globe" (MLB Advanced Media, 2003, para. 4). The live webcasts are streamed via a strategic relationship with RealNetworks, Inc., MLBAM's exclusive streaming media partner.

Thus, on March 16, 2003, MLB.TV viewers saw the Los Angeles Dodgers play the New York Mets in the weekend series in Mexico City. Similarly, the actual 2003 MLB Opening Game was to be played in the Tokyo Dome between the Seattle Mariners and the Oakland Athletics.[20] The Opening Day event would have come on the heels of a 2002-post season MLB All-Star series in Japan that drew about 400,000 for eight games. Those games pulled TV ratings of twenty-five or higher, meaning they were seen in more than 10 million homes per game (MLB Returns, 2002). As Paul Archey, the head of MLB International, has previously stated: "It's starting to come together, not only because of the obvious popularity of a guy like Ichiro, but because we have proof in the marketplace that you can use baseball to sell product" (King, 2002, p. 29).

Clearly, the competitiveness of MLB in this global market is coming to depend, not simply on the fortunes of the corporation as being a "national champion" and "American" but on the functions that it can perform – the value it adds – within the global economy. MLB is clearly in place with other multinational corporations (MNCs) where the market for their goods and services is increasingly globalized. This, as Castells (1996, p. 115) notes, " does not mean that all firms sell worldwide. But it does mean that the strategic aim of firms, large and small, is to sell wherever they can throughout the world, either directly or via their linkage with networks that operate in the world market. And, there are indeed, to a large extent thanks to new communication and transportation technologies, channels and opportunities to sell everywhere."

Nowhere is this more evident that in the 1997 purchase of the Los Angeles Dodgers for $311 million by Rupert Murdoch, Australian media baron and Chairman and CEO of News Corporation Ltd. One of the storied franchises of Major League Baseball, the Dodgers first entered the National League in 1890 as the Brooklyn Dodgers. A powerhouse franchise with six World Championships, twenty-one National League Pennants, eight Western Division titles, and over fifty members in the Hall of Fame, Walter O'Malley, president and chief stockholder, in arguably the most notorious MLB relocation decision, moved the Brooklyn Dodgers to the west coast in 1958 where they became the Los Angeles Dodgers.

For many the purchase price of the Dodgers was hailed as outrageous because *Financial World* magazine had only one year earlier valued the organization at $180 million. The problem here is that such a valuation measures the Dodgers under the historical "national champion" market conditions of artificial scarcity. It is true that the Dodgers were the last family owned MLB franchise and, are regarded as "one of the most successful organizations in Major League Baseball during the 20th century . . . a national institution and one of the most recognizable organizations in professional sports" (http://www.newscorp.com/management/dodgers.html). But the Dodgers represent something far more to Murdoch. That is what marks the sale's significance. Indeed, it may provide as much a turning point as the 1876 meetings that created the National League because it marks the beginning of a new relationship between baseball, global media distribution, value added production processes and television entertainment content – an alliance that is redefining the political economy of the game (Howell, 2002).

When he bought the Dodgers, Fox Broadcasting Company, one of Murdoch's many assets, had a $575 million, five-year national TV contract with baseball, a $43 million a year national cable deal, and local TV agreements with twenty-two of the thirty clubs through its Fox Sports Net organization, in a joint venture with TCI's Liberty Media. In 2001, when the national television contract ran out, Murdoch paid a staggering $2.5 billion for MLB broadcast rights through 2006. The strategic move of owning the team, and therefore controlling both programming content and distribution channel, appeared clear. For unlike any traditional owner, Murdoch buying a sports team gives him something far more important than a winning franchise. While it is true that buying the Dodgers helped Murdoch solidify his second cable sports channel in southern California, we should not be too terrestrial in our thinking. Murdoch's Dodgers were broadcast on his StarTV (Asia) and JskyB (Japan) satellite systems, giving him access to the magical international eighteen to forty-nine year old consumer audience, the most courted segment of television demographics.[21]

Thomas Hicks, the CEO of a private equity investment firm and a Texas billionaire, has used professional teams in similar ways. His intent when purchasing the Texas Rangers in 1998 for $250 million was to create a synergy between his entertainment and media holdings. Through his two communications companies, Chancellor Media and Capstar Broadcasting, he owns over 400 radio stations in seventy-seven markets. In addition, he is chairman of the board and owner of the National Hockey League's Dallas Stars. In discussing the purchase, Texas Ranger President Tom Scheffer stated: "While we could compete with just about anyone now, when you have Time Warner [Braves] and Disney [Anaheim Angels] and Fox [Dodgers] and Tribune [Cubs] coming in and owning teams, we felt to get better we were going to have to get bigger. We'd have to become more of an entertainment company than a baseball team" (Stone, 1998, para. 32).

Thus, in 2001 Hicks, along with Liberty Media International and Motorola created Digital Latin America, which will accelerate the launch of digital programing and Internet services to cable subscribers throughout Latin America. Similarly, in 2002, he, along with Fox Sports International and Liberty Media Corp., created Fox Pan American Sports LLC, a new holding company combining their interests in sports programming serving Latin America and the growing Spanish-language markets in the US. To complete the sport-media-entertainment package, in 2002 Hicks signed Seattle Mariner's shortstop, Alex Rodriguez, the most popular player in Latin America, to a blockbuster $252 million, 10-year deal, the largest contract in sports history. Of course, in considering this "acquisition of assets," the question as to who bought whom begs to be answered. In a celebrity culture where the sign-value attached to both player and team in cross-promotional strategies is essential, the inter-textual opportunities are obvious (Howell, 2002).[22]

There is little doubt that the league today operates within a new global economy where wealth creation is not just bound by the fixed assets and stocks, such as stadiums and teams, but rather by building on human capital resources. As one might imagine, this multi-national shift has had some unintended consequences. Owners who only think about local power, authority and control sow the seed of future MLB troubles. Put somewhat differently, a cartel is only as strong as its weakest member. These dysfunctions in the governance of the traditional model of franchise governance are causing serious discontent within MLB as it grows internationally.

First, in the midst of national economic turmoil, multi-national corporate owners are relatively quick to want to unload their assets. While an owner has responsibilities to fellow cartel members, and some would argue their consumer (fan) base, there remains an overriding obligation to another constituency: the parent company's shareholders. Therefore, it is hardly surprising that in the face of new economic forces, with earnings in trouble, entities such as News Corporation (Los Angeles Dodgers), The Walt Disney Company (Anaheim Angels) and AOL Time Warner (Atlanta Braves) are each discussing offloading their baseball entertainment assets. This perspective is entirely consistent with a corporation's duties of not just being motivated by production, but by profitability and the growth of value of its stocks (see Castells, 1996). Here, franchise decisions are tied to the shareholder's desire for profit, risk reduction and return on investment. It is quite different from the economic and social role of the "national champion" owner acting in the interest of the nation, or in this respect, the local community.

Second, in a post reserve clause era of free agency where winning baseball so often equates to open bidding on player salaries, market territory can have a determining impact on the payroll dollars owners have to bargain with. Before the 1996 season, MLB implemented a revenue sharing model to bridge the gap in revenues generated between large market and small market teams. Under the cartel's agreement, there were three sources of revenue for each MLB franchise. The first source was local revenues, which included gate receipts, local broadcasting revenues, ballpark concessions, advertising and publications, suite rentals, and post-season and spring training revenues. The second form of revenue was the central fund, made up of revenues MLB generates from national licensing and broadcast rights. Central fund revenue was distributed equally among all of the franchises. The third and final form of revenue came from a sharing pool, implemented to address the growing disparity in revenues among the franchises in MLB. For instance, each franchise in MLB contributed 20 percent of all its local revenues to a central pool, with 75 percent of the pooled funds then to be equally distributed among all of the teams. The remaining 25 percent was then divided on a sliding scale among all the teams that fell below the league average for local revenues.[23]

As an example, in 2001 the New York Yankees generated over $217.8 million in local operating revenue, with $57 million alone coming from their local broadcasting deals. In stark contrast to the New York Yankees were the Montreal Expos, who generated only $9.7 million in local revenues, with only $536,000 from local broadcasting rights (By the Number, 2003). Both teams received $24.40 million from the central fund, but while the New York Yankees paid $26.54 million to the revenue sharing pool, the Montreal Expos received $28.52 million from the pool. Ultimately, the New York Yankees had overall total local operating income after revenue sharing of $191.2 million while the Montreal Expos had revenues of only $38.3 million (By the Numbers, 2003).[24] Given this, it is hardly surprising that many franchises wish to play in US markets where they can increase local operating revenues via new stadium deals, particularly in terms of luxury suite revenue, and local broadcasting rights.

Third, cities recognize this too. With the increasing development of a post-industrial economy, many cities have attempted to revitalize their cores through the development of an "urban entertainment district" (Hannigan, 1998, p. 101) anchored by a sports stadium. If economic impact studies are to be believed, the argument is that the inclusion of a baseball franchise will add to the trickle down ideology of pro-growth. Its presence will "boost" other companies to make investment within that city's market and bureaucratic boundaries, thus increasing property and sales tax revenues.

But today, the stakes are higher. Increasingly, local economies are connected to the global entertainment enterprise web, meaning local governments have to adopt a form of "urban entrepreneurialism" (Harvey, 2001, p. 348) to compete for rare resources. As the rate of capital mobility accelerates and the global competition for investment tightens, local communities, become more vulnerable to external decisions that influence their future. To play on the global market they simply have to play the risky game of building out a new geography of value added production processes and enterprise networks and this increasingly means a web of interconnected global sports and entertainment facilities.[25] Thus the rash of new themed ballparks built in new gentrified urban zones in the US in the last decade.

This risky game can even be played by nations. Showing that simply having foreign players on the roster does not translate to immediate success in revenue generation, the Montreal Expos were sold to a limited partnership group made up of the other twenty-nine MLB teams in 2002. Currently, committees from Portland, Oregon, Washington DC, and Northern Virginia are vying for the rights to acquire the team and thus "buy" into the cartel. In the meantime, though, the Montreal Expos in 2003 played fifty-nine "home" games in Montreal and 22 "home" games at Hiram Bithorn Stadium in San Juan, Puerto Rico in 2003. As Jose Suarez, Executive Director of the Puerto Rico Tourism Company, puts it: "The Expos games in Puerto Rico extend America's love of the game of baseball to a warm weather destination that Americans love to visit . . . The games are generating considerable excitement and pride throughout the island and will allow us to showcase our first-class tourism destination to key markets in North America" (Batter Up, 2003).

The fourth major issue facing the MLB in this new global and multi-national era has to do with the acquisition of talent. There are three paths to the big leagues for ball players. First, for US citizens, Canadians and Puerto Ricans, there is the amateur draft. Second, for athletes from Mexico, Korea and Japan, there are formal agreements with MLB. Lastly, athletes from Central and South America sign with teams as free agents. Again, by way of example, in order to attain the right to negotiate a contract with a Japanese professional, MLB franchises must "post" sealed bids to the Japanese clubs that own the rights to the particular player. In the case of Ichiro Suzuki, the winning bidder, the Seattle Mariners, paid the Orix Blue Wave close to $13 million just for the right to negotiate a contract with Suzuki. Additionally, while it costs a major league team an average of $1.3 million to sign a first-round pick in the US amateur draft, players and their families in Latin America leap at the average signing bonuses of $5,000 to $8,000 (Guevara and Fidler, 2003). Now this should not really surprise or shock anyone familiar with globalization labor issues. Clearly, as Castells (1996) notes, labor is a global resource and multi-national enterprises may choose to locate in a variety of places worldwide to find the supply of labor they desire, whether it is for particular skills, costs, or social control. Currently, all thirty major league teams operate minor league facilities and summer league teams in the Dominican Republic, and twenty-eight major league teams have facilities in Venezuela (see Guevara and Fiddler, 2003).

To come to terms with this internationalization of the labor pool, MLB has proposed a world draft to instill equal competition for foreign recruits, lower labor bidding wars, and prevent special alliances among the pre-eminent franchises. However, despite the consensus agreeing on the need for a world draft, the negotiating parties have feuded on the conceptual details. Owners want to include international athletes along with domestic talent in a forty-round amateur draft. On the contrary, the Union desires a sixteen-round draft, consisting of eight rounds for international players and eight rounds for domestic talent, and the remaining athletes would be drafted as free agents. Nonetheless, the overall effectiveness of either plan remains murky (Rohman, 2003).[26]

The last issue brought on by the internationalization of the game has to do with symbolic analytical work. Castells (1996, p. 95) explains that a multinational corporation has to "find new markets able to absorb a growing productive capacity of goods and services" (p. 95); to create networks that "transcend national boundaries, identities and interest" but also remains "highly dependent on their national basis". As Bill King (2002) notes in his *Sport Business Journal* exposé appropriately titled "National pastime goes Multi-national", from "1990 to 2000, the Hispanic population increased by at least 100,000 in all but eight of the 24 U.S. baseball markets. It increased by more than 45,000 in all but four markets: Cincinnati, Cleveland, Pittsburgh and St. Louis. During that same 10-year span, Asian populations in seven markets increased by 100,000 or more, and by 45,000 or more in all but nine markets" (par. 15). With the diverse make up of MLB rosters, and the fact that "it is baseball, and not football or basketball, that is ingrained in the cultures of Latin America and Asia" (par. 12), it is of no surprise that MLB itself is developing domestic initiatives with business partners to provide Spanish-language print and TV coverage (MLB Reaches, 2001).

Commissioner Selig recognized this in his March 2003 keynote address at the *Sports Business Journal's* World Congress of Sports: "22 percent of our fans are African American or Hispanic. As the National Pastime, baseball should have a wider appeal to people of all ethnic groups" (Selig, 2003, para. 14). It appears they are on the right track. National demographic research shows that between 1995 and 2001, the Hispanic fan base increased by 361.3 percent, the Asian base by 43.7 percent. Meanwhile, there was a 12.4 percent and 8 percent decrease in the White and African American base, respectively (By the Numbers, 2003). This leads to an interesting dilemma for MLB. Given the increasing domestic and international demography, MLB is clearly promoting the game in a way that fits the cultural and historical context of the time? Whether this requires a new symbolic mythologizing of the game (for example, revisiting origins, international roots, diversity of ownership) remains to be seen.

Responding to those who decry such a shift, Jonathon Mayo, a senior writer for MLB.com, states that "these are people who cling to the *American* pastime and think they're protecting it. But all they're really doing is being unenlightened and myopic . . . The game can still be our pastime . . . Today's version is not the baseball our grandparents, or even parents, grew up with. It's already internationalized . . . 'Old school' isn't always the best school of thought" (Mayo, 2001, paras 9–10). In his World Congress of Sport address, Commissioner Selig was equally blunt:

> We have responded to the challenge over the last decade and have introduced more change to the game than we have seen in the previous 100 years combined. And it has not been easy. As mentioned earlier, bringing about change in any social institution is difficult. In baseball, because of the archaic and cumbersome league structure, which lasted through much of the 20th Century, and because of critics who were and continue to be resistant to change, it was treacherous going. (Selig, 2003, para. 18)

Selig having to "convince the clubs that they no longer could do business as they did in the 1940s, 50s, and 60s" (Selig, 2003, para. 21) brings me full circle to my introductory remarks regarding my travels from SBC Park to the Tokyo Dome. For there is no real irony in MLB, on one hand, having discussions of national contraction in some US cities while, simultaneously, seeking out strategies of international expansion. By extending its "global reach, integrating markets, and maximizing comparative advantages of location" (Castells, 1996, p. 96), MLB is simply operating under the conditions of a late capitalist global economy.

Postscript

In his analysis of the impact of shifting global forces on the US economy, Robert Reich (1992), the US Secretary of Labor during President Clinton's first term, told us that in the interconnected global networks of today "power and wealth flow to groups that have accumulated the most valuable skills in problem-solving, problem-identifying, and strategic brokering. Increasingly, such groups are to be found in many places around the globe other than the United States" (Reich, 1992). Six months after my first meeting with Jean Afterman in the Tokyo Dome, and three months after my second in SBC Park, the New York Yankees hired her as Assistant General Manager of Baseball Operations. Despite her non-traditional baseball managerial credentials, Brian Cashman, the Yankees General Manager stated: "Jean Afterman's abilities as a lawyer and negotiator, as well as her expertise in the Far East can only strengthen the abilities of the New York Yankees as we move forward in our quest to become World Champions once again" (Yankees Name, 2001, par. 3).

In February 2003, after an off-season in which the Yankees signed much sought after Japanese star Hideki Matsui to a three-year $21 million deal, Afterman was given the additional title of vice president of the New York Yankees. According to Yankees chief operating officer Lonn Trost, "The globalization of the New York Yankees is, in part, evidenced by her expertise and work ethic which has proven to be an invaluable resource to our baseball operations department" (Afterman Promoted, 2003, par. 3). In November 2003, Street and Smith's *Sport Business Journal* reported that MLB and Japanese advertising agency Dentsu Inc. signed a landmark six-year $275 million deal for the rights to broadcast MLB games in Japan, beginning with the 2004 season. Dentsu gets the rights to games and then subleases them to Japanese networks. This deal comes on the heels of a 2003 World Series that drew record ratings of over 75 million people, with over 19 million watching Game 1, the most watched MLB game ever in Japan (Kaplan, 2003). Of course, it is no coincidence that Hideki Matsui's New York Yankees were one of the competing teams. Clearly, in the two-way street that is globalization, not only are the local fortunes of MLB being increasingly shaped by global forces but local choices within the individual franchises are actively engaged in producing the global conditions out of which they emerge.

Notes

1. The JSM Group is composed of two companies. J. Sakazaki Marketing Ltd. matches sponsors and sports organizations, creates and runs sporting events, arranges television and other media coverage, and manages players and celebrities, helping companies find the right spokesperson for their products. MRM Inc. handles licensing of international brands and logos and is engaged in import and production licensing for sports, health, and leisure-related products and services.
2. Afterman worked with Nomura from 1994–9, and the agency's clients included Hideo Nomo, Hideki Irabu, Alfonso Soriano and Masato Yoshii. She moved on to manage the Law Offices of Jean Afterman, providing athlete representation and management with specialization in arbitration proceedings. She earned her law degree from the University of San Francisco in 1991.
3. For the first time, in 2001 MLB distributed 12 million All-Star ballots to the Dominican Republic, Japan, Puerto Rico, Venezuela and Canada, via their local title sponsors (MLB Takes, 2001). In Japan, the title sponsor of All-Star balloting, am/pm, distributed more than 5 million ballots with over 850,000 being returned. Ichiro clearly stimulated these results as he tallied 700,000 (excluding online votes) of his record-setting 3.37 million votes from Japan.
4. Current Major and Minor League player's come from: Australia, Aruba, Australia, Bahamas, Brazil, Canada, China, Columbia, Costa Rica, Cuba, Curacao, Dominican Republic, Ecuador, El Salvador, Germany, Guam, Honduras, Italy, Japan, Korea, Mexico, Netherlands, New Zealand, Nicaragua, Panama, Puerto Rico, Russia, South Africa, Taiwan, Venezuela, and the Virgin Islands (MLPI Business Plan, 2001).
5. As an Adjunct Professor, Jack Bair also teaches the legal issues course in the Sports Management graduate program at the University of San Francisco.

6. As part of the new collective bargaining agreement between MLB and the Players Union, all talks of contraction are now on hold until 2006, when the current agreement expires.
7. Although Hartford owner Morgan Bulkeley was the figurehead president in the NL's first year, Hulbert officially took over as president later that year. Hulbert's Hall of Fame plaque reads that he "is credited with establishing respectability, integrity and a sound foundation for the new league with his relentless opposition to betting, rowdiness and other prevalent abuses that threatened the sport" (William Hulbert, 2003).
8. For an excellent history of key dates in MLB history, visit www.baseballlibrary.com.
9. I am indebted to conversations with my colleague Robert Elias, Chair of the Politics Department at the University of San Francisco. His knowledge of baseball history and culture is astounding. Additionally, his book, *Baseball and the American Dream: Race, Class, Gender and the American Pastime* (Armonk NY: M.E. Sharpe, 2002) has been a valuable resource.
10. Spalding's Hall of Fame plaque acclaimed him as the "organizational genius of baseball's pioneer days" and as a star pitcher (Albert Spalding, 2003).
11. Operating with capital of $800, Spalding and his brother opened up their Chicago emporium that sold all kinds of baseball goods in 1876. In 1885 the first store outside of Chicago opened in New York City, and in 1889 new stores opened in Denver and Philadelphia. The company expanded rapidly over the succeeding years and grew to prominence as the largest and best-known company in its field (http://www.spalding.com/about/ag_Spalding.html).
12. There is obviously much debate about the mythmaking of Spalding. Nevertheless, and as the Baseball Hall of Fame notes: "Whatever may or may not be proved in the future concerning Baseball's true origin is in many respects irrelevant at this time. If baseball was not actually first played here in Cooperstown by Doubleday in 1839, it undoubtedly originated about that time in a similar rural atmosphere. The Hall of Fame is in Cooperstown to stay; and at the very least, the village is certainly an acceptable symbolic site for the game's origin" (http://www.baseball halloffame.org/about/history.htm).
13. While the Supreme Court did find against Standard Oil, it was one of only a handful of cases where antitrust was applied. The overwhelming majority of other cases failed, primarily due to the Supreme Court blocking the application.
14. Flood sat out the season and was subsequently traded to Washington where he retired one month into the season.
15. Although the National Labor Relations Act of 1935, known popularly as the Wagner Act, was designed to protect workers' rights to unionization, baseball players did not take that step until 1966, when they hired Marvin Miller, Chief Economic Advisor to the United Steelworkers of America as the first executive director of the Players' Association.
16. Whether an antitrust challenge would reveal that baseball is *not* protected in this area is unknown; it has never been explicitly challenged in court.

17. Many of these sources on the Seattle Mariner's were collected by University of San Francisco sport management graduate student Kris Rohman (2002) and can be found in his unpublished Master's Project entitled "Major League Baseball: International Players and Global Expansion".
18. This national protectionism was prevalent throughout the 1970s and 1980s. Indeed, as Reich (1992, p. 71) notes, by the end of the 1980s "almost a third of the standard goods manufactured in the United States, by value, were protected against international competition".
19. According to *Seattle Times* reporter Chris Judd (2001), Howard Lincoln, the Nintendo executive who later would rise to Mariner CEO status, recalled that when ratifying the purchase MLB owners had one question: "Who among the investors would be The Man, the owner's rep, the guy at the table who goes drinking with the guys after meetings? One owner reportedly scanned the group until his eyes rested on Minoru Arakawa, another Nintendo executive, and the only Japanese face at the table. Chewing on his cigar and nodding at Arakawa, about whom he knew little or nothing, he said: "*He* won't do" (para. 7–9).
20. The threat of war with Iraq caused MLB to cancel the game on Tuesday, March 18, 2003. Amazingly, this would have been owner Yamauchi's first live game involving the Seattle Mariner's.
21. It also helps explains why, in 1998, after purchasing the Los Angeles Dodgers, Rupert Murdoch's BskyB attempted to purchase Manchester United for $1 billion. After a six-month investigation, the British government's Monopolies and Mergers Commission blocked the sale arguing that the merger would adversely affect competition between broadcasters.
22. This also explains why the New York Yankees announced a strategic alliance with Manchester United of the English Premier League in February 2001. Owned by YankeeNets LLC, a premier integrated sports-based media company combining the ownership of the New York Yankees (MLB), the New Jersey Nets (NBA), and the New Jersey Devils (NHL) team, the New York Yankees will get cross promotional synergies with Manchester United's global brand name and international (particularly Asia) sponsorship and merchandizing skills (press release, 2001). Manchester United, on the other hand get access to the YankeeNets' YES Network, a cable channel that, in 2003, began showing United games on two-day delay.
23. I am indebted to USF graduate student Ken Kim for detailing this in such a clear manner.
24. A new collective bargaining agreement begins in 2003 and runs through 2006. Clubs will continue with revenue sharing. Here, 34 percent of net local revenue, after ballpark expenses, will go into a central fund to be split amongst all MLB teams. In addition $72.2 million will be transferred from payers to receivers based on the distance from the net local revenue mean. Additionally, teams will be taxed 17.5 percent on all payroll figures above $117 in 2003, with those thresholds increasing each year of the agreement. Economist Andrew Zimbalist (2003) points

out that the new agreement may not have the necessary results though. While the New York Yankees' revenue-sharing contribution will increase by nearly $20 million this year and their luxury tax will surpass $11 million, the projected Yankees' forty-man payroll for 2003 is $182 million, $7 million above last year. As Zimbalist (2003) continues, the Montreal Expos will see their revenue-sharing receipts rise by some $4 million, to more than $31 million. Nevertheless, their 2003 payroll remains at $40 million.

25. These interconnected features are evident in the building of San Francisco's SBC Park. The architect was HOK Sport the biggest sports design firm in the world, one with a portfolio that includes major league franchises like Cleveland's Jacobs Field, Baltimore's Oriole Park at Camden Yards, and Cincinnati's Great American Ballpark – one of the first traditional urban ballparks designed for a major league team in the modern stadium era (http://hoksport.com). In January 1999, HOK Sports merged with international sports design firm LOBB in an attempt to "be the first sports design firm in history to offer the combined knowledge from virtually every region of the world, to anywhere in the world . . . this merger is all about serving our clients as virtually every form of spectator experience spreads across oceans and cultures" (Global Connect, 1998). The constructor of SBC Park, Kajima USA, is itself a principal subsidiary of Kajima Corporation, based in Tokyo, Japan. As one of the biggest construction companies in the world, Kajima Corporation have fifty-three subsidiaries and more than 13,000 employees who span forty countries and four continents. Panasonic, based in Japan, also joined SBC Park's "global team" to provide fantastic audio and visual stimulation to fans, players and coaches.

26. The World Draft has been put on hold as part of the new collective bargaining agreement. There are clear issues to be resolved between MLB and the Union, let alone the restraints imposed by international labor laws.

References

Afterman Promoted by Yankees (2003), *The San Francisco Chronicle*, February 1. Retrieved March 3, 2003, from http://www.sfgate.com/cgi-bin/article.cgi?file=/news/archive/2003/02/11/sports1754EST0428.DTL.

Albert Spalding (2003). Retrieved October 3, 2002, from The Baseball Hall of Fame Website: http://www.baseballhalloffame.org/hofers%5Fand%5Fhonorees/plaques/spalding_al.htm.

Al Spalding (n.d.). Retrieved October 2002 from http://baseball-almanac.com/quotes/quospld.shtml.

Batter Up – See Your Favorite Major League Baseball Team Play In Puerto Rico This Season (2003), PR Newswire, March 11, 2003. Retrieved March 15 from http://www.puertorico-herald.org/issues/2003/vol7n12/BatterUp-en.shtml.

Brown, et al. v. Pro Football. dba Washington Redskins, et al. (1996). Retrieved March 12, 2003, from http://caselaw.lp.findlaw.com/scripts/getcase.pl?navby=search&court=US&case=/us/000/u20019.html.

By the Numbers (2003). Special edition. *Sport Business Journal*, 5(3): 1–160.

Castells, M. (1996), *The Rise of the Network Society*, second edition, Oxford: Blackwell.

Federal Club v. National League, 259 U.S. 200 (1922). Retrieved March, 2003, from http://caselaw.lp.findlaw.com/scripts/getcase.pl?navby=search&court=US&case=/us/259/200.html

Flood v. Kuhn, 407 U.S. 258 (1972). Retrieved March 12, 2003 from http://caselaw.lp.findlaw.com/scripts/getcase.pl?court=us8vol=4078invol258.

Goldstein, W. (1989). *Playing for Keeps: A History of Early Baseball*, Ithaca: Cornell University Press.

Greene, J. and Belson, K. (2001), The Mariner's Catch a Tsunami, *Business Week*, June 23. Retrieved October 21, 2002, from http://www.businessweek.com/@@J*GIPoYQM0CGxBAA/magazine/content/01_26/b3738105.htm.

Guevara, A. and Fidler, D. (2003), *Stealing Lives: The Globalization of Baseball and the Tragic Story of Alexis Quiroz*, Indiana: Indiana University Press.

Hannigan, J. (1998), *Fantasy City: Pleasure and Profit in the Postmodern Metropolis*, New York: Routledge.

Harvey, D. (2001), *Spaces of Capital: Towards a Critical Geography*, New York: Routledge.

Howell, J. (2002), Luring Teams, Building Stadiums. In Robert Elias (ed.), *Baseball and the American Dream: Race, Class, Gender and the American Pastime*, Armonk NY: M.E. Sharpe.

Ingham, A., Howell, J. and Schilperoot, T. (1987), Sport and Community: A Review and Exegesis. In K. Pandolf (ed.), *Exercise and Sport Sciences Review*, New York: Macmillan.

Judd, R. (2001), It Takes a Global Village to Open Owners' Minds, *The Seattle Times*, July 11. Retrieved October 15, 2002 from http://archives.seattletimes.nwsource.com/cgi-bin/texis.cgi/web/vortex/display?slug=judd11&date=20010711&query=judd+yamauchi

King, B. (2002), National Pastime Goes Multinational, *The Sports Business Journal*, 4(50): 23.

King, B. (2003), Japan TV Deal a Record, *The Sports Business Journal*, 6(28): 23.

Major League Baseball votes to contract two teams (2001), MLB press release, November 6. Retrieved October 12, 2002, from http://www.mlb.com/NASApp/mlb/mlb/news/mlb_news_story.jsp?article_id=mlb_20011106_ownersvote_pr&team_id=mlb.

Market Development (2001). Retrieved June 2, 2002 from http://cbs.sportsline.com/u/baseball/mlbcom/int/int_programs.htm.

Mariner's Report Second Highest MLB Profit (2001), *Puget Sound Business Journal*, December 6. Retrieved October 12, 2002, from http://seattle.bizjournals.com/seattle/stories/2001/12/03/daily36.html.

Mayo, J. (2001), International Relations. MLB.Com, March 26. Retrieved October 12, 2002, from http://mlb.mlb.com/NASApp/mlb/mlb/news/mlb_news_story.jsp?article_id=mlb_20010326_mayoopeningday_news&team_id=mlb.

McGuire, F. and Kou, J. (1995), The Baseball Strike, *Harvard Business Review*, 9: 796–059

Melville, T. (2001), *Early Baseball and the Rise of the National League*, Jefferson NC: McFarland & Co. Inc.

MLB Advanced Media Offers Fans Live TV on the Internet of 1,000 Out-of-Market Baseball Games for the 2003 Season (2003). PR Newswire, March 11, 2003. Retrieved March 15, 2003, from http://news.corporate.findlaw.com/prnewswire/20030311/11mar2003104142.html.

MLB Reaches Out to Bilingual Latino Baseball Fans in the United States (2001), MLB press release, March 15. Retrieved October 12, 2002 from http://www.mlb.com/NASApp/mlb/mlb/news/mlb_news_story.jsp?article_id=mlb_20010315_mlbespanol_pr&team_id=mlb.

MLB Returns for Japan Opener with a Big Star to Sell (2002), *The SportsBusiness Journal.* Retrieved January 12, 2003, from http://www.sportsbusinessjournal.com/article.cms?articleId=26633&s=1.

MLB Takes All-Star Balloting International (2001), MLB press release, April 25. Retrieved October 12, 2002, from http://www.mlb.com/NASApp/mlb/mlb/news/mlb_news_story.jsp?article_id=mlb_20010425_mlbiballot_pr&team_id=mlb.

MLBI to Broadcast the 2001 All-Star Game in High Definition Television (2001), MLB press release, July 5. Retrieved October 12, 2002, from http://www.mlb.com/NASApp/mlb/mlb/news/mlb_news_story.jsp?article_id=mlb_20010705_hdtv_pr&team_id=mlb.

Muscat, C. (2003), Selig Addresses Recent Issues. MLB.com, March 2. Retrieved March 7, 2003, from http://www.mlb.com/NASApp/mlb/mlb/news/mlb_news.jsp?ymd=20030302&content_id=208511&vkey=spt2003news&fext=.jsp.

Reich, R. (1992), *The Work of Nations*, New York NY: Vintage Books.

Rohman, K. (2002), Major League Baseball: International Players and Global Expansion. Unpublished Master's Project, Sport Management graduate program, University of San Francisco.

Rovell, D. (2002), Land of the Rising Revenue Stream. ESPN.com. Retrieved December 2002, from http://espn.go.com/gen/s/2002/0509/1380659.html.

Sage, G. (1990), *Power and Ideology in American Sport*, Champaign: Human Kinetics Press.

Schimmel, K., Ingham, A. and Howell (1993), Professional Team Sport and the American City: Urban Politics and Franchise Relocations. In Alan Ingham and John Loy (eds), *Sport in Social Development: Traditions, Transitions and Transformations*, Champaign: Human Kinetics.

Selig, B. (2003), Selig at World Congress of Sports. Retrieved March 15, 2003, http://toronto.bluejays.mlb.com/NASApp/mlb/mlb/news/mlb_news.jsp?ymd=20030313&content_id=218843&vkey=news_mlb&fext=.jsp.

Stone, L. (1998), *The Seattle Times*, June 10. Retrieved January 15, 2003, from http://www.texnews.com/1998/texsports/hicks0610.html.

Thiel, A. (2001), Ichiro is Music to M's Ears, *The Seattle Post-Intelligence*, March 30. Retrieved December 9, 2002 from http://seattlepi.nwsource.com/thiel/bbthiel.shtml.

Toolson v. New York Yankees, 346 U.S. 356 (1953). Retrieved March 3, 2003, from http://caselaw.lp.findlaw.com/cgi-bin/getcase.pl?navby=volpage&court=us&vol=346&page=357#357.

Voigt, D. (1983), *American Baseball: From the Gentleman's Sport to the Commissioner System*, University Park: Pennsylvania State University Press.

William Hulbert (2003), Retrieved October 3, 2002 from the Baseball Hall of Fame Website: http://www.baseballhalloffame.org/hofers%5Fand%5Fhonorees/plaques/hulbert_william.htm.

Yankees Name Afterman Assistant GM (2001). Retrieved December 12, 2002, from http://www.baseballamerica.com/today/news/yankees1205.html.

Yankees Try to Set Up Meeting with Free Agent Matsui (2002). Retrieved January 3, 2003, from http://espn.go.com/mlb/news/2002/1118/1462764.html.

Zimbalist, A. (2003), *MLB Goes 1-for-2 under New Labor Agreement*. Retrieved March 12, 2003, from thttp://www.sportsbusinessjournal.com/article.cms?articleId=28984&s.

12

Cultural Contradictions/ Contradicting Culture: Transnational Corporations and the Penetration of the Chinese Market[1]

Trevor Slack, Michael L. Silk and Fan Hong

Rujing ernjin; ruguo erwenshu; rumen erwenhui

[If you enter a region, ask what its prohibitions are;
If you visit a country, ask what its customs are;
If you cross a family's threshold, ask what its taboos are.]

Li Ji, *The Book of Rites*

Within this chapter we provide a preliminary analysis of the processes involved in the international restructuration of China through the lens of the Chinese sportingscape. We begin by contextualizing the broad global political, economic and cultural shifts that began in the 1970s and have, in some cases, led to the erosion of nation-states and national identity. For China, these transformations in political, economic and cultural life are particularly interesting given the potential clashes that may occur as Western capitalism and neo-liberal democracy meet deeply ingrained tradition and Confucian ideologies and practices. We explore these tensions, as they are manifest in the structure and operations of sport in China and the operations of transnational organizations seeking to penetrate the Chinese marketplace. In the first section of the paper we provide a discussion of the broad contextual shifts that are the driving forces of the new global economy. In the next section we look specifically at China and the attempts by transnationals (including some in the sport industry) seeking new markets and production sites, to penetrate the country and some of the issues and problems they have encountered when faced with the structure of the Chinese market, the traditional modes of operation that characterize China as a nation and the Chinese way of doing business. In the third section we focus specifically on sport and provide a short explanation of roots of the hierarchical and bureaucratic nature of the Chinese sport system. We then provide a few brief examples of the tensions that result when the efforts of transnationals that enter China clash with the deeply ingrained norms of traditional society that are held within the country. We finish with some concluding remarks.

Contextualizing Transnational Corporatism

Understanding national cultures such as China has become troublesome given increasing global trends towards economic restructuring, technological shifts and the movement of a more mobile form of capital. According to Held, McGrew, Goldblatt, and Perraton (1999, p. 16), globalization is "a process (or set of processes) which embodies a transformation in the spatial organization of social relations and transaction – assessed in terms of their extensity, intensity, velocity and impact – generating transcontinental or interregional flows and networks of activity, interaction and the exercise of power". Although most contemporary commentators (apart from Hirst and Thompson, 1996) would concur with Held et al.'s (1999) assertion as to the existence of globalizing economic, political, cultural, and technological processes, there is widespread disagreement as to manner in which they affect and are accepted in the host community. This is particularly true when considering the ramifications of globalization for individual nation-states, especially emerging economies, such as China, which have only recently begun to acknowledge, and perhaps engage with, transnational corporate capitalism.

Whereas many learned commentators decry the demise of the nation at the hands of rampant globalization, some display a steadfast belief in the enduring relevance of the nation as a source of identity and differentiation. This fracture is equally evident among those working in the global marketplace, particularly those within the marketing, advertising and strategic nodes of transnational companies (such as Sony, Volkswagen, and Disney), whose corporate footprints transcend the boundaries of nation-states and who operate "simultaneously in different countries around the world, on a global scale" (Morley and Robins, 1995, p. 223). To many, these types of arguments suggest that transnational forces are undermining significant aspects of the sovereignty once held by nations, thus rendering them increasingly obsolete economic and political entities within the all-prevailing global marketplace. The expanding range of information flows and the spatial reach of digital communications systems are, for example, argued by some social theorists to be leading to new kinds of social anomie, a "dissolution" of social relationships and the collapse of political, cultural and place-based identities that characterized the era of capitalist industrialism (Preston and Kerr, 2001). However, such apocalyptic visions can be challenged given the role of the nation-state and the salience of national/local specificities within a country such as China. In this particular locale, following the theoretical reasoning of Preston and Kerr (2001), and despite the global cosmopolitanism suggested within such literature, "geography still matters" in a very real sense as local and national specificities continue to shape production and consumption processes in many sectors in different ways. As such, and as many chapters in this text have pointed out, the somewhat hegemonic "borderless world" (Ohmae, 1990) rhetoric can be, at least to some degree, undermined – for our purposes this is especially the case when considering the engagement between global capitalism and the specificities of the Chinese "marketplace" and Chinese cultural identities.

Despite this qualification, it is possible to argue that, prefigured on the logic of increased interdependence and interconnectedness, contemporary conditions of advanced globalization have seriously undermined the economic and political autonomy that helped constitute the modern nation. Lash and Urry (1995) have designated the deconcentration of capital through globalized production, financing and distribution, a concomitant shift in the occupational structures of core and periphery economies and the growth of capitalism in the "developing" world "disorganized capitalism". Although its roots can be traced further back, and as was highlighted in the introduction to this volume, this process of "the withering away of the nation" (Hannerz, 1996, p. 81) began in earnest during the 1970s, when the confidence in Fordist/Keynesian economic policies that had held sway in many Western economies since the end of World War II began to unravel and corporations, aided and abetted of course by the Reagan and Thatcherite regimes of the time, began to operate beyond their own national boundaries. Prefigured on advances in telecommunications, flexible manufacturing and information technology, and a need to distance themselves from national accumulation and regulatory modes (Allen, 1992), corporations looked to rationalize and restructure. In fleeing rigid national labor, accumulation and regulatory regimes, corporations became internationally mobile, operating through a globally connected communications network and a financial system with floating exchange rates (Harvey, 1989). Castells (1989; 1996) has termed the organization, the operation and the import of information and services within the new global economy the "network society" that conditions the effectiveness of both firms and countries.

The transnational organization of this global market has centered on the instantaneous, real-time coordination of economic activity and the development of new information and communications technologies (Robins, 1997). Such significant shifts and transformations occurring within late capitalism have meant that the modes of development and modes of production have been transformed from material- and labor-oriented structures to those that are dependent upon information and knowledge (at least within Western economies). Passages from Fordism to post-Fordism, industrialism to a post-industrial society and from nationally grounded to post-national marketplaces for goods, services and production have led to an international economy based on networks of corporations (and nations) linked by fiber optics and satellites rather than concrete or steel, physical or tangible systems with information, as opposed to goods, circulating. These conditions have meant that many major corporate entities shifted from focusing on commodity production and capital accumulation (at least within core economies) within individual national markets to a more flexible approach within which the corporate footprint transcended national borders in the search for more rational and efficient commodity chains – an approach interrogated throughout the various contributions to this volume. Corporations such as McDonalds, IBM, Motorola, Procter and Gamble, Nike, News Corporation and IMG (International Management Group) have penetrated China through the economics and imagery of global capitalism and represent the latest and most sophisticated attempt by transnational corporations to command the widest possible market base and thereby accrue the benefits derived from the realization of colossal economies of scale (Luo, 2000).

Global Fordism has also created the "regulatory" environment for the establishment of free trade zones loosely regulated by quasi-governmental "have" nations that center on the primacy of free markets, deregulation, and unfettered international trade (Sassen, 2000). These have been institutionalized by the formation of transnational political structures, alliances, and treaties (such as the World Trade Organization, the International Monetary Fund, the North American Free Trade Agreement, the G8 and the Asian Pacific Economic Cooperation). Given these political and economic processes and the concomitant rise of the transnational capitalism, in conjunction with technological developments, political approval, deregulationist initiatives and lower trade tariff barriers, corporations have transcended national boundaries, redesigned their organizational structures, operations and promotional strategies in an effort to truly benefit from the massive economies of scale derived from the establishment of a truly global market. This allows transnational corporations, such as Nike, to move through Japan, Taiwan and Korea to the current major producers of sportswear – Indonesia, Vietnam and China (Van Dusen, 1998). Through its use of subcontractors, Nike, as a vertically disaggregated corporation, has established a manufacturing presence within China that could operate to gain incentives and tax breaks for Nike, and lower labor and environmental regulations within the nation. With corporations seeking out the most attractive global "business climate" in an effort to rationalize labor costs (a race to the bottom in regard to labor regulations, standards and conditions) and create new marketplaces, states are seeking to "short circuit the sequence of development" (Castells, 1989) by leapfrogging into a race to attract transnational investment.

Given the structure, organization and strategic functions of the global economy, and following the theoretical reasoning of Castells (1989), many countries, especially those like China on the fringes of the capitalist core, are attempting to connect themselves to networks by repositioning themselves as places that can attract the right sort of firms and be a part of the information infrastructure. These efforts of national development are driven both by corporate interests and by the Chinese governmental and political system. China represents what can be termed an "emerging economy". This previously closed (or perhaps centrally planned) economic and political system has undergone dramatic change and now shows evidence of a market led system characterized by a rapid pace of development, governmental policies that favor economic liberalization and the adoption of a free market system (Perkins, 1994; Hoskisson, Eden, Lau and Wright, 2000). Understanding this increasing internationalization of the flow of capital and commodities and the ways in which China articulates, engages with, rejects and operates within a new global ecumene is of crucial importance for addressing the impact that the globalizing forces of transnational corporations are having upon China and the Chinese sportingscape. While tempting to invoke Edward Said's (1978) *Orientalism*, particularly the concept of the "West defining the Rest", if we are to understand fully the impact of such forces we need to address the complex interactions and engagements between global capital and local cultures. As such, it is important to understand the new global economy and the emergence of transnational corporate capitalism prior to discussing the ways in which these movements have been met, embraced, rejected and contested within China. Specifically we are concerned about the possible transformation of the national sportingscape and indeed the possibilities for a resistant reassertion of national and regional cultural traditions and identities in the face of such encounters.

In tandem with these "internal" processes, which of course take place in relation to wider global political, economic and technological shifts, of particular interest for us in this chapter are the actions and strategies of transnational corporations who looking to engage with the Chinese marketplace. Specifically, we are interested in addressing these "mutually reinforcing" strategies to begin to address the ways in which these processes of national development and the presence of transnational corporate capitalism within China is impacting upon the organization, structure and operation of the Chinese sportingscape. It is in this way that we are addressing the "changing" of the Chinese nation, politically, economically and culturally, under the logics of transnational corporate capitalism (Hannerz, 1996). Of course, these changes may not go unchallenged; rather they may be resisted, rearticulated or engage in considerable patterns of interactions prior to cultural change. Especially for a country like China that has deeply entrenched traditions, values and political and cultural ideologies, the engagement with transnational corporatism may well invoke skepticism or resistance and any such transformations may well take time and significant (even misguided) effort on behalf of various corporations. For example, while Chinese political policy may well invite nomadic corporations to operate within Chinese borders, China may not have the physical, technological and indeed institutional requisites for the effective operation of transnational corporate capitalism. At this juncture, then, it is important to understand more about the emergent Chinese economy, market and infrastructure and the concomitant shifts within China's political, economic and cultural spheres. This will then provide us with an adequate context from which we can begin to understand the transformations, structure and operation of, and within, the Chinese sportingscape.

Transnational Corporatism and the Appropriation of the Chinese Marketplace

In 1978, following years of state control of all productive assets, China, under new leader Deng Xiaoping, began a program of market oriented economic reform. This involved a move away from the central economic planning of the past to a more market form of economy that included a place for the profit motive. Accomplishing this transformation meant China opening her doors to the world. As Premier Zhao Ziyang noted in November 1981 in his speech to the National People's Congress "By linking our country with the world market, expanding foreign trade, importing advanced technology, utilizing foreign capital, and entering into different forms of international economic and technological cooperation, we can use our strong points to make up for our weak points" (Schell, 1984, p. 90). The country officially opened up to foreign investment with the passage of a joint venture law in 1979. In the first four years of the country opening up, foreign direct investment (FDI) averaged just under $700 million per year. But, with foreign companies seeking to stake their claim on what they believed to be a potentially lucrative market FDI rose rapidly, particularly through the 1990s, and by the end of 1998 the Chinese authorities had given approval to over 300 foreign invested enterprises involving $522.4 billion of foreign capital (Luo, 2000).

In opening her doors, China has acknowledged and has begun to capitalize upon transnational corporate capitalism. Much of this capital came from large transnational corporations (Nokia, IBM, Motorola, General Motors, General Electric, Daimler-Benz, Fosters, McDonalds, and Ford), including some in the sport industry (Nike, IMG, and News Corporation through its Star Sport arm) anxious to gain a foothold in what they saw as potentially the world's biggest market. In addition to these transnational corporations such as Nike, IMG, and News Corporation, a number of the international governing bodies of sport have also shown designs on China. The most visible of these is the International Olympic Committee with its decision to award to 2008 Olympic Games to Beijing. There is much speculation as to the merits of the IOC decision it was undoubtedly assisted by transnational corporations, such as GM, Xerox, Heineken, and Fuji Film, who helped underwrite the cost of the Beijing bid (*Sports Illustrated*, 10 July, 2001). Transnational companies such as these saw the holding of the Olympics in China as a chance for them to penetrate the world's biggest market (at least in terms of population) and begin to accrue the benefits that can be derived from such economies of scale. While the IOC's involvement in China is the biggest and most visible initiative by an international sport governing body, a number of other bodies, such as the Federation internationale de l'automobile (the governing body of Formula 1 races) and MotoGP (motorcycle racing), have shown their designs on the Chinese marketplace.

Many Western transnationals, including a number directly involved in sport, seduced by the lure of the imagined size of the Chinese market, have arrived with an over simplistic view of the Chinese nation-state and a lack of knowledge about the enduring political, economic and cultural qualities of a country that until recently had followed a policy of isolation from the rest of the world. Many viewed China as a homogeneous nation waiting to be the recipient of Western values and a country with a culture designed to engage in the type of business practices that are routinely taught in the major MBA programs of North America and Western Europe. However, while some corporations seeking to penetrate global markets have tried "to neuter cultural differences through a strategic global uniformity, many corporations have realized that securing a profitable global presence necessitates negotiating with the local" (Silk and Andrews, 2001, p. 187).

McDonald's, for example, ensures that its operations, product and corporate structure are relevant to the Chinese marketplace through a strategy of "localization". Yan (1997), for example, points to the family orientation of the restaurant in China, ensuring each franchise is Chinese owned and operated, the introduction of "Aunt McDonald" to greet customers on entry (and perhaps more cynically create a database of young consumers), and the promotional strategizing focusing on the "Little Emperor" of the Chinese family. Targeting the Little Emperor, perhaps the most influential member of the Chinese family, especially in regard to influencing familial consumption, allows McDonalds to exploit the Chinese marketplace and gain the most effective economies of scale from their presence in China. While the presence of McDonald's may have caused a transformation in consumption patterns, and while McDonald's may have sought (however superficially or exploitatively) to engage with a certain element of the Chinese populace, the actual McDonald's experience appears to be rearticulated by Chinese consumers. McDonald's in China is a place to be seen, a place to relax and be seen, a romantic, clean and comfortable environment that "connects" younger, affluent (the cost is a sixth of a month's salary) to the outside world (Yan, 1997). As such, and following Yan (1997), McDonald's in China points to the complexity of the practices and presence of transnationals in China: a juxtapoition of *tu* (rustic, backward, traditional) and the *yang* (foreign). Transnationals seeking to enter countries like China have, for the most part, sought to be part of the local through the creation of localized spaces of identity and experiences that facilitate the continuity of flow between global production and local consumption but in doing so they have, as a result, had to engage with entrenched local practices and traditions. In the case of China it is here that some have failed or at least not realized their expected return on investment.

One of the first problems that transnationals seeking to operate in the Chinese market have had to deal with is the misconstruction of numbers. While it is true that the population of China is in the region of 1.3 billion, nearly 900 million of these people live in rural areas and have low-income levels. Estimates vary but the income of rural families is usually presented as less than $400 per year. Even in the more developed areas along the east coast and Yangtze River basin, per capita family incomes may only reach $2,000 to $3,000 per year (again estimates vary). While this certainly affects the potential of the Chinese markets for the producers of what might be construed as "luxury" goods (although those working to manufacture those goods with have little interest in, let alone the resources for, such goods) it has, as Studwell (2002) notes, also affected corporations seeking more broad-based consumer markets. Breweries such as Bass and Fosters lost considerable investment in China and Studwell (2002) cites a 1998 survey by management consultants A. T. Kearney that revealed that, of 229 foreign-invested businesses only 38 percent of all manufacturers were covering their operating costs.

In addition to miscalculating the size of the Chinese market, transnationals looking to engage with China often fail to recognize the specificities, and the deeply rooted importance, of local norms and traditional ways of doing business.

Unlike in the West, where there is a transaction-based business culture, Chinese business is based on relationships. As Chen (2001, p. 45) notes, "in the Chinese business context, relationships are a form of social capital, owned by businesspeople and associated with the companies they run." Key to these relationships is the concept of *guanxi*. While it is hard to define *guanxi*, it involves connections based on reciprocity, trust, mutual obligations, and shared experiences. For some *guanxi* is seen as a form of influence peddling but it is more than this and has it roots in Confucianism where social exchange and reciprocity are used to build and maintain interpersonal relationships. For transnationals entering China, *guanxi* is a key factor that will influence the development of private businesses during market reforms. However, it is also important for companies looking to do business in China to understand other complexities of local market conditions. As well the absence of commercial laws in many areas of operation, insecure property rights, internal trade barriers and problems of corruption and counterfeiting make globalizing companies forays into China all the more difficult.

In addition to understanding how businesses and business relationships work in China, attempts by global companies to enter the country will be shaped by the peculiar politics of China. As Studwell (2002, p. 170) notes "the biggest myth about China in the 1990s was that the country ceased to be socialist." The government showed a level of commitment to free-market enterprise and the involvement of transnationals, but China's own description of its economy as a fundamentally socialist country which was undergoing some Chinese modifications was an accurate depiction of the changes that were taking place. One of the biggest changes as a result of the move to a more market-led economy was the reform of state-owned enterprises. As Studwell (2002, p. 39) notes "as early as 1979 . . . China's State Council laid out plans for the reform of state-owned enterprises (SOEs) concentrated in the country's big urban centers. The objective was to introduce more market- and profit oriented behavior into state companies in order to improve their performance, this was to be done in the framework of centralized planning." These industries, formally protected from market forces, began to feel pressure from domestic as well as global market forces. The reform of previously SOEs is extremely difficult as there is still a level of government protection. Reforming these enterprises means displacing employees as well as the managers who have gained from their comfortable locations within the state apparatus. One of the consequences of this effort at transformation is that the Chinese market landscape is awash with quasi-governmental organizations and other mixed institutions. Even in the newly introduced private organizations the lack of developed capital markets, regulatory systems, and periods of macroeconomic instability have posed problems.

The problems highlighted above of a miscalculated market size, a lack of knowledge of how to do business in China, and a government that, despite showing some level of transition to a global market economy is still strongly entrenched within an ideology of socialism, have not failed to have an impact on the transnational companies within the sport industry and the international sport bodies that are seeking to secure their place in the Chinese market. Those transnational corporations that have sought to engage and appropriate the Chinese market have had to deal with these very real cultural, political, economic, operational and technological particularities and complexities in their efforts to operate in the global. Despite these obstacles, the presence and practices of transnational corporations in China have very real impacts upon the sportingscape and indeed the consumer logic of the Chinese marketplace. For example, through global expansion designed to accrue maximal profit from emergent markets, those sporting transnationals that have entered China have capitalized upon, and exploited, a cheap source of labor. Further, these corporations have sought engagement at a purely superficial level with those who "fit" their very specific corporate agendas, as opposed to connecting with the multifarious, diverse and rich cultures of China. However, it would be naïve to suggest that those transnational organizations that have engaged (at varying degrees of superficiality) with the Chinese marketplace have managed to easily secure a profitable presence through operating seamlessly within the nation. In the next section we provide some exploratory examples of the complexities sporting transnationals have confronted when attempting to appropriate and operate in a China that is looking to engage itself as a player on the global stage yet is still very much entrenched in peculiarly nationalist practices. Specifically, we focus on the operations, practices and relationships with the Chinese sportingscape of the NBA, FIFA, IMG, the English Premier League and Manchester United, the global sports media, and perhaps the most pervasive sporting transnational of all, Nike. From these brief sketches, we point to the ways in which the presence and practices of transnational organizations are involved (along with other important agencies such as the Chinese state) in the manufacture, or refinement, of the Chinese economy and cultural identities centered on mostly Western consumer capitalist discourse – a "changing" of the Chinese nation, politically, economically and culturally, under the logics of transnational corporate capitalism (Hannerz, 1996).

Cultural Contradictions: Transnational Corporatism and the Particularities of the Chinese Sportingscape

The bureaucratic and hierarchical system that characterizes China's sport system has its roots in the writings of the sage Confucius (551–479 BC) and his disciples.

Confucianism is more a system of ethics and morals than a religion. The core of Confucianism is "Li" (the rules of propriety), which are said to be based on the principle of benevolent control. In reality, in Chinese history, they were often nothing more than a manipulative means by which an absolute ruler enforced conformity. The rules of propriety were inflexible. They defined privileges and obligations in accordance with an individual's status and they were sanctioned by law. Confucianism held a dominant position in traditional culture for more than 2,000 years. Its "principle of hierarchy" governed political structure, social life and traditional ethics and can still be seen to be at work, in myriad of ways, in China today. China's political structure probably owes as much to Confucian heritage as it does to the Soviet Union, on which the People's Republic is largely modeled. Far from the "classless" organization of communist mythology, Chinese society is in fact strictly hierarchical, with rank and privileges clearly defined. People relate to one another not as individuals but rather according to their relative ranks. Decision-making is strictly from the top down, and little is accomplished without support from the higher echelons. Confucianism is an inherently conservative belief system. It does not facilitate innovation and does nothing whatsoever to encourage such practice. Indeed, a hierarchical, vertical system of government where decisions of even minor import must be referred upward does not provide an ideal setting for multi-nationals looking to do business.

As perhaps the prototypical sporting transnational entity, the NBA (see Andrews, 1997), with its allied and mutually reinforcing commodity signs firmly tucked under its arm, has had an interesting relationship with the specificities of the Chinese sportingscape. The NBA first sent a team of all-stars on an exhibition tour of China in 1984 but it was in the 1990s that their presence began to be felt. As Andrews (1997) has argued, the NBA outgrew the US market and, along with their corporate interests, most notably Nike and Coca-Cola, looked to cultivate the overseas market. Currently, the NBA has a broadcast foothold in 206 countries and some 550 million households (Miller et al., 2001). The NBA started to boom at about the same time as the forces of globalization were having their most significant impact on China. The NBA has sought to expand its global reach into China with the drafting of Wang Zhizhi by the Dallas Mavericks and the Houston Rockets making Yao Ming the number one draft choice in 2002.

The hierarchical system alluded to above has affected the relationship between the NBA and the reformed Chinese sports system. The drafting of 7 foot 6 inch Yao Ming in the 2002 National Basketball Association draft provides a classic example of the role that the state still plays in sport and the manner in which it exerts control over its operation. Yao, who first came to the attention of NBA scouts during the Sydney Olympics, was selected first overall in the 2002 draft by the Houston Rockets. However, far from being able to ply his trade freely within the marketplace Yao Ming's transition to the NBA had to be approved by the Chinese Basketball Association (CBA) and his team the Shanghai Sharks. The suggested agreement involved 50 percent of Yao's salary and endorsements being returned to China: 30 percent to the CBA, 10 percent to the government and 10 percent to his club. The CBA also wanted an assurance that he would be available for national team games. As CBA general secretary Xin Lancheng noted "They [the NBA and the Rockets] have to guarantee that Chinese players will be physically and mentally healthy. At the same time, our players should be able to play for their own country when they are needed" (*People's Daily*, June 25, 2002). After protracted negotiations with the CBA and the Sharks an agreement was eventually reached on the conditions of Yao being allowed to join the NBA, however the terms of the agreement were not revealed.

Additionally, and not surprisingly, the NBA have sought to capitalize upon the Chinese market through offering footage of NBA games to China Central Television (CCTV) in a deal that involved blanket coverage for the NBA on Chinese TV (Gluckman, 2002). In seeking to cultivate the league's global presence, the NBA have keyed their global televisual product on the lure held by the trappings of American consumer culture over the youth populace of the world (Alms, 1994). In this vein then, and despite rhetoric from the NBA about spreading the sport to China, it is as Michael Denzel, managing director of NBA Asia notes, about "more viewers [and] potentially more merchandise sales" (Gluckman, 2002).

In addition to the NBA, the "global game" (Guiliannotti, 1999), has seen China as a major market opportunity. FIFA, the world governing body of soccer is a transnational body that promotes globalization (and transnational capitalism) through its marketing and structuring (historically, imperialist) of the game worldwide (Sugden and Tomlinson, 1998). Within China for example there are more than seventy foreign players in the Chinese first and second divisions and more than ten foreign coaches. Further, Bora Milutinovic, a Serb, became a national hero in China when he coached the national team to the 2002 World Cup Finals. Along with the role of FIFA, in 1994 IMG signed an $8 million guarantee with the Chinese Football Assocation (CFA) to be the exclusive agent for advertising and television rights. Initial seed money for the IMG deal came from Philip Morris Inc., famous for its Marlboro brand. This new era of transnational engagement with the Chinese footballscape evolved into the Jia A and Jia B (the equivalent to the English Premier and First Divisions), the nationwide emergence of professional club networks, player transfers, agents, sponsorship, television rights and merchandising. By 2001 the total amount of revenue, which was being generated by the CFA, was $15 million, 70 percent of which, Ashton (2002) claims, is underwritten by IMG (Star TV, 2002).

At the same time, and as Sugden and Tomlinson (1998) point out, football continues to be a locus of local and parochial national voices. These tensions can be seen in the Chinese marketplace as tendencies towards a strong national governing body and national team articulate with the presence of transnationals such as IMG and FIFA. Although IMG set up the Chinese league system and organized seminars to teach "best practice" on day-to-day operations, there is a conflict between the Chinese sports system, a product of traditional culture and a planned economy, and the professional club system, a product of Western culture and a market economy. Lack of sponsorship, investment and audience has seen eleven of the twelve original clubs face bankruptcy. The famous Sichuan club, Jiannanchun, for example, changed ownership four times in seven years before eventually disappearing. The hierarchical system continues to dominate the Chinese sports system and, despite the presence of IMG, the structure of management at the CFA remains the same. The CFA and its provincial and local commissions make the major political and economic decisions for clubs and matches. This is rooted in the ownership of the clubs within China. When the Professional League started in 1994, the clubs came directly from established provincial teams. These former provincial teams were required to seek out private enterprise (sponsors and owners) to become professional clubs. However, the players and stadiums were still owned by the governing body through the local sport commissions. This situation changed when companies recognized that they needed more control and started to buy players from the sports commissions in the late 1990s. While most clubs now own their own players there is still a tension between professional clubs and the CFA. The CFA, as the governing body, is still the major decision maker, which vet minor changes in organization and structure of clubs and stands in the way of various transfers between provinces and clubs.

The presence of FIFA and IMG has clearly had a significant impact upon the Chinese footballscape. The structure of the sporting landscape has been changed by the practices and operations of these transnationals. Football also provides an interesting site from which to view the relationships between foreign organizations and Chinese businesses seeking to engage with foreign (*yang*) markets. The China Kejian Company, a maker of mobile phones, for example signed a shirt sponsorship deal with the English Premier League club Everton. This deal not only involves exposure for the China Kejian company throughout the globe via its symbolic association with a representative from the pinnacle of the global game, but included the loan of a Chinese player to Everton. Here is an example of the complexities involved in the fusion between the (reformed)

Chinese sportingscape, the CFA, Everton football club, a Chinese transnational and of course the symbolic delivery systems of News Corporation. Everton manager David Moyes originally selected midfielder Li Tie from the club Liaoning but much to Moyes surprise the player sent to Everton was Li Weifeng from Shenzhen Pingan. Liaoning were sponsored by a rival telephone manufacturer Bodao who objected to their rivals Kejian being able to reap publicity from the deal. Rather than create a conflict between the two clubs the strategy of avoiding a head-to-head confrontation advocated by the Chinese military strategist Sun Zi, whose work has continued to have a significant effect on Chinese thought and indeed on Western organizational strategists, was employed. Li Weifeng was drafted at the last minute, something even he knew nothing about, to meet the Chinese Football Association's obligation and then a compromise was reached between the two clubs and the telephone companies. Everton came out the winner in these negotiations, ending up with two Lis for the price of one (Northcroft, 2002, p. 13). Such Chinese business practices which involve a penchant for maintaining a low profile, are steadily changing and while many companies will be forced into head-to-head confrontations a number will continue to employ traditional practices. While doing business with the Chinese demands a knowledge of such practices, it also points to the promotional strategizing of organizations within China. Not only can the China Kejian company begin to appropriate the global market, the same symbolic delivery systems provide a focal point, or "representative subjectivity" (Marshall, 1997) in the form of Li Weifeng, for the Chinese media sport market. Such a relationship may well blossom into future promotional opportunities for Everton in China, for the China Kejian Company, and indeed for the continued impact of the English Premier League on the Chinese consumer. While hypothetical, such relationships point to both the complexities of the relationships between those organizations involved and to the transformation in the Chinese sportingscape under the logics of transnational corporate capitalism.

In addition to this impact on the Chinese football marketplace, there have been a number of other significant relationships between the Chinese sporting system and football – most notably, and least surprisingly, through the global, consumer oriented, mediated football product. The sports-media complex in China, which feeds an insatiable demand across its 1.26 billion population, takes place in relation to the hierarchical system. Direct broadcasting by foreign broadcasters is banned and domestic outlets can carry no more than 25 percent of non-Chinese content. The dominant figure in the Chinese sports media is the State-owned CCTV in Beijing. This is controlled by the State Administration for Radio, Film and Television, which is under the ultimate jurisdiction of the Ministry of Information Industry. CCTV has nine channels. One of these channels, CCTV 5, is wholly dedicated to sport and reaches 90 million households and around 360 million individuals. CCTV dominates the market and has first pick of both domestic and foreign sports properties. This Chinese media monopoly is resistant to change. It is a product of the top-down Confucian cultural inheritance and operates through State regulation to enhance State control through the control of publicity and preservation of the political system and public order. In stark contrast to the deregulated Western sport-media complex, legislation protects the position of CCTV; as a result Chinese broadcasters rarely pay significant rights fees – historically the organizers of sports competitions paid fees to CCTV for broadcasting their event.

In 1994, however, a significant transformation occurred in the Chinese system and Western media sport practices were mimicked. The CFA learned from England and negotiated a TV rights fee with CCTV. After a difficult process of negotiation, CCTV agreed to pay the CFA 1.1 million RMB (8 RMB = approximately US$1) over three years (1994–7). On average CCTV would pay the CFA 130,000 RMB (US$1,300) for each match (Feng, 2001). However, the CBA is not that fortunate. Compared with an NBA basketball team that makes 90 percent of its revenues from television rights, the CBA has not reached any agreement with CCTV, let alone local and regional television stations (Bai et. al., 2000). Transnational companies thus still face big obstacles in exploiting television rights in the Chinese sports marketplace as a result of the highly centralized control exerted by the State. As Guy Horne, the Director of Sports Rights at IEC in Sport notes, "there is an effective monopoly in place with CCTV as the dominant player. There is little opportunity for other stations to bid for major sports rights. Until deregulation occurs, Chinese sport will be starved of a much-needed source of investment. This is critical if sport business is to flourish" (cited in Ashton, 2002, p. 39).

Of course, the archetype for the twenty-first century global media firm (Herman and McChesney, 1997) entered Asia in 1991. Headed by the infamous Rupert Murdoch, News Corporation has a foothold on all six continents (owning and controlling various revenue-generating nodes of the sport-entertainment industry) and aims to create a vertically integrated and globally encompassing sport-media delivery system. In August 2002 its ESPN Star Sports signed a distribution agreement involving deals with over twenty regional television channels and national channel CCTV5. As a result of this deal over 100 million Chinese will be able to see 165 live English Premier League games. Thus, while global media oligopolies may face difficulty in controlling the media marketplace within China, they can ensure a presence by providing content such as the NBA and the English Premier League. This presence appears to be having an impact upon the strategizing of Chinese organizations, as we have seen with the case of the CBA and Yao Ming. Further, the opening of the global mediascape also has sparked interest among those at CCTV who are looking to capitalize upon the commodity signs attached to this foreign content.

Long prior to the establishment of Jia 1 and Jia 2 and the enhanced arrangement with ESPN Star Sports, English Premier League games have been seen weekly in China – leading to many Chinese supporting foreign clubs. The success of Manchester United in the 1990s in particular saw a large and loyal fan base (estimated to be 8 million) develop around the "Red Devils". Of course, Manchester United, ever keen to enhance and exploit its global ubiquity, was not shy in embracing its newfound fan base. In July 1999, 80,000 people watched Manchester United play at Shanghai football stadium while 100 million watched on CCTV. Tickets were sold out in hours and cost more than a peasant's annual income. People from President Jiang Zemin to school children reveled in wearing the logo. In 2002, and capitalizing upon its previous incursion into China, Manchester United successfully negotiated a deal with CCTV. The arrangement will see the content of MUTV broadcast on CCTV5 for 2 to 4 hours a week. CCTV plans to use the content to generate its own profits through the sale of Manchester United merchandizing, the launch of an associated Web site and the ever looming "Pay TV". Of course, the club plans to develop its chain of "Theatre of Dreams" stores, Red cafes and football academies across China to truly gain the benefits from their 8 million Chinese faithful.

Manchester United will have to face the dangers of miscalculating the size of the Chinese marketplace. While they may be phenomenally popular, the reality is that most Chinese would not be able to afford to purchase their Nike manufactured uniform (or indeed the counterfeit version). Nike itself has also faced the complexities of the local marketplace when it first entered China. In the early 1980s Nike, along with Reebok and Adidas, was one of the first entrants into the Chinese marketplace. It entered the country through a contractual joint venture. However, like others who do business in China, Nike encountered difficulty with the state apparatus. As Luo (2000, p. 233) notes "Nike tried to deal directly with state enterprises, but state-owned factories could not comprehend what Nike wanted in terms of price, quality and delivery. . . . Its American managers faced problems in dealing with China's public sector." As Chen (2001, p. 161) notes, China is still a socialist country where the Communist Party exerts a strong conservative influence and "foreign businesses forget this at their peril". As a result of the difficulties faced, Nike gradually wound down its agreements with the State-owned factories and moved to a situation where it subcontracted its operations thus shifting risks to the subcontractor. Today, Nike continues to engage with some of the peculiarities of doing business in China. For example, as with the CFA, the Chinese Basketball

Association still owns the players who play for various clubs. Nike were furious when the players of Nike-sponsored Shanghai Basketball Club were refused permission to engage in promotional activities such as signing autographs by the Shanghai Basketball Association (*People's Daily*, 1999). However, it is perhaps in the global Fordist regime of accumulation and mode of regulation that we can begin to see the complexities of the Chinese market as it engages in relationships with Western transnational capitalism.

Along with Indonesia, China produces two-thirds of Nike's footwear and is indicative of a transnational turning away from a rigid Western regulatory system towards a nation more willing to attract investment, offer incentives and "refine" labor laws and environmental regulations. The lure of a higher wage draws mostly females from rural areas to free trade zones or "export processing zones" (EPZ) as they are officially known in China (Klein, 1999); the reality, however, is very different given the well-documented working conditions, labor "rights" and human rights abuses (Landrum and Boje, 2002). These workers (the *Laobaixin)* struggle for economic survival and basic human rights in the factories within such EPZs. Even with this emergent population migration, while the country reports high levels of growth in gross national product actual income levels are, for the most part, still very low.

Not only is China appealing to Nike because of its cheap labor costs, but also because of its potential as a market for shoes. As Luo (2000, p. 229) notes, China has 2.6 billion consumer feet that Nike dream of covering. If it sells a pair of athletic shoes for every 11,812 people in China it will make profits equivalent to what could be realized if it sold one pair to every fourth person in the US. At the level of consumption, Nike has a very different group (as opposed to those who manufacture the product, the *laobaixin*) of the Chinese populace in mind. Nike has sought to connect itself to China's nouveau riche (*baofahu*) and it has set up stores in prosperous developed cities such as Shanghai, Beijing, and Guangzhou (Luo, 2000). While the *baofahu* may only make up a small portion of the Chinese market, the sheer size of the Chinese population is enough to encourage transnational corporations such as Nike into the Chinese market. Manchester United and Nike may well connect with the *baofahu*, but the *laobaixin* will remain disconnected from, and exploited by, the presence and strategizing of those transnationals who have engaged with the Chinese sportingscape.

Given the limited access to its goods, Nike, like many transnationals in China, have experienced problems as local citizens, anxious to obtain the trappings of Western wealth but unable to afford the high prices demanded by Western transnationals, have turned to buying counterfeit goods. Nike estimates its losses through counterfeiting at $15 million per year (Rae, 2002). Technically, with

World Trade Organization accession and new Chinese laws, counterfeiting is illegal and supposedly easier to prosecute. In reality however criminal prosecutions, which are handled by the Administrations of Commerce and Industry (AIC), are difficult to enforce, penalties are low and the AIC cannot grant compensation to the rights holder.

Coda

In this chapter we have provided a preliminary sketch of the practices of sporting transnationals as they have engaged, at various levels, with the Chinese marketplace. China is clearly seen as a place that can be penetrated by the economics and imagery of transnational corporate capitalism and is thus a prime site for the investigation of the impact of Western consumer capitalism upon local cultures. Of course, global interconnectedness does not necessarily imply some type of corporate imperialism or indeed a "Westernization" of the rest (Featherstone, 1995; Said, 1978). The very global communications systems, electronic highways, and instantaneous real time coordination of economic activity that has allowed for transnationals to operate in a footloose manner has been capitalized upon by those within China. The strategies of these corporations and governmental entities, such as CCTV's use of Manchester United, the relationship between the CBA and the NBA and the sponsorship of Everton by the China Kejian Company, can be seen as part of an effort to connect to a network economy and reposition China as a player in the global information infrastructure. Further, and as we have seen, "geography still matters" for those transnationals seeking to engage with the Chinese marketplace and understanding national and local peculiarities is extremely important for the structure, operation and practices of foreign entities within China. The particularities of a China entrenched in tradition and a move from central economic planning to market oriented economic reform have meant that transnationals operating within the nation have had to *negotiate* these specificities. This has been seen through localizing products to the Chinese market, operating in relation to *guanxi* and the hierarchical business system and developing relationships with quasi-governmental and mixed organizations.

In this sense, and returning to the outset of this chapter, transnationals looking to accrue mass economies of scale and the benefits of the marketplace must negotiate the prohibitions, customs and taboos of China – rather than the pervasiveness of the idea of a global, ubiquitous, transnational corporate capitalism it is better to conceive of the ways in which the very idea of transnational capitalism has itself been modified by powerful organizations in China. The fusion of tradition, socialism and transnationalism has created a unique sporting landscape, the particularities of which have only just begun to be played out. There will probably continue to be tension, contradiction and further transformations apparent in the Chinese sportingscape as transnationals attempt to engage and perhaps exploit the mass Chinese population. Further, as transnationals seek to accrue maximal profit, there may well be a further bifurcation in the Chinese marketplace – transnational presence in China appears twofold: those who provide cheap labor to produce and those who are targeted as consumers for those products. In Castells (1996) terms, and under the logics of transnational corporatism, certain populations may well become connected to an interconnected global culture of "real virtuality", while others will be disconnected, existing within the real time of a culture of tradition and place (although a place that has itself become changed through the manufacturing presence of vertically disaggregated corporations operating in a loosely regulated, unfettered international market). While those "connected" may be small in size in relation to the total Chinese population, it appears that the *baofahu* is significant enough in size for transnationals to seek it out and capitalize upon it. How this affects the symbolic promotional strategizing of TNCs, such as Nike, requires further exploration to determine any change, at least in an imagined sense, of external, commercially oriented representations of Chinese cultures. Indeed, the ways in which China attempts to promote a particular version of itself, which may well mask over various internal disruptions, through the intense intersection of national redevelopment, media, and sporting spectacle – the 2008 Beijing Olympics – may be a telling episode in China's attempts to connect to the global economy and leapfrog into the race to attract further transnational investment. What is perhaps clearer at this point is the current transformation in the Chinese sporting system that has taken place in relation to the international restructuration of China and the global economy. This has resulted, at the least, in a refinement, if not a re-contouring, of the Chinese sportingscape through Western consumer capitalist discourse – a "changing" of the nation under the logics of transnational corporate capitalism (Hannerz, 1996).

Notes

1. This chapter draws on a larger study being conducted by the authors in association with Dr John Amis (University of Memphis). Our discussion is based on a series of interviews conducted in 2000 and 2001 by the authors with individuals representing Chinese football clubs, the Chinese Football Association, Local and

Provincial Associations, the Chinese Sport Association, the Chinese Basketball Association and Chinese Sports Agents.

References

Allen, J. (1992). Post-industrialism and Post-fordism. In S. Hall, D. Held and A McGrew (eds), *Modernity and its Futures*, Cambridge: Polity, pp. 168–204.

Alms, R. (1994), Globe Trotters: NBA Takes a World View of Marketing, *Dallas Morning News,* November 1, p. 1D.

Andrews, D. (1997). The [trans]National Basketball Association: American Commodity-sign Culture and Global-local Conjuncturalism. In A Cvetovitch and D. Kellner (eds), *Articulating the Global and the Local: Globalization and Cultural Studies*, Boulder CO: Westview Press, pp. 72–101.

Ashton, C. (2002), *China: Opportunities in the Business of Sport*, London: SportBusiness.

Bai, X.L., Su Y.W., Zhang Y. and Yu, A.F. (2000), Current Situation and Strategy of Chinese Basketball Clubs [Zhongguo zhiye lanqiu julebu de jinying xianzhuan yu fazhang duice], *Journal of Beijing University* [Beijing daxue xuebao], 1*:* 1–4.

Castells, M. (1989), *The Informational City – Information Technology, Economic Restructuring and the Urban-regional Process*, Oxford: Blackwell.

Castells, M. (1996), *The Rise of the Network Society*, Cambridge MA: Blackwell.

Chen, Ming-Jer (2001), *Inside Chinese Business*, Boston MA: Harvard Business School Press.

Featherstone, M. (1995), *Undoing Culture: Globalisation, Postmodernism, and Identity*, London: Sage.

Feng, J.M. (2001), Interview conducted by Fan Hong in the Chinese Football Association in Beijing on September 2.

Gluckman, R. (2002), *Taking China to the Hoop*. Available at: http://www.gluckman.com/NBA.html (accessed, November 10, 2002).

Guilianotti, R. (1999), *Football: A Sociology of the Global Game*, Cambridge: Polity Press.

Hannerz, U. (1996), *Transnational Connections: Culture, People, Places*, London: Comedia.

Harvey, D. (1989), *The Condition of Postmodernity*, Oxford: Blackwell.

Held, D., McGrew, A., Goldblatt, D. and Perraton, J. (1999), *Global Transformations: Politics, Economics and Culture*, Cambridge: Polity Press.

Herman, E.S. and McChesney, R.W. (1997), *The Global Media: The New Missionaries of Corporate Capitalism*, London: Cassell.

Hirst, P. and Thompson, G. (1996), *Globalization in Question: The International Economy and the Possibilities of Governance*, Cambridge: Polity.

Hoskisson, R. E., Eden, L., Lau, C.M. and Wright, M. (2000). Strategy in Emerging Economies, *Academy of Management Journal*, 43: 249–67.

Klein, N. (1999), *No Logo: Taking Aim at the Brand Bullies*, New York: Picador.

Landrum, N. and Boje, D. (2002), Kairos: Strategies Just in Time in the Asian Athletic Footwear Industry. In U. Haley and F-J Richter (eds), *Asian Post-crisis Management: Corporate and Governmental Strategies for Sustainable Competitive Advantage*, New York NY: Palgrave Macmillan.

Lash, S. and Urry, J. (1987), *The End of Organized Capitalism*, Cambridge: Polity Press.

Luo, Yadong (2000), *How to Enter China: Choices and Lessons*, Ann Arbor: University of Michigan Press.

Marshall, P. (1997), *Celebrity and Power: Fame in Contemporary Culture*, Minneapolis MN: University of Minnesota Press.

Miller, T., Lawrence, G., McKay, J. and Rowe, D. (2001), *Globalization and Sport*, London: Sage.

Morley, D. and Robins, K. (1995), *Spaces of Identity: Global Media, Electronic Landscapes and Cultural Boundaries*, London: Routledge.

Northcroft, J. (2002), Moyes Solves Chinese puzzle, *The Sunday Times*, December 1.

Ohmae, K. (1990), *The Borderless World*, New York NY: HarperBusiness.

People's Daily (2002), *CBA Suggests Written Agreement on National Duty for NBA Team to Get Yao Ming*, June 25. Available at: http://english.peopledaily.com.cn/200206/25/eng20020625_98477.shtml (accessed, November 11, 2002).

Perkins, D.H. (1994), Completing China's Move to the Market, *Journal of Economic Perspectives*, 8: 23–46.

Preston, P. and Kerr, A. (2001), Digital Media, Nation States and Local Cultures: The Case of Multimedia "Content" Production, *Media, Culture and Society*, 23: 109–31.

Rae, S. (2002), *The American Chamber of Commerce People's Republic of China, The Fight to Protect US Brand Names and Intellectual Property*. Available at: http://www.amcham-china.org.cn/publications/brief/document/Counterfeiting5-00.htm (accessed, November 10, 2002).

Robins, K. (1997). What in the World is Going On? In P. DuGay (ed.), *Production of Cultures / Cultures of Production*, London: The Open University, pp. 11–66.

Said, E. (1978), *Orientalism*, Harmondsworth: Penguin.

Sassen, S. (2000), Whose City Is It? Globalization and the Formation of New Claims. In F. J. Lechner (ed.), *The Globalization Reader*, Malden MA: Blackwell, pp. 70–6.

Schell, O. (1984), The New Open Door, *The New Yorker*, November 19, p. 90.

Silk, M. and Andrews, D. (2001), Beyond a Boundary? Sport, Transnational Advertising and the Reimagining of National Culture, *Journal of Sport and Social Issues*, 25: 180–201.

Sports Illustrated (2001), *Olympics Mean Big Business for China, The World*. Available at: http://sportsillustrated.cnn.com/olympics/news/2001/07/10/china_bigbusiness_ap/ (accessed, November 11, 2002).

Star TV (2002). Star, About Us. Available at http://www.startv.com/eng/abus_milestone.cfm (accessed, November 11, 2002).

Studwell, J. (2002), *The China Dream*, London: Profile Books.

Sugden, J. and Tomlinson, A. (1998), *FIFA and the Contest for World Football: Who Rules the People's Game?* Cambridge: Polity Press.

Van Dusen, S. (1998), *The Manufacturing Practices of the Footwear Industry: Nike vs. the Competition*, Available at: http://www.unc.edu/~andrewsr/ints092/vandu.html (accessed, September 14, 2002).

Yan, Y. (1997). McDonald's in Beijing: The Localization of Americana. In J. L. Watson (ed.), *Golden Arches East: McDonald's in East Asia*, Stanford: Stanford University Press, pp. 39–76.

Index